Conundrums in Practical Theology

Theology in Practice

VOLUME 2

The titles published in this series are listed at *brill.com/thip*

Conundrums in Practical Theology

Edited by

Joyce Ann Mercer
Bonnie J. Miller-McLemore

BRILL

LEIDEN | BOSTON

Cover illustration: © Louise Roach, Dreamstime.com, St Francis Labyrinth.

Library of Congress Cataloging-in-Publication Data

Names: Miller-McLemore, Bonnie J., editor. | Mercer, Joyce Ann, editor.
Title: Conundrums in practical theology / edited by Bonnie J. Miller-McLemore, Joyce Ann Mercer.
Description: Leiden ; Boston : Brill, 2016. | Series: Theology in Practice ; ISSN 2352-9288, Volume 2 | Includes bibliographical references and index.
Identifiers: LCCN 2016036677 (print) | LCCN 2016037405 (ebook) | ISBN 9789004324237 (pbk. : alk. paper) | ISBN 9789004324244 (E-book)
Subjects: LCSH: Theology, Practical.
Classification: LCC BV2 .C66 2016 (print) | LCC BV2 (ebook) | DDC 230–dc23
LC record available at https://lccn.loc.gov/2016036677

Typeface for the Latin, Greek, and Cyrillic scripts: "Brill". See and download: brill.com/brill-typeface.

ISSN 2352-9288
ISBN 978-90-04-32423-7 (paperback)
ISBN 978-90-04-32424-4 (e-book)

This book is printed on acid-free paper and produced in a sustainable manner.

Printed by Printforce, the Netherlands

Contents

List of Figures

Notes on Contributors

Tom Beaudoin
Associate Professor of Religion, Fordham University

Eileen R. Campbell-Reed
Associate Professor of Practical Theology, Central Baptist Theological Seminary, Nashville, Tennessee

Faustino M. Cruz
Associate Dean of Academic Affairs, Associate Professor of Practical Theology and Leadership, Seattle University

Jaco Dreyer
Professor of Practical Theology, University of South Africa

Courtney T. Goto
Assistant Professor of Religious Education, Boston University School of Theology

Tone Stangeland Kaufman
Associate Professor of Practical Theology, MF Norwegian School of Theology, Oslo, Norway

Joyce Ann Mercer
Professor of Practical Theology and Pastoral Care, Yale Divinity School

Bonnie J. Miller-McLemore
E. Rhodes and Leona B. Carpenter Professor of Religion, Psychology, and Culture, Vanderbilt University Divinity School and Graduate Department of Religion

Phillis Isabella Sheppard
Associate Professor of Religion, Psychology, and Culture, Vanderbilt University Divinity School and Graduate Department of Religion

Katherine Turpin
Associate Professor of Religious Education, Iliff School of Theology

Claire E. Wolfteich
Associate Professor of Practical Theology and Spirituality Studies, Boston University School of Theology

Introduction

Bonnie J. Miller-McLemore and Joyce Ann Mercer

Practical theology has a complicated history and position within the academy and within religious life that raise powerful conundrums for those who draw on its resources. Indeed, by its very definition practical theology does not limit itself to the academy alone. The term *practical theology* has multivalent meanings that connect it, from the beginning, to the life of religious faith and the practices of religious communities. So, the term refers to both an academic discipline in its own right *and* an activity of faith and responsibility shared by all believers. Practical theology happens in everyday life among the faithful. But it has also accrued an important academic role in universities and seminaries where scholars seek to reconnect proclaimed beliefs to actions, scientific explanation to normative appraisal, intellectual theory to bodily practice, and theoretical ideas to practical and aesthetic knowing. To complicate matters further, academic practical theologians are especially attentive to concrete problems (e.g., immigration, marriage, violence), existential experiences (e.g., suffering, joy), and religious and spiritual practices (e.g., celebrating worship, taking care of children). Yet, to comprehend such matters adequately involves a potentially unlimited variety of sources and methods, requiring not only textual analysis but also study of living subjects as well as interdisciplinary work within religion (e.g., scriptural and historical study) and beyond religion (e.g., social sciences, philosophy). Ultimately, however, practical theologians hope not only to understand but, in the best of all circumstances, to effect change, enhancing individual and communal life based on convictions and norms from religious traditions and communities. The question then becomes: How does one align or combine all these aspirations with the expectations and limitations of the academy?

It should come as no surprise, therefore, given practical theology's complex location and aims, that scholars who profess expertise in the discipline encounter a variety of intellectual and practical conundrums as we do our work and live out our vocations. The challenges are not ours alone, however, but plague our scholarly peers *and* spill over into the lives of those who make their way from our schools into a diversity of professional roles that require practical embodiment of religious beliefs in concrete contexts. In other words, the problems explored in this book reflect wider biases and breakdowns in the academy and religious life at large—who possesses knowledge and how, who defines and wields power over religion, how does one know what one knows

 | DOI 10.1163/9789004324244_002

about religion and religious faith, and so forth. In a way, practical theologians are just the "canary in the coal mine" or the place where academic problems "come home to roost." Hence, how the conundrums in this book are recognized and managed has a reverberating effect beyond practical theology with implications not just for scholars but also for people struggling with their faith in religious communities in general.

Tackling Conundrums: Conceptual, Emotional, and Political Work

On first blush, little ambiguity surrounds the term *conundrum*. Quite simply, the word refers to *a confusing or difficult problem or question*. With our noses to the ground, fingers in many pots, and feet crossing multiple boundaries, the contributors to this volume had no problem identifying recurring challenges at the heart of our work. Since the book's inception, the subject elicited a commitment, cohesion, and energy among its authors that rarely obtains in edited collections. And in talking about the book with others, we received enthusiastic encouragement. The book title itself reflects this clarity. It names the subject matter concisely; it needs no tinkering.

Upon digging deeper into each conundrum, however, authors discovered that our analysis required more than expected. That is, few of us anticipated the intractable morass of personal, professional, and vocational problems into which we plunged. For, the conundrums in this volume hide within themselves qualities that make them enticing *and* confounding all at once.

First of all, genuine conundrums do not just *confuse*; they *refuse* easy answer. They have a kind of Catch-22 dynamic, which puts people in an aggravating and relentless damned-if-you-do, damned-if-you-don't-position. A conundrum is not just an issue; it entraps people in unresolvable problems or, better said, riddles, puzzles, paradoxes, and ironies. So, addressing a conundrum is inevitably maddening because one is essentially trying to solve an unsolvable problem. Many contributors felt as if we had opened up a hornet's nest, a Pandora's Box, better left undisturbed if we wanted peace of mind. Some of us found ourselves before a long list of scholarly publications outside our area of expertise that we needed to read to fathom properly the full range of the conundrum. We assumed wrongly that the book would have a unified bibliography. As the book evolved, it became clear that each chapter needed its own extensive collection of sources with minimal overlap between chapters.

Even more confounding, in contrast to the usual scholarly commitment to the logical world of rational discourse, examining conundrums raises unique emotional and political turmoil. That is, the problems addressed in this book are not simply conceptual, although they are indeed intellectually puzzling. The conceptual dilemmas almost always overflow into more deeply felt and lived quagmires, reflecting social inequities and political injustices that reverberate across academia and the marginalized publics to whom we hold ourselves especially accountable (e.g., ministers, ministry and doctoral students, practice faculty on the margins of professional degree programs, congregations, families, the racially oppressed, the religiously excluded). This spill-over quality of conundrums means that those whose work takes them into the midst of such puzzles do not simply walk away at the end of the day, unscathed and unfettered by our scholarly endeavors. Conundrums bring real costs. They implicate us within their tangled webs, sometimes at quite a personal level, provoking not just intellectual quandary but emotional reaction (e.g., frustration, inadequacy, discomfort, anger, depression, to name just a few) *and* ethical, political imperatives and responsibilities. As you will see in the chapters ahead, conundrums are about territory, status, boundaries, exclusions, recognition, discrimination, power, prejudice, knowledge, intellectual inadequacies, limitations, and much more. In short, this book takes up the unwieldy task of addressing subjects that do not easily exhaust themselves, that entangle us in contradictions and dead ends, and that put us in an awkward, even potentially conflictual position with scholars and colleagues whom we admire and appreciate and toward whom we mean no offense.

In a word, conundrums rub on raw spots. Readers may experience what authors felt in taking up these problems—an immediate interest and eagerness to remedy a fault *and* then a hesitation and a desire to refrain from naming a wound or pushing a growing edge. Tackling such conundrums requires a kind of honesty, self-reflexivity, and professional risk seldom demanded by even the most personal musings. To even begin to discuss such matters openly requires having a secure position in the academy that allows one to take up dicey matters that others have had less freedom to voice. Those less academically secure must have courage and assurance of support to venture out nevertheless into difficult terrain. Of course, the authors in this book naturally diverge in our positionality, in our writing style, and in the way and the extent to which we interpret and work with the idea of a conundrum. Some divergence stems from our differing subdisciplinary areas: we variously write out of expertise in constructive theology, religious education, pastoral care, spirituality, cultural studies, feminist theory, and sociology of religion, to name a few of our more specialized locations within the larger rubric of practical theology. In addition, some conundrums in the book are simply more conceptual with only indirect life consequences (e.g., Campbell-Reed, Kaufman, Turpin), while others are more life determining, especially chapters that name racism/white supremacy/colonialism (e.g., Dreyer, Goto, Sheppard), religious subjugation (e.g., Beaudoin, Wolfteich), and academic privilege, prejudice, and elitism (e.g., Cruz, Mercer, Miller-McLemore).

Location, Audience, and Aims

Even though conundrums display a seeming inevitability and intractability, they are like so much else in postmodernity—relative to our current climate, reflective of the narrow modern debates of a white Western academy—and will some day (we hope) seem no more relevant than conundrums that seemed pressing to early Christians (e.g., God's nature as simultaneously human and divine). As Tom Beaudoin points out in his chapter (p. 13), the conundrums in this volume show how a problem has surfaced and taken roost in one particular author's life at this point in theology's history. From this vantage point, we see even more clearly how the conundrums themselves reflect who has had the power and privilege to divide up disciplines and define complex terms like *theology, spirituality, faith, theory, race, knowledge, truth,* and *religious practice.*

Conundrums are not just negative markers of parochial squabbles, however. As Claire Wolfteich attests in her chapter in this volume, they also have positive sides "of creativity and growth" (pp. 278–279). Simply naming these conundrums out loud is itself a step toward addressing them, and part of the book's mission will be met merely by raising consciousness. The book also overflows with what French scholar Michel de Certeau calls *tactics,* many small moves and pathways by which we navigate the broader academic structures that shape and distort intellectual life. In addition, many of the chapters move from creative resistance on a small scale to consideration of wider structural systems that we hope to unsettle, even if ever so slightly. However, given the nature of the conundrums, their long history, and their systemic realities, the tactics and strategies in each chapter will not completely undo the impact of the problems. We hope that the small steps taken will contribute nonetheless to the larger ongoing work of others and that the contributions will outweigh the discomforts and risks incurred in speaking out.

To undo or "resolve" conundrums, wider forces and scholarly communities will have to be engaged. Hence, our imagined audience is not simply our colleagues in practical theology narrowly defined. This book will not have its full effect unless it reaches beyond this group. That is something of a conundrum itself: we write as practical theologians for a wider audience whose scholarship rarely considers or addresses our work. As border crossers, boundary walkers, and scavengers looking for truths in many places, practical theologians may feel the effect of conundrums more acutely and directly than our colleagues in other areas. Conundrums, such as the binary between theory and practice, discrimination against theological normativity, Christian-centrism, token inclusion of marginalized peoples, and invisibility of raced bodies, arise in acute form in our discipline. But these conundrums plague the entire theological school, and colleagues in other areas perpetuate them through neglect and inattention. Hence, we hope scholars in other disciplines will read this book and understand more fully what we are trying to accomplish in practical theology and the roadblocks that make our research and teaching particularly demanding. We also imagine the chapters helping seminary faculties at large think afresh about how curriculum evolves, how colleagues relate, how courses are structured, how problems in ministry and faith are addressed, and so forth.

We picture a more immediate and ready audience as well—the very ministry and doctoral students who have themselves raised the questions we take up. As we talked and wrote, we thought about ministry students who do senior projects and become immersed in precisely the kinds of complexity we explore—research involving interdisciplinary (e.g., Mercer), local knowledge (e.g., Turpin) that destabilizes assumptions about the relationship between theory and practice (e.g., Miller-McLemore). We thought about graduates who wonder about the motivations behind their hire (e.g., Cruz), the racial and racist undertones behind professional invitations (e.g., Goto), their disciplinary and vocational identity while pursuing multiple approaches to a subject (e.g., Mercer), their racial misrepresentation and physical erasure (e.g., Sheppard), and their justification for using only one in-depth case study as evidence for an argument (e.g., Campbell-Reed) or for choosing to serve through administrative leadership rather than publish (e.g., Cruz).

Themes, Ironies, and Support

None of the conundrums in the book is unique to practical theology, but authors explore why they surface acutely for practical theologians and how they take distinct shape within and beyond the discipline. As a consequence, common themes emerge across the essays. Several chapters reconsider how we define theology and broach larger questions of theological epistemology or what counts as knowledge, how we know what we know in theology, and who decides (e.g., Campbell-Reed, Cruz, Dreyer, Mercer, Miller-McLemore, Turpin). These chapters have implications for how we structure theological education and curriculum. Several chapters invite closer examination of practices *within* the academy itself and the perpetuation of patterns and habits endemic to distorted theologizing (e.g., Beaudoin, Goto, Miller-McLemore, Sheppard). Other chapters turn to methods and approaches within the field that keep us questioning our work and whether we are a discipline (e.g., Campbell-Reed, Mercer, Turpin). Several conundrums arise because practical theologians stand in multiple places with many commitments and strive to meet standards and loyalties required by each context (e.g., Cruz, Kaufman, Mercer, Wolfteich). Some chapters put into words concerns that have not been voiced out of fear that articulating problems such as the institutional hegemony of theory over practice, racist tokenism, christianicity, and Protestanticity will reify rather than defuse them (e.g., Beaudoin, Dreyer, Goto, Miller-McLemore, Sheppard, Wolfteich). Most of the conundrums have a kind of meta-quality, as Courtney Goto observes in her chapter in this volume, that runs well beyond specific subjects we study and teach. The "nature of the beast," as Goto remarks "is such that the same conundrum can trip up the researcher repeatedly and quite aside from a particular topic" (p. 110). In other words, the conundrums cross over specific research problems and effect diverse projects in the field. Even though we do not often talk about or deal explicitly with these problems, they inform our work every step of the way.

Finally, there are ironies that emerge from taking up conundrums. Tito Cruz, for example, writes a conventional scholarly essay while questioning the idealization of conventional scholarship for those called to service and leadership; Courtney Goto claims her racial location while naming the injustices surrounding race identification; Jaco Dreyer uses his "advantaged" position to question colonial power and privilege only to inadvertently reassert it in his effort to be reflexive; Bonnie Miller-McLemore resurrects an old hegemonic binary between practice and theory while trying to undo it; Joyce Ann Mercer draws on multiple disciplines to explore the risk of interdisciplinary work; Phillis Sheppard resorts to words to describe a problem that can only be addressed adequately if we acknowledge its most powerful inchoate apparitions in physical images, bodies, and habits; Claire Wolfteich wants to welcome Catholic and Protestant engagement while highlighting each party's limitation and negligence.

Our work together fostered a solidarity that allowed us to persist nonetheless. The book began where much good practical theology begins—in conversation and community. Because the work was hard and laid bare questions about our scholarly identity and vocation, we benefited immensely from the collaboration and associations that characterized this endeavor from its beginnings during a meeting at the Association of Practical Theology (APT) in 2014. We met prior to the American Academy of Religion (AAR) that fall, reading drafts and offering feedback. Connections through email, occasional academic meetings, and a shared Dropbox folder provided company and support.

For official support, we have institutions and persons to thank, including our own institutions (Vanderbilt University, a sabbatical home at the Collegeville Institute at St. John's University, Virginia Theological Seminary, and Yale Divinity School), the academic societies that provided space for conversation (APT, AAR, International Academy of Practical Theology), and the colleagues, family members, and friends who listened to authors labor over their conundrums, all of whom cannot be listed but make up the much wider collegium of people interested in and committed to theology in practice. We thank authors for hard work under tight time constraints, and we also thank Mirjam Elbers at Brill Publishers for her confidence in and support for this book and the Brill book series in Theology and Practice as a whole, her assistant Ingrid Heijckers, and Kishundra King, PhD student at Vanderbilt University for editorial assistance.

At no point in laying out the book did the editors or authors presume any kind of comprehensive coverage. The table of contents grew out of the interests and investments of contributors, and chapters are arranged alphabetically by author's surname rather than by some larger overarching rationale. Our hope is that this arrangement makes the volume more invitational. We invite readers to ask themselves the same question we raised for ourselves: Is there a frustrating problem you encounter again and again as you do your work that baffles and annoys you, that seems difficult to resolve, that needs further attention and exploration, and that might help other students and scholars with their own puzzlements in ministry, teaching, and research? Perhaps tackling such matters will assume a life of its own for you as it did for each of us.

CHAPTER 1

Why Does Practice Matter Theologically?

Tom Beaudoin

In a recent book on Catholic practical theology, Julie Hanlon Rubio discusses "family ethics" in terms of "practices of love and solidarity." She presents a "vision" for an activist-style practice of "resistance" by way of everyday family practices grounded in Catholic and, more broadly, Christian theological claims. It looks like it all holds together quite well. In the last few pages of the chapter, however, Rubio honestly states that "as [her] children grew up, it began to unravel." Her children took up other life-models than Jesus, rendering her family effectively "interfaith."[1] She suggests that much of the way Christian theology speaks of practice cannot accommodate the "mixed families" like the one hers became when her children grew up and went their own way. This is because most of our inherited theologies of families imagine a religiously homogeneous faith situation, wherein parenting is normatively Christian and children are meant to stay within the Christian fold.[2] It is a poignant, although very common and increasingly typical, story for Catholicism in particular and mainline Christianity in general in the United States.

Rubio's story, as well as my own experience attempting to re-situate my Catholic heritage within a larger frame, and the larger familiar patterns of religious switching and deconversion in the United States, have made me curious about why and whether practical theology has to make its prime task the discovery of Christian significance in practice. I wonder if practices modeled from the outset as having pre-Christian, Christian, and post-Christian dimensions, or practice construed as "empty of"/"indifferent toward" Christianity, might help things go differently for families like hers and all of us who find ourselves at times outside religion or declining affiliation. Rubio gestures toward the possibility of imagining a kind of Christian parenting that does not further Christian affiliation, a situation of "respecting where each person is,

1 Julie Hanlon Rubio, "Practices of Love and Solidarity: Family Ethics," in *Invitation to Practical Theology: Catholic Voices and Visions*, ed. Claire E. Wolfteich (New York: Paulist, 2014), 227.

2 Rubio suggests that theology inherits two influential trajectories regarding family: the shared-faith model, emphasizing the importance of maintaining the family religious tradition through parenting practices; and the missionary model, emphasizing adults as evangelizers with less of an emphasis on parenting practices ("Practices of Love," p. 228).

 | DOI 10.1163/9789004324244_003

asking not for total agreement but for companionship on the way, and agreeing to support each other in the quest for truth." She suggests that this practice might be one of "living together in a loving community that respects, honors, and supports differences"—including differences of religion and spirituality.[3] Indeed, families that are able to accommodate the "breaking" of affiliation and end up able to affirm its importance and goodness probably have some way of interpreting practice along the lines I end up suggesting in this chapter. It will take understanding how and how much (Christian) practical theology has practiced an investment in the reproduction of Christianity—a phenomenon that I will later refer to as "christianicity"—and then of imagining doing something different with practical theology's Christian heritage, something more along the lines of "respecting, honoring, and supporting difference."

So what is it about practice?[4] Energy for responding to this question unites practical theologies. The actual responses, however, divide them. No practical theology avoids presuming or arguing that practice is of vital importance. In the renewal of practical theology of recent decades, that conviction became the working assumption of the field and remains central to its distinctiveness among academic theological enterprises.

The definitions of "practice" in practical theology are many, and I am using "practice" in this chapter to stand for a complex matrix of overlapping concepts used in the field: practice, praxis, action, performance, experience. Practice, however understood, is that domain of life in relation to which the practical theologian intentionally makes her moves. And by suggesting that practical theologies take practice to be of "vital importance," I mean that practice is taken to be theologically significant. For every practical theology, and for a range of reasons always traceable in principle to an account of God, practice is a crucial theological focus. The practical theologian's distinctiveness becomes manifest in the capacity to show how practice constitutes theological material. This means that practice "signifies" (that is, it bears/carries or indicates/points-to) some essential relation to *theos*. This signifying can take place "directly" or "indirectly" in relation to God-related material, such as experience-concepts that point toward God, such as Jesus, sacrament, Spirit, anthropology, grace, sin, saints, virtue, mercy, or incarnation. In short, practical theologies render practice as divine material. This understanding of theol-

3 Rubio, "Practices of Love," 228.

4 I am grateful for comments on an earlier draft of this chapter from all the co-authors of this book, and in particular from the editors, Bonnie J. Miller-McLemore and Joyce Ann Mercer. In addition, Leonard Cassuto and Moshe Gold of Fordham University provided helpful feedback as I drafted the middle sections of the chapter.

ogy's work is precisely what attracted me to practical theology when I was in graduate school in the 1990s. In order to make the present need to respect religious (and nonreligious) difference into a theologically coherent program that relates creatively to practical theology's distinctiveness, I will discuss the deep theologically significant shifts I have experienced. In the wake of those defamiliarizations, I explore what theology can expect from the study of conundrums and then present the notion of "christianicity" and look at its function in practical theology. This allows me to return to Rubio's challenge to practical theology, as I reformulate practical theology's task away from continuing Christianity and toward a wider arena of inquiry and impact, including but not limited to Christianity.

Three Disorientations

After twenty years in practical theology, I face a conundrum about the theological significance of practice and the place of Christianity in practical theology. This conundrum is related to three interwoven long-term disorientations in my work as a practical theologian that are caught up in larger developments in the field.

Questioning Practice

First, practical theology as a disciplinary home has also come to seem something like a hall of mirrors, with multiple reflections and refractions of practice but difficulty finding where these images "begin" theologically. Not that we need one starting point, to be sure, but I find myself curious that practice cannot also be a weak and broken concept instead of a foundation, however diversely defined, for the field. I mean that it is no longer obvious to me that practice is the kind of thing that is susceptible to the assignments of theological meaning typical of our field. Instead of only seeing the overlapping consensus about the theological significance of practice as an attractive distinction about our work, I also wonder what this consensus means, and what the practice of its perpetual reinforcement causes or keeps from happening. This sounds paradoxical, but I am no longer sure practical theologians should be encouraging religious practice.[5] More on

5 There are historical reasons for the valorization of religious/faith practice: practical theology as an academic discipline has commonly distinguished itself from other theological disciplines that do not take action, experience, or practice with sufficient seriousness. Attention to this important background exceeds the scope of this chapter.

this below.[6] Thinking this way gives me a substantial challenge to "start over," seeing the basic questions of practical theology as if from the beginning.

Questioning Whiteness

The second disorientation is my recognition, as a white scholar, of the deeply white-racialized character of my practical theology, and of practical theology as a field. This critical vantage exposes practical theology as a profoundly racial project whose whiteness inclines it to racist ways of operating that must be actively resisted. I must become more able to look at the colonialism coming through my teaching and research and find new ways of working with this heritage. This is not separable from my position as a man within the 'boys club' of a Jesuit university, and as married to a woman within the 'officially heterosexual' climate of my (Catholic) university. All of these confer advantages that have shaped and also distorted my sense for what theology should be.[7]

As a field, we do not yet understand sufficiently how whiteness has been allied to the need to find practice theologically significant, although we have longstanding research from scholars of color and recent research from white scholars that can contribute to this understanding. This deep theological question can be difficult to face. Herein is a second reckoning with the need to "start over," to imagine practical theology as if from the beginning, as a racially diverse field in its very foundations, yes, but also to let the whiteness of practical theology loosen the very stability often given to this kind of theology as a "field" or "discipline." As was true for the first disorientation regarding the repetition of the significance of practice, nothing less than a relativizing of practi-

---

6 I give personal examples and theoretical reflection on this question in several recent works. For example, Tom Beaudoin, *Witness to Dispossession: The Vocation of a Postmodern Theologian* (Maryknoll: Orbis, 2008); Beaudoin, "Everyday Life in a Scandalized Church: A Theological Perspective," in *Religion, Media, and Culture: A Reader*, ed. Gordon Lynch, Jolyon Mitchell, and Anna Strhan (New York: Routledge, 2011), 236–243; Beaudoin, "Postmodern Practical Theology," in *Opening the Field of Practical Theology: An Introduction*, ed. Kathleen A. Cahalan and Gordon S. Mikoski (New York: Rowman and Littlefield, 2014), 187–202, especially pp. 198–202.

7 See the reflection and examples in Tom Beaudoin and Katherine Turpin, "White Practical Theology," in *Opening the Field of Practical Theology*, 251–269. Among recent publications that explicitly and implicitly put the matter of race to the majority of white academic practical theologians, see Phillis Isabella Sheppard's chapter in this volume, and her *Self, Culture, and Others in Womanist Practical Theology* (New York: Palgrave Macmillan, 2011), and Dale Andrews, "Race and Racism," in *The Wiley-Blackwell Companion to Practical Theology*, ed. Bonnie J. Miller-McLemore (Malden: Blackwell, 2012), 401–411.

cal theology's grounds, methods, and purposes can acknowledge the depth of the matters at stake in the disorientation that surfacing whiteness introduces, especially for white scholars.

Questioning "Christian-Centrism"

Third, the impact of interreligious and intersecular developments in the study of religion has made its way into my understandings of practice and of theology, not only from the outside in—as Christian accounts of practice meet non-Christian accounts—but also from the inside out: as Christian theological understandings of practice get read back down to the non-Christian religio-cultural formations ingredient to Christian practice. This disorientation has shown me that practical theology (in the USA) has been too untroubled in its Christian confidence. It has not done well enough at letting the religious "other" into the theological sense it makes of practice; neither has it allowed in much wisdom and experience from nonaffiliated/secular persons.[8] It is tempting for theologians to narrow their religious focus by doing theology for Christian communities, but this often shuts out the religious and nonreligious "others" within Christian communities and in the Christian tradition itself. It is threatening for many practical theologians to imagine releasing a Christian center for practical theology, but that is exactly what confronts us, with no guarantee of what comes next.[9] This disorientation has convinced me

---

8 Reflecting a major finding of recent research in sociology of religion, in a recent study of religious affiliation in the USA, sociologist Darren Sherkat concludes that the "most important substantial trend in religious identification is the rejection of religious identity." See Sherkat, *Changing Faith: The Dynamics and Consequences of Americans' Shifting Religious Identities* (New York: NYU Press, 2014), 181. Hosffman Ospino and Elsie Miranda note the complications this poses for the growing Latino/a influence in U.S. Christianity, referring to the "second and third generation [...] children of immigrants who are rapidly integrating into mainstream culture and do not feel compelled to serve in their ecclesial communities." (See Ospino and Miranda, "Hispanic Ministry and Leadership Formation," in *Hispanic Ministry in the 21st Century: Present and Future*, ed. Hosffman Ospino (Miami: Convivium, 2010), 181.

9 See Kathleen J. Greider, "Religious Pluralism and Christian-Centrism," in *The Wiley-Blackwell Companion*, 452–461. As I argued in *Witness to Dispossession*, "Christian theology has its own duty to divest itself, through interrogation of its own history and practices, of—in principle—all claims to ahistoricity, first, and uniqueness, second," which involves detachment from an investment in experiencing Christian practices as if they "derive from an inner-ecclesial history and can be practiced in ways that are *sui generis* Christian. On the contrary, every Christian exercise of making defensible sense of culture... is a releasement to 'paganism,' a reliance on being and registering the world that represents a profound otherness

that without a deep understanding of a second religious (or nonreligious/secular) tradition, there is no adequate understanding of a first religious tradition, which means that more than ever, what practical theologians predicate of divinity in practice must carry on at least an implicit dialectic with religious/nonreligious "others."[10] This disorientation, like the first two, is more than enough grounds for "starting over." It is a demand arising from the indifference, and even the violence, involved in making Christian sense of practice apart from other secular and religious senses "outside" of and "within" Christian theology. These three disorientations add up to a conundrum for practical theology. To understand *that* and *how* they do so requires attention to the meaning and function of conundrums in theology.

Reframing Theological Conundrums

This chapter is part of a book about conundrums in practical theology. At first glance, it might seem that a conundrum is a usefully clear concept, along the lines of "something perpetually difficult to figure out." However, it is important to remember that many things once considered "conundrums" in reflection on religious traditions, including Christian theology, are no longer considered to be so—not because they were "solved," but because the psycho-spiritual-cultural framework in which the conundrum seemed urgent fell away and no longer felt significant or made a living difference. Imagine a catalogue of Christian theological conundrums, each with its birthdate and expiration date: Can Gentiles join the people of Israel? Can Jews comprehend a savior who includes Gentiles? Can meat be sacrificed to idols? What of the Law is binding on those who follow Jesus? Are Christians who fell away during persecutions to be welcomed back? Is *homoousios* or *homoiousios* more fitting? Are women and men fundamentally equal? Can a Christian own slaves? A nearly endless list like this is a sobering lesson in the historical and cultural relativity of what we consider conundrums today.

already within" (p. 62). See also my discussion on the problem of the construction of an "amiable past" for Christian practices (p. 144).

10 See David R. Brockman, *No Longer the Same: Religious Others and the Liberation of Christian Theology* (New York: Palgrave Macmillan, 2011). Brockman argues that "while necessary, boundary drawing can easily become a way to stop thinking about the true complexity of reality. Christian theology can blind itself by creating an illusion of internal consistency, giving the impression that it has thereby attained truth" (p. 20).

Given the evanescence—and the corresponding political stakes—of the display and handling of theological conundrums, it is incumbent on practical theologians in particular and religionists in general to appreciate the psycho-religio-cultural work that the assertion of a conundrum may accomplish. In other words, the problem of the conundrum in practical theology is another way of talking about the question that animates this chapter: why does any practice matter theologically? The very idea of a conundrum in practical theology is a theological conundrum, that is to say, the generation of a conundrum with theological heft is a performance of the academic theologian that gains theological significance under certain conditions that we should be able to study for the sake of a richer understanding of how practices make important things happen—in academic disciplines and in life writ large. This kind of critical reflection on the very notion of conundrum—or the practice of generating and theologically substantiating a conundrum—is an instance of asking the bigger question about why practice is theologically significant.

It is true that one common way of defining a conundrum is: What has the field of practical theology been resistant to grasp? But if the history of theology suggests that what are identified as conundrums in the moment turn out to be ways of being embedded in construals of reality that generated the conundrum in the first place, then to organize theological work around the notion of conundrums risks repeating the basic terms that make sense of reality in a specific cultural moment.

A different way of articulating a conundrum would be to resist the terms laid out by the field for specifying what matters (that is, what the field likes to talk about but has not adequately addressed) and instead to wonder about the field's silences (that is, what the field does not like to talk about and which might be holding back progress at the edge of the discourse).[11] This latter approach would be a risk-taking care for who and what has been "off-limits," sharing in the spirit of Marcella Althaus-Reid's concept of the "obscene," which is the stuff that seems naturally not to fit with what we know to be true, evoking feelings of confusion, repulsion, or guardianship over threatened theological material. This is a "grace dis-covering obscenity" that aids the theological work of "affirming reality."[12] This way of rendering a conundrum, which integrates more overt responsibility for the creative dimension of what gets called

11 This is not to suggest that the centers and margins of the field/discipline will not be simultaneously constructed and contested, open and veiled.

12 Marcella Althaus-Reid, *Indecent Theology: Theological Perversions in Sex, Gender, and Politics* (New York: Routledge, 2000), 111. On Althaus-Reid for practical theology, see my "Postmodern Practical Theology," 194, 198. See also Lisa Isherwood and Mark D. Jordan, eds.,

a conundrum, would be to move research forward in ways heterogeneous to the established parameters for progress in the field. Critical theological work on conundrums then becomes wondering about the lack of conundrums on deeply taken-for-granted matters.

Such wondering means practical theologians admitting that we are always already articulating the novel, being heralds of the new in ways that take the measure of—while renewing—the freedom promised in practical theology. This is the thinking that stands behind my articulation of the present conundrum.

My conundrum has to do with why practical theology has not been troubled by substantial friendly dissent from within about its working consensus (implicit or explicit, assumed or argued) regarding the theological significance of practice. Practical theologians might expect a deep troubling of this working consensus to come from "outside" discourses like (speculative) systematics or (text-fetish) biblical studies, or any number of purveyors of "theory-to-practice" theology. But I think it is raised by the work of practical theology itself. Here, then, is my practical-theological conundrum: Why is practice theologically significant? What is going on when we do what we do best: theologically criticize and appreciate practice? Practice, after all, is not "self-evidently" theologically significant. Something has to happen to practice to allow it to gain a theological registration.

For what can we hope in addressing this conundrum? Not an "answer" to it, because this conundrum is as reproductory of its cultural situation as the specification of any conundrum. Because the very specification of a conundrum is a way of advancing a particular theological project with respect to the rhetorical parameters and political stakes of a historical moment, my approach in this chapter is to show why it matters for practical theology that we imagine this particular conundrum.

Predication and Affordance in Practical Theology

If conundrums represent evanescent puzzles, with real-life effects, about the ways practical theology has inherited of making theological sense of reality, then in considering the present conundrum we should pay attention to the dynamics by which theological work is related to larger cultural forces. In

---

Dancing Theology in Fetish Boots: Essays in Honor of Marcella Althaus-Reid (London: SCM, 2010).

other words, we should look carefully at conundrums in relation to, and as an example of, cultural practice. This is a way we can approach why practice matters theologically as the specific content of the rest of this chapter. Insofar as this approach to practical theological content is "under pressure" from the three disorientations sketched above, then two aspects present themselves that make this theological practice also a cultural practice.[13] First is the work of "predication," and second is the work of "affordance" in practical theology.

By "predication," I mean that practical theology typically works by assigning a theological significance to practice in a way that backgrounds just how "made"—how creative, political, historical, and invented—the assignation truly is. Even though this working is essential to how practical theology finds practice theologically significant, such an intervention is normally framed in a theologically naturalized or essentialized fashion, such as claims about God-material showing itself in, through, or in relation to practice, along these familiar lines: God cares about X, Jesus is concerned with Y, the Spirit is known through Z. Appeals to material drawn from religious beings, beliefs, or books typically are thought to secure the theological importance of practice. These appeals are couched in terms of fidelity: to the grammar of the faith, the hermeneutical process, or the liberation of the oppressed. Why is predication so important in practical theology? Because this field distinguishes itself by its connections to lived experience in religion and society. Predication authorizes a range of actions bearing on practice for pastoral and academic workers. Specifically, it helps these workers give critical care for lived religion; specify normative religious practices; facilitate communal discernment; intervene in marginalizations; and support pastoral leadership. The fiction of predication is crucial for the curation of action, which is ingredient to practical theology's self-understanding.

Predication, as a politically charged act in a cultural situation, is emotionally laden. Practical theological forms of predication, including academic varieties, work through forms of argument that are factories of affordance. I borrow the term "affordances" from music criticism. It refers to the range of "affective spaces" that specific forms of music make possible, or "afford," for those who experience the music. The notion of "affordances" implies that the en-

13 These disorientations can put people who share these aspects of my history "under pressure": "It's the terror of knowing what this world is about," as "love dares you to care for the people on the edge of the night" and "love dares you to change the way of caring about ourselves" (Queen, "Under Pressure," *Hot Space* (EMI, 1982)).

counter with music is fundamentally a matter of feelingly imaginative landscapes, offering an emotional climate in which to live at least while the music endures. That emotional climate generates the possibility that creative things may happen that bear on identity in everyday life: memories are recalled, pains and losses are forgotten or indulged, decisions are contemplated, desires are evoked or quelled, wonders and joys are savored. The specific kind of landscape brought up will be pre-framed for individual/social experience based on the cultural history of associations in circulation about the music. This history is always striated by the effective markers of advantage or disadvantage in a setting, such as social class, race, ethnicity, gender, sex, ability, geography, and religion. Musical significance as affordance, in sum, means that different kinds of music afford different affective spaces, which are then more or less negotiated creatively by the listener in consenting to and/or resisting the given framing emotional landscape.[14]

When practice gains a theological predication, which is the work of practical theology, that work is generated by, expressed in, and given out through, affordances. The ways that practical theologies "feel" to readers/hearers, is—like music—often evident only on reflection after the critical-intellectual response has been worked through. This feeling-sense has to do with how recipients have been trained to experience certain theological productions. This "training" is the outcome of a specific history, individual and social, that allows the hearer a margin of freedom to complicate and consent to that larger social-emotional landscape-framing. The experience of practical theology is analogous to the experience of music in just this way: their pleasures, disappointments, boredoms, or indifferences are ways of being reached by and reaching forces of cultural power that are already making and unmaking the lives of individuals and communities and in relation to which people reach for some bearing to come to terms with life.

Practical Theology and "Christianicity"

In practical theology, the theological confection of practice through predication and affordance has come through a form of theology closely allied to Christian identity and to the work of the churches. In different cultural contexts, practical theology has begun promoting non-ecclesial and non-Christian

14 See Christopher Partridge, *The Lyre of Orpheus: Popular Music, the Sacred, and the Profane* (New York: Oxford, 2013), 44–47.

paths,[15] but in the USA, and in the larger practical theological tradition globally, Christian-ecclesial traditions remain not only the main focus for action but supply the intellectual resources for theological work. Practical theology is still quite far, in general, from being able to relate with the depth of creativity and criticality to its Christian heritage that a postcolonial, two-thirds-world-attentive global situation requires. Predication and affordance are pitched toward making practice a continuation of Christianity, and making Christianity live continually in practice. This active ongoing invention of Christian experience goes by the name "christianicity" in recent scholarship in historical and philosophical studies of religion.[16] Understanding the meaning and mechanics of christianicity in some of this research will help us make progress on our practical theological conundrum. If we want to understand that and how we predicate and afford theological significance to practice, it helps to understand how christianicity is functioning in those practical theological dynamics. That in turn may allow practical theology to do something different that is more fitting to both the contemporary situation and to Christianity itself.

Daniel Boyarin on Christianicity

Christianicity is a term appearing in contemporary works in the philosophy of religion and historical studies of Christianity. Its meaning varies, but has to do with the historical-philosophical generation and management of the core of Christian experience and identity. While it is similar to a word like "Christianness," christianicity points to what is taken to be real for Christians and how

---

15 Heinz Streib, Ralph W. Hood, Jr., *et al.*, *Deconversion: Qualitative and Quantitative Results from Cross-Cultural Research in Germany and the United States of America* (Göttingen, Vandenhoeck and Ruprecht, 2009), develop a multiple-trajectory approach for appreciating how and why study participants in Germany and the USA left their "home" religion for something different; Jeff Astley, *Ordinary Theology: Looking, Listening, and Learning in Theology* (Aldershot: Ashgate, 2003), develops a multi-pronged approach from England out of the distinctiveness of personal narratives to get at how faith "comes and goes." Both books provide resources for the promotion of multiple paths rather than a full-fledged theological argument for a multipath approach. Given the Western-Christian history of the field, such practical theological foregroundings of the religious/nonreligious "other" are rare.

16 Christianicity is sometimes capitalized in the historical and philosophical literature. Doing so emphasizes that the term is putting on identity, but also can leave the impression of something static and settled rather than a dynamic process of religious identity building. For this reason, I do not capitalize christianicity (apart from headings) unless quoting directly from an author who capitalizes the term.

that being-taken is generated. It can mean a distinctive way of thinking the relationship between history and transcendence, as in the work of philosopher Hent de Vries.[17] In historical studies, christianicity has a strongly constructed and culturally situated sense. For instance, for historians of antiquity Daniel Boyarin and Catherine Chin, the term describes how early influential Christian theologians created a category for existing in which people were to recognize themselves as Christians. These theologians helped fashion a form of experience that could count as legitimately Christian.

For Boyarin, christianicity comes about as early thinkers attempted to manage the ambiguous relationship between Jewish followers of Jesus and non-Jewish followers of Jesus; the very idea of making belief the marker of the Jesus-follower is a way of marking out "Christians" from "Jews" and—crucially—of creating and sustaining those categories in the very marking-out process. Christianicity is a product of a painful and complex identity-sorting by Christian thinkers that made the management of boundaries, always against "Judaism," the way that "Christians" were to measure who they were. Christianicity itself is an historical artifact bound to heresiology—the invention of the notion of "heresy" as a way of ruling people in and out based on religious belief and practice.

Christianicity describes how it was that one influential strand of early Jesus-following came to define something called being a Christian. Justin Martyr, Boyarin argues, inaugurates a way of construing identity that is "entirely novel," wherein "Christianity" is considered not as nation, tribe, country, or language, but as "a new thing, a community defined by adherence to a certain canon of doctrine and practice."[18] Christianicity suggests that "Christianity" is in some sense a misnomer if it gives the impression of being a religion with a conceptually consistent historical through-line.

Boyarin uses "christianicity" to emphasize that Christianity is always a rhetorical invocation intended to establish and manage the border between what is Christian and what is not Christian. In other words, the "-ity" as the suffix for "Christian," Christian*ity*, is formed by taking an adjective, "Christian," and abstracting from it so as to make it seem like something that has a solid

17 See Hent de Vries, *Philosophy and the Turn to Religion* (Baltimore: Johns Hopkins University, 2001), and *Religion and Violence: Philosophical Perspectives from Kant to Derrida* (Baltimore: Johns Hopkins University, 2001).

18 Daniel Boyarin, *Border Lines: The Partition of Judaeo-Christianity* (Philadelphia: University of Pennsylvania Press, 2004), 17. The mention is brief but the term does significant symbolic work for Boyarin's overall argument about the contestations of and in "Christian" identity in antiquity.

state. It is an "abstract noun." Boyarin is suggesting that an "abstract noun," however, is simply not sufficient. It covers over too much. Hence Boyarin's use of "christianicity," akin to "Christianness," that emphasizes the active making and sustaining dimension of identity.

This making and sustaining is also a "partitioning," in Boyarin's language, a creation of Christianity's "other" as part of the security of a Christian identity. Christianity is pictured as a religion over against the religions of others. It is this christianicity, Boyarin argues, that contributes decisively to the constituting of Judaism as a "religion" in antiquity. To be a Christian is to manifest practices (actions and confessions) that are "not Jewish" and "not Greek/pagan." "For these Christian thinkers, the question of who's in and who's out became the primary way of thinking about Christianicity."[19] "This notion that identity is achieved"—practical theologians would say "practiced"—"and not given by birth, history, language, and geographical location was the novum that produced religion."[20] This is a relevant background and conceptual frame for what became practical theology and its investment in practice as the performance, manifestation, or experience of Christian identity.

Catherine Chin on Christianicity

For Chin, "christianicity" describes Christian life as a utopic experience in letters written from Jerome to Paulinus in the late fourth century. Jerome pictures the way that Christians can live within biblical texts, traveling their pathways word by word and phrase by phrase, visiting vocabularies as stations on a pilgrimage, and experiencing commentary as a way of getting about in the holy land of the page. In being whisked from locale to locale in the scriptural accounts, the reader is to travel a road of literate enjoyment while never in fact leaving, because it is Christ who is encountered in every place the reader might go. Chin characterizes Jerome as ushering readers into experiencing the places in scripture as an "essential sameness" because of the way a kernel of Christian identity is being subtly elaborated in Jerome's theologizing: "It is the elusive quality of 'being Christian' that is evoked," a "Christianicity," instead of a "specific set of Christian teachings or practices."[21] Chin explains that she means "Christianicity" as something like "Italianicity" in the work of literary theorist Roland Barthes. Just as, for Barthes, "Italianicity" is "the condensed essence of

19 Boyarin, *Border Lines*, 17.

20 Boyarin, *Border Lines*, 17.

21 Catherine M. Chin, "Through the Looking Glass Darkly: Jerome Inside the Book," in *The Early Christian Book*, ed. William E. Klingshirn and Linda Safran (Washington: Catholic University of America, 2007), 105.

everything that could be Italian," "Christianicity" is "the condensed essence of everything that could be seen as within the purview of the Christian." Here, christianicity is a way of experiencing, through a sacred writing, that reflects being trained to anticipate and recognize Christ "from Egypt to Nineveh."[22]

There is an appreciative, but also a critical, sense in which Chin uses christianicity. She argues that Jerome disseminates a kind of Christian wherewithal that is not reducible to a specific act or idea; yet at the same time this distinctive quality is built on the cordoning of sensibility, and in a sense *is* the cordoning of sensibility, trading on the duality of essential sameness and essential difference. Christian readers cannot, for example, be thinking of the holy land as it existed in their time; they must be conformed rather to the "abstraction."[23] The practice of reading draws from and leads toward the securing of Christian identity, the "ideal space" that is "Christianicity."[24] The "-icity" suffix of Chin's formulation suggests a state of being that keeps asserting its presence. The suffix suggests the ongoing valorization of an essence, and indeed this is evident in Chin's discussion of Jerome's unease around the maintenance of Christian identity. Jerome is famously an admirer of the accomplishments of the "heterodox" theologian Origen. But is his fondness for Origen evidence of a way into, or a derailment from, being-manifesting Christianness? Not, according to Jerome, if Origen's interpretive practices are followed, while Origen's doctrines are disavowed.[25] The Christian labor of denominating salvific ideality, of creating and maintaining a center that can be experienced as natural and must be rhetorically tended through practices that share a "fantastic space"[26]—this labor begins to describe Chin's concept of "Christianicity."

Why Christianicity Matters for Practical Theology

I find this concept helpful for the way it induces in practical theologians an awareness for the precariousness of our work. Those who work in a context conditioned by a Christian heritage inherit and participate in this fictive setting of terms for experience and identity called christianicity. Instead of seeing Christianity as a ready-made thing that is available to be practiced or the invocation of which can condition others' practice, we can see our traffic in Chris-

22 Chin, "Through the Looking Glass Darkly," 105, n. 17, with reference to Roland Barthes, *Image, Music, Text*, trans. Stephen Heath (New York: Hill and Wang, 1977), 48.

23 Chin, "Through the Looking Glass Darkly," 105: "Christianicity is abstracted from fourth-century Palestine."

24 Chin, "Through the Looking Glass Darkly," 106.

25 Chin, "Through the Looking Glass Darkly," 114–115.

26 Chin, "Through the Looking Glass Darkly," 106.

tian materials as a practice of christianicity. The conduct of this practice is ethically important in a cultural situation in which the multiplication of sites of religious/nonreligious practice is important. It is theologically important because there is no way to valorize a "Christian tradition" as something related to practice without at the same time proposing a way of experiencing/identifying as Christian. Holding the dynamic of christianicity critically is an imperative for the practical theologian who wishes to bring the power dynamics of the history of this work to bear more critically and consciously.

Christianicity as the ordering of conduct to fit divine revelation; to keep connected to a sense of "center" and to maintain an "outside" and "outsiders"; the notion that it is beliefs and practices that place one inside or outside of Christianity; that these beliefs and practices will be a test or display of faithfulness and the depth of Christian life/identity: all this seems to date at least to the late second and early third century. This heritage is part of the discourse of practical theology as the theological discipline that takes care for Christian life and for Christian "care of souls."[27] "Christianicity" is meant to remind the reader that "Christianity" is much less a description of a state or condition (an abstract noun) than a kind of display of identity in a certain time and place, a way of designating and fostering an experience of recognizing one's own or another's essential Christian-ness as resident in beliefs and practices, in an over-against relationship with the "others" of "Christianity," that is neither essential nor unchosen. The idea of there being Christian practice is a political choice for one of many possible "Christianities" that naturalizes its action by establishing continuity with a Christian past and laying down track toward a Christian future. Christianicity as a way of thinking about the performance of religious identity means that to declare someone "Christian," through the theological significance of their practice or belief, is to sustain a characterization of that person by way of disembedding him or her from and re-embedding him or her in beliefs and practices that are thought to protect or secure Christianness.[28]

---

27 The "care of souls" language is a crucial semantic link between contemporary understandings of practical theology and the ancient Western world in the philosophical schools, as one of which an influential strand of ancient Christianity presented itself. See Pierre Hadot, *What is Ancient Philosophy?*, trans. Michael Chase (Cambridge: Harvard University Press, 2004); Hadot, *Philosophy as a Way of Life: Spiritual Exercises from Socrates to Foucault*, trans. Michael Chase (Oxford: Blackwell, 1995), 126–144.

28 Whereas in earlier work I have used the alternative term "Christianities" to foreground the way that—and the problem of the significance of—substantially different conceptual contents and forms of experience go forward as animating life and faith named "Chris-

It makes sense that predication and affordance are put into the service of furthering a form of experience called and felt as "Christian" (or "Catholic" or other Christian markers). There is a mutual reinforcement between assigning Christian meaning to an assigned domain called *practice*, feeling relatively at home in a religious world of texts, concepts, and experiences, and thinking the task of the theologian is to keep what feels like forward motion going, to reproduce its essential characteristics in a new generation and to restore fidelity to it in the present by finding ever-anew a hospitable religious past that funds contemporary practice.[29] The question is whether this Christianicity is adequate to a more critical theological account of the Christian tradition itself and to the range of needs of contemporary persons for choosing integral lives that make sense to them. When we name and question the Christianicity in practical theology, we are able to see that practical theology "evangelizes" frequently by implicitly and explicitly disambiguating theological from nontheological material, prising apart theological, religious, spiritual, or sacred practice, action, performance, or experience from what is invented as its other: nontheological, nonreligious, nonspiritual, nonsacred practice, action, performance, or experience.[30] Practical theology works up special material (for example, "religious practice"), often through the velvet gloves of "recognition" (honoring what is "already going on"). Under the pressure of the three developments outlined at the beginning of this chapter (questioning practice, whiteness,

---

tian," in more recent work I have experimented with "christianicity." First, I attempted to work with "christianicity" as a way of making sense of different theological interpretations of music in my chapter "Introduction: Theology of Popular Music as a Theological Exercise," in *Secular Music and Sacred Theology*, ed. Tom Beaudoin (Collegeville: Liturgical Press, 2013), xxii–xxiii, with reference to theology's concern for cultural capitulation, for hermeneutics, and for liberation. Second, I used the notion as a way of understanding the rhetorical moves made by some postmodern practical theologies that take postmodern analyses as occasions to reground Christian identity foundationally, in "Postmodern Practical Theology," 192.

29 For example: "[T]he very reason for practical theology is to promote discipleship" that "calls forth long-term commitment from disciples and faithful communities," in Kathleen A. Cahalan and James R. Nieman, "Mapping the Field of Practical Theology," in *For Life Abundant: Practical Theology, Theological Education, and Christian Ministry*, ed. Dorothy C. Bass and Craig Dykstra (Grand Rapids: Eerdmans, 2008), 84.

30 For example: "Just about any activity, if it is *performed regularly and with a shared understanding of religious intent or meaning*, can be considered a religious practice [...] Nothing can be deemed too secular to study, because the *secular and the sacred, like the intellect and the spirit, and like theology and practice, dwell in us together.*" Mary Clark Moschella, *Ethnography as a Pastoral Practice: An Introduction* (Cleveland: Pilgrim, 2008), 51, emphasis added.

and Christian-centrism), this theological dynamic is the kind of theological propriety (property-making/-(s)taking) that can and should be brought to crisis[31]—or that can be understood now as the habitation of a crisis always there but glossed over by theological glue that stabilizes significance in service of techniques and politics of Christian continuities.

Beyond Christianicity in Practical Theology

The force of the conundrum under consideration, through its constituent dynamics of predication, affordance, and christianicity, necessitates a search for other ways for practical theology to elaborate its Christian heritage that can enable practical theology to proceed differently in the present cultural landscape. Insofar as Christianity as practice-experience is generated by and readable back down to "non-Christian" elements that are backgrounded in order for christianicity to "take place," emergence from the conundrum is a matter of dispossessing the need to maintain a Christian center. Resisting christianicity will energize new forms of religious/nonreligious ways of life out of Christian materials, and also out of the non-Christian materials that make up the heritage of Christian theology, including its practices and concepts.

As philosopher of religion Daniel Colucciello Barber has argued, Christianity has understood itself in terms of an assertion of difference with what it constitutes as "Judaism" and worked diligently to maintain the religious-political importance of that difference. But having become itself by being "over against" something it called "Judaism," Christianity then proceeded to deny difference as Christians asserted salvific preeminence among religions and revelations. "Christian religion," Barber argues, would do well to recall that "it is the heir of discontinuity," so that it can better "affirm this discontinuity" as it confronts difference within and outside itself.[32] To be constituted by "discontinuity" would be for practical theology to acknowledge the strangeness of the Christian heritage—its "queer" assemblage of materials and forms of life—

31 The theologian who works well "knows how to seize the moment, or better to create the moment in which a given theology is brought to crisis by a new historical or social development.... Angling for change, the theologian determines which theological materials do the most work in a particular theological configuration and how much interpretive leeway already surrounds them." Kathryn Tanner, *Theories of Culture: A New Agenda for Theology* (Philadelphia: Fortress, 1997), 90.

32 Daniel Colucciello Barber, *On Diaspora: Christianity, Religion, and Secularity* (Eugene, OR: Cascade, 2011), 97–98.

and to advocate strangeness as a possible way of life for the souls for which it cares.[33]

Scoring Practice

When practical theologians work to grant practice a theological registration, then what counts as practice is always "scored." This scoring is what the predications and affordances enact. To respond to the three disorientations and thus to detour from the christianicity of practical theology, it is important to understand the common ways that practical theology is engaged in scoring cultural events as practice and to inquire, as I began to do above, how practice can be scored differently. "Scoring" has four simultaneous meanings that suit well a deeper understanding of practical theology.

First, to "score" is to mark, as in scoring leather or wood. Notches are made that serve aesthetic or utilitarian purposes. Practice is marked by practical theologians as they bring theological frameworks that generate what counts as practice and that grant that practice a theological voice. Second, to "score" a musical or a film, for example, is to give it a soundtrack that cues and communicates the significance of what we are seeing. To score is to musically frame the interpretation of the production for the audience.[34] Practical theology provides just this sort of meaning-framing for practice, heard through the poetics of theology, which limns (or, less subtly, asserts) the quality of the religious-spiritual truth of practice. To "score," thirdly, is also to grade, rate, and evaluate, as in scoring tests. Practical theology has innovated numerous ways of

---

33 Practice-minded theological work along this construal of Christianity is already being done. See, for example, Michelle Gonzalez on Catholic practices as "indistinguishable" from Santeria and "evil eye" in Guatemala, in Gonzalez, "If It Is Not Catholic, Is It Still Popular Religion? Evil Eye, Espiritismo, and Santeria: Latino/a Religion Within Latino/a Theology," in *Decolonizing Epistemologies: Latina/o Theology and Philosophy*, ed. Ada María Isasi-Díaz and Eduardo Mendieta (New York: Fordham, 2011), 151–168; Marion Grau on the changes in the meanings of gospel in Anglican missions among the Zulu in South Africa from "pre" to "post" evangelization, in Grau, *Rethinking Mission in the Postcolony: Salvation, Society, and Subversion* (New York: Continuum, 2011); and Emmanuel Lartey on the marks of postcolonial pastoral theology through an interpretation of a Ghanaian healing ritual involving Muslim, Christian, and traditional African religious leaders, in Lartey, "Postcolonial African Practical Theology," *Journal of Pastoral Theology* 21:2 (2011): 1–17.

34 Pop music scholar Simon Frith quotes Schopenhauer to this effect: "Suitable music played to any scene, action, event or surrounding seems to disclose to us its most secret meaning, and appears as the most accurate and distinct commentary upon it." Schopenhauer in Simon Frith, *Performing Rites: On the Value of Popular Music* (Cambridge: Harvard, 1998), 111.

critically adjudicating the faithfulness of practice. A fourth related meaning of "scoring" is to achieve points in sports, such as scoring a goal in football/soccer. Practical theology has valorized practice as the way of living the faithful Christian life and celebrates such performances.

What are the ways of scoring practice as theologically significant? They center on liberation (a discourse of freedom), situation (a discourse of context), formation (a discourse of shaping persons), and correlation (a discourse of relating faith and culture). When applied with practical theological skill, they make practice theological, or "show" practice as a theological carrier. They stabilize the otherwise threatening multivocality of what has come before and what could come after and authorize action in pastoral and social settings.

What the foregoing line of argument suggests is that the deeply animating conviction in practical theology that practices are "theory-laden," inherited from the justly influential work of Don Browning, needs to be rethought. Browning, and all who inherited his liberal-correlational approach to practical theology, substantially advanced the field with his contention that practices are weighted with constituent forces that can be framed theoretically and addressed theologically.[35] The argument of this chapter takes a different tack. Instead of imagining practices as theory-laden, the strongly fictive and creative character of practical theological work on practices comes to the fore, known through the practices of predication and affordance in the light of the incitement to christianicity. It would not be appropriate, then, to speak of practices as theory-laden. Theologically significant practices have competing centers/outsides that are "unladen" of some material in order for the theologian to read them as "laden" with other material. The identification of a practice in practical theology is a symptom of an essentially contested christianicity. The "normative" moment in practical theology is a ritual invocation of a boundary to be able to get things done. But when necessary, that boundary can be read back into (heterogeneous accounts of) its component parts for the sake of furthering (non)religious strangenesses that open onto more life, that offer living significance today. It is a matter of handing over the co-

35 "By using the phrase *theory-laden*, I mean to rule out in advance the widely held assumption that theory is distinct from practice. All our practices, even our religious practices, have theories *behind* and *within* them" (emphasis added). Practical theology sensitizes the theologian in the capacity to "abstract the theory from the practice." Don S. Browning, *A Fundamental Practical Theology: Descriptive and Strategic Proposals* (Minneapolis: Fortress, 1991), 6. The relation (and debt) of my proposal in this chapter to Browning's foundational work in the field will be further elaborated in future publications.

ordinates of "the faith" to the service of a truth not yet comprehended by the faith.

Christian Practice Beyond Christian Hermeneutical Control

When one is a Christian, or when Christianity has some bearing on one's life or identity, then one is already related to possibilities "outside" Christianity and placed within the process of the very generation and maintenance of an "inside" and an "outside." To be related to Christianity is at the same time to be not related to Christianity, insofar as it is also to be a person inheriting the heritage of other faiths, other cultures, other times, other values, other practices. What counts as Christian practice is always generated out of local inherited available materials, conscious and personally/culturally unconscious. When we anchor a practice in a Christian notion, we necessarily disembed that notion from its current and historic non-Christian grounds or dimensions. We usually do this because we want to support the practice of faith, but it is important to recognize this for the invention that it is, however unaware of its fictive character we are. We rehearse an idea of continuity from there to here and expect that the disembedded Christian material guarantees that continuity. "Jesus Christ is the same yesterday and today and forever."[36] For movement beyond this conundrum, it is better to see our work in practical theology for the christianicity that it is. And then, once we acknowledge that seam, to ask whether acknowledgement is enough. Or whether we can appreciate the strangeness of the theological material of practice. "What if the strangenesses out of which Christianities were made continue to strangeness Christianities?"[37]

To practice Christianity or otherwise employ Christian resources is to be subtly hypercontextual, in the sense of thinking and doing things that are more than twenty centuries' residue for the present moment—not all equally formative and never merely "available" to us, of course. This is why Michel Foucault charges that practices hold "not a timeless and essential secret but the secret that they have no essence, or that their essence was fabricated in a piecemeal fashion from alien forms."[38] Every element of Christian practice and belief is an inside keeping back—and simultaneously building on—an outside, through the predications and affordances that have enacted christianicity. That "fic-

36 Heb. 13:8, New Revised Standard Version.

37 Beaudoin, *Witness to Dispossession*, 144.

38 Michel Foucault, "Nietzsche, Genealogy, History," in Michel Foucault, *Aesthetics, Method, and Epistemology*, ed. James D. Faubion, trans. Robert Hurley et al. (New York: New Press, 1998), 371.

tion of the others" that religion creates lets us know that Christians are also all that they are not. They thus can acknowledge the fictions that maintain the grounds of Christian practice.[39]

Is practical theology left with empty hands? No—or rather, Yes: practical theology is left with hands that become theological by how they give away what was never the property of Christianity to begin with. This giving away is an acknowledgement that there is no "here" of proper Christian practice that is against a "there" of non-Christian practice. Christian practice depends on and is open (usually via resistance) to living "outside religion." Christianity runs through practical theology when theologians let the dichotomies and component histories that structure theological registrations of practice run through our hands. In doing so, we learn more about what religious practice is "about."[40]

What does this mean for the theological significance of practice? It means rethinking the grounding indicative/imperative rhetoric in practical theology and opening up the theological significance of practice beyond Christian governance of theological material. Such indicative/imperative rhetoric is common and indicates the inflation of a normative bumper that is a defensive theological strategy, along the lines of "If Christians are incarnational, then in this circumstance they should live like this," or "If God is merciful, then practice should go this way." The investment in the "if" is substantial; in a way, it is everything. Practical theology does not commonly see it as its task to substantiate the grounding claims brought in for this normative bumpering.

Practical theology can hold open pre-Christian, Christian, post-Christian, and non-Christian meanings all at once, and let those meanings be non-exclusive to each other. Gospel—as "good news"—has meanings before, during, after, and apart from Christianity. Speaking of gospel: Holding open such

---

39 What is excluded as Christian material in theology not only sits "outside" as non-theological material. It is more fundamentally the "ground of being" of the notion of "the Christian" (practice, idea, object, etc.) as such. "Religious others are constitutive of the Christian situation." See the discussion in Brockman, *No Longer the Same*, 28ff. Brockman's important argument focuses on the ways that religious others are included (through discursive exclusion) in Christian self-understanding; I am focusing on the ways that "religious" and "nonreligious" others are, similarly, already "within" Christian self-understanding, understood in terms of practice, in a way that bears not only on Christian self-understanding but that reformulates the task of Christian-heritage practical theology into a "multireligious" and "multisecular" work.

40 This paragraph is adapted and revised from Tom Beaudoin, *Witness to Dispossession*, 143–154, which represents an earlier articulation of the present argument.

diverse meanings will necessarily revise the account of ultimate reality to which practical theologians tie practice. The cost of not doing so is enough to threaten the very work of practical theology: failing to adequately fit theology to the present and profoundly impoverishing what can be learned of "God" through practice.

From Publics to Futures

My wager is that this way of dealing with the conundrum aids practical theology in addressing the three disorientations with which I began this chapter. In other words, it renders practical theology more hospitable to the variety of spiritual habitations made today, attempting to make practical theology a practice of hospitality toward the religious/nonreligious "other," analogous to the practice of hospitality as a practice recommended to churches and other religious institutions in multireligious and secular outreach approaches.[41] Hospitality becomes a problem when practical theology presumes that the freedom practical theology is after will be assimilable to Christianity, instead of also "transcending" Christianity, standing "indifferent" toward it—or more. Theologically significant practices always make a new spiritual situation—irreducible to what has come before.

In this way, practical theology can move more fully from a concern to address "publics" to inventing "futures." It may do this through a critical search for ancestry. In opening the theological significance of practice to pre-Christian, Christian, post-Christian, and non-Christian meanings, which is a result of seeing Christianity itself as a jerrybuilt pastiche of cultural materials, of cultural practices rendered as religious/faith/Christian practices, practical theology keeps its curiosity permanent regarding the heritage of practice. This is a political imperative that cuts across the three disorientations. The future will be and should be multiply religious and nonreligious and multiply racial/ethnic. As Gerben Heitink argues with regard to practical theology, "It is not a matter of building on the past, but of anticipating the future, and from there critically remembering the past."[42]

---

41 Sheryl A. Kujawa-Holbrook, *God Beyond Borders: Interreligious Learning Among Faith Communities* (Eugene: Pickwick, 2014), 12–14.

42 Gerben Heitink, *Practical Theology: History, Theory, Action Domains*, trans. Reinder Bruinsma (Grand Rapids: Eerdmans, 1999), 134.

Bibliography

Althaus-Reid, Marcella. *Indecent Theology: Theological Perversions in Sex, Gender, and Politics*. New York: Routledge, 2000.

Andrews, Dale. "Race and Racism." In *The Wiley-Blackwell Companion to Practical Theology*, edited by Bonnie J. Miller-McLemore, 401–411. Malden: Blackwell, 2012.

Astley, Jeff. *Ordinary Theology: Looking, Listening, and Learning in Theology*. Aldershot: Ashgate, 2003.

Barber, Daniel Colucciello. *On Diaspora: Christianity, Religion, and Secularity*. Eugene, OR: Cascade, 2011.

Beaudoin, Tom. *Witness to Dispossession: The Vocation of a Postmodern Theologian*. Maryknoll: Orbis, 2008.

Beaudoin, Tom. "Everyday Life in a Scandalized Church: A Theological Perspective." In *Religion, Media, and Culture: A Reader*, edited by Gordon Lynch, Jolyon Mitchell, and Anna Strhan, 236–243. New York: Routledge, 2011.

Beaudoin, Tom. "Introduction: Theology of Popular Music as a Theological Exercise." In *Secular Music and Sacred Theology*, edited by Tom Beaudoin, ix–xxiv. Collegeville: Liturgical Press, 2013.

Beaudoin, Tom. "Postmodern Practical Theology." In *Opening the Field of Practical Theology: An Introduction*, edited by Kathleen A. Cahalan and Gordon S. Mikoski, 187–202. New York: Rowman and Littlefield, 2014.

Beaudoin, Tom and Katherine Turpin. "White Practical Theology." In *Opening the Field of Practical Theology: An Introduction*, edited by Kathleen A. Cahalan and Gordon S. Mikoski, 251–269. New York: Rowman and Littlefield, 2014.

Boyarin, Daniel. *Border Lines: The Partition of Judaeo-Christianity*. Philadelphia: University of Pennsylvania Press, 2004.

Brockman, David R. *No Longer the Same: Religious Others and the Liberation of Christian Theology*. New York: Palgrave Macmillan, 2011.

Browning, Don S. *A Fundamental Practical Theology: Descriptive and Strategic Proposals*. Minneapolis: Fortress, 1991.

Cahalan, Kathleen A., and Gordon S. Mikoski, eds. *Opening the Field of Practical Theology: An Introduction*. New York: Rowman and Littlefield, 2014.

Cahalan, Kathleen A., and James R. Nieman. "Mapping the Field of Practical Theology." In *For Life Abundant: Practical Theology, Theological Education, and Christian Ministry*, edited by Dorothy C. Bass and Craig Dykstra, 62–85. Grand Rapids: Eerdmans, 2008.

Chin, Catherine M. "Through the Looking Glass Darkly: Jerome Inside the Book." In *The Early Christian Book*, edited by William E. Klingshirn and Linda Safran, 101–116. Washington: Catholic University of America, 2007.

Foucault, Michel. "Nietzsche, Genealogy, History." In Michel Foucault, *Aesthetics, Method, and Epistemology*, edited by James D. Faubion, translated by Robert Hurley *et al.*, 369–391. New York: New Press, 1998.
Frith, Simon. *Performing Rites: On the Value of Popular Music*. Cambridge: Harvard, 1998.
Gonzalez, Michelle. "If It Is Not Catholic, Is It Still Popular Religion? Evil Eye, Espiritismo, and Santeria: Latino/a Religion Within Latino/a Theology." In *Decolonizing Epistemologies: Latina/o Theology and Philosophy*, edited by Ada María Isasi-Díaz and Eduardo Mendieta, 151–168. New York: Fordham, 2011.
Grau, Marion. *Rethinking Mission in the Postcolony: Salvation, Society, and Subversion*. New York: Continuum, 2011.
Greider, Kathleen. "Religious Pluralism and Christian-Centrism." In *The Wiley-Blackwell Companion to Practical Theology*, edited by Bonnie J. Miller-McLemore, 452–461. Malden: Blackwell, 2012.
Hadot, Pierre. *Philosophy as a Way of Life: Spiritual Exercises from Socrates to Foucault*, translated by Michael Chase. Oxford: Blackwell, 1995.
Hadot, Pierre. *What is Ancient Philosophy?*, translated by Michael Chase. Cambridge: Harvard University Press, 2004.
Isherwood, Lisa, and Mark D. Jordan, eds. *Dancing Theology in Fetish Boots: Essays in Honor of Marcella Althaus-Reid*. London: SCM, 2010.
Kujawa-Holbrook, Sheryl A. *God Beyond Borders: Interreligious Learning Among Faith Communities*. Eugene: Pickwick, 2014.
Lartey, Emmanuel Y. *Postcolonializing God: An African Practical Theology*. London: SCM, 2013.
Moschella, Mary Clark. *Ethnography as a Pastoral Practice: An Introduction*. Cleveland: Pilgrim, 2008.
Ospino, Hosffman and Elsie Miranda. "Hispanic Ministry and Leadership Formation." In *Hispanic Ministry in the 21st Century: Present and Future*, edited by Hosffman Ospino, 175–200. Miami: Convivium, 2010.
Partridge, Christopher. *The Lyre of Orpheus: Popular Music, the Sacred, and the Profane*. New York: Oxford, 2013.
Queen, "Under Pressure." *Hot Space*. EMI, 1982.
Rubio, Julie Hanlon. "Practices of Love and Solidarity: Family Ethics." In *Invitation to Practical Theology: Catholic Voices and Visions*, edited by Claire E. Wolfteich, 215–233. New York: Paulist, 2014.
Sheppard, Phillis Isabella. *Self, Culture, and Others in Womanist Practical Theology*. New York: Palgrave Macmillan, 2011.
Sherkat, Darren. *Changing Faith: The Dynamics and Consequences of Americans' Shifting Religious Identities*. New York: NYU Press, 2014.

Streib, Heinz, Ralph W. Hood, Jr., Barbara Keller, Rosina-Martha Csöff, Christopher F. Silver, *Deconversion: Qualitative and Quantitative Results from Cross-Cultural Research in Germany and the United States of America*. Göttingen: Vandenhoeck & Ruprecht, 2009.

Tanner, Kathryn. *Theories of Culture: A New Agenda for Theology*. Philadelphia: Fortress, 1997.

de Vries, Hent. *Philosophy and the Turn to Religion*. Baltimore: Johns Hopkins University, 2001.

de Vries, Hent. *Religion and Violence: Philosophical Perspectives from Kant to Derrida*. Baltimore: Johns Hopkins University, 2001.

CHAPTER 2

The Power and Danger of a Single Case Study in Practical Theological Research

Eileen R. Campbell-Reed

> *It is impossible to talk about the single story without talking about power… How they are told, who tells them, when they're told, how many stories are told, are really dependent on power.*
>
> CHIMAMANDA NGOZI ADICHIE, "The Danger of a Single Story"[1]

A single case study in practical theological research and writing can be extraordinarily powerful for showing the richness of a complex situation or a person's life or an entire social or spiritual phenomenon. A single case study can provide an instance of practical wisdom, and it can contribute to complex human learning or assist with urgent needs for discernment in multifaceted and demanding situations. Yet a single case study can also mislead or misdirect readers to stereotypes, one-sided assessments, or oversimplified analysis. The dangers of a single case study are always present, and thus cases in practical theological scholarship involve risk and require great care in their construction.

Beginning with a personal case that entails misunderstandings about one of my own research proposals, this essay explores the challenge of using a single case study for how it may instantiate powerful wisdom and how it may also be troublesome or even dangerous. To see why single cases present a conundrum at this juncture in history, I offer a brief recounting of the use of case studies in theological education and situate their use in the longer post-Reformation history of *casuistry* or the case-by-case deliberation over moral dilemmas. By exploring a series of misunderstandings over the use of case studies in the social sciences, I draw out implications for practical theologians who wish to overcome their aversion to using single or small numbers of case studies. For

1 Chimamanda Ngozi Adichie, "The Danger of a Single Story" TED Talk, July 2009, accessed July 24, 2015, http://www.ted.com/talks/chimamanda_adichie_the_danger_of_a_single_story/transcript?language=en. A case study is not simply a story, although it often includes one or more stories.

 | DOI 10.1163/9789004324244_004

cases to be useful, practical theologians need a wide range of methodological tools, and they need to attend to uses, misuses, and possible abuses of power within the situations under study, including their own social location and personal interests in the case. Cases are essential to all forms of advanced human learning, and thus they hold potential for practical, important, and wise outcomes; yet they deserve and demand care in their formulation and use, so as to avoid potential dangers and harms. Finally, I will suggest some guidance for the construction and use of cases by practical theologians in their research and writing.

A Case of Misunderstood Methodology

Not long ago I got one of those dreaded letters in the mail. My research proposal to further my study of clergywomen in the United States would not receive funding. After the holidays and several pressing deadlines, I contacted the staff person at the granting agency who had initiated more conversation in my notification letter. Over the phone I learned some reasons reviewers were reluctant. The reviewers apparently liked my proposal generally, but were "not convinced that the methodology works." Other reviewer misgivings fleshed out the methodological concerns.[2] They wondered, "Could I make a claim based on a limited group?" They also worried that some study participants already know me through a longitudinal study that I have directed since 2009, and they wondered if I should take a "fresh look" and/or choose new study participants. The reviewers were suspicious about the methods of interviewing small groups of pastors and laity. They feared participants would not get "equal participation in the conversation." Reviewers were also concerned that the proposal "tilted toward the positive" with "no room for the negative" aspects of what it could mean to be a female pastor in twenty-first century America. Possibly more troubling, they raised a concern over my asking questions about ministry that might allow or even cause me to "essentialize different types of experiences of men and women." They worried that my hypothesis was "too big a claim" or the wrong claim for the fieldwork I proposed. They said the fieldwork would be important, but wondered if I might aim for a project that "came in somewhere between case studies and history and the bigger

2 Phrases in quotes come from my notes taken during the conversation with the staff person. The ideas surely include interpretation and filtering of what reviewers actually said. Nevertheless the critiques are fairly direct in relationship to qualitative research and case studies.

enterprise" of changes to women's leadership in the church in the last fifty years.

Many of the reviewers' concerns go to the heart of the conundrum of using case studies (or any small-scale qualitative research design) in the work of constructing new knowledge, a challenge that most practical theologians face at some point. Reflecting later, I saw how my proposal assumed too much and how I might take more responsibility to interpret my use of case studies. I assumed that reviewers would see the power of the cases I planned to construct, and I did not adequately address the dangers nor how I would avoid or mitigate them. For example, I did not show how cases might offer a pathway into larger arguments about the history of Christian clergywomen since 1960.[3] As a practical theologian, I assume the significance of contextualization, historicity, and social analysis as well as the integration of theological reflection into my scholarship, but I could have done more to spell out these assumptions in my proposal. In fact, I could have defined what I meant by cases more carefully.

Case Studies Defined

Case studies are instances of research focusing on a particular person, group, or situation over a defined period of time. They are based in a distinct set of research questions, shaped by explicit parameters, and set within socio-political, historical, and theological context. Nearly all case studies, whether for classroom learning, field education, or scholarly investigations, include background, description of the event or situation, and evaluation and/or analysis.[4] Research-based case studies can be constructed in various ways and always require a selection of materials that includes some features and leaves out others. What holds cases together are the questions that shape the research, questions open enough to allow the person or situation to define itself, rather than being defined solely by the researcher. Like many creative and constructive acts, the work of writing case studies is one of participating with others, and it involves both creating and discovering the narratives and analysis.

Teaching the practice of ministry and theological reflection about ministry is done well through the use of cases, and many practical theologians use

3 I make extensive connections between individual cases of clergywomen and the wider history of Baptists in my recent book, *Anatomy of a Schism: How Clergywomen's Narratives Reinterpret the Fracturing of the Southern Baptist Convention* (Knoxville, TN: University Press, 2016).

4 Glen H. Asquith, Jr. "Case Study Method," in *The Dictionary of Pastoral Care and Counseling*, ed. Rodney J. Hunter (Nashville, TN: Abingdon, 1990), 125.

case studies in their teaching.[5] In a seminary course on Interpersonal Skills for Ministry, I asked my class to consider two cases from the Learning Pastoral Imagination (LPI) Project, a national, ecumenical, and longitudinal study of ministry in the United States.[6] In the cases, new ministers Asha and Malinda, each twenty-six years old, are moving from seminary graduation to a first call in ministry.[7] The cases give background about each woman, and I provided my students several open-ended questions: What skills and gifts are *available* and *needed* as each woman begins her ministry? How does her social location impact her call? What else would you need to know to make a fuller assessment of her present situation? After a thirty-minute discussion one woman said, "You're asking us to think about what else we would need to know to understand this case because that's the kind of question we should be asking in our own situations of ministry!" Yes, exactly.

By comparing the two stories, my students could see differences and similarities in each woman's life, especially related to social location. Asha expressed fear about taking church leadership, having grown up in what she called a "hierarchical black-church tradition." Malinda described a sense of calling in her encounter with God while spending time alone in a wilderness area. Upon sharing her call, she found a welcome in her white congregation as well as an invitation to be a summer ministry intern. Additional observations, personal identifications, and questions about Melinda and Asha became touch points for the remainder of the class. The narratives helped students hold on to the learning.

Case studies also invite a multi-layered integrating practice of formation for students beyond single classes or subject areas. For example, practical theologian Kathleen Cahalan uses case studies to help her students "gain an appreci-

5 For an example, see the series of open-source ministry cases by Scott Cormode, "Almond Springs," accessed February 17, 2015, http://www.christianleaders.org/Almond_Springs/index.htm.

6 Chris Scharen and I are co-directors of the Learning (LPI) Project, funded by the Lilly Endowment (2008–16). The study asks: *How is pastoral imagination formed through practice in ministry over time?* It follows fifty seminary graduates from ten schools across five regions of the United States. For findings at the five-year mark, see Christian A.B. Scharen and Eileen R. Campbell-Reed, *Learning Pastoral Imagination: A Five-Year Report on How New Ministers Learn in Practice* (New York: Auburn Seminary, 2016).

7 All names in the LPI research protocol are changed to guard the identities of participants. Reference to Asha's story appears in Eileen R. Campbell-Reed and Christian Scharen, "'Holy Cow! This Stuff is Real!' From Imagining Ministry to Pastoral Imagination" in *Teaching Theology and Religion* 14, no. 4 (2011): 323–42, and Malinda's story appears at in Eileen R. Campbell-Reed and Christian Scharen, "Ministry as Spiritual Practice: How Pastors Learn to See and Respond to the 'More' of a Situation," *Journal of Religious Leadership* 12, no. 2 (2013): 125–44.

ation for how to think theologically and practically" across multiple skills and areas of ministry, experiencing how they "interconnect in real time."[8] Practical theologian Daniel Schipani agrees: "case study methodology serves very well as an empirically grounded, patterned, disciplined, and praxis-focused way of doing mid-level practical theology for the sake of theological and ministerial formation."[9] By "mid-level," Schipani follows Leonardo and Clodovis Boff in their interpretation of the mid-level or "pastoral" level of liberation theology as a bridge between popular (grassroots) and professional (academic) theology. He suggests that case studies are mainly useful for pastors to learn and reflect on instances of ministry. There is a deep congruence between the method of case study and the discipline of practical theology itself. Schipani sums up the good of case studies, saying they are "empirically grounded, contextually situated; they are hermeneutical in character, fundamentally evaluative and normative, and pragmatically and strategically oriented."[10] However, when it comes to using case studies in scholarly writing, Schipani is more cautious, warning about the lack of clear limits on data gathering, the problem of "generalizing from one case to another," and bias on the part of the researcher.[11]

Other practical theologians construct case studies about their teaching in order to explore pedagogical wisdom. For example, James R. Neiman engages a "solitary case" of teaching the course "Liturgy and Life" to offer a "broader constellation of proposals in the field of practical theology." Similarly, John D. Witvliet writes about an approach to teaching as "a pedagogy of and for deep participation" that moves beyond techniques and objectives of worship "to an approach that forms students in the constellation of knowledge, wisdom, skills, and capacities needed for faithful practice."[12]

In the same way case studies foster understanding in classrooms, and in scholarship on pedagogy, so constructing, writing up, and reflecting on case studies also fits well as a mode of practical theological scholarship. One key to understanding the power of case studies in teaching, learning, research, and

8 Kathleen Cahalan, "Introducing Ministry and Fostering Integration" in *For Life Abundant: Practical Theology, Theological Education, and Christian Ministry*, ed. Dorothy C. Bass and Craig R. Dykstra (Grand Rapids: Eerdmans, 2008), 97.

9 Daniel Schipani, "Case Study Method," in *The Wiley-Blackwell Companion to Practical Theology*, ed. Bonnie J. Miller-McLemore (Malden, MA: Blackwell Publishing, 2012), 99.

10 Schipani, "Case Study Method," 100.

11 Schipani, "Case Study Method," 99.

12 See James R. Neiman, "Liturgy and Life: An Account of Teaching Ritual Practices" and John D. Witvliet, "Teaching Worship as a Christian Practice," in *For Life Abundant: Practical Theology, Theological Education and Christian Ministry*, ed. Dorothy C. Bass and Craig Dykstra (Grand Rapids: Eerdmans, 2008), 150–51, 117–18.

writing is *context*. Practical theology is nothing without a context. Whatever it tries to be without context will be neither practical nor theology.[13] Without context, the questions, problems, discernment, wisdom, or any hoped-for remedies would make little sense. To write practical theology, "theology that matters" to the people and places where it is situated, practical theologians make use of case studies to allow careful historical, social, and theological contextualization, descriptions, and analysis, designed to avoid the dangers of reductionism and stereotyping of the people or situations they want to understand.[14]

The Paradox of Using Cases in Practical Theological Research

The paradox of using single or small numbers of cases studies is that although human beings need single cases for understanding the complexity and intensity of a situation, single cases are constantly suspect because of their limitations, perceived or real bias, and their novelty. In practical theological research, case studies are useful for articulating complex, context-dependent knowledge, revising belief and practice, offering practical wisdom or helpful discernment about situations, and showing how change happens over time. However, because of the potential trouble or danger of single (or a small numbers of) cases, they are often viewed as mainly illustrative, heuristic, suggestive for building research agendas, or even decorative, rather than as substantive or *real research*. Precisely because cases are powerful and necessary for human learning, there is a danger of misuse of their power by the researcher. Thus, practical theological researchers hold a special responsibility as they construct cases. They need to articulate realities with care, and they need to set research agendas that avoid harm whenever possible, attending to the dynamics of power in the situation.[15]

---

13 In her 2011 presidential address to the International Association of Practical Theology, Bonnie Miller-McLemore summarized practical theology as a robust *academic discipline* as well as "an *activity* of believers seeking to sustain a life of reflective faith in the everyday, a *method* or way of analyzing theology in practice... a *curricular area* in theological education." The four overlapping definitions "are connected and interdependent... and reflect the range and complexity of practical theology today." Bonnie J. Miller-McLemore, "Five Misunderstandings about Practical Theology," *International Journal of Practical Theology* 16, no. 1 (2012): 19–20.

14 The phrase "practical theology that matters" emerged in conversation with Chris Scharen about our research in the LPI Project and expresses a conviction about attending to urgent needs of people and situations.

15 Feminist practical theologians like Elaine Graham and Bonnie Miller-McLemore insist the descriptive and empirical turn by practical theologians should include greater atten-

In case-study based research, what is feared to be bias by some may actually be practical wisdom or expertise on the part of the researcher who understands the case at hand based on years of observation, research, and writing about the subject. My dilemma as a researcher is to present my work with both sufficient accounting for the point of view (the "bias") and adequate description of the sources of my wisdom about it. Such transparency is a delicate, sometimes impossible, tight rope to walk.

Thus, case studies are also a conundrum for practical theologians because one needs a wide range of skills, knowledge, and expertise to execute them well. For example, practical theologians need an immersion in academic theology (to speak to our colleagues); awareness of everyday demands on people of faith; a sense of history, common practices, and the ideas and concepts that inform and interact with those practices; a good sense of the whole picture of the situation under study; informed and focused questions about what needs understanding, description, or change; and a healthy sense of the limits of our work as researchers and/or practitioners (clinicians, pastors, teachers). The demands of writing case studies for research are steep and may account for some of the aversion by researchers to the approach. However, a longer history of the trouble and perceived dangers of case studies also shapes the research agendas of practical theologians.

The Historical Use of Cases in Moral and Pastoral Guidance

In the history of the Western church, the need for making moral judgments about everyday practical issues or "cases of conscience" grew over centuries into a practice of "casuistry." This case-by-case consideration of moral situations allowed pastors and priests to give guidance and to interpret certain exceptions and exemptions regarding the keeping of church rites. As a kind of pre- and early modern practical theology, casuistry grew into a pastoral, practical, and eventually formal set of case-based guidelines and literature.[16] Ro-

---

tion to the power differentials and dynamics in their scholarship. See Graham, *Transforming Practice: Pastoral Theology in an Age of Uncertainty* (London: Mowbray, 1996) and Miller-McLemore, "The Living Human Web" in *Through the Eyes of Women: Insights for Pastoral Care* (Minneapolis, MN: Fortress Press, 1996), 9–26. See also Eileen R. Campbell-Reed and Christian Scharen, "Ethnography on Holy Ground: How Qualitative Interviewing is Practical Theological Work," *International Journal of Practical Theology* 17, no. 2 (2013): 232–59.

16 For histories of casuistry, see E. Brooks Holifield "Casuistry, Protestant" and Jean Porter "Casuistry, Roman Catholic" in *The Dictionary of Pastoral Care and Counseling*, ed. Rodney J. Hunter (Nashville, TN: Abingdon, 1990), 126–29.

man Catholic priests, particularly Jesuits, and later Protestant pastors became the arbiters of these judgments. Catholic casuistry was often tied to both the "sacrament of penance" and to the church's canon law.[17] From the early church to the Middle Ages, pastorally focused questions arose regularly in the areas of "truth-telling, self-defense, wealth and commerce, and marriage and family life."[18] Between the Reformation and the opening of the eighteenth century, both Catholics and Protestants practiced casuistry robustly, guiding parishioners through ambiguous moral situations.

A crisis over the dangers of casuistry arose in the seventeenth century as Albert Jonsen and Stephen Toulmin describe in their book, *The Abuse of Casuistry*.[19] At this time, one's public standing and one's church standing were synonymous in France (and all of Europe). Even royalty and public officials participated in church rites (communion, confession and absolution), and they were subject to open scrutiny. During this period, Jesuits in France who took the confessions of monarchs, courtiers, and commoners alike came into controversy with the Jansenists, a small reform-minded sect of Catholic clergy and laity. The two groups became embroiled in a controversy over the use (and abuse) of casuistry.[20] Mathematician, philosopher, and religious prodigy Blaise Pascal was sympathetic to the Jansenists (his sister Jacqueline was a nun in the convent at Port-Royal), and he wrote a series of public critiques under a pen name that eviscerated the use of cases—not just the poorly handled ones, but any and all cases. Pascal's critiques of casuistry were rooted in his own preference for certainty about all things, even the complex and challenging everyday problems that the casuists were employed to help parishioners think through. He used satire and wit to expose the casuists as too simple, too dependent on reason (not God), and too lax on tough moral issues. His powerful critique undermined the entire enterprise. The public disgrace of casuistry combined with other philosophical thinking of the day highlighted, among other things, the problem of personal bias influencing places of public power. The residue of that controversy continues to fuel suspicion even now in many domains, including research and other situations calling for practical judgment.

In sixteenth-century Europe and America, Protestant casuistry books focused on salvation and sanctification, offering pastoral guidance for one's in-

---

17 Porter, "Casuistry, Roman Catholic," 128.

18 Porter, "Casuistry, Roman Catholic," 128. These moral concerns endure into the twenty-first century.

19 Albert R. Jonsen and Stephen Toulmin, *The Abuse of Casuistry: A History of Moral Reasoning* (Berkley, CA: University of California Press, 1988), 11–16.

20 Jonsen and Toulmin, *The Abuse of Casuistry*, 231–49.

terior spiritual life and direction for "how to apply general ethical principles to specific ambiguous cases."[21] In the United States, the Protestant use of casuistic manuals lasted longer, declining in the mid-eighteenth century for various reasons including: the growth of populist forms of ministry, which depended on the Bible alone for guidance in ministry and morality; the emergence of moral philosophies and ethics that did not make use of case-based considerations; and the increasing specialization of pastoral literature that dropped its concern for case-by-case moral deliberations. In the twentieth century, the residual use of cases moved forward with Christian ethicists who continued using cases to test moral principles.[22]

In the 1920s and 1930s, case-based learning re-entered theological education through a side door. Protestant theological education and ministry came under the scrutiny of several studies, which pointed out numerous deficits of ministry preparation.[23] These studies called for new standards, effectiveness, and professionalism in seminaries and a new organization to oversee them: the American Association of Theological Schools (AATS).[24] At the same time, in hospitals and mental health facilities Russell Dicks, Anton Boisen, Richard Cabot, Helen Flanders Dunbar, and others were pioneering a new "clinical training" for ministry, utilizing the case study method as their main technique for teaching and learning.[25] In 1936 the AATS recommended the new Clinical Pastoral Education (CPE) become a seminary requirement.[26] However, the schools never fully integrated CPE into the curricula.[27] Case study teaching and learning remained affiliated with training outside core seminary courses, although it eventually gained more of a foothold in the requirements of field

21 Holifield "Casuistry, Protestant," 127.

22 Holifield "Casuistry, Protestant," 127–28.

23 E. Brooks Holifield, *God's Ambassadors: A History of the Christian Clergy in America* (Grand Rapids, MI: Eerdmans, 2010), 215–17. Holifield identifies a number of studies including: William Adams Brown, Mark A. May and Frank K. Shuttleworth, *The Education of American Ministers*, 4 volumes (New York: Institute of Social and Religious Research, 1934) and Benjamin E. Mays and Joseph W. Nicholson, *The Negro's Church* (New York, Institute of Social and Religious Research, 1933).

24 Holifield, *God's Ambassadors*, 230–32. The following factors also exerted pressure on the structures and curriculum of theological schools: the impact of modernism; expanding university ideals of academic disciplines, research, and specialization; and the growth of other professions like law, medicine, and social work.

25 Asquith, "Case Study Method," 123–26.

26 Holifield, *God's Ambassadors*, 233.

27 Holifield, *God's Ambassadors*, 232–34.

education.[28] Cases were not adopted widely in the research agendas of theological educators until the resurgence of practical theology in the 1980s and since.[29] Among other important things that CPE, field education, and the renaissance of practical theology did for ministry students and the wider theological academy was to bring a new emphasis to the strength of learning that comes from looking carefully at single instances or cases taken from life. That power does not come without problems, yet the significance of the learning is hard to deny.[30]

The Significance of Cases in Human Learning

Everybody uses practical reasoning every day and learns what to do through repeated experiences in a variety of situations. Yet single cases can misdirect learners, emphasizing the need for multiple cases in both every-day learning and research protocol.[31] However, colleagues in the social sciences help explain how human learning depends on single cases despite the potential dangers. Danish planning expert and philosopher of social science Bent Flyvbjerg wrote *Making Social Science Matter* in response to the "Science Wars" of the late 1990s. For years, American and European social and natural scientists debated the value of social sciences.[32] In his book, Flyvbjerg follows

---

28 A group who met to discuss "field work" in theological education between 1946 and 1957 identified a "need for a more holistic, integrated approach to theological education." Thus began a new (adjunct) curricular area called "field education." See Robert T. O'Gorman, Kathleen Talvacchia, and W. Michael Smith, "Teaching from a Community Context: The Role of the Field Educator in Theological Education," in *Theological Education*, 37, no. 2 (2001): 3. See also W. Clark Gilpin, *A Preface to Theology* (Chicago: University of Chicago Press, 1996), 87. Gilpin reports the first call for internships to be part of seminary training came in 1899.

29 Bonnie Miller-McLemore traces this history briefly in her introduction to *The Wiley-Blackwell Companion to Practical Theology*, ed. Bonnie J. Miller-McLemore (Malden, MA: Blackwell Publishing, 2012), 1–4.

30 When we asked recent seminary graduates in the LPI Project about their "Aha!" learning moments in ministry, they consistently named stories from CPE, internships, and field education rather than classroom or text book learning. See Campbell-Reed and Scharen, "Holy Cow! This Stuff is Real!" 338.

31 The need for multiple stories to prevent stereotyping, bias, and misunderstandings is the main point in Adichie's TED talk, "The Danger of a Single Story."

32 Bent Flyvbjerg, *Making Social Science Matter: Why Social Inquiry Fails and How it Can Succeed Again* (New York: Cambridge, 2001), 1–5.

American philosopher Hubert Dreyfus in exploring how the Aristotelian notion of *phronesis* or practical wisdom is an appropriate paradigm for social sciences, which study human situations and problems, entailing vested interests, researcher engagement, and human values. He extends the significance of phronesis by revising the classic Aristotelian questions: "Where are we going? Is it desirable? What should be done?" Demonstrating his own attunement to power dynamics, an interest practical theologians share, he adds: "Who gains, and who loses? Through what kinds of power relations? What possibilities are available to change existing power relations? And is it desirable to do so? Of what kinds of power relations are those asking these questions themselves a part?"[33]

Flyvbjerg works to show how human learning and genuine expertise in everyday activities and among advanced professionals depend on hundreds and thousands of concrete cases.[34] Everyday examples of expertise include "social, technical, and intellectual skills" such as driving a car, packing a lunch, or recognizing a face on a video. Most adults in U.S. society are expert at these things, not because they know the rules or theories about them, nor because they conduct elaborate experiments, but through exposure to countless instances of seeing and doing these activities.[35] The exposure alone is not enough. Actions like driving a car require the embodied and relational experiences of doing, fraught with emotion, risk, and responsibility, to establish learning in the bodies and minds of learners. Most of the beginning rules and maxims are long forgotten in any conscious way, and learners perceive the doing to be "intuitive."[36] This kind of embedded, embodied, relational knowing is basic for helping practitioners make wise judgments in all sorts of important moments and settings.[37]

Advanced human learning in areas as diverse as practical theology, sociology, physics, and biblical studies depend in significant ways on such embedded, embodied, relational knowing. A number of practical theologians draw

---

33 Flyvbjerg, *Making Social Science Matter*, 131.

34 Bent Flyvbjerg, "Five Misunderstandings about Case-Study Research," *Qualitative Inquiry* 12, no. 2 (2006): 219–221.

35 Flyvbjerg, "Five Misunderstandings," 219–221.

36 Hubert L. Dreyfus and Stuart E. Dreyfus, "Peripheral Vision: Expertise in Real World Contexts," *Organization Studies* 26 (2005): 779–92.

37 See Shaun Gallagher, "Philosophical Antecedents of Situated Cognition" (chapter 3) in *The Cambridge Handbook of Situated Cognition*, ed. Philip Robbins and Murat Aydede (New York: Cambridge University Press, 2009). See also Jean Lave and Etienne Wenger, *Situated Learning: Legitimate Peripheral Participation* (New York, N.Y.: Cambridge University Press, 1991).

on the philosophies put forward by Flyvbjerg, Dreyfus, and others to show how human learning and practical theological wisdom converge.[38] Flyvbjerg argues that the highest learning for practitioners who deal with human lives and social worlds is not decontextualized knowledge that is universally applicable, a value held by many in the natural and social sciences as well as the general public, but context-dependent knowledge. Such knowledge is of far greater value than either the beginner's rules for practice or context-independent knowledge and the analytical-rational thinking that goes with it. Only beginners find rational deliberation helpful in learning how to play a game, drive a car, or navigate a ship. Experts in these areas do not stop to deliberate about each move; they move intuitively, as if "without thinking." Stuart and Hubert Dreyfus show how deliberation is still useful to experts, but mainly for the sake of "improving intuition, not replacing it."[39]

According to Dreyfus and Dreyfus, this way of understanding human learning, expertise, and intuition goes against much of what Western education advocated about the value of knowledge for two centuries or more. Since French philosopher René Descartes, the notion that humans "make progress by mastering our emotions and being as detached and objective as possible" has regulated formal education.[40] Despite these stated values, emotional, relational, and embodied "involvement" in learning is absolutely necessary for the full development of expertise and wise judgment. The idea of wise judgment or making a choice in the moment that fits what the situation calls for is how Aristotle envisioned *phronesis*.[41] Learning to act phronetically may begin with learning the rules and theories about how something works or what to do in a situation. However, phronesis is only enacted through active involvement over time with the area in which one is emotionally invested and responsible for action. One learns wise judgment through experiencing case after case in situations that allow for an accumulation of knowledge and call for particular kinds of judgments.

Thus, cases are not merely illustrations for bigger and more important theories or theologies. They do not solely set agendas, offer opportunities for

38 For example see Kathleen Cahalan, *Introducing the Practice of Ministry* (Collegeville, MN: Liturgical Press, 2010), 118–48; Miller-McLemore, "Five Misunderstandings about Practical Theology"; and Campbell-Reed and Scharen, "'Holy Cow! This Stuff is Real!'" 327.

39 Dreyfus and Dreyfus, "Peripheral Vision," 779.

40 Dreyfus and Dreyfus, "Peripheral Vision," 785.

41 Aristotle, *The Nicomachean Ethics*, trans. David Ross, ed. Leslie Brown (New York: Oxford University Press, 2009). For an elaboration of the meaning and uses of phronesis by Aristotle, see Jonsen and Toulmin, *The Abuse of Casuistry*, 58–74; see also Flyvbjerg, *Making Social Science Matter*, 53–60.

"mid-level" reflection, or make points of comparison. Cases of context-specific situations are valuable, even essential, for the highest form of expertise and wise judgment in the study of human beings and their social worlds. Flyvbjerg makes an extended argument in his book to compel social scientists to make more and greater use of single case studies. In his effort to address a variety of misunderstandings about cases, he identifies concerns similar to those raised by the reviewers of my grant proposal and faced by practical theologians who want to use cases.

Reinterpreting the Limits of Case Studies

To compel social scientists to reconsider their ambivalent view of cases, Flyvbjerg takes on what he calls five misunderstandings about "case-study research" and turns the social science research paradigm on its head. He observes: "Social science has not succeeded in producing general, context-independent theory and, thus, has in the final instance nothing else to offer than concrete, context-dependent knowledge. The case study is especially well suited to produce this knowledge."[42] The five misunderstandings are the following: "(a) theoretical knowledge is more valuable than practical knowledge; (b) one cannot generalize from a single case, therefore, the single-case study cannot contribute to scientific development; (c) the case study is most useful for generating hypotheses, whereas other methods are more suitable for hypotheses testing and theory building; (d) the case study contains a bias toward verification; and (e) it is often difficult to summarize specific case studies."[43]

As Flyvbjerg addresses these common misperceptions, he affirms the value of adopting case studies as a primary form of research and writing for social scientists. The parallels are strikingly useful for case studies in practical theology. Along with exploring each misunderstanding, I will note where the misunderstandings overlap with the worries reviewers suggested about my research proposal and restate each misunderstanding constructively for the contribution it makes to practical theological scholarship, emphasizing how the dilemmas remain, but should not paralyze practical theologians from using single cases in their research and writing.

The first misunderstanding Flyvbjerg identifies is: "General, theoretical (context-independent) knowledge is more valuable than concrete, practi-

42 Flyvbjerg "Five Misunderstandings," 223.
43 Flyvbjerg "Five Misunderstandings," 219.

cal (context-dependent) knowledge."[44] Reviewers of my proposal reportedly doubted my use of case studies, and they questioned the value of data gathering that attends to concrete, lived experience of clergywomen through interviews, observations, and small group conversations. The first misunderstanding frames an epistemological concern: What counts as knowledge? And it is also a political problem: Who gets to decide what counts? As Flyvbjerg explores at greater length in his book, beginning with Socrates and running up to the Enlightenment, a way of thinking about "theory" evolved into a powerful set of cultural assumptions, which hold that the best and most valuable knowledge is: 1) explicit; 2) universal; 3) abstract; 4) discrete ("formulated only with the aid of context-independent elements, which do not refer to human interests, traditions, institutions, etc."); and 5) systematic ("it must constitute a whole, in which context-independent elements [properties, factors] are related to each other by rules or laws"). Modern natural sciences added the final element to "ideal theory": 6) it must be complete and predictive.[45] The work of "theory" is thus to explain and predict within a given domain. This is what the paradigm of normal science upholds as the highest kind of knowledge in the twenty-first century.[46]

What practical theologians and many social scientists call "theory" does not match the rigorous definition of "explanation and prediction" that Flyvbjerg (and the Dreyfus brothers) describe. Psychiatrist and scholar of religion and psychology Volney Gay puts the problem in another light. He says, "Using the magnifying lens, we can distinguish two types of object: one type (objects amenable to natural science) can sustain magnification; the other type (objects typical of humanistic inquiry) cannot.... we can investigate the form and structure of natural objects to the very limits of imaging capacity. They can be magnified to any desired size without losing signal: there is always more to see. The opposite is true of what I've termed cultural objects: they *cannot* be magnified." Gay explains that "mere magnification after two or three times fails to produce anything useful or descriptive in art, religion, or literature."[47]

In the recently published landmark *The Wiley-Blackwell Companion to Practical Theology*, contributors use the term *theory* a great deal, but on the whole

44 Flyvbjerg, "Five Misunderstandings," 221.

45 Flyvbjerg, *Making Social Science Matter*, 38–39.

46 Thomas S. Kuhn, *The Structure of Scientific Revolutions* (4th ed.) (Chicago: University of Chicago Press, 1962/2012), 5–8.

47 Volney Gay, *Progress and Values in the Humanities: Comparing Culture and Science* (New York: Columbia University Press, 2010), 8–9.

they are not using it like Flyvbjerg, Gay, or most scientists. Practical theologian Ted Smith describes *practice* as "a word to conjure with, a potent tangle of meanings that has been deployed for a wide variety of purposes."[48] I think we could give a similar description of the way *theory* is used by practical theologians. Theory ends up being a catchall of concepts, definitions, heuristic and interpretive frameworks—anything that serves as a counterweight to practice. Often practical theologians lump together these various meanings and include theology itself. Much of what academic practical theologians call theory would better be described as practical wisdom or phronesis, which cases studies are so well suited to explore through attention to complexity and change over time. Additionally, continuing to use the term *theory* uncritically in social sciences or practical theology over-promises or mis-promises what can be delivered, and it keeps the split between *theory* and *practice* going. Without greater care in writing about these terms when speaking to academic audiences outside the narrow confines of our discipline, practical theologians may also foreclose conversation with colleagues in the social sciences and in other theological disciplines.[49]

In his book, Flyvbjerg summarizes why the kind of "theory" which is explanatory and predictive is incompatible with the study of human beings and social systems: "A social science theory of the kind which imitates the natural sciences, that is, a theory which makes possible explanation and prediction, requires that the concrete context of everyday human activity be excluded, but this very exclusion of context makes explanation and prediction impossible."[50] In other words, the problem of using case studies rests within a "fundamental paradox" in the social and political sciences, and we can add practical theology.[51] Following Flyvbjerg, we can restate the value of the use of case studies this way: A search in the scholarship of practical theology for universal, predictive theories is in vain. The most valuable knowledge is the context-dependent knowledge found in concrete cases.

Flyvbjerg states the second misunderstanding about case studies this way: "One cannot generalize on the basis of an individual case; therefore, the case

48 Ted A. Smith, "Theories of Practice" in *The Wiley-Blackwell Companion to Practical Theology*, ed. Bonnie J. Miller-McLemore, 2012 (Malden, MA: Blackwell Publishing, 2012), 244–54.

49 See Bonnie Miller-McLemore's chapter 8 in this volume for reflection on the "theory-practice split" (pp. 190–215) and Joyce Mercer's chapter 7 for exploration of the interdisciplinary character of practical theology (pp. 163–189).

50 Flyvbjerg, *Making Social Science Matter*, 40.

51 Flyvbjerg, *Making Social Science Matter*, 40.

study cannot contribute to scientific development."[52] For example, the reviewers who read my proposal wondered: "could I make a claim based on a limited group?" These reviewers also described a concern over my asking questions about ministry that might allow or cause me to "essentialize different types of experience." In other words, they worried on one hand that I *could not* generalize from my sample of forty clergywomen in a helpful, valid, or compelling way, and on the other hand they worried that I might generalize and reach poor or damaging conclusions.

Flyvbjerg makes two important points in his argument against this misunderstanding. First, he shows how a number of powerful scientific breakthroughs essentially were discoveries found in a single case (i.e., Galileo's discovery that gravity is not determined by weight). Large-scale experiments that call for randomized samples and "double blind" participation are attempts to generalize, verify, or replicate what is already known. Pastoral theologian Robert Dykstra tells the story of Barbara McClintock who won the 1983 Nobel Prize in Physiology or Medicine "for her discovery of mobile genetic elements."[53] She made her discovery through decades of immersion with corn plants. She learned the corn so well both under the microscope and in the field that she "could walk through a cornfield and simply by natural observation of any particular plant determine its precise, peculiar, chromosomal structure." Her expertise reflects practical wisdom gained through participation over time with her objects of study.[54]

Flyvbjerg goes on to show how generalization is also one skill among many needed for doing the work of discovery. While it is valuable, if generalization is accepted as the only or the highest form of "scientific innovation," it limits the variety of ways scientific knowledge is accumulated. And, Flyvbjerg adds, many kinds of knowledge that cannot be generalized are extremely important for scientific discovery. For example, scientists must know how to operate specific lab equipment, gather and store data for their particular experiments, and interact with their area of study in ways unique to their particular study, like McClintock's interaction with the corn plants. Each of these aspects of knowledge is essential for discovery, but they are not widely generalizable when decontextualized. In the natural sciences, generalization from

52 Flyvbjerg, "Five Misunderstandings," 221.

53 "The Nobel Prize in Physiology or Medicine 1983, Barbara McClintock," accessed June 24, 2015, http://www.nobelprize.org/nobel_prizes/medicine/laureates/1983/mcclintock-facts.html.

54 Robert C. Dykstra, *Discovering a Sermon: Personal Pastoral Preaching* (St. Louis, MO: Chalice Press, 2001), 80–81ff.

a single case is also extremely useful when seeking to falsify or disprove a theory.[55]

Restating the misunderstanding to reflect the reinterpretation, we can affirm: One can generalize on the basis of a single or small numbers of cases in the natural sciences (i.e. Galileo's discoveries about the moon or gravity), in the social sciences (Freud's Rat Man or Dora; Patricia Benner's study of exemplary nursing teachers), and in practical theology (ethnographies like Carroll et al.'s *Being There* and Moschella's *Living Devotions*).[56] The examples of ethnographic studies in practical theology and related fields of pastoral theology (Moschella) and congregational studies (Carroll et al.) provide a generalized knowledge about devotional practices and seminaries respectively, without being reductive or attempting to offer explanatory and predictive theory. They become part of a growing number of cases that contribute to broader knowledge and understanding about lived religion, thanks to their specificity and complexity in presenting the situations. To be sure, not everything in any exemplary study can or should be generalized and some aspects can be unhelpfully generalized, highlighting the need for multiple cases that together build practical wisdom over time.

The third misunderstanding that Flyvbjerg identifies is this: "The case study is most useful for generating hypotheses; that is, in the first stage of a total research process, whereas other methods are more suitable for hypotheses testing and theory building."[57] The reviewers of my research proposal did not think I should set up a study based on an assumption that renewing the church was the only trajectory of ministry, worrying that my hypothesis was "too big" or the wrong claim for my fieldwork. I was actually aiming to show *how* the renewal of churches is a trajectory of ministry. "How" studies are especially

---

55 Flyvbjerg, "Five Misunderstandings," 224–28. Some procedural knowledge can be generalized, but not to all types of study, and some technical/procedural knowledge is specific or limited to one or more research paradigms.

56 See Patricia E. Benner, *From Novice to Expert: Excellence and Power in Clinical Nurse Practice* (Paramus, NJ: Prentice Hall, 2000); Jackson W. Carroll et al., *Being There: Culture and Formation in Two Theological Schools* (New York: Oxford University Press, 1997); and Mary Clark Moschella, *Living Devotions: Reflections on Immigration, Identity, and Religious Imagination* (Eugene, OR: Pickwick Publications, 2008). Freud illustrates how single cases are both powerful and dangerous. Feminist theorists argue that his stereotypes and misperceptions about women are both wrong and harmful. See Jane Flax, *Thinking Fragments: Psychoanalysis, Feminism, and Postmodernism in the Contemporary West*. Los Angeles: University of California Press, 1990, 73–77.

57 Flyvbjerg, "Five Misunderstandings," 221.

helpful in social sciences and practical theology because they can show the complexity of change over time with tremendous subtlety. To correct this misunderstanding about cases, Flyvbjerg develops two broad strategies for choosing samples and cases for a study: 1) random selection and 2) information-oriented selection. In randomized selections, the explicit purpose is "to avoid systematic biases in the sample" and to choose a size sample that "is decisive for generalization." The information-oriented selections are designed "to maximize the utility of information from small samples and single cases. Cases are selected on the basis of expectations about their information content." Flyvbjerg suggest four varieties of information-oriented cases: extreme/deviant cases, maximum verification cases, critical cases, and paradigmatic cases.[58]

This taxonomy of sampling and case type holds great potential for guiding practical theological researchers who want to use single or small numbers of case studies to cultivate understanding and build knowledge about a whole range of issues. Christian education scholar Charles Foster and his team presented paradigmatic cases of exemplary teachers in theological education in *Educating Clergy*. Foster's research team identified four signature pedagogies (formation, interpretation, contextualization, and performance) that are now widely utilized to frame the work of theological curricula in U.S. seminaries and rabbinical schools.[59] Practical theologian Christian Scharen's ethnographic study, *Public Worship, Public Work*, compares three congregations in the greater Atlanta area offering cases with "maximum variation" in their approach to liturgy, ethics and character formation.[60] Feminist and practical theologian Mary McClintock Fulkerson's *Places of Redemption* offers a shining example of an "extreme case" of one unique and highly diverse congregation in Durham, North Carolina.[61] Her participant observation and theological reflection with the Methodist congregation (self-described "African American, White American, Asian, Native American, Latino, Mentally and Physically Challenged") may also constitute a "critical case" on Flyvbjerg's terms because it examined what most churches only aspire to, but this congregation managed to embody and sustain for several years. Practical theologian Phillis Sheppard presents cases of several African American women, bearing

58 Flyvbjerg, "Five Misunderstandings," 230.

59 See Charles R. Foster et al., *Educating Clergy: Teaching Practices and Pastoral Imagination* (San Francisco: Jossey-Bass, 2006).

60 Christian Batalden Scharen, *Public Worship, Public Work: Character and Commitment in Local Congregational Life* (Collegeville, MN: The Liturgical Press, 2004).

61 Mary McClintock Fulkerson, *Places of Redemption: Theology for a Worldly Church* (New York: Oxford University Press, 2007).

witness to the state of womanist practical theology and the complex intersections of gender, race, sexuality, class and power in black churches.[62] My study of five clergywomen offers their narratives as paradigmatic cases of what it was like to live through a period of schism in Southern Baptist life, demonstrating both the theological and psychological character of a denominational split.[63] In terms of practical theological research, we may affirm that while case studies can test hypotheses, they can also demonstrate (and sometimes disprove) new knowledge.

The fourth misunderstanding identified and overturned by Flyvbjerg is: "The case study contains a bias toward verification, that is, a tendency to confirm the researcher's preconceived notions." Schipani also warned that case studies face distortions of perception and researcher bias.[64] The reviewers who looked at my proposal worried about my preconceived notions and how I as a researcher would manage my "bias." Apparently, they had little way of imagining how my "bias" might actually be a kind of practical wisdom or expertise in understanding the practice of ministry or women's experience in church leadership based on years of ministry experience, teaching, research, and writing.[65] The critique of "bias toward verification" reflects a general problem built into the human powers of observation and interpretation. Human beings, including all researchers, must be aware of the tendency to see that for which they are looking. Even researchers in the natural sciences can make misjudgments and allow their bias to enter into projects that lead to wrong conclusions.[66]

Pascal's critique of casuistry demonstrated the dangers of using single cases as real and complex, even if his critique, based on a desire for certitude, overstated some concerns. However, researchers who spend long years of immersion in a field of study, may develop a kind of recognition of variances and learn not to dismiss them out of hand. Like Barbara McClintock, they learn their field of study so well as to be able to walk through it and identify even the smallest anomalies. Naturalist and scientist Charles Darwin made a disciplined habit (what he called his "golden rule") of noticing and writing up any

62 Phillis Isabella Sheppard, *Self, Culture, and Others in Womanist Practical Theology* (*Black Religion/Womanist Thought/Social Justice*) (New York: Palgrave Macmillan, 2011).

63 Campbell-Reed, *Anatomy of a Schism*.

64 Flyvbjerg, "Five Misunderstandings," 221; Schipani, "Case Study Method," 99.

65 This kind of experience and expertise is difficult to show and undervalued by the academy generally. And my proposal did not spell out steps I take in my research protocol to minimize potential bias.

66 See Gay, *Progress and Values in the Humanities*, 184–87 for examples of scientists so convinced of their viewpoint that they made mistakes and reported false findings.

contradictory observation or thought that challenged his research findings, anticipating many scholarly objections and managing his own "bias toward verification."[67]

The strategy Darwin used is one kind of reflexivity that careful ethnographers, anthropologists, and practical theologians utilize in their work consistently.[68] By noticing everything, including one's own participation, reactions, feelings, and conclusions in a situation under study, one comes closer to articulating the human situation through the case. Flyvbjerg suggests an opposite problem: the specificity one finds when plowing into a situation often challenges and revises the initial ideas and conceptual frames that case study researchers bring with them. Thus, falsification is more often the result of in-depth case studies, argues Flyvbjerg, than verification. Worth noting, subjectivism or verification bias can also occur in quantitative surveys. The questions frame issues in ways that do not capture the experience of study participants, yet no mechanism for feeding back the lack of resonance is available, thus missing the complexity of lived situations. Conclusions in such studies can verify what quantitative researchers mistakenly coded into their questionnaires.

Flyvbjerg concludes that more new discoveries arise from close examination of lived reality than quantitative studies of large numbers of people taken at a distance.[69] A practical theological restatement of the misunderstanding about the verification bias could go like this: through close proximity and participation in a context, in-depth case studies provide ample opportunities for cultivating practical theological knowledge and wisdom, as well as multiple chances to falsify inadequate concepts and conclusions one might bring to the situation. An example of this comes up in the LPI Project. Common sense about learning the practice of ministry assumes that ministers will each be so different in terms of denomination or tradition and in terms of the idiosyncrasy of individual ministers that little can be concluded about their commonalities. However, our engagement with seventy-five pastors, following fifty of them over five years' time, falsified that common sense, discovering a remarkable amount of resonance among ministers. To be sure, differences remain,

---

67 Charles Darwin, *The Autobiography of Charles Darwin* (New York: Norton, 1958), 123, as reported in Flyvbjerg, "Five Misunderstandings," 234.

68 On reflexivity in theological research, see Christian Scharen and Aana Marie Vigen, *Ethnography as Christian Theology and Ethics* (New York: Continuum, 2011); Mary Clark Moschella, *Ethnography as Pastoral Practice: An Introduction* (Cleveland, OH: Pilgrim, 2008); John Swinton and Harriet Mowat, *Practical Theology and Qualitative Research* (London: SCM Press, 2006).

69 Flyvbjerg, "Five Misunderstandings," 236.

but commonalities in learning the practice of ministry are more striking. And complications to individual stories of learning ministry are more often gathered around differences of gender, race, and sexual orientation than around denomination or tradition.[70]

Flyvbjerg identifies a fifth misunderstanding: "It is often difficult to summarize and develop general propositions and theories on the basis of specific case studies."[71] Similarly, the reviewers for my research project worried that I was making either "too big a claim" or the wrong claim for the fieldwork I proposed, which they saw as falling between "case studies and history." Closely related, Schipani offers this critique: "The researcher often has no clear limits on data gathering or on writing" potentially making the task "aimless or limitless."[72] These critiques assume case studies are too tightly bound and self-referential, unable to do any work beyond the situation they reflect, or they are too diffuse and lack adequate boundaries of time and place.

Case studies need to be set in their proper and full context, giving a "thick description" of the situation, so they make a kind of sense that conveys adequate information.[73] Context includes long-term history; social factors; relationships; overt and subtle influences of gender, race, sexuality, and class; power dynamics; geography; landscape and architectural setting; economic and class constraints; religious beliefs and practices; ritual character of the situation; psychological factors, etc. Not every one of these features is key to every case presented; however, adequate interpretation calls for attention to what sets the case in relation to larger questions, problems, and situations. Conversation with other practical theologians, qualitative researchers, anthropologists, and ethnographers provides a sounding board and a rich set of research practices and practical wisdom for the work of case study building.

Nursing scholar Patricia Benner gives the example of the habits of a starfish. Just because one gathers information about the singular life of one starfish does not mean one is not still talking about starfish in a common or even universal way. And by following a full lifecycle of a single starfish, one can learn far more than depending solely on the data of measurements, geographical

---

70 Scharen and Campbell-Reed, *Learning Pastoral Imagination*, 10–14.

71 Flyvbjerg, "Five Misunderstandings," 221.

72 Schipani, "Case Study Method," 99.

73 Many ethnographers and practical theologians take Clifford Geertz's "thick description" as a point of departure. See Geertz, *The Interpretation of Cultures* (New York: Basic Books, 1973). See also Don S. Browning, *A Fundamental Practical Theology* (Minneapolis, MN: Fortress Press, 1991), 107; and Miller-McLemore, "The Living Human Web," 24.

location, gestation period, or total number of starfish in the Atlantic Ocean. Both kinds of knowledge contribute to understanding starfish.[74]

Analogously, human diversity and particularity should not prevent the usefulness of cases. To the contrary, the ambiguity and uncertainty of human lives and lived religion provide the fodder for richer understandings of particular cases. Flyvbjerg says, "I avoid linking the case with the theories of any one academic specialization. Instead I relate the case to broader philosophical positions that cut across specializations.... The goal is not to make the case study be all things to all people. The goal is to allow the study to be different things to different people."[75] For practical theologians, the narratives themselves, along with appropriate interpretation, become the end of the research, and if well told, a form of practical wisdom. Summarizing or reducing the findings to propositions is not just challenging, but unnecessary.

Using Single Cases in Practical Theological Scholarship

Case studies continue functioning in theological education primarily as a pathway for "mid-level" theological reflection in classroom learning and field education, yet they remain dubious at the point of research. Critics wonder if cases are robust or "universal" enough, reflecting a mistake of thinking that concepts and "theory" are always superior to other kinds of knowledge. A long history of suspicion about case knowledge in moral reasoning in the seventeenth and eighteenth centuries contributed to making case approaches in research suspect of abuse and personal bias, ignoring the everyday use of cases in all kinds of practical reasoning and discernment. All of these problems contribute to an aversion to single case studies in practical theological scholarship. Yet, methodologically, case studies provide a powerful and complex form of knowing, rooted in context and interpretation. The potential troubles with cases cannot be eliminated, yet people of faith and a suffering world urgently need the practical wisdom afforded by cases. Researchers can benefit from shared wisdom and guidance for navigating the potential dangers by considering the following brief guidelines, injunctions, and implications from the analysis in this chapter.

1. Practical theological scholarship can and should take the risk of using single case studies for their power as instances of practical wisdom, while taking

74 Patricia Benner, email to author, February, 2012.

75 Flyvbjerg, "Five Misunderstandings," 238.

care to mitigate dangers such as personal bias, overgeneralizing, and lack of attention to power dynamics, including a researcher's own role in the situation. Learning requires risk *and* responsibility, and if practical theological research and writing are to embody new knowledge and practical wisdom, then single case studies are a powerful method, and researchers can take responsibility for how they handle the material of each case.

2. Case studies should reflect the relational and participatory character of practical wisdom. The audiences for practical theological scholarship, anyone in a study and those who may learn from it, need a place in the construction of case studies. Case studies should generate "knowledge useful to practitioners," and practical theologians can aim to make an impact or difference in the most practical, local, and contextual ways.[76] A primary audience needs to be the particular local people, social groups, and/or geographical places under study with all their specificity in terms of history, language, culture, religion, and traditions. Audiences may include other practical theologians, theological educators and researchers, disciples and believers, perhaps seminary students, pastors, or other ministers, and researchers and practitioners in other (or no) faith traditions. Those who agree to be part of a study deserve the researcher's careful, reflexive attention to concrete details and experience-near narratives. The study participants' questions and concerns must play a vital role in the work, including, when possible, opportunities to interact and give feedback to the cases. All methods for data collection are a form of participation and deserve theological attention and reflection from start to finish. Such research practices resist the dangers of misdirecting or failing to articulate the experience and learning of others.
3. In addition to the local accountability to participants, researchers must also situate cases studies historically, socially, politically, and theologically. Questions about the power dynamics in the research, including the social location of the researcher, are crucial when observing and writing up case studies. The stakes, the players, and the means of action in a situation can be challenging to see and articulate, yet they can illuminate a great deal of practical wisdom. Context-setting required for good social science and also for practical theology go a long way in helping researchers choose an appropriate kind of case and the right scale of analysis.

76 Inge Mette Kirkeby, "Transferable Knowledge: An Interview with Bent Flyvbjerg," *Architectural Research Quarterly* 15, no. 1 (2011): 9, accessed June 1, 2015. http://papers.ssrn.com/sol3/papers.cfm?abstract_id=2237933. See also Katherine Turpin's chapter 10 in this volume (pp. 250–275) about local knowledge in practical theological research and writing.

4. Navigating case studies requires practical theologians to cultivate a bicultural expertise. Over several decades, nursing scholar Patricia Benner became a leading voice in the scholarship of teaching and learning for the profession of nursing.[77] In her research, she utilizes paradigmatic cases that feature first-hand, experience-near narratives to show how learning takes place and expertise grows over time. Canadian philosopher Charles Taylor says Benner assumed two apprenticeships. In nursing she became an expert in the practice of caring for human health, and in the academy she cultivated expertise in making connections among whole overlapping fields of medical care and ethics. Over time she achieved a "bicultural" identity, leading her to a scholarly collaboration between practical experts and philosophers of knowledge. Both medical practitioners and philosophers need the knowledge that becomes possible in this collaboration, and, says Taylor, they need to be "able to speak usefully to each other."[78] Such is an apt goal for practical theologians. Finally, we must speak fruitfully and generatively to our colleagues, audiences, and especially to partners for whom our research matters.

Bibliography

Adichie, Chimamanda Ngozi. "The Danger of a Single Story" TED Talk, July 2009. Accessed July 24, 2015. http://www.ted.com/talks/chimamanda_adichie_the_danger_of_a_single_story/transcript?language=en.

Aristotle, *The Nicomachean Ethics*. Translated by David Ross. Edited by Leslie Brown. New York: Oxford University Press, 2009.

Asquith, Glen H. Jr. "Case Study Method." In *The Dictionary of Pastoral Care and Counseling*, edited by Rodney J. Hunter, 123–26. Nashville, TN: Abingdon, 1990.

Benner, Patricia E. *From Novice to Expert: Excellence and Power in Clinical Nurse Practice*. Paramus, NJ: Prentice Hall, 2000.

Benner, Patricia E., Molly Sutphen, Victoria Leonard, Lisa Day, and Lee S. Shulman. *Educating Nurses: A Call for Radical Transformation*. San Francisco: Jossey-Bass, 2010.

77 Benner, *From Novice to Expert*. See also Patricia E. Benner, Molly Sutphen, Victoria Leonard, Lisa Day, and Lee S. Shulman. *Educating Nurses: A Call for Radical Transformation* (San Francisco: Jossey-Bass, 2010).

78 Charles Taylor, "Part VI. Reply and Re-Articulation: Charles Taylor Replies" in *Philosophy in an Age of Pluralism: The Philosophy of Charles Taylor in Question*, ed. James Tully and Daniel M. Weinstock (New York: Cambridge University Press, 1995), 246.

Brown, William Adams, Mark A. May and Frank K. Shuttleworth. *The Education of American Ministers*, 4 volumes. New York: Institute of Social and Religious Research, 1934.

Browning, Don S. *A Fundamental Practical Theology*. Minneapolis, MN: Fortress Press, 1991.

Cahalan, Kathleen. "Introducing Ministry and Fostering Integration." In *For Life Abundant: Practical Theology, Theological Education, and Christian Ministry*, edited by Dorothy C. Bass and Craig R. Dykstra, 91–116. Grand Rapids, MI: Eerdmans, 2008.

Cahalan, Kathleen. *Introducing the Practice of Ministry*. Collegeville, MN: Liturgical Press, 2010.

Campbell-Reed, Eileen R. *Anatomy of a Schism: How Clergywomen's Narratives Reinterpret the Fracturing of the Southern Baptist Convention*. Knoxville, TN: University of Tennessee Press, 2016.

Campbell-Reed, Eileen R. and Christian Scharen. "'Holy Cow! This Stuff is Real!' From Imagining Ministry to Pastoral Imagination." *Teaching Theology and Religion* 14, no. 4 (2011): 323–42.

Campbell-Reed, Eileen R. and Christian Scharen. "Ethnography on Holy Ground: How Qualitative Interviewing is Practical Theological Work." *International Journal of Practical Theology* 17, no. 2 (2013): 232–59.

Campbell-Reed, Eileen R. and Christian Scharen. "Ministry as Spiritual Practice: How Pastors Learn to See and Respond to the 'More' of a Situation." *Journal of Religious Leadership* 12, no. 2 (2013): 125–44.

Carroll, Jackson W., Barbara G. Wheeler, Daniel O. Aleshire, and Penny Long Marler. *Being There: Culture and Formation in Two Theological Schools*. New York: Oxford University Press, 1997.

Cormode, Scott. The "Almond Springs" Cases. Accessed February 17, 2015. http://www.christianleaders.org/Almond_Springs/index.htm.

Darwin, Charles. *The Autobiography of Charles Darwin*. New York: Norton, 1958.

Dreyfus, Hubert L. and Stuart E. Dreyfus. "Peripheral Vision: Expertise in Real World Contexts." *Organization Studies* 26:5 (2005): 779–92.

Dykstra, Robert C. *Discovering a Sermon: Personal Pastoral Preaching*. St. Louis, MO: Chalice Press, 2001.

Flax, Jane. *Thinking Fragments: Psychoanalysis, Feminism, and Postmodernism in the Contemporary West*. Los Angeles: University of California Press, 1990.

Flyvbjerg, Bent. "Five Misunderstandings about Case-Study Research." *Qualitative Inquiry* 12, no. 2 (April 2006): 219–45.

Flyvbjerg, Bent. *Making Social Science Matter: Why Social Inquiry Fails and How it Can Succeed Again*. New York: Cambridge, 2001.

Foster, Charles R., Lisa E. Dahill, Lawrence A. Golemon, and Barbara Wang Tolentino. *Educating Clergy: Teaching Practices and Pastoral Imagination.* San Francisco: Jossey-Bass, 2006.

Fulkerson, Mary McClintock. *Places of Redemption: Theology for a Worldly Church.* New York: Oxford University Press, 2007.

Gallagher, Shaun. "Philosophical Antecedents of Situated Cognition." In *The Cambridge Handbook of Situated Cognition*, edited by Philip Robbins and Murat Aydede. New York: Cambridge University Press, 2009.

Gay, Volney. *Progress and Values in the Humanities: Comparing Culture and Science.* New York: Columbia University Press, 2010.

Geertz, Clifford. *The Interpretation of Cultures.* New York: Basic Books, 1973.

Gilpin, W. Clark. *A Preface to Theology.* Chicago: University of Chicago Press, 1996.

Graham, Elaine. *Transforming Practice: Pastoral Theology in an Age of Uncertainty.* London: Mowbray, 1996.

Holifield, E. Brooks. "Casuistry, Protestant." In *The Dictionary of Pastoral Care and Counseling*, edited by Rodney J. Hunter, 126–28. Nashville, TN: Abingdon, 1990.

Holifield, E. Brooks. *God's Ambassadors: A History of the Christian Clergy in America.* Grand Rapids, MI: Eerdmans, 2010.

Jonsen, Albert R. and Stephen Toulmin. *The Abuse of Casuistry: A History of Moral Reasoning.* Los Angeles: University of California Press, 1988.

Kirkeby, Inge Mette. "Transferable Knowledge: An Interview with Bent Flyvbjerg." *Architectural Research Quarterly* 15, no. 1 (2011): 9–14. Accessed June 1, 2015. http://papers.ssrn.com/sol3/papers.cfm?abstract_id=2237933.

Kuhn, Thomas S. *The Structure of Scientific Revolutions* (4th ed.). Chicago: University of Chicago Press, 1962/2012.

Lave, Jean and Etienne Wenger. *Situated Learning: Legitimate Peripheral Participation.* New York: Cambridge University Press, 1991.

Mays, Benjamin E. and Joseph W. Nicholson. *The Negro's Church.* New York: Institute of Social and Religious Research, 1933.

Miller-McLemore, Bonnie J. "Five Misunderstandings about Practical Theology." *International Journal of Practical Theology* 16, no. 1 (2012): 5–26.

Miller-McLemore, Bonnie J. "Introduction: The Contributions of Practical Theology." In *The Wiley-Blackwell Companion to Practical Theology*, edited by Bonnie J. Miller-McLemore, 1–20. Malden, MA: Blackwell Publishing, 2012.

Miller-McLemore, Bonnie J. "The Living Human Web: Pastoral Theology at the Turn of the Century." In *Through the Eyes of Women: Insights for Pastoral Care*, ed. Jeanne Stephenson Moessner 9–26. Minneapolis, MN: Fortress, 1996.

Moschella, Mary Clark. *Ethnography as Pastoral Practice: An Introduction.* Cleveland, OH: Pilgrim, 2008.

Moschella, Mary Clark. *Living Devotions: Reflections on Immigration, Identity, and Religious Imagination.* Eugene, OR: Pickwick Publications, 2008.

Neiman, James R. "Liturgy and Life: An Account of Teaching Ritual Practices." In *For Life Abundant: Practical Theology, Theological Education and Christian Ministry,* edited by Dorothy C. Bass and Craig Dykstra, 150–67. Grand Rapids: Eerdmans, 2008.

"The Nobel Prize in Physiology or Medicine 1983, Barbara McClintock." Accessed June 24, 2015. http://www.nobelprize.org/nobel_prizes/medicine/laureates/1983/mcclintock-facts.html.

O'Gorman, Robert T., Kathleen Talvacchia and W. Michael Smith. "Teaching from a Community Context: The Role of the Field Educator in Theological Education." *Theological Education,* 37, no. 2 (2001): 1–57.

Porter, Jean. "Casuistry, Roman Catholic." In *The Dictionary of Pastoral Care and Counseling,* edited by Rodney J. Hunter, 128–29. Nashville, TN: Abingdon, 1990.

Schipani, Daniel. "Case Study Method." In *Wiley-Blackwell Companion to Practical Theology,* edited by Bonnie J. Miller-McLemore, 91–101. Malden, MA: Blackwell Publishing, 2012.

Scharen, Christian Batalden. *Public Worship, Public Work: Character and Commitment in Local Congregational Life.* Collegeville, MN: The Liturgical Press, 2004.

Scharen, Christian and Aana Marie Vigen. *Ethnography as Christian Theology and Ethics.* New York: Continuum, 2011.

Scharen, Christian A. B. and Eileen R. Campbell-Reed. *Learning Pastoral Imagination: A Five-Year Report on How New Ministers Learn in Practice.* New York: Auburn Seminary, 2016.

Sheppard, Phillis Isabella. *Self, Culture, and Others in Womanist Practical Theology (Black Religion/Womanist Thought/Social Justice).* New York: Palgrave Macmillan, 2011.

Smith, Ted A. "Theories of Practice." In *The Wiley-Blackwell Companion to Practical Theology,* edited by Bonnie J. Miller-McLemore, 244–54. Malden, MA: Blackwell Publishing, 2012.

Swinton, John and Harriet Mowat. *Practical Theology and Qualitative Research.* London: SCM Press, 2006.

Taylor, Charles. "Part VI. Reply and Re-Articulation: Charles Taylor Replies." In *Philosophy in an Age of Pluralism: The Philosophy of Charles Taylor in Question,* edited by James Tully and Daniel M. Weinstock, 213–57. New York: Cambridge University Press, 1995.

Witvliet, John. D. "Teaching Worship as a Christian Practice." In *For Life Abundant: Practical Theology, Theological Education and Christian Ministry,* edited by Dorothy C. Bass and Craig Dykstra, 117–48. Grand Rapids: Eerdmans, 2008.

CHAPTER 3

The Tension between Scholarship and Service

Faustino M. Cruz

The annual conferences of the American Academy of Religion, the Catholic Theological Society of America, and other professional guilds constantly remind me that tension exists between scholarship and service. I used to feel like an impostor walking down aisles of book exhibits profoundly contrite for "what I have failed to do." I do not have a single-authored work to display. Worse still, a few senior colleagues have recited publicly a litany of admonitions berating my lack of accountability to the academic community: "Tito, you have to publish." "It's publish or perish." "We need a Filipino voice, write!" Not even two successive academic dean appointments—at a free-standing seminary and at a university—can exonerate me from the offense of not having authored a book. In fact, some of my critical friends still adamantly oppose my having accepted administrative jobs perceived to be serious deterrents to scholarship. At some point, I might convince myself that whatever I do or whoever I become will not matter much to the academy—not until I commit to research and writing more intentionally.

Over the years, mentors and colleagues have written letters of recommendation endorsing my application for various faculty positions. Consistently, each recommender—intent at convincing a search committee that I was going to publish—underscored my potential as a scholar. Yet, not a single academic emphasized my capacity to serve a hiring institution generously and effectively. Practical theologians tend to be scholar-practitioners with particular sets of skills needed by academic institutions—skills such as organizing programs and people; relating to diverse constituencies; and designing and setting-in-motion strategic planning toward an institution's educational mission. Clearly, practical theologians are not the only ones in the academy to have such skills. But for many of us, applying our leadership capacities to serve the greater wellbeing of people and institutions constitutes a vital aspect of an academic vocation that rewards practice. At the same time, however, engaging in such service often works against performing other tasks considered definitive of membership in the academy, such as research and publishing. Thus, I examine in this essay the nature of the tension between scholarship and service perceived through the lens of an immigrant reflective practitioner, an empathic knower who performs between and betwixt the standards of scholar-

 | DOI 10.1163/9789004324244_005

ship and the norms of service in the academy. I explore alternative approaches of these embodied and performed practices toward the advancement of service within community-engaged scholarship.

Academic Service Reconsidered

Academic institutions in the United States traditionally classify expressions of faculty practice based on the tripartite roles of teaching, scholarship, and service. Over the past twenty years, attempts have been made to expand the meaning of scholarship and reform the practice of teaching; however, service remains the most contested and least regarded role.[1]

The term *service* has been defined in various vague and imprecise ways, and expectations regarding what it constitutes are loosely articulated in faculty handbooks in modes challenging to assess.[2] Consequently, the lack of consensus on the meaning of the term, as well as the academy's proclivity to privilege research and publishing, impel institutions to value scholarship—followed by teaching effectiveness—over service during tenure, promotion, contract renewal, or annual performance reviews.[3] This mode of assessment poses a conundrum particularly to academic professionals for whom service is a constitutive element and fundamental expression of our embodied and performed scholarship. For practical theologians, this tension resides between the vocation to practice service and the institutional obligation to publish.

In general, faculty service includes but is not limited to applying one's leadership potential to serve others, sharing knowledge, using professional expertise beyond the classroom for reasons other than investigative research, and performing acts that are not specified in a faculty job-description. Involvement with accreditation commissions, regulatory boards, religious congregations, and professional guilds, as well as commitments to community organizing and advocacy are some of the most common examples of service beyond one's home institution. The term *service* is also widely used to refer to anything faculty offers gratis. Yet, for whom and for what is service?

1 Thomas Schnaubelt and Anne Statham, "Faculty Perceptions of Service as a Mode of Scholarship," *Michigan Journal of Community Service Learning* (Fall 2007): 29.

2 Schnaubelt and Statham, "Faculty Perceptions," 24.

3 Robert Green, "Tenure and Promotion Decisions: The Relative Importance of Teaching, Scholarship, and Service," *Journal of Social Work Education* 44, no. 2 (Spring/Summer, 2008): 117.

Anthropologists, social workers, and nurses have explored ways to clarify the difference between *service for responsible citizenship* in the academy and *professional service*.[4] On one hand, service for responsible citizenship profiles a faculty participating in university governance, advising students, mentoring newly hired colleagues, serving on the rank and tenure committee, chairing a faculty search, and contributing to a charitable appeal. These acts do not necessarily require knowledge and competencies in the faculty's academic area of specialization. Faculty usually draws knowledge from previous academic and professional work; for instance, a professor of Spanish literature and a former accountant assists the department in managing a National Endowment for the Humanities grant.

On the other hand, professional service "connects thought to action" and demands the application of a faculty's specialized academic training. Ernest Boyer, former president of The Carnegie Foundation for the Advancement of Teaching, correlates this type of service to the formation of faculty-engaged scholars who "connect the rich resources of the university to our most pressing social, civic, and ethical problems, to our children, to our schools, to our teachers and to our cities," in such a way that the academy becomes a "staging ground for action."[5] For instance, a professor of public health provides community-based preventive care education to Vietnamese immigrant women who have one of the highest rates of cervical cancer among ethnic groups.[6] Similarly, a Seattle University team of scholars of environmental justice and sustainability—including a practical theologian—helps create a carbon neutral campus that utilizes renewable and sustainable energy, reduces emission of greenhouse gases, and regulates energy consumption. The team inspired participation across administrative units and colleges by facilitating interdisciplinary conversations on Pope Francis's encyclical *Laudato Sí* [On Care for Our Common Home], which calls "every person living on this planet" to an inclusive dialogue on how to care for the earth, our common home.[7]

4 Lori J. Vogelgesang, Nida Denson, and Uma M. Jayakumar, "What Determines Faculty-Engaged Scholarship?" *The Review of Higher Education* 33, no. 4 (Summer 2010): 438.

5 Ernest L. Boyer, "The Scholarship of Engagement," *Journal of Public Service and Outreach* 1, no. 1 (1996): 19–20.

6 Cathy Pascual, "Culture Puts Vietnamese Women at Increased Cancer Risk," *Los Angeles Times*, October 12, 2000, accessed July 27, 2015, http://articles.latimes.com/2000/oct/12/local/me-35544. Center for Disease Control and Prevention, "Cervical Cancer Rates by Race and Ethnicity," accessed July 27, 2015, http://www.cdc.gov/cancer/cervical/statistics/race.htm.

7 Pope Francis, *Laudato Sí* [*On Care for Our Common Home*], 2015, accessed October 1, 2015, http://www.usccb.org/about/leadership/holy-see/francis/pope-francis-encyclical-laudato-si-on-environment.cfm.

Faculty in various disciplines have attempted to repackage creative products (what they do) beyond the academy, in order for institutions to recognize such work as legitimate scholarship and faculty members as authentic scholars.

Addressing the issue of "service or scholarship" in nursing education, Rheba de Tornyay claims that "many problems of society require the application of knowledge that expert faculty members can and should provide. Connecting thought to action is the approach that scholars use in solving problems. These service activities must come directly from the faculty member's special field of knowledge to be considered evidence of scholarship." De Tornyay argues that "service related to expertise is serious, demanding work and requires the rigor and accountability traditionally associated with research activities." She proposes that "faculty must develop criteria and exemplars for excellence in these professional activities," underscoring that "the reward structure for faculty engaged in such activities does not imply a reduction in the importance of traditional scholarship. Instead, traditional scholarship is enhanced through externally oriented professional activities."[8]

Lamentably, theological schools tend to classify professional service (which requires the application of a faculty's specialized training) either as an expression of *responsible citizenship* (which generally does not incorporate a theologian's academic expertise) or as an instance of one of the vague and imprecise definitions of service mentioned above. This tendency exacerbates the tension between scholarship and service by negating scholarship as an essential ingredient of professional service, thus bifurcating further two expressions of faculty practice that are not mutually exclusive.

In reality, practical theologians in the academy serve a broad ecology of theological education both within and extending beyond the walls of their schools as preachers, administrators, spiritual directors, religious educators, pastoral counselors, liturgists, and community organizers. Whether in the context of a free-standing or university-based seminary, we encounter the conundrum of being caught between the *standards by which we must live*—the values by which we could not help but live if we were to promote the integrity of who we are and what we do as reflective practitioners—and *norms about what we must do*—expectations that are generally determined by institutional policies, regulatory boards, and employment contracts.

Inspired by poet William Stafford's invitation to "ask me whether what I have done is my life," author and educator Parker Palmer invites us to ask ourselves, "What am I meant to do? Who am I meant to be? What calling do I

8 Rheba de Tornyay, "Service or Scholarship?" *Journal of Nursing Education* 30, no. 3 (March 1991): 101.

hear?"[9] My vocation as a reflective practitioner, therefore, comes from listening "to my life telling me who I am. I must listen for the truths and values at the heart of my own identity, not the standards by which I *must* live—but the standards by which I cannot help but live if I am living my own life."[10] As practical theologians, whose lives are we living? To what extent do communities of accountability, i.e., seminaries, universities, and professional guilds enable us to practice "what we are meant to do" and to listen to "who we are meant to be"? In what ways do these institutions either legitimize or invalidate our practice as reflective practitioners?[11]

The Vocation of a Reflective Practitioner

Among forty-nine U.S. based members of the International Academy of Practical Theology, only seven explicitly indicate Practical Theology in their faculty title. Others self-identify as professionals in various fields including pastoral theology, religion, contextual education, theology, leadership, constructive theology, spirituality, pastoral care and counseling, psychology and culture, mission and evangelism, and Christian education. While calling ourselves each by a different name, we all share a common commitment to reflexive practice.

My public identity as a practical theologian grew out of a collaborative writing project led by biblical scholar Diane Bergant of the Catholic Theological Union. In a pastoral resource for theological reflection published in 2004 by the Center for the Study of Religious Life, we defined ourselves:

> Practical theologians are nothing more than *reflective Christian practitioners*, people who look deeply into the heart of the Christian religious tradition in order to interpret contemporary situations from a Christian perspective. As practical theologians, we not only reflect on life experience, but we do this *within* the very experience of life itself, and we do it as part of a believing community. In other words, we are praxis-oriented.... We do this with insight into the contemporary world, knowledge of and commitment to our religious tradition, reflective skills that

9 Parker Palmer, *Let Your Life Speak: Listening for the Voice of Vocation* (San Francisco: Jossey-Bass, 2000), 1–2.

10 Palmer, *Let Your Life Speak*, 4–5.

11 Donald A. Schön, *The Reflective Practitioner: How Professionals Think in Action* (New York: Basic Books, 1983).

> enable us to bring the world and the tradition together in creative transformative ways, and practical sense and the ability to form prudent judgments and decisions to act.[12]

Here, the term *reflective* denotes our ability to apply intellectual discipline, imagination, intuition, affect, bodily knowing, and other forms of meaning-making to (a) examine the socio-historical presuppositions upon which spiritual, religious, or theological assertions and traditions lie; (b) analyze and interpret biblical, doctrinal, canonical, and devotional texts; and (c) explore effective and alternative approaches of knowledge construction, discernment, and decision-making.

As reflective practitioners, our role is to perceive with eyes of faith the complexities of the human condition, uncovering what is of critical value and significance. By engaging in social analysis, we unveil systems and structures that shape lived realities in order to reframe them, toward imagining, proposing, and performing a transformative response. Thus, we reflect not only on faith but upon the process during and within which we live such faith.[13] In the academy, our lives as reflective practitioners are principally located between and betwixt, in the conundrum of scholarship and service. Who we are as practical theologians impels us to reflect intentionally on our own practice. Palmer calls this "listening to life."[14]

Listening to My Story, Our Story

Following seminary formation, I pastored for six years in an inner-city, multilingual immigrant church with a parochial school and taught in a diocesan institute for pastoral formation. Subsequently, I pursued an interdisciplinary PhD in Religion and Education at Boston College in tandem with multiple academic and pastoral obligations, constantly living the tension between scholarship and service.

To illustrate, I was flying to Bogotá, Colombia for a meeting at the Conference of Latin American Catholic Bishops and I had to miss the last hour of Dr. Maryanne Confoy's class on adult faith development. Granting me permission, she implicitly exposed the conundrum of practical theologians having

12 Diane Bergant, et al., *Theological Reflection for Transformation* (Chicago: Center for the Study of Religious Life, 2004), 13.

13 Bergant, et al., *Theological Reflection*, 15.

14 Palmer, *Let Your Life Speak*, 3.

to choose habitually between the classroom of scholarship and the classroom of service. "You would gain more insights from your trip than this class could possibly give you, and the impact of your work with the bishops would touch many more lives and communities." Her directive sounded more like the Great Commission—Go therefore! Indirectly, I heard her say, "serve."

By the time I completed my doctorate in 2001, I had applied to at least three institutions for a full-time faculty appointment. However, there simply were no job openings in the field of religion and education, specifically at Roman Catholic institutions, so I pursued postings in disparate areas such as pastoral care, faith and culture, and theology. Consequently, my professional identity was virtually in flux and contingent upon what prospective employers demanded. In addition, the extent to which I could creatively appropriate recently acquired interdisciplinary competencies to meet the minimum qualifications set by jobs that I considered was still in question. I had to highlight what marketing professionals would call my "differentiators," referring to what sets me apart from competing products, brands, or applicants.

As a Filipino immigrant student, I was a prominent "poster child" during a concurrent period of affirmative action and job scarcity in higher education. In addition to such "unearned privilege," what clearly differentiated me from my peers was my *practice*—a comprehensive knowledge of and experience in multi-lingual immigrant ministry at parish, regional, and national levels. At that time, the Association of Theological Schools of the United States and Canada (ATS) was aggressively challenging member schools to foster a more inclusive community life; to recruit students, faculty, and staff from under-represented groups; and to develop culturally and contextually appropriate programs. This vision increased my viability for employment.

Subsequently, I was hired at the Franciscan School of Theology (FST) in Berkeley, California, then a member school of the Graduate Theological Union (GTU). FST had the institutional capacity to reframe its mission, providing a canvas on which to reimagine theological education for a multicultural church and society. Educational leadership of this institutional endeavor, rather than teaching and research, evolved as my primary practice.

I facilitated adaptive change across the curriculum by serving as co-director of a new program that intentionally engaged faith and culture.[15] While this role was at the very core of a religious educator's vocation, my teaching and

---

15 Ronald Heifetz, Alexander Grashow, and Marty Linsky, *The Practice of Adaptive Leadership: Tools and Tactics for Changing Your Organization and the World* (Boston: Harvard Business Press, 2009), 15. These authors emphasize that adaptive leadership aims "to engage people in distinguishing what is essential to preserve from the organization's her-

research remained unfocused and de-emphasized for many years. Regrettably, there was no room to teach in my primary area of specialization (religious education), and my research interests did not directly correlate with the core content of the courses I facilitated. Administrative oversight, a form of *service for responsible citizenship* to the institution that came with a disproportionate amount of student advising, generated an ambiguous hybrid professor-administrator position that further marginalized my scholarship. If I ceased to specialize in a particular branch of learning, would I still be a scholar? Is what I do "scholarship" or "service"?

Moreover, the three Roman Catholic seminaries at the GTU did not require courses in religious education, unlike most Protestant member schools in the consortium. Instead, my faculty load included four seminars that provided the theoretical underpinnings of field-based ministerial formation, which required professional service to church and society. Regrettably, some of the more research-focused faculty categorically assumed that such courses, while essential to educating the whole person, were "light-weight" both theologically and scholarly.[16]

To illustrate, I assumed the title Assistant Professor of Practical Theology and Education when I was hired, but a year later changed my field to Theology and Education. Why? Otherwise, the GTU would not have recognized the courses I taught as "theology."[17] As a result, students in programs requiring either a thesis or dissertation would not fulfill degree requirements by subscribing to my courses, following the dictum that "anything ministerial or formative is not academic." Therefore, I was constantly in search of professional validation and an "academic home." To this day, my search for identity within the academy directly correlates to such a tenuous relationship between scholarship and service.

In July 2005, a month after I had been promoted to Associate Professor with a permanent contract (the tenure system was only implemented the follow-

---

itage from what is expendable. They claim that "the most effective leadership anchors change in the values, competencies, and strategic orientations that should endure in the organization."

16 See Bonnie Miller-McLemore's chapter 8 in this volume for reflection on the "politics of practical knowledge" (pp. 190–218).

17 Joyce Ann Mercer, "Feminist and Womanist Practical Theology," in *Opening the Field of Practical Theology: An Introduction*, eds. Kathleen A. Cahalan and Gordon Mikoski (Lanham, MD: Rowman and Littlefield, 2014), 97–114. She argues that, for some women, naming as a *practical theologian* can be especially problematic because such self-identification further locates them in a marginal and unrecognized position within the academy, when they are already marginalized and unrecognized persons.

ing year), I began a six year term as Executive Vice President and Academic Dean of the Franciscan School of Theology. I had just been with the school for five years, having earned a doctorate four years previously. At forty-three, I was the youngest and only foreign-born member of the faculty. The seemingly accelerated process of promotion and contract renewal was the result of two unforeseen transitions within the administrative team, namely the appointment of a new seminary President and resignation of the Academic Dean. My willingness to serve was informed by three vocational insights. First, I was deeply convinced that the school's decision to appoint me to leadership had nothing to do with affirmative action, unlike my underlying suspicion of why I was initially hired on the faculty. Second, I made a conscious choice to teach leadership by leading. Third, I embraced the role of dean as *diakonia*.

With the assistance of the Wabash Center for Teaching and Learning in Theology and Religion, a national center for faculty development, I achieved excellence in course design, student advising, assessment, and facilitation. However, my academic publications were limited; my contributions were mainly to pastoral and episcopal resources. Nevertheless, one of the distinctive strengths I brought to this administrative position was my life-long commitment to *praxis*.

Essentially, administration is regarded as *service for responsible citizenship* that does not require an educator's use of specialized academic knowledge and competencies. For instance, associate deans of academic affairs at Seattle University where I currently work generally do not go up for promotion in rank from associate professor to professor until we return to full-time teaching. The university regards promotion in rank as recognition of excellence in teaching, scholarship, and service. Thus, academic administrators who maintain a significantly reduced teaching load (most do not even teach a single course) allegedly lack sufficient evidence, such as student course evaluations and syllabi, to demonstrate growth in teaching effectiveness. Moreover, most of our faculty administrators rarely publish due to the demands of our positions. Unlike regular faculty on nine-month contracts who engage in summer research and writing, administrators are employed for the entire year, giving us little or no time for scholarship.

However, a growing number of teacher-scholar-practitioners across disciplines contest such bifurcation between service and scholarship, which is often imposed by institutions. They maintain that service can be scholarly and scholarship about service must be promoted more vigilantly. For instance, an academic dean can use social scientific research methodologies in gathering information to propose and validate a critical policy change, thereby providing data-based evidence that replaces anecdotal examples typically used at faculty meetings.[18] Subsequently, a case study and critical reflection on faculty governance could be published as a scholarship about service based on one administrator's leadership practice. Yet, one must reside within the tension between scholarship and service to integrate this dualistic reality.

Chief academic officers of theological schools have begun affirming what we do as scholarly, specifically as scholarship of academic administration. Academic dean at Wartburg Theological Seminary Craig Nessan reflects on how deans should view work involving "the composition and editing of many kinds of documents necessary for the operation, assessment, and improvement of the school." He argues that schools should cultivate a dean's vocational self-understanding by valuing the research and writing of administrative documents as an integral component of one's creative products and scholarship, especially during performance, tenure, or promotion reviews.[19] Academic administration as service also engenders interdisciplinary practice and incorporates knowledge, skills, and competencies acquired prior to seminary and doctoral studies. Therefore, every expression of academic service, whether in the form of responsible citizenship or professional practice, has an implicit scholarly dimension.

However, the tension between service and scholarship is further intensified for me as a practical theologian by my social location and formation, which have deeply shaped my epistemology and, hence, my understanding of what counts as "scholarly" knowledge. To explain this more clearly, I must turn to Filipino indigenous psychology to examine how Filipinos as empathic knowers are socialized to make meaning in relatedness, and why we construct knowledge primarily to serve the common good. Such an examination further underscores that aspect of the service-scholarship conundrum related to the over-deployment of marginalized persons in service-rich academic labor positions. The academy capitalizes on the commitment of marginalized persons to the common good, including their advocacy for social justice on behalf of others, all the while devaluing service in the academy.[20]

---

18 E. Suzanne Lee, "Scholarly Service and the Scholarship of Service," *American Association of University Professors*, accessed July 25, 2015, http://www.aaup.org/article/scholarly-service-and-scholarship-service#.VdUMevlViko.

19 Craig Nessan, "The Dean as Teacher and Scholar," in *C(H)AOS Theory: Reflections of Chief Academic Officers in Theological Education*, eds. Kathleen D. Billman and Bruce Birch (Grand Rapids, MI: Eerdmans Publishing Company, 2011), 184.

20 Audrey Williams June, "The Invisible Labor of Minority Professors," *Chronicle of Higher Education*, November 8, 2015, accessed November 10, 2015, http://chronicle.com.proxy.seattleu.edu/article/The-Invisible-Labor-of/234098?cid=trend_right_h.

Service as Empathic Knowing

Filipino psychology (*Sikolohiyang Pilipino*) is born out of cultural revalidation. This process, which some western scholars describe as indigenization, searches for indigenous psychology from within the culture, as opposed to "clothing a foreign body with a local dress."[21] Filipinos understand service in the academy through the lens of empathic knowing. Both women and men are traditionally socialized toward empathy, learning to make meaning reflexively in connected ways. Filipinos have an acute sense of *pakikipagkapwa-tao* (care of neighbor) and its corollary *damayan* (attentive expression and reflexive sharing of suffering and loss).[22] These connected ways of knowing strengthen a person's propensity to understand more fully the reality of another (*unawa*) and combine with other ways of knowing that collectively constitute genuine wisdom: intellect as power of knowing (*pag-iisip*), reason (*dunong, katwiran*), judgment (*hatol*), comprehension (*talino*), and intelligence (*kaalaman*). This convergence affirms the unitive essence and performance of empathy as dynamic knowing "in relatedness."[23]

In Filipino epistemology, "to know" implies discerning acutely what others feel for the purpose of sharing the same feeling with them. Thus, to be *manhid* (apathetic) is a serious psychosocial dysfunction.[24] This construction of knowledge represents what cross-cultural psychologists call "social intelligence." In some societies, the cognitive expressions of intelligence (e.g., literacy, memory, and the ability to process information efficiently) that Western epistemology has often idealized are considered inherently futile unless they are intended for the common good and betterment of the community. As in Japanese and other Asian cultures, Filipino "meaning making" demands this

---

21 Rogelia Pe-Pua, "From Decolonizing Psychology to the Development of a Cross-Indigenous Perspective in Methodology: The Philippine Experience," in *Indigenous and Cultural Psychology: Understanding People in Context*, eds. Uichol Kim, Kuo-Shu Yang and Kwang-Kuo Hwang (New York: Springer, 2006), 110–111.

22 Kevin Nadal, *Filipino American Psychology: A Handbook of Theory, Research, and Clinical Practice* (Hoboken, NJ: John Wiley and Sons, 2011) and F. Landa Jocano, *Working with Filipinos: A Cross-cultural Encounter* (Manila: Punlad Research House, 2001).

23 José de Mesa, *In Solidarity with the Culture: Studies in Theological Re-rooting*, Maryhill Studies 4 (Quezon City, Philippines: Maryhill School of Theology, 1991) and Albert E. Alejo, *Tao pô! Tulóy! Isang Landas ng Pag-unawa sa Loob ng Tao* (Quezon City, Philippines: Ateneo de Manila University, 1990).

24 Ed Lapiz, *Paano Maging Pilipinong Kristiano* [Becoming a Filipino Christian] (Makati City, Philippines: Kaloob, 1997), 14.

moral dimension of knowing, whereby cognitive performance must be nurtured together with an empathic dimension; thus, knowledge is understood also as serviceableness, responsibility, perseverance, politeness, and obedience.[25] In other words, it would be difficult, if not impossible, for someone with such an epistemology to pursue knowledge merely as an end in itself or to separate the pursuit of knowledge from the moral imperative to serve the wider social good.

For Filipinos, scholarly knowledge requires and assumes empathy—the ability "to see with the eyes of another, to hear with the ears of another, and to feel with the heart of another." Empathy, whether expressed as attentive love or maternal thinking, is a deep structure in the development of connected ways of knowing.[26] When teaching and learning with Filipinos, educators must recognize the centrality of empathic knowing and four representative values that are intrinsic to a Filipino person, family, and society: *kapwa, utang na loob, hiya,* and *pakikisama.*

Kapwa signifies that Filipinos view themselves as *persons-in-relationship* rather than as individuals. It is the essence of "care of neighbor" for the sake of the common good (*pakikipagkapwa-tao*). A person is derided for not having compassion for others (*walang malasakit sa kapwa*). *Kapwa* expands the scope (*sakop*) of one's village, tribe, family, country, or clan in order to embrace difference and otherness. *Utang na loob,* commonly translated as debt of gratitude, depicts a person's acute ability to recognize a giver and receive a gift with thankfulness that swells from the depths of one's being (*loob*). The gift one receives, usually given at a time of dire need, is regarded as too valuable, expensive, or precious to replicate—like the gift of life. While one tries to reciprocate, nothing will ever be equal to the gift. Unlike a debt that is measurable, quantifiable, and payable, this type of gift is irreplaceable and freely given without recompense. *Hiya* (shame) and "saving face" are commonly experienced by Filipinos and other Asians. While it profoundly affects the person, shame has adverse implications for family, community, clan, and groups because of our interwoven identities and affiliations in church and society. Finally, *pakikisama* is a constitutive trait of a person with empathy. It requires the ability to think reflectively and act freely for the sake of a common good. It engenders social acceptance and promotes collaboration that results from

25 Pierre Dasen, "Cross-cultural Study of Intelligence: Piaget and the Baoulé," *International Journal of Psychology* 19 (1984): 407–34.

26 Mary Field Belenky et al., *Women's Ways of Knowing: The Development of Self, Voice, and Mind* (New York: Basic Books, 1997), 143 and Sara Ruddick, *Maternal Thinking: Toward a Politics of Peace* (Boston: Beacon Press, 1995).

one's decision to conform and carry out the "group think." *Pakikisama* defies individualism, one of the "habits of the heart" pervasive in the American ethos, as deficient in genuine concern for the common good.[27]

Effectively, it is in the movement from isolation to participation that the four values converge. Persons-in-relationship (*kapwa*) engage in mutual gift giving (*utang na loob*) to restore dignity (*hiya*, shame is overcome) by thinking reflectively and acting freely for the sake of the common good (*pakikisama*). Upon these four values, service as empathic knowing is embodied and performed. Not to act in relation to these values—in other words, *not* to serve—constitutes an insurmountable violation of personhood formed in and through Filipino culture. The conundrum is therefore amplified even further: the negation of service, alongside the elevation of a particular form of scholarship (i.e., academic publishing) at the expense of service, requires acceptance of a foreign set of cultural norms in order to have membership in the academy. In this conundrum, to be counted as a *real* scholar in my discipline and in the academy, I must put aside key elements of my own identity, becoming *unreal* as a Filipino.

"No" is Not an Option!

On March 14, 2015, at an ATS consultation for students and recent graduates of the Preparing for 2040 Schools Project, one of the participants, a person of color, asked me how I became an academic dean and what inspired me to become an administrator. My immediate response was, "When people like you and me are invited to lead, 'No' is not an option." Why? Because until immigrant professors become more fully integrated into the leadership structures of our institutions, decision makers will continue to "talk about us rather than with us." Thus, we must discern what skills, competencies, and attributes we have that could enhance our practices of teaching, scholarship, and service.[28] Where must we then locate service today?

For Asian immigrant scholars, a primary locus of service is an academy that perpetuates what Mia Tuan calls the lives of "forever foreigners or honorary

---

27 Michael Himes and Kenneth Himes, *Fullness of Faith: The Public Significance of Theology* (Mahwah, NY: Paulist Press, 1993), 54.

28 Faustino M. Cruz, "Formal and Informal Religious Leadership in the U.S. Context: Catholic Multicultural Trends," in *Religious Leadership: A Reference Handbook*, ed. Sharon Henderson Callahan (Thousand Oaks, CA: Sage, 2013), 62.

whites."[29] I am reminded of a white male administrator's remark as he was reviewing my application for contract renewal. "I will support you with all my clout." What I heard him say was, "on the basis of merit alone you will not make it, but with my political influence, I can make you become one of us." His message carried a subtext. Since I had made a conscious decision to nurture a vocation to serve as a reflective practitioner, I was an alien to an academic community that expected faculty to live fully the obligation to publish as scholars almost at the exclusion of serving church and society. I was also a foreigner to a teaching and learning community that privileged printed words as the embodiment of constructed knowledge. This *assumption of foreignness* negates the very core of "what I am meant to do" and "who I am meant to be" in the academy—a devastation of identity and belonging that only magnifies the tension between scholarship and service. The assumption of tokenism further exacerbates this conundrum.[30]

One of the "bittersweet successes" of scholars of color is tokenism: "the assumption is that minority faculty are 'mere tokens… hired without the appropriate credentials, experience, or qualifications…. [Thus] there is unspoken pressure put on minority academics to continually prove that they are as good as white academics."[31] Such was the case when a white male graduate student in his thirties and a former business investor bluntly asked me, "Do you think you are competent enough to teach white people like me?" I leaned forward and gently replied, "What do you think?" Ironically, tokenism validates that "I do exist." While such value, attitude, and behavior presuppose my "abnormality," insinuating that I may endanger an institution's normative system of teaching, learning, assessment, leadership, and common life, it liberates me to seize the opportunity to embody and perform what I teach, i.e., reflective practice—and do it very well! However, I must still strive to be in both worlds of scholarship and service. Choosing one over the other is not an option for persons in minority-related positions.

Another "bittersweet success" is the typecasting syndrome, the assumption that we can only or should occupy minority-related positions. That is probably one of the reasons why each time I transition into an academic dean's

29 Mia Tuan, *Forever Foreigners or Honorary Whites: The Asian Ethnic Experience Today* (New Brunswick, NJ: Rutgers University Press, 2001), 18.

30 See Courtney Goto's chapter 5 in this volume for reflection on "coercive mimeticism" (pp. 110–133).

31 Caroline Sotello Viernes Turner and Samuel L. Myers, Jr., *Faculty of Color in Academe: Bittersweet Success* (Boston: Allyn and Bacon, 2000).

position, I find a Manila folder on file clearly tabbed "Minority Hires." Such administrative practice is a constant and painful reminder of an existing hidden and subversive culture of racial and ethnic labeling in the academy that "puts us where they believe we rightfully belong." The roles faculty of color play in the academy, both as scholars and purveyors of service, are determined by how prominently institutions are willing to locate us.

During my first summer at Seattle University, I went up to the library information desk to inquire where the faculty lounge was located. The young student worker politely responded, "It's on the sixth floor, *but* you have to be faculty to use it." Apparently, faculty is a "majority-related position," and on the basis of my profile, the staff decided "you do not qualify." There is still a world out there that is not used to witnessing people of color in positions of teaching and academic leadership. To reverse this tragedy, faculty of color must intentionally transgress dominant systems that impede full, mutual, and equitable participation in teaching, scholarship, and service.

Women and faculty of color contribute a disproportionate level of service to the academy. Scholars use terms such as "cultural taxation" and "identity taxation" to demonstrate how various cultural and social identities may result in additional non-academic service commitments for certain faculty, on the basis of race, ethnicity, gender, and sexual orientation.[32] I am keenly mindful that, each time I get invited to publish or to serve on professional committees, colleagues purposefully recognize the distinctive tone and hue I represent guiding their discernment.[33]

In a 2011 ATS survey on changes in faculty work, respondents identified increases in administrative responsibilities (i.e., service) as one of the most significant shifts in faculty work. Participants in a consultation that ensued talked about "off the grid" commitments, referring to "work that is essential (they hope!) for the school's mission but that doesn't fit neatly—or at all—into the grid of work that is recognized or rewarded." Unfortunately, these responsibilities as mentioned above "may fall most heavily on female, racial/ethnic, and junior faculty."[34] The remarkable increase in service commitments may also be attributed to the dramatic decline in full-time faculty positions. However, a pervasive attitude of "presumed invisibility" toward women and minority faculty impedes their ability to serve.

32 Laura E. Hirshfield and Tiffany D. Joseph, "'We Need a Woman, We Need a Black Woman': Gender, Race, and Identity Taxation in the Academy," *Gender and Education* 24:2 (March 2012): 213–227.

33 See Goto's chapter 5 in this volume (pp. 110–133).

34 Stephen Graham, "Changes in Faculty Work," *Colloquy* (Fall 2011): 38–40.

To illustrate, a national organization attempting vigorously to appoint persons of color to the executive board could only surface names of two white males. One of the women in leadership contested, "If we are wanting to increase diversity, in what ways will these two individuals increase diversity?" Frustrated and hopeless, the chair replied, "But we have not had any success in finding people who are able and willing to serve in this capacity. We want to increase diversity, but we also need to fill the seats on the committee." My gut reaction was, "Where have you been looking? You will not find people of color in exclusively white enclaves." So I crafted a response: "If we were fully committed to diversity, we should make it happen intentionally. While it might take us longer to identify viable candidates, there are certainly colleagues out there who are waiting to be invited and included." By the end of the day, I had contacted three colleagues of color across the country who agreed to be nominated.

While I am undoubtedly chosen to diversify the roster of contributors or participants, given my distinctive non U.S. born and immigrant of color positionalities, I have disrupted dominant-minority related assumptive sets by contesting marginality—the pervasive and gnawing feeling of being an "outsider from within"—and by moving toward a position of integrated liminality.[35] This disposition is essentially the movement from *I am my culture* to *I have a culture*. It signifies the transcendence from my *embeddedness in liminality* to *my relationship with liminality*, which creates our *in-both* selves. As I have argued in another context, this integrated liminality facilitates "interrelating with multiple identities and affiliations, crossing borders and spaces, as well as engaging in public empathic conversations that advance a more authentic struggle for justice and the common good (right action-in-relationship)."[36] For this reason, my scholarship and practice must never be uprooted from the daily life and struggle of the people I serve. While scholars are viewed generally as learned persons who specialize in a particular branch of study through creative work, the noble purpose of all the systematized methods, disciplines, and attainment we utilize to demonstrate accuracy, critical ability, and thoroughness is service. This conviction is deeply rooted in Filipino indigenous understanding of service as empathic knowing.

35 Faustino M. Cruz, "Locating Multiple Immigrant Identities and Belonging in Relatedness: Insights for Intercultural Leadership," in *C(H)AOS Theory: Reflections of Chief Academic Officers in Theological Education*, eds. Kathleen D. Billman and Bruce C. Birch (Grand Rapids: Eerdmans Publishing, 2011), 217.

36 Cruz, "Locating," 219.

Scholarship and Service: Exploring the New Normal

During a period of consistent and rapid decline in tenure-track positions in the academy, colleges and universities have increasingly appointed "professors of practice," full-time non-tenure track colleagues hired initially in non-academic fields for their skills and expertise. The American Association of University Professors (AAUP) reports that in 2001 alone, over thirty-percent of full-time faculty are professors of practice. These academics engage primarily in teaching. Lamentably, they are denied the procedural protection provided by tenure generally reserved to research scholars, making their appointments contingent and unsecured. Professors of practice fear losing their employment, at times for simply teaching materials that are too controversial or because tenured faculty are threatened by diminishing enrollment. Practice faculty are at the behest of senior colleagues and administrators who deliberate on their reappointment, potentially creating a caste system within the academy.

Critics of such non-tenure track appointments argue that severing the connection between teaching and tenure ineluctably impairs the freedom to teach—the fundamental academic freedom vital for protecting the rights of the educator. Citing the *1940 Statement of Principles of Academic Freedom and Tenure*, they maintain that tenure is "indispensable to the success of an institution in fulfilling its obligation to its students and to society."[37] While a significant number of free-standing seminaries offer either permanent or long-term renewable contracts, the status of professors of practice are comparable to those in colleges and universities when it comes to teaching in skill-based disciplines. Practical theologians in clinical and contextual education programs, regardless of their highest educational attainment, are often hired on non-tenure track lines. Institutions typically view their practice beyond the academy as service, and rarely advance their scholarly pursuits.

University-based theological schools, also known as embedded seminaries, are beginning to experience a decline in the percentage of tenured or tenure-track positions and a growth in part-time and non-tenured faculty hires—a phenomenon that may soon hit free-standing seminaries, given what Stephen Graham predicts as the "new normal" in theological education. Faculty size will be cumulatively smaller and institutions will be leaner. At this time, close to sixty-percent of ATS faculty head count is part-time, a figure

---

37 Subcommittee on Academic Freedom and Tenure of the American Association of University Professors, "Professors of Practice," American Association of University Professors, accessed July 30, 2015, http://www.aaup.org/report/professors-practice.

above the national average of fifty-percent for all postsecondary faculty in the United States.[38]

Tenure lines once held by retired colleagues are now replaced by full-time contractual appointments awarded to lecturers and instructors, many of whom are not eligible for promotion in rank. In addition to teaching, these junior faculty are obliged to serve other roles for which graduate programs do not generally prepare them, such as advising students, participating in faculty governance, engaging in accreditation work, or serving on committees. Yet, they are not expected to do less research. Ironically, faculty are sensing that they are doing less of what they have come to see as their central role—research—and more of what they often do not know—to serve both the academy and society.[39] However, economic benefits are undeniably deterrents against service and motivators of scholarship.

Education professor Gert Biesta of the University of Luxembourg argues that, despite the proliferation of open access libraries, academic publishing and global capitalism remain inextricably conjoined, underscoring that "major publishers of academic journals and books are global companies with wide and deep networks all over the world." He maintains that "the 'logic' of academic publishing itself is increasingly becoming a matter of the production of intellectual commodities—articles and chapters—with the aim of establishing a position in the academic market (known as 'impact')."[40] Furthermore, he contends that "the transformation of academic activity into a process of production of intellectual commodities is further exacerbated by funding regimes that reward quantity over quality—such as those cases where universities, departments, or even individual scholars get paid directly for each publication they produce."[41] At the 2015 biennial conference of the International Academy of Practical Theology held at the University of Pretoria and the University of South Africa, some of our local hosts revealed receiving from their departments supplemental income based on the international ranking of the journal that publishes their work.

---

38 Tom Tanner, "Tenure and Other Faculty Facts at ATS Member Schools," *The Association of Theological Schools and the Commission on Accrediting*, June 2, 2015, accessed July 30, 2015, http://www.ats.edu/uploads/resources/publications-presentations/documents/tenure-and-other-faculty-facts-part-1.pdf.

39 William G. Tierney, *The Responsive University* (Baltimore: Johns Hopkins University Press, 1998), 2.

40 Gert Biesta, "Editorial: On Academic Generosity," *Studies in Philosophy and Education* 33 (2014): 1.

41 Biesta, "Editorial," 1.

Yet, scholarship and service remain inextricably conjoined. Biesta reminds us that service, expressed as academic generosity, is unquestionably an intrinsic component of scholarship. For example, we have colleagues who willingly serve as peer reviewers to assess and maintain the quality of academic work, whose contributions we rarely, if ever, recognize. He highlights the formative dimension of peer reviews, the collegial and dialogical process that allows manuscripts to grow in depth and breadth due to the transformative power of faculty service.[42]

Junior colleagues, in particular, typically choose scholarship over service. They intuit that rarely are contracts terminated based on a professor's failure to serve. And should they ever need to find another academic home, future employers prefer candidates with demonstrated teaching effectiveness and a record of refereed publication (as long as there is no clear evidence of incivility or egregious behavior) over those who have been uber-benevolent servants at the expense of teaching and research. Notwithstanding, some professors must learn to say "No," a generative term that enhances self-care, professional boundaries, and life-work balance, yet undervalued by some over demanding and recalcitrant administrators.

Without faculty service—responsible citizenship—there is no academy. Service is essential to enhance student-centered learning. This principle ascertains that even the practice of teaching has a constitutive service component, as demonstrated, for instance, by our attitudes toward students and course assignments. Many of us have received feedback from students who deeply appreciate the substantive comments we write on margins whenever we assess their creative work, taking the extra step in a posture of mutual teaching and learning, in contrast to moments when we might "grade" papers without even engaging with the student. Indeed, service is grounded in empathic knowing, embodied and performed.

Scholarship and Service: Embodied and Performed

In class, I once handed out five sheets of post-it notes to each participant. On each sheet, they were to write an error they had made as a leader. The activity ensued and I started writing my own responses on each of my five sheets. One by one, participants read out examples of leadership failure and posted them on the board. And so did I. Toward the end of the session, a student was astonished that I had been contributing to the exercise. So I asked, "What

42 Biesta, "Editorial," 2.

message would I have given you if I had just sat down while waiting for you to finish writing?" A few retorted in unison, "It's like telling us that you have never failed." I have learned that, mainly with students in their twenties and early thirties, transparency and authenticity (being and doing) have become increasingly non-negotiable. They know when you are faking it, and they also know when you are "going through life with them."

So, one of the leadership failures I had indicated was precisely my compulsion to resolve an unsolvable conundrum, rather than choosing to live within and work through the tension between scholarship and service among faculty. As academic dean, I oversee programs "dedicated to educating the whole person, to professional formation, and to empowering leaders for a just and humane world,"[43] by providing a curriculum that integrates academic, pastoral, and spiritual formation. However, I have not fully encouraged faculty to commit to the same integrative practices in which we expect our students to engage. As a reflective practitioner, I must strive to embody and perform the foundational theories in which I embed the courses I teach. Two of the leadership challenges that experts James Kouzes and Barry Posner identify as necessary for making extraordinary things happen are modeling the way and challenging the process.[44] Organizational theorists Richard Boyatzis and Annie McKee agree that leaders can "counter the inevitable 'power stress' of the leadership role... by stepping out of destructive patterns and renewing themselves physically, mentally, and emotionally."[45] According to Donna J. Markham, strong leaders are able to affirm that, in the midst of turmoil and chaos, "there is at work in our world and within our organizations a life-generating energy straining to author a new global communion."[46] When we educate to transform, we teach and write about what we know by doing it.[47] That is why I never require my students to do anything that I am not willing to do, especially *with* them. Hence, I am inspired by Kouzes and Posner to model

---

43 Seattle University, "Mission of Seattle University," accessed August 1, 2015, https://www.seattleu.edu/about/mission/.

44 James M. Kouzes and Barry Z. Posner, *The Leadership Challenge: How to Make Extraordinary Things Happen in Organizations* (San Francisco: Jossey-Bass, 2012).

45 Richard Boyatzis and Annie McKee, *Resonant Leadership: Renewing Yourself and Connecting with Others through Mindfulness, Hope, and Compassion* (Boston: Harvard Business School Press, 2005).

46 Donna J. Markham, *Spiritlinking Leadership: Working through Resistance to Organizational Change* (New York: Paulist Press, 1999), 18.

47 Jane Vella, *Learning to Listen, Learning to Teach: The Power of Dialogue in Educating Adults* (San Francisco: Jossey-Bass, 2002).

the way and challenge the process; by Boyatzis and McKee to step out of my own destructive patterns and renew myself physically, mentally, and emotionally; and by Markham to welcome a life-generating energy from which a new paradigm flows in the midst of institutional chaos.

Through the lens of Howard Gardner's theories of multiple intelligences[48] and five minds for the future,[49] I am also cognizant of the ways in which I have privileged certain ways of knowing, particularly linguistic (use of words) and logical-mathematical (reasoning and calculating), even though I seek to promote indigenous and other ways of knowing. I have not (yet) become what I teach. Sadly, I have participated in making decisions that have alienated "embodied performers" who were subsequently denied tenure or contract renewal. Recalcitrant institutions of which I have been a part were unwilling to accept new forms of scholarship, such as educational phone apps, videos, visual art, or computer software programs as "scholarship," in lieu of traditional published, refereed work.

The call to authenticity and transparency has implications for faculty development, specifically of younger scholars. My colleague, Mark Hearn, a Korean American scholar who has just finished year one of his first full time faculty appointment, asked me about how I write (I was actually sharing with him my manuscript on the tension between service and scholarship). He asked, "Do you still feel you need to footnote everything you say, to back it up with theory or an expert's opinion?" I pulled off the shelf a refereed journal and said, "See, this article is inundated with citations. I had to prove I could use a library." Thumbing through a book chapter, I exclaimed, "Here, I have begun expressing my own voice. It has taken me several years to realize that, if I were to become overly dependent on references, I would never be able to claim a thought unless validated by dominant perspectives. It is taking a lifetime to declutter my colonized mind." By unpacking with a fellow male scholar of color that, on one hand we benefit from certain unearned privileges as academics and on another hand we still lack the freedom to embody and perform from the margins our indigenous ways of knowing, I was exposing the complex intersectionality among racial-ethnic identities, immigrant narrative, colonial history, and gender that inform scholarship and service.

Despite my deficiencies, exercising formal academic leadership at my institution has enabled me to live grace-fully the tension between scholarship and

---

48 Howard Gardner, *Multiple Intelligences: New Horizons in Theory and Practice* (New York: Basic Books, 2006).

49 Howard Gardner, *Five Minds for the Future* (Cambridge: Harvard Business Review Press, 2009).

service. As a result, more faculty of color are hired; more students from underrepresented groups are recruited; faculty integrates texts written by women and scholars from Asian, Latin America, and Africa; community life is enlivened; international students are eligible for scholarships; participatory and collaborative leadership is now the norm; opportunities once reserved for faculty—such as retreats and educational travel abroad, and participation in governance—are extended to staff; and the institution embraces a resurgence of life-generating energy and spirit. These accomplishments and steps have helped moderate the tension between service and scholarship for myself and for others. Living between the tension requires these kinds of adaptive changes. Making space for adaptive change is one of the most challenging roles leaders play, especially in times of institutional transition in our patterns of teaching, service, and scholarship.

Service and Community-Engaged Scholarship

The tension between scholarship and service persists even though traditional tripartite categories of teaching, scholarship, and service are no longer sustainable. Given the changing nature of faculty work load, the erosion of tenure and long-term contracts places greater demand on hybrid positions that create an imbalance in faculty workload. Empathic knowing enkindles a culture of generosity to serve, and reflective practitioners must embody and perform what they teach. However, adaptive change in the academy may alleviate such pervasive tension by advancing community-engaged scholarship, bridging service and service learning, promoting life-long civic engagement through curriculum reform, reframing faculty perception of service as scholarship of service, including community partners in faculty performance review and the contract renewal process, accepting multiple forms of scholarship,[50] and providing effective mechanisms for assessment.[51]

Community-engaged scholarship supports the notion of service as empathic knowing toward "right action" (*pakikipagkapwa-tao*). It advances collaboration between institutions of higher education and the wider community for the mutual exchange of knowledge and resources in a context of partnership and reciprocity. The purpose of community engagement is to enrich

50 Kerry Ann O'Meara, "Encouraging Multiple Forms of Scholarship in Faculty Reward Systems: Does It Make a Difference?" *Research in Higher Education* 46, no. 5 (August 2005): 479–510.

51 Green, "Tenure and Promotion Decisions," 117.

scholarship, research, and creative activity; enhance curriculum, teaching and learning; prepare more formally educated and engaged citizens; strengthen democratic values and civic responsibility; address critical social issues; and contribute to the public good.[52] Such practice is rooted in a commitment to keep communities growing. Thus, the production and socialization of knowledge is fundamentally for the common good of the people, and practical wisdom (phronesis) for transformation is its telos. This approach poses specific challenges to community-engaged faculty.[53]

Since doctoral studies, I have realized that I tend to generate more data than my research colleagues whenever we engage in collaborative participatory action research. Apparently, within certain religiously-affiliated Hispanic and Asian neighborhoods, respondents and informants conflate my roles as priest, immigrant, and researcher, and so they open up to me more readily. This situation ineluctably shifts conversations from testimonial to confessional, triggering an ethical obligation for me as scholar to suspend or limit my access to people's narratives. Even a university's institutional review board (IRB) would not have predicted my dilemma. This experience has clarified that as a scholar, there will be times when publishing the findings of research in a refereed journal article is an untenable goal. What is possible, however, is community engagement—utilizing my professional skills and competencies with the people for the common good.

Recognizing faculty as a wealth of untapped resource, service learning and faculty professional service must be conjoined, particularly when colleges and universities can play a significant role in addressing and resolving local and global issues. Scholars argue that "faculty professional service is the bridge that links the realm of service and experiential learning with proponents of rethinking scholarship and faculty roles. Widespread acceptance of experiential learning as well as faculty service and outreach will both flourish when they are recognized as two essential, mutually reinforcing facets of an institutional commitment to link theory and practice, campus and community."[54]

However, such initiative requires a reframing of the current system of promotion, tenure, and contract renewal that either limits or hinders faculty in-

---

52 Carnegie Classification of Institutions of Higher Education, accessed July 30, 2015, http://carnegieclassifications.iu.edu/.

53 Elmer Freeman, Susan Gust, and Deborah Aloshen, "Why Faculty Promotion and Tenure Matters to Community Partners," *Metropolitan Universities* 20:2 (2009): 87–103.

54 Deborah Hirsh and Ernest Lynton, "Bridging Two Worlds: Professional Service and Service Learning," New England Resource Center for Higher Education, University of Massachusetts at Boston, Working Paper 17, 1995.

volvement in community outreach and the deployment of academic units and centers.[55] This is particularly crucial in enabling faculty of color to engage in activities that advance racial and ethnic communities through race research and minority-related community service.[56] Those committed to service learning value the opportunity to put interdisciplinarity into action, gain from the learning outcomes intended for all teacher-learners, and incite curriculum reform by advancing life-long civic engagement. Lamentably, any attempt to engage mutually service learning and faculty professional service is disrupted by the chronic tension between scholarship and service.

A case in point: In July 2011, the Bill and Melinda Gates Foundation awarded Seattle University School of Theology and Ministry (STM) a grant to implement the Faith and Family Homelessness Initiative (FFH). In partnership with Jewish, Muslim, Catholic, Protestant, and Evangelical congregations from King, Pierce, and Snohomish counties, FFH has led efforts to end homelessness through community engagement, service, and advocacy. Together with hundreds of fledgling homelessness advocates, the initiative has ignited local and national interest and energy for engaging faith communities, policy makers, and service providers in dialogue, understanding, and action. FFH conducts research on the most effective approaches to congregation-based efforts, such as the rapid rehousing of people experiencing homelessness and recruitment of religiously affiliated private landlords. FFH also creates and disseminates educational and new landlord recruitment materials, provides assistance in establishing local faith based resource and training centers, and conducts poverty workshops. Poverty workshops simulate the experiences of low-income families who struggle to live from month to month, in order to conscientize participants into the realities of urban poverty and homelessness. The three-hour activity allows participants to reflect critically on their experience and identify concrete ways through which they could participate intentionally in addressing the crisis of family homelessness in their community through faith-based engagement. After over one hundred and fifty training sessions and events, the university has awakened new prophetic voices that embody and perform the mission of the project.[57]

However, while sponsored and directed by a school of theology and ministry, it has taken four years for the first cohort of faculty—composed exclu-

55 Hirsh and Lynton, "Bridging Two Worlds."

56 Benjamin Baez, "Negotiating and Resisting Racism: How Faculty of Color Construct Promotion and Tenure," Georgia State University, January 11, 1998, available on ERIC.

57 Seattle University School of Theology and Ministry. "Faith and Family Homelessness Project," accessed June 25, 2015, http://faithandfamilyhomelessness.com/.

sively of practical theologians—to participate in FFH, a project initially regarded as community service with no academic or scholarly import. While such assumption was clearly contrary to the primary intent of the Gates Foundation grant to promote public theology, the lack of faculty participation was triggered by unwarranted fears that only faculty commitments yielding scholarly products could advance cases for promotion, tenure, or contract renewal. The recent appointment of a practical theologian as associate dean of academic affairs has facilitated institutional change and curricular reform, and FFH service activities are now integrated in leadership and contextual education courses. Nevertheless, the tension between scholarship and service persists.

Undoubtedly, faculty perception of service (for responsible citizenship) must shift toward scholarship of service. To help faculty negotiate the tensions between conventional scholarship and service, we must affirm multiple forms of scholarship,[58] provide effective tools for assessing community engagement, and reimagine the procedure for performance review and professional advancement.[59] We must ensure institutional support precisely since financial resources are required to induce faculty engagement in service learning.

Advocates of scholarship of service through community engagement firmly believe that the community and all those whose lives would be affected by the impact and significance of the common work should be involved in the assessment process. The perspective and input of community partners should be sought and valued as peers in the process: (a) identifying promising practices at existing colleges and universities that involve community partners; (b) serving on committees as external experts on community engagement; and (c) defining and assessing impact of community-engaged faculty on the community.[60]

To illustrate, Community-Campus Partnerships for Health (CCPH), a national organization promoting health equity and social justice through partnerships between communities and higher education institutions, supports scholarship of service through a program called Faculty for the Engaged Campus. This initiative aims to intensify "community-engaged career paths in the academy by developing innovative competency-based models of faculty development, facilitating peer review and dissemination of products of community-engaged scholarship, and supporting community-engaged faculty members

58 O'Meara, "Encouraging Multiple Forms of Scholarship," 479–510.

59 J.R. Cooper, "Ten Years in the Trenches: Faculty Perspectives on Sustaining Service-Learning," *Journal of Experiential Education* 37, no. 4 (2014): 415–428.

60 Freeman, Gust and Aloshen, "Why Faculty Promotion," 99–100.

through the promotion and tenure process."[61] Expressed as empathic knowing, scholarship of service through community engagement seeks justice and social transformation for the common good:

> The production of knowledge through community engagement, whether by communities or academic institutions, will help to promote social justice and social change for the common good, but the sharing of that knowledge will help us to determine the practices that will be most beneficial and strategic in serving the common good. To share knowledge, one must build models of shared power and shared governance. Therefore, community participation in the promotion and tenure process is the next logical step in building such models of community-engaged scholarship so these models of partnership may grow and be sustained.[62]

In other words, empathic knowing requires the creation of new ways to evaluate scholarship.

In conclusion, the lack of consensus on the meaning of the term *service* impels institutions to value scholarship, followed by teaching effectiveness, over service during tenure, promotion, contract renewal, or annual performance reviews. This mode of assessment poses a conundrum particularly to academic professionals for whom service is a constitutive element and fundamental expression of one's embodied and performed scholarship. For practical theologians in particular, this tension resides between the vocation to practice service as reflective practitioners and the institutional obligation to publish as scholars. Such tensions become even greater for practical theologians of color, whose cultural identities often include a strong imperative to practice service as a necessary element of one's personhood. Adaptive change in the academy may alleviate, even if it cannot wholly resolve, such pervasive tensions.

Bibliography

Alejo, Albert E. *Tao pô! Tulóy! Isang Landas ng Pag-unawa sa Loob ng Tao*. Quezon City, Philippines: Ateneo de Manila University, 1990.

61 Sarena D. Seifer, Lynn W. Blanchard, Catherine Jordan, Sherril Gelmon, and Piper McGinley, "Faculty for the Engaged Campus: Advancing Community-Engaged Careers in the Academy," *Journal of Higher Education Outreach and Engagement* 16, no. 1 (2012): 5–19.

62 Freeman, Gust, and Aloshen, "Why Faculty Promotion," 101.

Baez, Benjamin. "Negotiating and Resisting Racism: How Faculty of Color Construct Promotion and Tenure." Georgia State University, January 11, 1998. Available on ERIC.

Belenky, Mary, Blythe Clinchy, Nancy Rule Goldberger, and Jill Mattuck Tarule. *Women's Ways of Knowing: The Development of Self, Voice, and Mind.* New York: Basic Books, 1997.

Bergant, Diane, Faustino M. Cruz, Kathleen Dorsey-Bellow, Bernard Lee, and Maureen R. O'Brien. *Theological Reflection for Transformation.* Chicago: Center for the Study of Religious Life, 2004.

Biesta, Gert. "Editorial: On Academic Generosity." *Studies in Philosophy and Education* 33 (2014): 1–3.

Boyatzis, Richard and Annie McKee. *Resonant Leadership: Renewing Yourself and Connecting with Others through Mindfulness, Hope, and Compassion.* Boston: Harvard Business School Press, 2005.

Boyer, Ernest L. "The Scholarship of Engagement." *Journal of Public Service and Outreach* 1, no. 1 (1996): 11–20.

Center for Disease Control and Prevention. "Cervical Cancer Rates by Race and Ethnicity." Accessed July 27, 2015. http://www.cdc.gov/cancer/cervical/statistics/race.htm.

Cooper, J.R. "Ten Years in the Trenches: Faculty Perspectives on Sustaining Service-Learning." *Journal of Experiential Education* 37, no. 4 (2014): 415–428.

Cruz, Faustino M. "Formal and Informal Religious Leadership in the U.S. Context: Catholic Multicultural Trends." In *Religious Leadership: A Reference Handbook,* edited by Sharon Henderson Callahan, 56–64. Thousand Oaks, CA: Sage, 2013.

Cruz, Faustino M. "Locating Multiple Immigrant Identities and Belonging in Relatedness: Insights for Intercultural Leadership." In *C(H)AOS Theory: Reflections of Chief Academic Officers in Theological Education,* edited by Kathleen D. Billman and Bruce C. Birch, 208–220. Grand Rapids: Eerdmans Publishing, 2011.

Dasen, Pierre. "Cross-cultural Study of Intelligence: Piaget and the Baoulé." *International Journal of Psychology* 19 (1984): 407–34.

De Mesa, José. *In Solidarity with the Culture: Studies in Theological Re-rooting.* Maryhill Studies 4. Quezon City, Philippines: Maryhill School of Theology, 1991.

De Tornyay, Rheba. "Service or Scholarship?" *Journal of Nursing Education* 30, no. 3 (March 1991): 101.

Freeman, Elmer, Susan Gust, and Deborah Aloshen. "Why Faculty Promotion and Tenure Matters to Community Partners." *Metropolitan Universities* 20, no. 2 (2009): 87–103.

Gardner, Howard. *Five Minds for the Future.* Cambridge: Harvard Business Review Press, 2009.

Gardner, Howard. *Multiple Intelligences: New Horizons in Theory and Practice.* New York: Basic Books, 2006.

Graham, Stephen. “Changes in Faculty Work.” *Colloquy* (Fall 2011): 38–43.

Green, Robert. “Tenure and Promotion Decisions: The Relative Importance of Teaching, Scholarship, and Service.” *Journal of Social Work Education* 44, no. 2 (2008): 117–127.

Heifetz, Ronald, Alexander Grashow, and Marty Linsky. *The Practice of Adaptive Leadership: Tools and Tactics for Changing Your Organization and the World.* Boston: Harvard Business Press, 2009.

Himes, Michael and Kenneth Himes. *Fullness of Faith: The Public Significance of Theology*. Mahwah, NY: Paulist Press, 1993.

Hirsh, Deborah and Ernest Lynton. “Bridging Two Worlds: Professional Service and Service Learning.” New England Resource Center for Higher Education, University of Massachusetts at Boston. Working Paper 17, 1995.

Hirshfield, Laura E. and Tiffany D. Joseph. “‘We Need a Woman, We Need a Black Woman’: Gender, Race, and Identity Taxation in the Academy.” *Gender and Education* 24, no. 2 (2012): 213–227.

Jocano, F. Landa. *Working with Filipinos: A Cross-cultural Encounter*. Manila: Punlad Research House, 2001.

June, Audrey Williams. “The Invisible Labor of Minority Professors.” *Chronicle of Higher Education*, November 8, 2015. Accessed November 10, 2015. http://chronicle.com.proxy.seattleu.edu/article/The-Invisible-Labor-of/234098?cid=trend_right_h.

Kouzes James M. and Barry Z. Posner. *The Leadership Challenge: How to Make Extraordinary Things Happen in Organizations*. San Francisco: Jossey-Bass, 2012.

Lapiz, Ed. *Paano Maging Pilipinong Kristiano* [Becoming a Filipino Christian]. Makati City, Philippines: Kaloob, 1997.

Lee, E. Suzanne. “Scholarly Service and the Scholarship of Service.” *American Association of University Professors*. Accessed July 25, 2015. http://www.aaup.org/article/scholarly-service-and-scholarship-service#.VdUMevlViko.

Markham, Donna J. *Spiritlinking Leadership: Working through Resistance to Organizational Change*. New York: Paulist Press, 1999.

Mercer, Joyce Ann. “Feminist and Womanist Practical Theology.” In *Opening the Field of Practical Theology: An Introduction*, edited by Kathleen A. Cahalan and Gordon Mikoski, 97–114. Lanham, MD: Rowman and Littlefield, 2014.

Nadal, Kevin. *Filipino American Psychology: A Handbook of Theory, Research, and Clinical Practice*. Hoboken, NJ: John Wiley and Sons, 2011.

Nessan, Craig. “The Dean as Teacher and Scholar.” In *C(H)AOS Theory: Reflections of Chief Academic Officers in Theological Education*, edited by Kathleen D. Billman and Bruce Birch, 175–187. Grand Rapids, MI: Eerdmans Publishing Company, 2011.

O’Meara, Kerry Ann. “Encouraging Multiple Forms of Scholarship in Faculty Reward Systems: Does It Make a Difference?” *Research in Higher Education* 46, no. 5 (August 2005): 479–510.

Palmer, Parker. *Let Your Life Speak: Listening for the Voice of Vocation*. San Francisco: Jossey-Bass, 2000.

Pascual, Cathy. “Culture Puts Vietnamese Women at Increased Cancer Risk.” *Los Angeles Times*, October 12, 2000. Accessed July 27, 2015. http://articles.latimes.com/2000/oct/12/local/me-35544.

Pe-Pua, Rogelia. “From Decolonizing Psychology to the Development of a Cross-Indigenous Perspective in Methodology.” In *Indigenous and Cultural Psychology: Understanding People in Context*, edited by Uichol Kim, Kuo-Shu Yang and Kwang-Kuo Hwang, 109–137. New York: Springer, 2006.

Pope Francis. *Laudato Sí [On Care for Our Common Home]*, 2015. Accessed October 1, 2015. http://www.usccb.org/about/leadership/holy-see/francis/pope-francis-encyclical-laudato-si-on-environment.cfm.

Ruddick, Sara. *Maternal Thinking: Toward a Politics of Peace*. Boston: Beacon Press, 1995.

Schnaubelt, Thomas and Anne Statham. “Faculty Perceptions of Service as a Mode of Scholarship.” *Michigan Journal of Community Service Learning* (Fall 2007): 18–31.

Schön, Donald A. *The Reflective Practitioner: How Professionals Think in Action*. New York: Basic Books, 1983.

Seattle University. “Mission of Seattle University.” Accessed August 1, 2015. https://www.seattleu.edu/about/mission/.

Seattle University School of Theology and Ministry. “Faith and Family Homelessness Project.” Accessed June 25, 2015. http://faithandfamilyhomelessness.com/.

Seifer, Sarena D., Lynn W. Blanchard, Catherine Jordan, Sherril Gelmon, and Piper McGinley. “Faculty for the Engaged Campus: Advancing Community-Engaged Careers in the Academy.” *Journal of Higher Education Outreach and Engagement* 16, no. 1 (2012): 5–19.

Subcommittee on Academic Freedom and Tenure of the American Association of University Professors. “Professors of Practice.” American Association of University Professors. Accessed July 30, 2015. http://www.aaup.org/report/professors-practice.

Tanner, Tom. “Tenure and Other Faculty Facts at ATS Member Schools.” *The Association of Theological Schools and the Commission on Accrediting*, June 2, 2015. Accessed July 30, 2015. http://www.ats.edu/uploads/resources/publications-presentations/documents/tenure-and-other-faculty-facts-part-1.pdf.

Tierney, William G. *The Responsive University*. Baltimore: Johns Hopkins University Press, 1998.

Tuan, Mia. *Forever Foreigners or Honorary Whites: The Asian Ethnic Experience Today*. New Brunswick, NJ: Rutgers University Press, 2001.

Turner, Caroline Sotello Viernes and Samuel L. Myers, Jr. *Faculty of Color in Academe: Bittersweet Success*. Boston: Allyn and Bacon, 2000.

Vella, Jane. *Learning to Listen, Learning to Teach: The Power of Dialogue in Educating Adults*. San Francisco: Jossey-Bass, 2002.

Vogelgesang, Lori J., Nida Denson, and Uma M. Jayakumar. "What Determines Faculty-Engaged Scholarship?" *The Review of Higher Education* 33, no. 4 (Summer 2010): 437–472.

CHAPTER 4

Knowledge, Subjectivity, (De)Coloniality, and the Conundrum of Reflexivity

Jaco S. Dreyer

An important task of every academic practical theologian is to do research and to contribute to the discipline's knowledge base. We thus do research by tracing the sacred; by exploring, describing, and explaining religious practices of religious actors in particular locations.[1] Our research efforts usually result in a description, explanation, or a theory of lived religion of people, whether in Baltimore, Bangalore, Belhar, Brisbane, or Brussels. Research is not complete if it does not result in some form of communication of the "research findings," that is, our interpretations and constructions of our research efforts. Whatever form the communication of the research results take, it always entails some kind of interpretation and representation of whatever was researched.

Positivistic approaches want us to believe that our research results can in some way be an accurate representation of what we research. It is the researcher's task to give an exact representation of the "facts." If you follow the same procedure, you should be able to replicate the "findings" of other researchers. The assumption is that the researcher is "neutral" regarding the "study object" and that "objective" researchers should arrive at the same representations. Researchers therefore have to strive to eliminate subjectivity (bias and "observation errors") and to maintain objectivity.

For a long time human science researchers tried to emulate this scientific model of the natural sciences with its perceived objectivity.[2] Knowledge could only be credible to the extent that the researcher's influence is eliminated.[3]

1 R. Ruard Ganzevoort, "Forks in the Road when Tracing the Sacred: Practical Theology as Hermeneutics of Lived Religion," Presidential Address to the Ninth Conference of the International Academy of Practical Theology, Chicago, Aug. 3, 2009.

2 Due to the limitations of this essay, it is not possible to give a more nuanced description of the various methodological approaches in the human and social sciences. See Norman Blaikie, *Approaches to Social Enquiry* (Cambridge: Polity Press, 1993), 11–50, for an overview of some classical approaches in the social sciences.

3 This created epistemological and ontological challenges for theologians who have to "bracket" their faith in the research process.

 | DOI 10.1163/9789004324244_006

One way to do this was to focus on "better" (e.g. highly standardized) research instruments and methods. However, despite all efforts to establish the human and social sciences as *sciences*, the criticism from "interpretivist" scholars remained as a constant thorn in the flesh of positivists.

This positivist philosophy of science was slowly eroded and replaced by philosophies of science that made more room for the unique challenges and opportunities of human science research. Scholars came to realize that it is not possible to escape our "horizon of understanding" as German philosopher Hans-Georg Gadamer has so eloquently described it in his magnum opus *Truth and Method*.[4] The poststructuralist and postmodern philosophies of science problematized the Cartesian subject-object dualism and destroyed the idea of objectivity. This acknowledgement of the researcher's subjectivity in the research process opened a Pandora's box[5] regarding the use and abuse of research and the role of knowledge and human interests.[6] Feminist scholars further contributed to this discrediting of the researcher's objectivity with their "standpoint theories" that, amongst other things, emphasize the importance of power issues and the researcher's "positionality" in the research context.[7] The representation of research findings lost its presumed innocence and became a very contested area.

This situation, namely that all knowledge is mediated knowledge, that there is a conflict of interpretations, and that bias, researcher subjectivity, and positionality play a role in these interpretations, is a basic epistemological dilemma in all research endeavors and the starting point of this chapter.

The usual way to deal with this epistemological dilemma is to advocate some form of reflexivity. French sociologist Pierre Bourdieu describes the epistemological dilemma and the role of reflexivity in the following way:

> The positivist dream of an epistemological state of perfect innocence has the consequence of masking the fact that the crucial difference is not between a science which effects a construction and one which does not, but

4 Hans-Georg Gadamer, *Truth and Method*, 2nd rev. ed., trans. Joel Weinsheimer and Donald G. Marshall (London: Sheed & Ward, 1989), 300–307.

5 "The moment that the researcher distances him- or herself from the conventional belief of positivism, he or she opens Pandora's box by blurring genres and producing messy research texts," writes Stefanos Mantzoukas, "Issues of Representation within Qualitative Inquiry," *Qualitative Health Research* 14, no. 7 (2004): 1000, doi:10.1177/1049732304265959.

6 Jürgen Habermas, *Knowledge and Human Interests*, trans. Jeremy J. Shapiro (Boston: Beacon Press, 1971).

7 See Sandra Harding, ed., *The Feminist Standpoint Theory Reader* (New York and London: Routledge, 2004).

> between a science which does this without knowing it and one which, being aware of this, attempts to discover and master as completely as possible the nature of its inevitable acts of construction and the equally inevitable effects which they produce.[8]

The conscious deliberations on the acts of knowledge construction that Bourdieu refers to is today a standard practice in most research endeavors. Researchers are aware that there are no unmediated knowledge claims.

The point of this chapter is that reflexivity cannot heal the "epistemological wound" of researcher subjectivity, bias, and positionality.[9] It could help researchers to better understand some of the factors that may influence the knowledge constructed, and it could make them more sensitive to the possible "violence" in the act of representing others by means of research as well as the many ambiguities related to research practices. However, due to our existential "situatedness," our horizons of understanding, we will never be able to escape from our subjectivities.[10] This is the "*crisis* of the cogito," the *shattered* Cartesian cogito that we are left with today, according to French philosopher Paul Ricoeur.[11] Just as we cannot see others from an "objective" or "God's eye view," we cannot see ourselves from this vantage point. Reflecting on our reflexivity will thus continue indefinitely, with no possibility of reaching a final point. Just as the mirage of water in the desert recedes when the thirsty traveler tries to reach for it, it is an illusion to think that you could objectify your subjectivity. Our reflexive efforts will therefore always be trapped between "apodictic certainty" and "perpetual suspicion."[12] This is the *conundrum of reflexivity* and the topic of my exploration in this chapter.

I use the term "reflexivity conundrum" here as shorthand for the difficulties and dilemmas related to reflexivity. Scholars in other disciplines, such

---

8 Pierre Bourdieu, "Understanding," *Theory, Culture & Society* 13, no. 2 (1996): 18.

9 Terry Evens, Don Handelman and Christopher Roberts, "Introduction: Reflexivity and Selfhood," in *Reflecting on Reflexivity: The Human Condition as an Ontological Surprise*, ed. Terry Evens, Don Handelman and Christopher Roberts (New York: Berghahn Books, 2016), 4.

10 Bourdieu's view, quoted above, regarding the attempts to discover and *master* the acts of knowledge construction as completely as possible seems to still carry some leftovers of the Cartesian cogito.

11 Paul Ricoeur, *Oneself as Another*, trans. Kathleen Blamey (Chicago: University of Chicago Press, 1992), 1–25.

12 Charles E. Reagan, "Personal Identity," in *Ricoeur as Another: The Ethics of Subjectivity*, ed. Richard A. Cohen and James L. Marsh (New York: State University of New York, 2002), 7.

as historians of psychology Wade E. Pickren and Alexandra Rutherford, have noted this problem. In their historical study, they observe, "We attempt to highlight some implications of the subject–object or reflexivity conundrum as they have influenced the development of psychological theory and practice throughout our account."[13] English literature professor Ilana Shiloh writes in a similar vein about the conundrum of self-reflexivity: "Recursion is also the attribute of self-reflexivity, of consciousness contemplating itself. The conundrum of self-reflexivity has a long history of philosophical inquiry."[14] As these examples suggest, the conundrum of reflexivity can be analyzed or discussed from many different angles and approaches. I choose to first describe my personal grappling with the issue of researcher subjectivity, bias, and positionality as part of my knowledge-generating activity. I do this to illustrate the continuous discovery of new layers of subjectivity and bias in my personal knowledge-generating practices and to illustrate the role of the researcher's selfhood in such an endeavor. Next, I describe and evaluate the three dimensions of Bourdieu's epistemic reflexivity. I will argue that epistemic reflexivity a la Bourdieu is a necessary but insufficient way to deal with researcher subjectivity and bias. The problem is that the subject of epistemic reflexivity is not doing this reflexivity from some kind of "neutral" or disinterested "rational" position. Researchers' reflexive efforts reflect their interests, experiences, values, emotions, and competencies. Epistemic reflexivity is thus rooted in the researcher's worldview or ontology. However, I will demonstrate that attending to the person of the researcher and to his or her ontologies still does not provide a solution to the conundrum of reflexivity. Finally, I turn to Ricoeur's hermeneutics of the self and his view on attestation as a possible response to the conundrum of reflexivity.

Dilemmas of Researcher Subjectivity, Bias, and Positionality: An Autobiographical Account

The difficulties created by the subjectivity of the researcher have concerned me from an early stage of my academic life. My initial training in empirical research methods was in the social sciences. Much emphasis was placed on

13 Wade E. Pickren and Alexandra Rutherford, *A History of Modern Psychology in Context* (New Jersey: Wiley, 2010), xix.

14 Ilana Shiloh, *The Double, the Labyrinth and the Locked Room: Metaphors of Paradox in Crime Fiction and Film* (New York: Peter Lang, 2011), 142.

quantitative research methods, statistics, and the elimination of researcher subjectivity (e.g. sampling, observation, and measurement errors in statistical terms). There was a course in phenomenological psychology in my psychology honors program where things were different. The prescribed material for this course included two books that made me start to doubt the "standard" (neo-positivist) view of research at that time.[15] Dreyer Kruger wrote, for example, about challenging the "traditional natural scientific approach" in psychology and about research as an *intersubjective* process.[16] This was a very different approach to research than what I had learned in the research methodology courses.

Despite the cracks that started to appear regarding "the scientific method" and the problematic relationship of the researcher and the researched, I started my research career at the Human Sciences Research Council (HSRC) in Pretoria before joining the University of South Africa as a junior lecturer in 1989. There I conducted my first research firmly within a neo-positivist frame of mind. The subjectivity of the researcher had to be minimized as far as possible, even in the writing of the research report where writing in the third person was considered the standard. I enjoyed the statistical calculations and the thrill of finding statistically significant correlations. As I was teaching research methodology to our practical theology students, I decided to explore qualitative research approaches. This choice was pragmatic, as almost all our students did not have a sufficient background in mathematics to do the statistics required in quantitative research, and few students showed interest in doing quantitative research. Due to the importance of the person of the researcher in qualitative research, I now became convinced of the importance of intersubjectivity. The subjectivity of the researcher is important, but it has to be checked by other researchers and even the research participants.

Dealing with researcher subjectivity did, however, still pose a significant problem for me. I realized that objective knowledge in the positivist sense was a chimera, but I was concerned with the researcher's subjective choices

---

15 Dreyer Kruger, *An Introduction to Phenomenological psychology*, 2nd rev. ed. (Cape Town: Juta, 1988); Mary Stewart van Leeuwen, *The Person in Psychology* (Grand Rapids, Michigan: Eerdmans, 1985). We also studied some texts from Amedeo Giorgi.

16 Kruger, *An Introduction to Phenomenological Psychology*, 208 gives the following definition: "Psychology is an intersubjective, communicative science, systematically studying the structures of individual human existence by explicating lived (historical) experience of our problematic presence to the world."

and interpretations. The focus was still on controlling (or perhaps policing?) the subjectivity of the researcher. The researcher's subjectivity and bias were thus still seen as a major obstacle in the construction of (scientific) knowledge. My focus was still methodological and epistemological rather than ontological.

During that time, I was very much interested in critical theory (Habermas) and hermeneutics (Gadamer and Ricoeur) and later also the critical sociology of Bourdieu. Jürgen Habermas' *Knowledge and Human Interests*, Gadamer's *Truth and Method*, Ricoeur's *From Text to Action*, and Bourdieu and Loïc Wacquant's *An Invitation to Reflexive Sociology* helped to shape my understanding of the importance of the researcher's subjectivity, and of reflexivity, in doing research.[17] In articles such as "The Researcher: Engaged Participant or Detached Observer?" and "Participation and Distanciation in the Study of Religion" I engaged with these issues.[18]

In recent years I became aware of an additional, deeper, and even more complicated layer that adds another dimension to the problem of the researcher's subjectivity and bias in the research context that twentieth-century European philosophers only partly anticipated. I am a middle-aged practical theologian working at a public university in postcolonial South Africa. This may not seem particularly interesting. However, if I say that I am a white person who lived the greater part of my life in the apartheid era, the reader may sense the difficult situation that I find myself in. If I add that I am a male, Afrikaans-speaking[19] and a member of the Dutch Reformed Church,[20] those with some knowledge of the South African context will understand why I experience this situation as problematic.

---

17 Habermas, *Knowledge and Human Interests*. Gadamer, *Truth and Method*. Paul Ricoeur, *From Text to Action: Essays in Hermeneutics, II*, trans. Kathleen Blamey and John B. Thompson (London: Athlone Press, 1991). Pierre Bourdieu and Loïc J.D. Wacquant, *An Invitation to Reflexive Sociology* (Cambridge: Polity Press, 1992).

18 Jaco S. Dreyer, "The Researcher: Engaged Participant or Detached Observer?," *Journal of Empirical Theology* 11, no. 2 (1998): 5–22. Jaco S. Dreyer, "Participation and Distanciation in the Study of Religion" in *Religion: Immediate Experience and the Mediacy of Research*, ed. Hans-Günter Heimbrock and Christopher P. Scholtz (Göttingen: Vandenhoeck & Ruprecht, 2007), 189–211.

19 Afrikaans was seen as the language of the oppressor. The 1976 Soweto uprisings started as protest against Afrikaans as a compulsory subject in township schools.

20 The Dutch Reformed Church (DRC) was a close ally of the apartheid government and also gave theological legitimation to the policy of separate development.

I belong to the group of "white settlers" who colonized South Africa and who are held responsible for its colonial heritage.[21] Due to my whiteness I have benefited from apartheid. I grew up in a middle class family, had a decent education, and had access to resources and experiences that were not available to most black[22] people in South Africa before the transition to a democratic South Africa. It also meant access to resources and educational and other opportunities that others were excluded from purely on the basis of race. Although things have changed in postcolonial South Africa, many of the structural issues of the apartheid legacy are still prevalent.[23] In a material sense, the enduring effects of colonialism are present in the vast disparities in economic power between the different racial groups of South Africa, the lack of infrastructure, poor housing, and inadequate access to good health care and education. It is, of course, too simplistic to view everything through the lens of colonialism. There is, however, a good argument to be made that many of the current economic disparities between groups have their origin in colonialism and apartheid as a specific form of continuation of colonialism. Being a middle-aged white male, who grew up in the apartheid years, puts me in a category of "previously advantaged."

I must confess: it has been incredibly difficult for me to write this chapter. This is not in the first place due to the complexity of the issues raised, but due to the questioning of my professional identity and my position as scholar and researcher in post-apartheid South Africa. Being a privileged, white person confronts me and challenges me in my work as a practical theologian at a public university. How can I, from my position as "settler colonizer,"[24] responsibly

21 The term "settler" is often used to indicate the colonial baggage of white people. See Anna Johnston and Alan Lawson, "Settler Colonies," in *A Companion to Postcolonial Studies*, ed. Henry Schwarz and Sangeeta Ray (Malden: Blackwell, 2005), 360–376.

22 I use the term "black" here in a generic sense to indicate people of all races who were denied political and other rights due to the color of their skins. The term "previously or historically disadvantaged" overlaps with this category, but also includes those disadvantaged due to gender discrimination (thus white women).

23 Ironically, while I was working on this chapter, students in South Africa protested against the continuing legacies of colonialism (#RhodesMustFall) and the enduring inequalities and lack of access to higher education (#FeesMustFall).

24 I do not analyze the relation between my "settler subjectivity" and my "colonized subjectivity" in this contribution. See for example Jack Harrington, "Between Colonizer and Colonized: The Political Subjectivity of the Settler." https://www.opendemocracy.net/jack-harrington/between-colonizer-and-colonized-political-subjectivity-of-settler, accessed May 1, 2016.

fulfill my duties as a practical theologian with a subjectivity tainted by colonialism and apartheid? Living and working in postcolonial and post-apartheid South Africa thus sensitize me to my historical situation and my whiteness and how these aspects contribute to my position as "colonizer."[25]

Although I was aware of these issues related to my subjectivity and tried to account for that in earlier work as described above, I did not, and still cannot, fully understand the effects of the "inscriptions of the past," my colonial heritage, and my whiteness on my research and knowledge-generating practices.[26] A multitude of experiences and events over many years helped me to become aware of even more complex layers of this problem and sensitized me to the huge challenges that I, a white Afrikaner male, face when I do my scholarly work in this postcolonial context.[27] I cannot escape my colonial baggage in a postcolonial context. This colonial baggage is an important part of my subjectivity as researcher and colors every action that I take.

I came to realize that whiteness entails much more than the color of my skin. It implies a worldview shaped by the legacy of colonialism. My own theological training was thoroughly Western or Eurocentric. Many if not most of our prescribed books came from the Northern hemisphere (Europe and the USA), and only in a discipline such as "Missiology" did we really read anything from our African colleagues. Many discussions with colleagues and the emphasis of the university where I am employed to "Africanize" the curriculum and to become a truly "African university" helped me to realize how "Eurocentric" my theological imagination is, and how little I know about the epistemologies, ontologies, methodologies, and axiologies of my African colleagues. It slowly dawned on me that my practical theological research in many ways continues the colonial legacies of the past due to my "Western-centered" paradigm. I started to understand my complicity in the marginalization of epistemologies, ontologies, and methodologies that differ from my (Western-centered) research paradigm and the ongoing racism that this entails. My interest in the issue of researcher subjectivity and bias thus expanded

25 The white "Afrikaner" was until the early 20th century under Dutch or British colonial rule. The Afrikaner was regarded as backward and unsophisticated by the English establishment. However, when the Afrikaner gained political power, the colonized quickly became the colonizers. This demonstrates some of the difficulties of the binary colonizer/colonized.

26 Amal Treacher, "On Postcolonial Subjectivity," *Group Analysis* 38, no. 1 (2005): 49. doi:10.1177/0533316405049365.

27 A workshop "Difficult Conversations: 'Race,' Racism, and Transformation" at the beginning of 2013 was a particularly significant event.

from concerns primarily about research approaches and methods to concerns about ethical issues related to power and knowledge, whiteness, coloniality, and the knowledge system itself.[28]

Bourdieu's Epistemic Reflexivity

The autobiographical account in the previous section describes my ongoing engagement with the issue of researcher subjectivity and bias as part of my research and knowledge-generating activities. In this section, I will use some ideas from Bourdieu to examine my reflections more systematically, that is, to engage in the art and practice of reflexivity, in view of the conundrum of reflexivity that I described in the introduction of this chapter.

The reader may ask why I engage with the ideas of Bourdieu when we have learnt so much from feminist and postcolonial theorists regarding the importance a researcher's locality, positionality, and intersectionality, and the importance of the practice of reflexivity. I chose Bourdieu mainly because of the central role that the notion of reflexivity plays in his writings. Loïc Wacquant, a student and colleague of Bourdieu, wrote in *An Invitation to Reflexive Sociology* that, "If there is a single feature that makes Bourdieu stand out in the landscape of contemporary social theory, it is his signature obsession with reflexivity."[29] I will argue below that Bourdieu is also interesting for our purposes due to his concern with "transformative research" and the values and personhood of the researcher. This does not mean that Bourdieu is unique in this regard. I could have engaged with the work of many other scholars regarding these issues. The point here is not to try to give an overview of the different approaches to reflexivity, but to demonstrate that Bourdieu's epistemic reflexivity, despite is comprehensiveness, is not really a way out of the conundrum of reflexivity.

28 Problems of colonialism, white supremacy, and racism have only recently moved to the foreground in practical theology. See, for example, Emmanuel Yartekwei Amugi Lartey, *Postcolonializing God: New Perspectives on Pastoral and Practical Theology* (London: SCM Press, 2013); Melinda A. McGarrah Sharp, *Misunderstanding Stories: Toward a Postcolonial Pastoral Theology* (Eugene, OR: Pickwick Publications, 2013); Melinda A. McGarrah Sharp, "Globalization, Colonialism, and Postcolonialism," in *Wiley-Blackwell Companion to Practical Theology*, ed. Bonnie J. Miller-McLemore (Malden: Blackwell, 2012), 422–431; and Tom Beaudoin and Katherine Turpin, "White Practical Theology," in *Opening the Field of Practical Theology*, ed. Kathleen A. Cahalan and Gordon S. Mikoski (Lanham, Maryland: Rowman & Littlefield, 2014), 251–269.

29 Bourdieu and Wacquant, *An Invitation to Reflexive Sociology*, 36.

How could Bourdieu help us in our reflection on reflexivity? I make use here of the three types of biases that stand out in Bourdieu's epistemic reflexivity,[30] namely the researcher's *social* location ("the *social* origins and coordinates (class, gender, ethnicity, etc.) of the individual researcher"), the researcher's position in the *academic* field ("the objective space of possible intellectual positions offered to him or her at a given moment, and, beyond, in the field of power"), and the *intellectualist bias* ("to construe the world as a *spectacle*, as a set of significations to be interpreted rather than as concrete problems to be solved practically").[31]

The first bias, namely social location, is the one that is most often discussed in research textbooks. In my personal account, it is clear that my social location plays an important role. I am working in post-apartheid South Africa where aspects such as my gender (male), race (white), class (upper middle-class in the South African context; part of the privileged who are employed on a full-time basis at a public university) definitely shape my view of the world and influence my relationship with research participants. From a religious perspective, it is also significant that I grew up in and still am a member of the Dutch Reformed Church.[32] It is one thing to acknowledge the influence of social location on one's research and knowledge-generating activities, but another to understand how the different "coordinates" influence one's research activities. Even at this level, we reach the threshold of personal insight into one's situation.[33] In spite of provocative titles such as "The Transparent Self,"[34] it is clear that it is only by taking the detour from the self to the self via others that we get some insight into our views, values, and prejudices. The conundrum of reflexivity is thus already fully present at this level.

The second bias, namely the researcher's position in the academic field, is less often considered.[35] It is, however, fairly obvious that the researcher's position in the academic field will play an important part with regard to research

30 Loïc J.D. Wacquant, "Toward a Social Praxeology: The Structure and Logic of Bourdieu's Sociology," in Pierre Bourdieu and Loïc J.D. Wacquant, *An Invitation to Reflexive Sociology*, 39.

31 Wacquant, "Toward a Social Praxeology," 39.

32 My father and my grandfather were pastors in the Dutch Reformed Church. It goes beyond this text to reflect on the formative influence of these "significant others" on me.

33 See chapters 5 and 9 in this volume by Courtney Goto (pp. 110–133) and Phillis Sheppard (pp. 219–249) for further reflection on the limitations of such self-identifications.

34 Sidney M Jourard, *The Transparent Self*, rev. ed. (New York: Van Nostrand Reinhold, 1971).

35 Wacquant, "Toward a Social Praxeology," 39. See chapter 8 by Bonnie Miller-McLemore in this volume on academic hierarchies encountered by practical theologians (pp. 190–218)

and knowledge generation. The researcher's position in the academic hierarchy (whether you are, for instance, a junior lecturer or research assistant at a small university versus a full professor at a highly-ranked international university) is often an important factor in who gets published, who gets invited to participate in conferences, who becomes part of research networks, who gets funding, who is elected to serve on editorial and other scholarly boards, and so forth. But Bourdieu also refers here to other aspects such as the relative place of the discipline in the academic hierarchy (e.g., theology versus the medical or economic and business management sciences) as discussed in his *Homo Academicus*.[36] Most importantly, as mentioned in the personal account above, one also has to reflect on one's position regarding the "Western knowledge systems"[37] and the enduring legacy of colonialism as highlighted so distinctly by postcolonial and decolonial theorists. These theorists help us to recognize how the "colonizers" and the "colonized" are influenced by the enduring legacy of colonialism. It does, however, seem to be quite difficult to break the shackles of self-colonization or to recognize your colonizing and patronizing tendencies. The slowness to recognize my entanglement in the colonial system of apartheid and my complicity in the marginalization of knowledge systems that differ from my own bear testimony to the many resistances and difficulties that our reflexive efforts face. The conundrum of reflexivity, namely that we cannot *not* reflect on our prejudices and biases, but that complete discovery and mastery of these prejudices and biases always eludes us, is thus also fully present at this level.

The third bias, namely the intellectualist bias, or "scholastic illusion,"[38] is the most original contribution of Bourdieu's epistemic reflexivity.[39] This refers to the risk of "theoreticism," of formulating theories that have lost their connection with or grounding in actual practices due to the researcher's privileged and scholarly position.[40] Epistemic reflexivity can be of great value here to

---

36 Pierre Bourdieu, *Homo Academicus*, trans. Peter Collier (Cambridge: Polity Press, 1988).

37 Dale Wallace, "Rethinking Religion, Magic and Witchcraft in South Africa: From Colonial Coherence to Postcolonial Conundrum," *Journal for the Study of Religion* 28, no. 1 (2015): 48.

38 Pierre Bourdieu, *Science of Science and Reflexivity*, trans. Richard Nice (Chicago: University of Chicago Press, 2004), 37.

39 Wacquant, "Toward a Social Praxeology," 39.

40 Shaun Rawolle and Bob Lingard, "Bourdieu and Educational Research: Thinking Tools, Relational Thinking, Beyond Epistemological Innocence," in *Social Theory and Education Research: Understanding Foucault, Habermas, Bourdieu and Derrida*, ed. Mark Murphy (Routledge: New York, 2013), 117.

prevent our theories from becoming totally detached from the lifeworld of the researched. However, we also run into the limitations of reflexivity. We cannot undo our privileged positions and frameworks of interpretation as scholars, and we thus could easily advantage our intellectualist interpretations over the views, interpretations, and concerns of the researched.

Bourdieu's epistemic reflexivity is helpful as it expands the reflexive task to issues that are often neglected and highlights the dangers and limitations of academic research. Engaging in epistemic reflexivity does not, however, unravel the conundrum of reflexivity. I can reflect on my social location as a white, male researcher in post-apartheid and postcolonial South Africa and all the complications and issues that are raised by this particular social location. I can reflect on my position as a professor of practical theology at a state university in South Africa and on the enduring legacy of colonialism in this context. I can reflect on my privileged position as a scholar and on the danger of intellectualizing faith and faith experiences due to this position. Hopefully, all these reflexive efforts will sensitize me and will help me steer away from abusive research practices and subjective knowledge claims. But how will one know? Who benefits from my research efforts? Will the "knowledge" gained make any difference in the lives of the researched?

Reflexivity: From Epistemology to Ontology

These last questions expose the limits of epistemic reflexivity. The researcher's reflexive efforts do not come from nowhere. It is not the result of some kind of universal or disengaged or disinterested rationality. No, to use another Bourdieusian term, it flows from the researcher's "habitus," from the specific interests, experiences, competences, and values of the researcher. Reflexivity helps us to see how our biases and prejudices shape our epistemology, our research practices, and our knowledge-construction efforts, but these reflexive efforts are themselves influenced by bias and subjectivity. Even when we reflect on bias, it is not done without bias. We can never escape from our "horizon of understanding," not even when we reflect on our "horizon of understanding." Put in another way, "*the subject is not the master of meaning*."[41] This is the conundrum of reflexivity explored in this chapter.

41 Johann Michel, *Ricoeur and the Post-Structuralists: Bourdieu, Derrida, Deleuze, Foucault, Castoriadis*, trans. Scott Davidson (London: Rowman & Littlefield, 2015), 102.

This situation, namely that reflexivity does not solve the problem of the "epistemological wound"[42] and that it does not provide a basis to compare or adjudicate between different approaches to knowledge construction or different epistemologies, brings us to the precipice of subjectivism and anarchy. How can we respond to this situation? Here I would like to draw on the insight of feminist scholars such as Liz Stanley and Sue Wise and also Sandra Harding about the relation between epistemology and ontology. Their insights do not solve the conundrum of reflexivity, but they help us see a possible way to deal with the conundrum through a consideration of the crucial role of the *person* of the researcher in all research and knowledge-generating activities.

I start with Stanley and Wise's feminist perspective on the relation between epistemology and ontology. They discuss this relation at length in the new edition of their classic book *Breaking Out: Feminist Epistemology and Ontology*.[43] I quote here one of the key passages in which they describe the relationship between epistemology and ontology:

> Our insistence upon the ontological basis of knowledge, and thus of the valid existence of varieties of feminist epistemology, brings us full circle in our discussion of recent feminist debates concerning the kinds of issues and questions discussed in the first edition of *Breaking Out*. Here, as in *Breaking Out*, we have argued throughout for the symbiotic relationship between ontology and epistemology. Proclamation of the reflexivity of feminist research processes; acknowledgement of the contextual specificity of feminist as of all other knowledge; recognition that who a researcher is, in terms of their sex, race, class and sexuality, affects what they 'find' in research is as true for feminist as any other researchers: these and other components of feminist epistemology emphasize the *necessarily* ontological basis of knowledge-production.[44]

Recognizing the ontological basis of our knowledge-production efforts places the spotlight firmly on the "who" of the research, the person of the researcher, and on his or her "being" and view of the world. It is thus not only the "what" of the researcher (what is your race, gender, scholarly position, etc.), his or

42 Evens, Handelman, and Roberts, "Introduction: Reflexivity and Selfhood," 4.

43 Liz Stanley and Sue Wise, *Breaking Out Again: Feminist Ontology and Epistemology*, Taylor & Francis e-Library, 2002, accessed May 1, 2016. https://cdn.preterhuman.net/texts/thought_and_writing/philosophy/breaking%20out%20again.pdf.

44 Stanley and Wise, *Breaking Out Again*, 228.

her positionality in terms of social location, academic position, and scholarly privilege that is important, but the *self* or *personhood* of the researcher.

The importance of the person of the researcher is widely accepted today in research methodology discussions, especially in poststructuralist and feminist discourses and social justice research approaches. How does a consideration of the *self* or *personhood* of the researcher help us to respond to the conundrum of reflexivity? It is in this regard that Harding's insights are valuable. She describes the importance of the values and selfhood of researchers in a chapter, "After Mr. Nowhere: New Proper Scientific Selves," in her recently published work *Objectivity and Diversity: Another Logic of Scientific Research*.[45] The need for proper scientific selves seem to be particularly important due to the diversity that is such a characteristic of our current research context. How can we do research that does not only benefit the researcher, but also the researched? This is one of the key questions that researchers face today and also a question that continues to haunt me when I do research in postcolonial South Africa. The ideal (or illusion) of value-neutral research has to give way to value-based research. Harding stresses that this stance does not mean "everything goes" and that there is no room for objectivity as a scientific value. Research skills and methodology are still important, but the quality of the research also depends on the person and values of the researcher. Dealing with the researcher's subjectivity and positionality is thus not only an epistemological matter, but also of ethics and ontology.

This crucial role of the researcher's *self* in the research process is also acknowledged by Bourdieu. In a remarkable passage in his essay on "Understanding," he wrote about the "welcoming disposition" of the researcher.

> Thus, at the risk of shocking both the rigorous methodologist and the inspired hermeneutic scholar, I would say that the interview can be considered a sort of *spiritual exercise* that, through *forgetfulness of self*, aims at a *true conversion of the way we look at* other people in the ordinary circumstances of life. The welcoming disposition, which leads one to make the respondent's problems one's own, the capacity to take that person and understand them just as they are in their distinctive necessity, is a sort of *intellectual love*: a gaze that consents to necessity in the manner of

45 Sandra Harding, *Objectivity and Diversity: Another Logic of Scientific Research*, chapter 7, e-book, accessed November 8, 2015. https://www.scribd.com/read/260842713/Objectivity-and-Diversity-Another-Logic-of-Scientific-Research.

> the "intellectual love of God," that is, of the natural order, which Spinoza held to be the supreme form of knowledge.[46]

Bourdieu's words here are not just idle talk. His research, especially as published in *The Weight of the World: Social Suffering in Contemporary Society*, is an example of this type of transformative research. His research was always characterized not just by strong epistemic values, but also by an equally strong commitment to research that will make a difference in the lives of the researched.

What is the implication of this for the focus of this chapter, namely the role of researcher subjectivity and bias in research and knowledge practices, and the conundrum of reflexivity? It implies, in my view, that we have to reflect on the social location of the researcher, the researcher's position in the academic field, as well as the researcher's privileged position as a scholar. However, and this is the main point here, reflexivity has to be more than a reflection on the researcher's positioning in terms of social location or academic position. It also has to include a reflection on the ontological starting point of the research as crystallized in the researcher's self and as expressed in the values, interests, commitments, and the worldview of the researcher.

Ricoeur's Hermeneutics of the Self and Attestation

The broadening of our reflexivity to include ontological aspects such as the researcher's worldview and values may seem to be a way out of the conundrum of reflexivity. However, this is not the case. We face the same conundrum again, namely that the researcher is not the master of meaning, and that there is no direct route or privileged access to his or her ontological commitments and values. Is this not just another possible place for self-deception?

It is at this point that the futility of striving to arrive at an ultimate foundation for our reflexive efforts is quite obvious. The certainty claimed by cogito philosophies has been shattered.[47] There is no way to escape from the conundrum of reflexivity due to fragmentary nature of selfhood and the broken promises that are so characteristic of us as human beings. Our reflexive efforts

46 Pierre Bourdieu, "Understanding," in *The Weight of the World: Social Suffering in Contemporary Society*, Pierre Bourdieu et al. (Cambridge: Polity Press, 1999), 614, emphasis in the original.

47 Ricoeur, *Oneself as Another*, 21.

will always be "provisional, tentative, a task rather than a fait accompli, a wager rather than a possession."[48]

Should we give up our reflexive efforts and give in to despair? Is the "humiliated subject" of Nietzsche the only possible response to Dilthey's "exalted subject"?[49] I do not think so. Ricoeur's hermeneutical anthropology, with his view of the capable and responsible self, could provide another avenue to respond to the troubling conundrum of reflexivity. Ricoeur's hermeneutical theory of the self provides rich insights into selfhood that could be applied to the self of the researcher as an acting and suffering person. There is no space here to discuss the main features of Ricoeur's hermeneutical anthropology. I just point out one aspect of his hermeneutics of the self that seems to me particularly relevant with regards to the conundrum of reflexivity. It is the type of certainty that we could aspire to regarding our reflexive efforts.

The conundrum of reflexivity lies in the lack of a basis on which to decide whether our reflexive efforts are biased or not, whether they are true or false. For example, I can reflect on my position of whiteness in post-apartheid South Africa and the possible distortions and biases that could flow from this position. I can do this as honestly as possible, reflecting on the hidden meanings and privileges of whiteness, and on strategies to interpret and to deal with this threat to objectivity in the research encounter. However, despite my best efforts, I could still continue to keep my privileged position intact through a variety of strategies or "moves to innocence" as described by Janet Mawhimey.[50] How could we decide on "the 'truth' from our position"?[51] What criteria could we use to test our truth claims?

It is in this context that Ricoeur's notion of *attestation* could be a way forward.[52] Ricoeur describes attestation as the *type of certainty* that is appropriate for a hermeneutics of the self that does not exalt the subject (Descartes) nor humiliate the subject (Nietzsche). He contrasts the type of certainty of attestation with the absolute certainty of the exalted cogito and the total lack of

48 Richard Kearney, "Introduction," in *Paul Ricoeur: The Hermeneutics of Action*, ed. Richard Kearney (London: Sage, 1996), 1–2.

49 Ricoeur, *Oneself as Another*, 1–23.

50 Janet Mawhimey, "'Giving up the Ghost': Disrupting the Reproduction of White Privilege in Anti-Racist Pedagogy and Organizational Change," MA thesis, Ontario Institute for Studies in Education of the University of Toronto, 1998, 94–120.

51 Mawhimey, "'Giving up the Ghost,'" 120.

52 Ricoeur mentions in a footnote in the ninth study of his "Oneself as Another" that "attestation" is "the password for this entire book." Paul Ricoeur, *Oneself as Another*, 289 (footnote 82).

certainty of the humiliated cogito. Attestation is not the certainty "claimed by the cogito" of "self-founding knowledge," that is, the certainty belonging to an ultimate foundation. But it is also not the uncertainty of perpetual doubt and suspicion as a result of a humiliated cogito.[53] Ricoeur says that attestation

> constitutes the instance of judgment that stands over against suspicion, in all those circumstances where the self designates itself, either as the author of its words, or as the agent of its action, or as the narrator of a story, or as a subject accountable for its acts. The heart of hearts then appears as the site of intimate assurance that, in some particular circumstance, sweeps away doubts, hesitations, the suspicion of inauthenticity, of hypocrisy, of self-complacency, of self-deception, and authorizes the acting and suffering human to say: *here I stand*.[54]

By "heart of hearts," Ricoeur refers to one of what he calls the three "registers of alterity": the *flesh* that mediates between the self and a world, the *stranger* that mediates between self and others, and the *heart of hearts* that is the voice of conscience that addresses oneself from deep within oneself.[55] Attestation is thus the kind of certainty of a self that recognizes its limitations and fallibility, but that acts with conscience and integrity, with the "*assurance of being oneself acting and suffering*."[56] It is not the kind of certainty that comes from an overly confident or self-possessed person, but from a person that recognizes the fragility and vulnerability of its claims and the "permanent threat of suspicion."[57] It is a kind of certainty that flows from trust in the ability to speak, to act, to do, and to live together in just relations and just institutions. It is the kind of certainty of a self that makes and keeps promises, that acts with self-esteem and conviction whilst always being aware of its fragility and its responsibility towards the self and others. As Ricoeur remarks, "There is no recourse against suspicion but a more reliable attestation."[58] In this way, attestation could provide the courage and endurance to continue to face the conundrum of reflexivity in our research encounters.

---

53 Ricoeur, *Oneself as Another*, 21.

54 Paul Ricoeur, *Philosophical Anthropology: Writings and Lectures, Volume 3*, ed. Johann Michel and Jérôme Porée, trans. David Pellauer (Cambridge, Polity Press 2016), 267.

55 Ricoeur, *Philosophical Anthropology*, 259.

56 Ricoeur, *Oneself as Another*, 22, emphasis in the original.

57 Ricoeur, *Oneself as Another*, 22.

58 Ricoeur, *Oneself as Another*, 22.

In the end, the conundrum of reflexivity cannot be solved. Researcher subjectivity and bias will always be part and parcel of our research practices and our attempts to make these subjectivities and biases transparent, though our reflexive efforts will always remain suspect. We are not masters of ourselves. However, all is not lost. The certainty of our reflexive efforts depends on the extent to which we do our research with integrity, with ethical imagination, and with a genuine concern for the wellbeing of the researched. This is what our practical theological research endeavors have to attest to.

Bibliography

Beaudoin, Tom and Katherine Turpin. "White Practical Theology." In *Opening the Field of Practical Theology*, edited by Kathleen A. Cahalan and Grodon S. Mikoski, 251–269. Lanham, Maryland: Rowman & Littlefield, 2014.

Blaikie, Norman. *Approaches to Social Enquiry*. Cambridge: Polity Press, 1993.

Bourdieu, Pierre. *Homo Academicus*, translated by Peter Collier. Cambridge: Polity Press, 1988.

Bourdieu, Pierre. "Understanding," *Theory, Culture & Society* 13, no. 2 (1996): 17–37.

Bourdieu, Pierre. "Understanding." In *The Weight of the World: Social Suffering in Contemporary Society*, Pierre Bourdieu et al., 607–626. Cambridge: Polity Press, 1999.

Bourdieu, Pierre. *Science of Science and Reflexivity*, translated by Richard Nice. Chicago: University of Chicago Press, 2004.

Bourdieu, Pierre and Loïc J.D. Wacquant. *An Invitation to Reflexive Sociology*. Cambridge: Polity Press, 1992.

Dreyer, Jaco S. "The Researcher: Engaged Participant or Detached Observer?," *Journal of Empirical Theology* 11, no. 2 (1998): 5–22.

Dreyer, Jaco S. "Participation and Distanciation in the Study of Religion." In *Religion: Immediate Experience and the Mediacy of Research*, edited by Hans-Günter Heimbrock and Christopher P. Scholtz, 189–211. Göttingen: Vandenhoeck & Ruprecht, 2007.

Evens, Terry, Don Handelman, and Christopher Roberts. "Introduction: Reflexivity and Selfhood." In *Reflecting on Reflexivity: The Human Condition as an Ontological Surprise*, edited by Terry Evens, Don Handelman and Christopher Roberts, 1–20. New York: Berghahn Books, 2016.

Gadamer, Hans-Georg. *Truth and Method*, 2nd rev. ed., translated by Joel Weinsheimer and Donald G. Marshall. London: Sheed & Ward, 1989.

Ganzevoort, R. Ruard. "Forks in the Road when Tracing the Sacred: Practical Theology as Hermeneutics of Lived Religion." Presidential Address to the Ninth Conference of the International Academy of Practical Theology, Chicago, Aug. 3, 2009.

Habermas, Jürgen. *Knowledge and Human Interests*, translated by Jeremy J. Shapiro. Boston: Beacon Press, 1971.

Harding, Sandra, ed. *The Feminist Standpoint Theory Reader*. New York and London: Routledge, 2004.

Harding, Sandra. *Objectivity and Diversity: Another Logic of Scientific Research*, chapter 7, e-book, accessed November 8, 2015. https://www.scribd.com/read/260842713/Objectivity-and-Diversity-Another-Logic-of-Scientific-Research.

Harrington, Jack. "Between Colonizer and Colonized: The Political Subjectivity of the Settler," accessed May 1, 2016. https://www.opendemocracy.net/jack-harrington/between-colonizer-and-colonized-political-subjectivity-of-settler.

Johnston, Anna and Alan Lawson. "Settler Colonies." In *A Companion to Postcolonial Studies*, edited by Henry Schwarz and Sangeeta Ray, 360–376. Malden: Blackwell, 2005.

Jourard, Sidney M. *The Transparent Self*, rev. ed. New York: Van Nostrand Reinhold, 1971.

Kearney, Richard. "Introduction." In *Paul Ricoeur: The Hermeneutics of Action*, edited by Richard Kearney, 1–2. London: Sage, 1996.

Kruger, Dreyer. *An Introduction to Phenomenological Psychology*, 2nd rev. ed. Cape Town: Juta, 1988.

Lartey, Emmanuel Y.A. *Postcolonializing God: New Perspectives on Pastoral and Practical Theology*. London: SCM Press, 2013.

Mantzoukas, Stefanos. "Issues of Representation within Qualitative Inquiry," *Qualitative Health Research* 14, no. 7 (2004): 994–1007. doi:10.1177/1049732304265959.

Mawhimey, Janet. "'Giving up the Ghost': Disrupting the Reproduction of White Privilege in Anti-Racist Pedagogy and Organizational Change." MA thesis, Ontario Institute for Studies in Education of the University of Toronto, 1998.

McGarrah Sharp, Melinda A. *Misunderstanding Stories: Toward a Postcolonial Pastoral Theology*. Eugene, OR: Pickwick Publications, 2013.

McGarrah Sharp, Melinda A. "Globalization, Colonialism, and Postcolonialism." In *Wiley-Blackwell Companion to Practical Theology*, edited by Bonnie J. Miller-McLemore, 422–431. Malden: Blackwell, 2012.

Michel, Johann. *Ricoeur and the Post-Structuralists: Bourdieu, Derrida, Deleuze, Foucault, Castoriadis*, translated by Scott Davidson. London: Rowman & Littlefield, 2015.

Pickren, Wade E. and Alexandra Rutherford. *A History of Modern Psychology in Context*. New Jersey: Wiley, 2010.

Rawolle, Shaun and Bob Lingard. "Bourdieu and Educational Research: Thinking Tools, Relational Thinking, beyond Epistemological Innocence." In *Social Theory and Education Research: Understanding Foucault, Habermas, Bourdieu and Derrida*, edited by Mark Murphy, 117–137. New York: Routledge, 2013.

Reagan, Charles. "Personal Identity." In *Ricoeur as Another: The Ethics of Subjectivity*, edited by Richard A. Cohen and James L. Marsh, 3–31. New York: State University of New York, 2002.

Ricoeur, Paul. *Oneself as Another*, translated by Kathleen Blamey. Chicago: University of Chicago Press, 1992.

Ricoeur, Paul. *Philosophical Anthropology: Writings and Lectures, Volume 3*, edited by Johann Michel and Jérôme Porée and translated by David Pellauer. Cambridge, Polity Press, 2016.

Shiloh, Ilana. *The Double, the Labyrinth and the Locked Room: Metaphors of Paradox in Crime Fiction and Film*. New York: Peter Lang, 2011.

Stanley, Liz and Sue Wise. *Breaking Out Again: Feminist Ontology and Epistemology*, Taylor & Francis e-Library, 2002, accessed May 1, 2016. https://cdn.preterhuman.net/texts/thought_and_writing/philosophy/breaking%20out%20again.pdf.

Treacher, Amal. "On Postcolonial Subjectivity," *Group Analysis* 38, no. 1 (2005): 43–57. doi:10.1177/0533316405049365.

Van Leeuwen, Mary Stewart. *The Person in Psychology*. Grand Rapids, Michigan: Eerdmans, 1985.

Wacquant, Loïc J.D. "Toward a Social Praxeology: The Structure and Logic of Bourdieu's Sociology." In *An Invitation to Reflexive Sociology*, Pierre Bourdieu and Loïc J.D. Wacquant, 1–59. Cambridge: Polity Press, 1992.

Wallace, Dale. "Rethinking Religion, Magic and Witchcraft in South Africa: From Colonial Coherence to Postcolonial Conundrum," *Journal for the Study of Religion* 28, no. 1 (2015): 23–51.

CHAPTER 5

Writing in Compliance with the Racialized "Zoo" of Practical Theology

Courtney T. Goto

In the context of the academy, a conundrum is a persistent, perduring dilemma that is enmeshed in the process of producing knowledge (in this case practical theology). It is deeper than a research question on a particular subject, when a scholar doggedly wrestles with a formidable problem and neither will let go. Many questions and their permutations have their seasons. However, the nature of the beast is such that the same conundrum can trip up the researcher repeatedly and quite aside from a particular topic of research. (Sometimes when a conundrum is so irksome, a practical theologian makes it a subject of research.) A conundrum entangles a person in a perennial quandary because it evokes something at stake for the researcher beyond filling gaps or addressing problems in the literature. For some of my colleagues in this volume, conundrums are limited to the work itself. When these theorists close their books and shut down their computer, the conundrum remains in the world of ideas. However, other conundrums such as the one I describe impinge in a more personal, existential way—not because of what I think but because of the status I am assigned as a person of color.

In this chapter, I present a conundrum in practical theology as well as the wider academy that reflects the racism of the larger culture in which it is embedded. The discussion shares intersections with Phillis Sheppard's chapter on racism as well as Jaco Dreyer's chapter on reflexivity.[1] Like other authors, I take a practical theological approach to the conundrum I describe, using multiple disciplines to analyze it, in my case drawing on postcolonial, Asian American, psychoanalytic, and theological perspectives. I then identify some areas of work in which the practical theology community can respond collectively to coercive mimeticism.

1 See Jaco Dreyer's chapter 4 (pp. 91–109) and Phillis I. Sheppard's chapter 9 (pp. 219–249) in this volume.

 | DOI 10.1163/9789004324244_007

The Emergence of a Conundrum

I was invited to write the Asian American chapter for *Opening the Field of Practical Theology* (Rowman & Littlefield, 2014).[2] This introductory textbook was designed to help students explore the breadth of trajectories in practical theology. Each chapter (fifteen in all) features a different perspective, including, for example, feminist, hermeneutical, liberationist, and contextual approaches to the field. Three "racial chapters" were originally intended to be included in the book (African American, US Latino/a, and Asian American).

As much as I was delighted to be asked to write a chapter for *Opening the Field*, it raised some troubling issues about which I wrote and discussed with colleagues as we engaged the work.[3] I appreciated that the editors wanted to include diverse perspectives, reflecting differences in race, gender, theology, and method. Asian American approaches to practical theology are not well known by scholars and students in the field. At the same time, I wondered why only scholars of color were asked to write the racial chapters, while white colleagues were invited to address approaches that are central to (meaning "well studied in") the discipline. Their request was not the result of conscious racism on anyone's part but a result that is consistent with larger patterns of unconscious marginalization of scholars of color in the academy and in the wider culture. To their credit, many of my white colleagues in the project cited literature authored by scholars of color. Many are mindful of the need for diverse perspectives. However, this does not erase an unwitting division of labor that implies and reinforces an assumption that those with power and privilege in the field speak about what is privileged (often without realizing that the field itself and they are in fact privileged), while those who are historically marginalized address what is often treated as marginal. As Dale Andrews, another contributor to the volume, writes, "We have not escaped the marginalization of studying the marginalized."[4] I was also disturbed that unlike scholars of color, my white colleagues in the project and in general were not expected to account for dynamics of power, privilege, and whiteness in their research and teaching. When I shared my concerns at our first authors' meeting, Tom

2 Kathleen A. Cahalan and Gordon S. Mikoski, eds., *Opening the Field of Practical Theology: An Introduction* (Lanham, MD: Rowman & Littlefield, 2014).

3 Courtney T. Goto, "Asian American Practical Theologies," in *Opening the Field of Practical Theology: An Introduction*, ed. Kathleen A. Cahalan and Gordon S. Mikoski (Lanham, MD: Rowman & Littlefield, 2014), 31–44.

4 Dale P. Andrews, "African American Practical Theology," in *Opening the Field of Practical Theology: An Introduction*, ed. Kathleen A. Cahalan and Gordon S. Mikoski (Lanham, MD: Rowman & Littlefield, 2014), 27.

Beaudoin and Katherine Turpin were inspired to write the "White Practical Theology" chapter.[5] Unfortunately, even this contribution could not solve a larger structural problem of the book.[6] The design of the volume assumes that the field is divisible into broad approaches that are seemingly untouched by race, while the work of addressing issues of race is assigned to isolated chapters coded as such.[7] The "racial chapters" reduce people to racial identity and "exoticize" those who are "other."

In writing my first draft of the chapter, I was reminded of cultural critic Rey Chow's discussion of John Berger's work, in which he characterizes tokenism and marginalization as zookeeping.[8] At the zoo, exotic animals are kept in captivity for the entertainment and education of visitors. Reflecting on the metaphor, Berger observes that zoo animals are subject to a gaze through which they are not seen truly. In fact, it is impossible to see wild animals as they *really* are because they are, of course, in captivity. What is seen is a distorted (imprisoned) version of animals in the wild. Worse yet, says Berger, zoo animals are completely dependent on their keepers or trainers.[9] I would add that sometimes dolphins and other animals are even trained to perform tricks that make them appear to be more like their captors. They are given food incentives and verbal praise to perform in ways that are pleasing.

Reflecting on Berger's metaphor, Chow likens the gaze of visitors at the zoo to the critical gaze of white readers in the academy. Especially when white Western readers interrogate literary texts or other cultural artifacts of developing countries, she argues, their gaze or reading becomes "a critical part of

5 Tom Beaudoin and Katherine Turpin, "White Practical Theology," in *Opening the Field of Practical Theology: An Introduction*, eds. Kathleen A. Cahalan and Gordon S. Mikoski (Lanham, MD: Rowman & Littlefield, 2014), 251–269.

6 Bonnie Miller-McLemore, Authors' meeting for *Conundrums in Practical Theology*, San Diego, November 21, 2014.

7 Another example of this pattern is Serene Jones and Paul Lakeland, eds., *Constructive Theology: A Contemporary Approach to Classical Themes* (Minneapolis: Fortress, 2005). Elaine Robinson points out that in this book substantive reflection on race in relation to human being is left to Shawn Copeland's chapter, "such that the white theologians need not wrestle deeply with their own white privilege." This approach "projects an 'additive' method in which the white theological tradition might appear to be normative and supplemented by theologians of color. No doubt this was not the intention of the authors. But the printed text, in fact, may belie the goal of presenting diverse perspectives as authoritative alongside more traditional ones." Elaine A. Robinson, *Race and Theology* (Nashville: Abingdon, 2012), 52.

8 Rey Chow, *The Protestant Ethnic and the Spirit of Capitalism* (New York: Columbia University Press, 2002), 95–96.

9 John Berger, *About Looking* (New York: Pantheon, 1980), 1–26, cited by Chow, *The Protestant Ethnic*, 96.

the image—and the imagining—of third world cultural productions."[10] Chow expresses the sense of captivity I experienced in writing my chapter, a feeling with which other scholars of color are likely familiar. I am seen and cannot help but come to see myself in terms of a destructive gaze, thinking and producing scholarship that responds to how I am seen by those in power. Chow writes about the imbalance of power between those who are seen as subjects of research (i.e., ethnics in so-called "developing countries") and those who have the power to define and construct with their looking (i.e., scholars from countries with a history of imperialism).[11] Through images, those without power are constructed in the imagination of those in authority, while the oppressed lack the agency to do the same.

I want to be clear that as an Asian American scholar, I have considerably more power than those who live in a developing country with less education and resources. As an author, I have some power to shape others' perceptions of me and to combat stereotypes about Asian Americans (as I am doing at this very moment). It might seem that if I wrote something true to my experience as an Asian American, readers could see me (and by implication other Asian Americans) as we "truly" are, but that is not possible. The assumption that people of color can represent or reveal what is "authentic" about their culture is a misperception that perpetuates the zoo.

No colleague of mine, and certainly none of my colleagues with whom I was collaborating on the *Opening* book project, would ever knowingly play the role of a zookeeper or want anything to do with a project that tokenizes or marginalizes anyone. The zoo image is as difficult to take in as it is for me to express. However, Chow's metaphor of the zoo helps to explain the bind that I and other scholars of color experience when we are asked to write an ethnic chapter representing "our people."

Naming the Conundrum: Coercive Mimeticism

My experience of the book project illustrates a conundrum that is insidious, systemic, and chronic, not only in practical theology but also in the academy, a

10 Chow, *Protestant Ethnic*, 100.

11 The binary of developing and developed countries implies a hierarchy, but I use it here to highlight the mentality that Chow criticizes. Nicholas Mirzoeff also discusses how colonized peoples have often been deprived of the "right to look" (in the words of Derrida). Nicholas Mirzoeff, *The Right to Look: A Counterhistory of Visuality* (Duraham, NC: Duke University, 2011), 1.

conundrum that expresses the racism and colonialism that characterize Western (and other) culture(s). It is not simply painful to feel tokenized. It is that I, and other scholars of color who aspire to be successful in the academy, are required to participate—one could properly say *trained* to participate—in making our own cages in conformity with white expectations. Chow would regard these practices as expressive of "coercive mimeticism," which is "a process (identitarian, existential, cultural or textual) in which those who are marginal to mainstream Western culture are expected, by way of what Albert Memmi calls 'the mark of the plural,' to resemble and replicate the very banal preconceptions that have been appended to them, a process in which they are expected to objectify themselves in accordance with the already seen and thus to authenticate the familiar and imagings of them as ethnics."[12] In other words, a person of color, whether as a research subject or as a research scholar, is expected to participate in being and becoming who his/her "captors" (i.e., members of one or more dominant cultures) deem this ethnic person to be.

Coercive mimeticism is a conundrum with a series of interlocking parts. First, I am handed the role of Asian American, and I feel obligated to play the part because there are consequences if I do not and incentives if I do. If I do not comply, I forgo the opportunity to be seen and heard at all. Not only does noncompliance hold me back professionally, it hurts others in my community who suffer the same chronic sense of invisibility and marginalization. However, accepting the invitation has its dangers as well, which leads to a second part of the bind. The term *Asian American* is problematic as I and many voices in Asian American studies and theology have discussed.[13] Writing a chapter on "my people" is liable to reinforce common assumptions that there is an essence to which the category "Asian American" refers, which of course there is not. Asian American identities are fluid and evolving, expressed and known only as they are performed at intersections of multiple histories, political commitments, and communal memories that do not necessarily meet easily or

12 Albert Memmi, *The Colonizer and the Colonized*, expanded ed., trans. Howard Greenfeld, introduction by Jean-Paul Sartre, afterword by Susan Gilson Miller (Boston: Beacon, 1991), 85. Cited in Chow, *Protestant Ethic*, 107.

13 See HyeRan Kim-Cragg, "Between and Beyond Asian-ness: A Voice of a Postcolonial Hybrid Korean-Canadian Diaspora," in *What Young Asian Theologians Are Thinking*, ed. Leow Theng Huat (Singapore: Trinity Theological College, 2015); Nami Kim, "The 'Indigestible' Asian: The Unifying Term 'Asian' in Theological Discourse," in *Off the Menu: Asian and Asian North American Women's Religion and Theology*, ed. Rita Nakashima Brock et al. (Louisville, KY: Westminster John Knox, 2007), 24.

consistently.[14] This leads me to the third part of the quandary. Asian American experiences are so vastly varied in terms of language, culture, religion, history, and levels of assimilation that one must question whether one can say anything meaningful about what Asian Americans experience, even though it is politically necessary to do so. I am forced to choose among no-win options—to be someone less than or largely other than myself in order to be accepted in white circles of discourse, not to participate at all, or to risk being called out by members of my community for misrepresentation.

In writing an Asian American chapter, I am constantly aware of how it will be viewed by my Asian American counterparts, colleagues of color, as well as my white peers. This affects both what and how I write. I am accountable to Asian American colleagues and communities because I have an opportunity to be seen and heard by those with power and by a wider audience. Sometimes I write in a self-referential way to speak as one person rather than speaking on behalf of all Asian Americans. However, one cannot make a political argument about power dynamics on a cultural level by speaking from personal experience alone. I agree with theorists such as Lisa Lowe and Gayatri Spivak who resign themselves to "strategic essentialism."[15] While recognizing that words can collapse differences and thereby disempower, referring to a "pan-ethnic"[16] or a "coalitional"[17] identity is in service of forming a critical mass that challenges oppressive norms and practices.

At the same time, I write with an acute awareness of how my writing will be seen by white colleagues. Their perceptions have an even greater impact on my professional advancement than those of my Asian American colleagues. According to Chow, scholars of color are never unaware of the power of the white gaze to define and shape them and their work, whereas white colleagues who

---

14 Tat-Siong Benny Liew, *What Is Asian American Biblical Hermeneutics? Reading the New Testament* (Honolulu: University of Hawai'i Press; Los Angeles: UCLA Asian American Studies Center, 2008), 16; Lisa Lowe, *Immigrant Acts: On Asian American Cultural Politics* (Durham: Duke University Press, 1996), 65.

15 Gayri Chakravorty Spivak, "Subaltern Studies: Deconstructing Historiography," in *In Other Worlds: Essays in Cultural Politics* (New York: Routledge, 1988), 205; Lowe, *Immigrant Acts*, 82.

16 Yen Le Espiritu, "Asian American Panethnicity: Challenges and Possibilities," in *The State of Asian America: Trajectory of Civic and Political Engagement; A Public Policy Report*, ed. Paul M. Ong (Los Angeles: LEAP Asian Pacific American Public Policy Institute, 2008), 119–36.

17 Kamala Visweswaran, "Predicaments of the Hyphen," in *Our Feet Walk the Sky: Women of the South Asian Diaspora*, ed. Women of South Asian Descent Collective (San Francisco: Aunt Lute, 1993), 305. Cited in Liew, *Asian American Biblical Hermeneutics*, 14.

live in countries that privilege whiteness do not experience a racializing gaze.[18] What I experience is a version of W.E.B. Du Bois' "double-consciousness," "this sense of always looking at one's self through the eyes of others."[19] In his context, he writes that one "measure[s] one's soul by the tape of a world that looks on in amused contempt and pity."[20] However, in the company of white liberals in the academy, I gauge my scholarly worth according to the unspoken cultural rubrics of white peers who unconsciously expect conformity to white images—even images about "diversity."

After years of living in the zoo, I resist yet have internalized a white imaging of being Asian American. Granted, every representation of self is a performance of one degree or another regardless of race; however, it is especially problematic for scholars of color. In order to continue to be "kept" or "fed" in the academic zoo, I have internalized and even aspire to a "model minority" image and perform in ways that confirm the image in others' minds (as well as my own) because that is what is rewarded both in the academy and in the wider culture.

The term *model minority* was coined by sociologist William Petersen in a 1966 *New York Times Magazine* article, "Success Story: Japanese American Style."[21] Petersen portrayed Japanese Americans as an exemplary immigrant group worthy of emulation because they were successfully combatting discrimination through hard work, an ethic supported by family structure and cultural values. Similar "success stories" of other Asian American groups validated the impression that Asian Americans were (because of values, ethics, and even genetics) more capable of succeeding in the U.S. than other minorities.[22] As others have written, the model minority is a myth in that not all Asian Americans are high achievers, highly assimilated, or highly successful.[23] High poverty, low education, low rates of insurance, and/or lack of political representation characterize many Asian American communities.[24]

---

18 Chow, *Protestant Ethnic*, 107.

19 W.E.B. Du Bois, *The Souls of Black Folk* (Rockville, MD: Arc Manor, 2008), 12.

20 Du Bois, *The Souls of Black Folk*, 12.

21 S. Cheryan and G.V. Bodenhausen, "Model Minority," in *Routledge Companion to Race & Ethnicity*, ed. S.M. Caliendo & C.D. McIlwain (New York: Routledge, 2011), 173–76.

22 Chervan and Bodenhausen, "Model Minority," 173–76.

23 For an influential essay on this issue, see Keith Osajima, "Asian Americans as the Model Minority: An Analysis of the Popular Press Image in the 1960s and 1980s," in *Reflections on Shattered Windows: Promises and Prospects for Asian American Studies*, ed. Gary Okihiro et al. (Pullman: Washington State University Press, 1988), 164–74.

24 Chervan and Bodenhausen, "Model Minority," 173–76.

I am encouraged to perform an assimilated Asian American who can move easily in white circles of discourse yet still be able to speak about her racial identity. Ironically, even as I wrote about Asian American practical theologies, particularly about what makes them unique and different, to some extent I was writing in ways that practiced conformity and reinforced a myth. What frightens me—speaking honestly even if it is potentially off-putting—is that I have been so thoroughly socialized by the academic zoo (and the larger zoo created by multiple dominant cultures), I am not always aware of the compromises I have made and even *continue* to make in participating in coercive mimeticism. While white colleagues may also be required to practice conformity and perhaps even inauthenticity in their scholarship toward tenure, this is not as pervasive and perennial as never knowing life outside of the zoo.

In the *Opening* project, my own experience of the zoo was heightened by being given a template of subheadings that determined the structure of the writing. These were good categories to use from the standpoint of the field—recognizable and foundational to many discussions. However, the issues and categories provided were not necessarily the categories and questions that Asian American practical theologians might have started with or carried forward. In essence, I was asked to *play* "Asian American" (adding exoticism to white perspectives), yet conform to a template that was taken for granted as neutral, ensuring that my contribution would be recognizable and matched with others (in other words, exotic but not too exotic). Other authors expressed concern about the limitations of standardizing the structure of chapters, but I could not aggressively challenge what had been decided, acutely aware that I was part of the project at the good grace of others. In scholarly discourse at the center of the field with white colleagues whose names are well known, I am constantly aware that my participation is precarious and contingent because it is by invitation and affirmation that I remain.

Even now there is also risk and danger to calling attention to the cage I willingly put myself in or to the whole zoo system that is the academy. It could signal to my senior colleagues: "Does not play well with others" and even less savory: "Angry Asian woman." I can/could hardly afford to embarrass or alienate any colleague, let alone those who are eminent in the field. This would be tantamount to committing professional suicide.

Coercive mimeticism is a set-up for everyone involved if I do not wish to be an exotic zoo animal, and if no person of good conscience and liberal training wants unwittingly to be a zookeeper. Some of the tragic irony of all this is that including racial chapters in the *Opening* book was intended to honor and embody diversity. Despite noble intentions, instances of coercive mimeticism crop up repeatedly because the problem of racism is structural. Consider a different but related situation. A panel at the American Academy of Religion was organized to introduce the book, focusing on issues of unequal power, scholarly writing, and the implications for practical theology.[25] There were good colleagues who proposed the panel because they felt that these issues needed to be explored and opened up. However, even in envisioning this session, at first I was the only person of color invited to serve on the panel. The zoo is replicated without thought and sometimes without question. Even in writing this chapter, I have used the tools of the academy to challenge oppressive, implicit norms, but in doing so I implicitly legitimize the academy that I critique.[26]

While coercive mimeticism is found in every academic field, it is of particular concern in practical theology because it is a field that emerged from concerns about honoring diverse ways of knowing. Rather than allowing theology to be dominated by those who work mainly on a conceptual level, scholars in the late twentieth century who put a name to practical theology advocated for taking seriously lived experience. In a perverse way, coercive mimeticism has obscured lived experiences of marginalization *within* practical theology by not examining *our own* contexts and lived experiences. It leads to the domestication of contributions by scholars of color to practical theology, which undermines the field's historic commitment to broadening theological epistemologies. As long as research and writing by scholars of color are subject to sterilization and homogenization, the field continues to be shaped predominantly by white sensibilities, priorities, questions, and assumptions. Ultimately, unchecked racism, power, and privilege not only distort the labors of those in the field but also do violence to those we serve in the academy, in churches, or in the public sphere.

Analyzing the Conundrum

In describing the conundrum, I have relied on postcolonial and Asian American perspectives, but I turn to sociology, psychoanalytic theory, theology, and social psychology to point to the formative and damaging role of images in coercive mimeticism. Underlying the conundrum is a general principle about

---

25 "*Opening the Field of Practical Theology* (Rowman and Littlefield, 2014): Exploring a New Textbook through Intersectionality," Panel session at the American Academy of Religion, San Diego, November 22, 2014.

26 This is a concern raised from the perspective of Asian women in Yoko Arisaka, "Asian Women: Invisibility, Locations, and Claims to Philosophy," in *Women of Color in Philosophy*, ed. Naomi Zack (New York: Blackwell), 219.

the formation and impact of images on the self, which sociologist Charles Horton Cooley theorized early in the twentieth century. He coined the notion of the "looking-glass self,"[27] which describes how a person comes to see herself through the eyes of others. She learns to relate to herself in ways that reflect how she imagines others have experienced and evaluated her, based on her experience of them.[28] Other people's images of her become her own, which is especially problematic if one is minoritized.

From a psychoanalytic perspective, the looking-glass self (and thereby the potential for coercive mimeticism) begins to form early in life and continues into adulthood. Pediatrician and psychoanalyst D.W. Winnicott noticed that children who were raised in coercive environments where parents were overbearing or controlling could not be spontaneous or creative. He observed this of adults as well, where adults were *less alive* because they felt compelled to conform to what was expected of them.[29] An expectation is an image that is not only waiting to be fulfilled but can also convey the weight of obligation to conform.

Conforming to what is expected in order to be pleasing is normal to a degree, though chronic compliance has devastating psychological effects. It all but destroys the possibility of forming authentic self images while contributing to the formation of distorted self images. In this regard, racism that gives rise to mimeticism inevitably fosters a version of "illness" in minoritized communities. Of course, sometimes it feels necessary to conform to routines or to social norms that one believes will avoid the disapproval of others. Healthy individuals do this some of the time. However, less healthy people consistently and unconsciously perform a self that conforms to what they believe will be acceptable to others, with little room for creativity or spontaneity. Winnicott associates these ways of being with what he calls "false self."[30] A person is always negotiating between more and less false self according to what feels safe and appropriate at a given moment. If one feels the constant need for false self, it can lead to feeling dead, not real, or inauthentic, but false self cannot be

27 Charles Horton Cooley, *Human Nature and the Social Order* (New York: Charles Scribner's Sons, 1902); see also George Herbert Mead, *Mind, Self and Society* (Chicago: University of Chicago Press, 1934).

28 Leigh S. Shaffer, "From Mirror to Self-Recognition to the Looking-Glass Self: Exploring the Justification Hypothesis," *Journal of Clinical Psychology* 61 (2005): 54.

29 D.W. Winnicott, *Home Is Where We Start From*, ed. Clare Winnicott, Ray Sheperd and Madeleine Davis (New York: Norton, 1986), 39–54.

30 D.W. Winnicott, *The Maturational Processes and the Facilitating Environment; Studies in the Theory of Emotional Development* (New York: International Universities Press, 1965), 142–43.

banished. For those who are marginalized, coercive mimeticism is performing false self but also with the obligation to objectify oneself in ways that confirm what is expected. Even more, coercive mimeticism involves not letting oneself (let alone others) know that one is performing false self. As a minoritized person, one's self image becomes more and more based on deception.

In addition to thinking psychoanalytically about the role of images in coercive mimeticism, I find the notion of *imago Dei* (image of God) helpful in reflecting theologically. The sheer idea that human beings are created in God's image is a radical one. In contrast to formative social images that are ubiquitous and in many cases damaging (e.g., stereotypes), the notion of *imago Dei* helps us to fathom the possibility of a divine image within us that may be hidden but is never destroyed. Coercive mimeticsm opposes and obscures *imago Dei* within the powerful as well as the minoritized, forming all of us with unholy images.

As a doctrine, *imago Dei* has a long history of usage and has many meanings, but I am drawn to Rubén Rosario Rodríguez's argument that understanding *imago Dei* should be based on the "other." He retrieves how the Cappadocian Fathers in early Christianity into the fourth century understood slaves to reflect the image of God, elevating their status in ways that challenged cultural norms. Forming a theological response to racism, Rodríguez uses this historical theology, as well as drawing on 16th century Calvinism and the example of Jesus, to reaffirm an understanding of *imago Dei* that is oriented toward the other.[31] From this perspective, the notion of *imago Dei* implies that one of the ways that a person is created in God's image is insofar as (s)he has "the freedom and capacity to transform the world through [his/her] work," drawing on critical, creative gifts.[32] In this view, the recognition and empowerment of the other are vital to the image of God being seen and known.

Imago Dei cannot be experienced and known in itself, unmediated, but only as it is mediated socially. My overall self-image, and thereby my indirect sense of *imago Dei*, have been misshaped by being forced constantly to decode images of what I am not—not a perpetual foreigner, not a model minority, and not an as-good-as-white academic. *My experience of God's image within me is distorted by a lifetime of experiences of being seen by others who see me as "other" and who have the power to construct, and more particularly, the power to construct me, by their gaze.* Being "othered" makes it difficult for me to embody God's image in transforming the world. As various dominant cultures enact

31 Rubén Rosario Rodríguez, *Racism and God-Talk: A Latino/a Perspective* (New York: New York University Press, 2008), 148–49.

32 Rodríguez, *Racism and God-Talk*, 173.

images that ostensibly reflect who I am, I am mirrored as "different from," "less than," or "needing to conform to," the "right" (dominant) images. No matter how much accurate mirroring one receives, it is difficult to undo internalized stereotypes.

Coercive mimeticism gives white colleagues false images of themselves that obscure historic, ongoing, unexamined habits of racism. Many colleagues have the impression that they are "celebrating the diversity" by adding people of color to their midst but without examining deeper and more threatening issues of unequal power in the academy and elsewhere. As it is commonly used, the language of "embracing diversity" assumes that God's image, captured in the richness and variety of humanity, can be witnessed and experienced first-hand and without contradiction. The assumption that we just need to "be ourselves" suggests no awareness of how truly futile it is for those who are racially labeled as "other." Liberal colleagues often take the mere presence of Asian Americans (and other scholars of color) among them as evidence of embracing diversity and seeing them "truly." Coercive mimeticism deforms and harms white colleagues through a lack of critical self-awareness of their role in the zoo.

Coercive mimeticism is incubated by a larger system of white supremacy that allows practical theologians (and Christians more broadly) to base assumptions about the collective "we" on white experiences, captured and represented in images that are taken for granted yet have profound power. This is a problem that practical theologians share with the wider theological academy. As a source of theological normativity, church history has long been read, studied, and taught as if North-Atlantic-Europe and North American were the center of Christianity.[33] There has been a historic assumption that "we" are "intellectual, spiritual, and even genetic heirs" to the unproblematic melding of a movement inspired by a radical Jew from Galilee, with Greco-Roman culture in Hellenistic times, followed by the conversion of Germanic peoples.[34] By separating mission studies from church history, this skewed view of church history teaches white people to imagine that the people of God have been those who are like "us," and everyone else is understood to have assimilated into a dominant history and identity.[35] Likewise, theologians (including practical theologians) have been trained in historical critical methods that inter-

33 Justo L. Gonzáles, *The Changing Shape of Church History* (St. Louis, MO: Chalice, 2002), 9.

34 Gonzáles, *The Changing Shape of Church History*, 16.

35 For an African American view of the racist nature of Christian imagination, see Willie James Jennings, *The Christian Imagination: Theology and the Origins of Race* (New Haven, CT: Yale University Press, 2010).

pret the biblical text from Eurocentric perspectives.[36] Such methods have long been assumed to be neutral, perhaps even lending a social scientific (read: scientific, "objective") air to hermeneutics. Although biblical hermeneutics are dominated by white perspectives, they are not marked as "white biblical hermeneutics."[37] To do their work, practical theologians habitually turn to theological disciplines without considering their racial bias, which reinforces the felt rightness and normalcy of the zoo.

Widening the analysis, one can argue that coercive mimeticism in practical theology is fueled by larger social patterns, drawing from an unconscious well of biased images. The Implicit Project at Harvard University has produced numerous studies, some of which address the implicit nature of racial bias and racial understanding. An important finding of the Project is that our behavior is less predicated on explicit beliefs about race than on implicit associations with social groups, which I understand to be images.[38] For example, one study finds, "In whom we trust is not only a reflection of who is worthy; it is also a reflection of who we are."[39] An unfamiliar white face is found to be more trustworthy than an unfamiliar African American face, not because respondents were white, but because respondents of different races hold certain associations (images) of whites and blacks that influence their perceptions.[40] An implication for our discussion is that biased images about what is good and right seep into everyday decisions, no matter how liberal or enlightened our beliefs may be.

Responding Collectively to Coercive Mimeticism

Coercive mimeticism is the responsibility of everyone in the practical theology community; it is a conundrum that harms everyone and must be addressed collectively. A single theorist cannot legislate a grand plan for responding to coercive mimeticism. Eventually all members of the practical theology

36 Kwok Pui Lan draws on studies that document how Western biblical interpretation has been historically shaped by a European Orientalist agenda. Kwok Pui-lan, *Postcolonial Imagination and Feminist Theology* (Louisville: Westminster John Knox, 2005), 4–5.

37 Liew, *Asian American Biblical Hermeneutics*, 3.

38 Damian A. Stanley et al., "Implicit Race Attitudes Predict Trustworthiness Judgments and Economic Trust Decisions," *Proceedings of the National Academy of Sciences* 108, no. 19 (May 10, 2011), 7713. doi:10.1073/pnas.1014345108. http://www.pnas.org/content/108/19/7710.abstract.

39 Stanley et al., "Implicit Race Attitudes," 7714.

40 Stanley et al., "Implicit Race Attitudes," 7713.

community must be involved in discerning collaborative action in the many settings in which the conundrum arises. Of course, the practical theology community does not only involve scholars; but coercive mimeticism is an academic conundrum. My hope is that as a practical theology community, we can become more culturally competent, empathic, and capable of empowering one another.

Given its systemic, historic, institutionalized nature, coercive mimeticism cannot easily be solved. Like other scholars, we practical theologians do not know how to operate within the academy without coercive mimeticism. For now, practical theologians must work from the modest places where we stand, feeling our way toward being a more life-giving scholarly community. In what follows, I propose three areas of work that involve small steps toward building a practical theology community less singularly on our scholarship, which is the foundation of the current community, but also more focused on how we relate to one another in ways that make us better servants.

Acknowledging the Mess We Are In

Admitting to ourselves and to one another that we are complicit in creating and maintaining a harmful, chronic conundrum involves taking the same baby steps repeatedly. The problem is that no one wants to keep in the forefront his/her role in the zoo of which Chow and Berger speak. For practical theologians who belong to the dominant group, being a zookeeper is shaming and embarrassing. Few people in the field, if any, intentionally practice racism, colonialism, or other forms of prejudice. These activities run counter to what many of my white colleagues espouse and which some actively seek to redress. Many white colleagues tire of acknowledging and implicitly feeling responsible for the alienation that unconscious representation, difference, and unequal power create. At the same time, minoritized scholars are weary not only of being zoo animals but also of continuing to acknowledge being oppressed. Change happens all too slowly, and it requires persistent vulnerability and enormous energy to name, much less engage, what few if any want to discuss. These are all good reasons that have kept practical theologians from becoming aware of coercive mimeticism. As importantly, these same reasons will continue to give us incentive to *minimize*, *forget*, or *ignore* the mess we are in despite its deleterious effects.

Acknowledging the ugliness of our situation entails being dedicated to learning, after the fact, how we avoid the hard work of addressing difference, power, and privilege and why we are motivated not to see, not to know, and not to discuss them. It means taking the time to notice and reflect when we have unwittingly returned to business as usual, slipping back into obliviousness about the zoo despite our best intentions. For example, we might begin to discern a pattern of silences among colleagues when issues of "diversity" arise and explore together what the silences mean. Some might feel that they do not know enough about racism to speak competently about it. Others might feel that academic life should focus on ideas, not on personal dynamics between and among people. Some might feel that we should avoid discussing divisive issues that threaten the sense of community that we make efforts to build. Others still might feel that it is too dangerous or futile to speak about race, power, and privilege because no one can be trusted and nothing seems to change.

We need ongoing conversations that help us to stay with and patiently return to issues of racism and how it manifests as coercive mimeticism. Significant growth through dialogue cannot happen on a large scale in the field—not yet at least.

Creating Alliances across Difference

Honest, open conversations between and among people across race and power differentials can only be practiced one-on-one or in small groups of people where trust and shared commitment can, over time, gradually deepen and grow organically and authentically. Of course, nearly everyone has friends, family members, or colleagues who are of another race. However, we need more than the acquaintanceships and the kind of functional relationships that we have with most colleagues, which require little personal investment or risk. Merely being in mixed company, even if habitually, is not enough. In fact, primarily cultivating "professional" and "non-personal" relationships only serves to inhibit if not foreclose the kinds of conversations and work that must take place.

We need to partner individually with someone of a different social location to help us see what we cannot and do not want to see. What I have in mind is deep, regular engagement across difference as we practice anti-racism and empathy on an everyday basis, as we go about the work of practical theology. By developing such close relationships, we can increasingly serve as a staunch ally, gadfly, and muse to one another. We need an ally who is trustworthy, who is committed to helping us address our complicity with racism, and who mirrors to us our capacity to be better. We need a colleague who we feel understands what it is like, for example, to be white and held accountable for power and privilege we never asked for, or to be minoritzed and forced to participate in our own captivity. We need a loving gadfly to challenge our assumptions about race and bring us consistently and gently back to tension that we would rather not face within ourselves and between us. We need a muse to inspire us to speak more powerfully from our own experiences of race and culture. Of course, our partner(s) needs all the same things from us. If a reader manages to develop a relationship with *one* colleague in practical theology (or elsewhere) with whom to engage this work, the reader will have achieved a vital accomplishment.

New alliances that bridge differences in race and power can also be formed within small groups. Of course, participating in small groups that help people become more culturally competent is a more challenging venture than working one-on-one. Pastoral theologian Sharon Thornton provides a simple example when she describes being a white pastor at a Japanese American church in Chicago. Over time, Thornton is "adopted" by this small community.[41] She writes, "As I grew within my new community, I was changed, not by choice or necessarily by design, but through a gradual process that involved having my previous worldview challenged, modified, and complicated. Becoming adopted by my new community involved relinquishing some of the assumptions I had grown up with [in a family of British descent]."[42] Thornton admits that the process of relinquishing assumptions is not easy because it involves a sense of grief, as one loses "what is given, stable, and secure."[43] However, relinquishment is nothing less than an act of faith that can be enlivening, as one gains new eyes for beholding, appreciating, and being influenced by the life worlds of others.[44] Few of us may have the experience of being a minority in an unfamiliar culture for long periods of time or being "adopted" by another community. However, the challenge of relinquishing the familiar confronts us every time we research faith communities that are "other" to us.[45]

Ultimately, we are working toward forming alliances within small groups constituted of diverse members, which is the most challenging task of all. Each

---

41 Thornton could not write as eloquently about pastoring a Japanese American church had she not fallen in love with Fumitaka Matsuoka, who is Japanese American. Likewise, in writing about racism, Matsuoka would be less able to reach a wide audience had he not been in the habit of practicing conversation with Thornton across race. Thornton and Matsuoka model the kind of deep one-on-one relationship that I describe.

42 Sharon G. Thornton, "America of the Broken Heart," in *Realizing the America of Our Hearts: Theological Voices of Asian Americans*, ed. Fumitaka Matsuoka and Eleazar S. Fernandez (St. Louis, MO: Chalice, 2003), 204.

43 Thornton, "America of the Broken Heart," 204.

44 Thornton, "America of the Broken Heart," 204.

45 For an example of a theorist who is challenged and informed by the "otherness" of the faith community that she studies, see Mary McClintock Fulkerson, *Places of Redemption: Theology for a Worldly Church* (Oxford: Oxford University Press, 2010).

person will tend to work, however consciously, to create and sustain group cohesion, often at the expense of addressing issues that create tension. Diverse small groups become settings in which to practice the cultural competence, empathy, and sensitivity learned in more established relationships where we have given and received much support.

Creating new alliances that traverse race and power destabilizes the politics of "cross-ethnic representation" that Chow describes. Some "taken-to-be-true" images of the "other" may be revealed, explored, and tested. While many of us will likely continue, at moments, to operate in terms of familiar images, we have the opportunity to revise them. As Thornton describes her own process of relinquishing Eurocentric assumptions, the process is neither "smooth" nor "seamless" nor completely "voluntary" nor "rational."[46] Her insights suggest that images of the "other" cannot be reasoned or shifted entirely, but must be altered through the slow process of cultivating intimate relationships with those who do not share our perspectives and experiences in terms of race. In "living experiences together," as Winnicott would say, we know the possibility of *continuing* to explore and amend what we have taken to be the case.

For most of us (practical theologians), continuing to acknowledge the painful predicament of coercive mimeticism and cultivating alliances across race in intimate settings are the work of a lifetime. The most important decision each of us must make is whether or not cultivating deep relationships across difference is optional. It is within the power of each person to decide how open we are to encounters with those who do not share our social location and how much time and energy we are willing to devote to making alliances across difference. One can come up with any number of excuses, which are among the many resistances to relinquishing what we know and are used to.

Identifying and Challenging Racializing Practices

A practical theology community that is gaining strength by acknowledging our complicity with racism and by building new alliances across difference has the simultaneous task of learning to identify and challenge racializing practices—both after they emerge and as they arise. Racializing practices are those that race people according to various dominant cultures, often while being taken for granted.

Racializing practices shape the dynamics of "rhetorical spaces" in practical theology. Feminist theorist Lorraine Code writes, "Rhetorical spaces… are

46 Thornton, "America of the Broken Heart," 204.

fictive but not fanciful or fixed locations, whose (tacit, rarely spoken) territorial imperatives structure and limit the kinds of utterances that can be voiced within them with a reasonable expectation of uptake and 'choral support': an expectation of being heard, understood, taken seriously."[47] In rhetorical spaces, argues Code, *who* is making claims, *where*, and *why* determine how reality is construed, as certain claims about experience are acknowledged while others are ignored, critiqued or discounted.[48] Code describes the dynamics of negotiating rhetorical spaces in terms of voicing claims, being heard, and support for claims being "echoed" (my words) in the process of determining what counts as knowledge. These auditory images are a version of Winnicott's notion of mirroring (a visual image which conveys the importance of being seen in a way that contributes to one feeling alive).[49] In both cases, Code and Winnicott draw attention to the importance of validation and the intersubjective nature of human knowing (in the case of Code) and relational nature of human maturing (in the case of Winnicott).

Uncovering the racializing practices within practical theological discourse in both speaking and writing requires recognizing how we are all affected by racism. Focused exclusively on "the work," we persistently ignore or forget that the field is shaped not only by the content of what is presented or published but also by a hidden layer of politics that determine what is written or taught, how the field is narrated, and who are understood to be the major players. Code helps us to consider how the processes of discourse in practical theology actually "remake and alter" representations of experience or reality.[50] To unmask and challenge racializing practices, conversation partners working across difference would need to help one another become sensitive to the unspoken, normative principles by which knowledge is produced.

Mostly without conscious thought, normative principles are operationalized through cultural practices that give white scholars (perhaps men more than women) confidence in the "choral support" they receive for their ideas. They have reasonable expectations that they will be "seen" by their white peers

47 Lorraine Code, *Rhetorical Spaces: Essays on Gendered Locations* (New York: Routledge, 1995), ix.

48 Code, *Rhetorical Spaces*, x.

49 Winnicott is attentive to the impact of images in one's environment that form a human being, particularly the image of mother's face as she responds with loving attentiveness, distractedly, or not at all. As if looking in a mirror, we see her face and by her response to us we sense who we are. D.W. Winnicott, *Playing and Reality* (London; New York: Routledge, 2005), 151.

50 Code, *Rhetorical Spaces*, x.

in ways that help to maintain their sense of authority, encourage their development as scholars, and ground them in a sense of belonging to rhetorical spaces in practical theology. Beaudoin and Turpin identify some of these taken-for-granted practices in their chapter on white practical theology in *Opening the Field*, for example, a focus on the individual, white supremacy, and orderliness and procedural clarity.[51] In addition, there are myriad, subtle practices that communicate to nonwhite scholars what language, values, and assumptions will allow their scholarship to be recognized and appreciated by white readers of practical theology. Scholars of color who have climbed the ranks of the academy have been so well trained in these practices that these habits may be difficult to identify. Colleagues working across difference can help one another see what one's own group is perhaps less able to see.

Writing confessionally about race is an example of a racializing practice. Chow argues that Asian Americans and other scholars of color are expected to "confess" repeatedly, in this case, expected to divulge the "ethnic secrets" of their group.[52] This chapter is a form of public confession, as I try to open up my experience of writing the Asian American practical theologies chapter in *Opening the Field*. Similarly, the *Opening* chapter attempts to provide an inside view of Asian American approaches to practical theology.

In practical theology, there is particular openness to confessional forms of writing because experience is taken seriously as a basis for understanding practices. Confession can be found in spiritual autobiographies,[53] narratives or testimonies in preaching and teaching,[54] and practical theological methods that accommodate the subjective.[55] It is not unusual for scholars to write personally and even vulnerably as part of their approach to practical theology.[56] Chow writes that in the West there has been a turn toward the self-referential, especially as a response to the rejection of metanarratives in postmodernity.[57]

51 Beaudoin and Turpin, "White Practical Theology," 255–59.

52 Chow, *Protestant Ethnic*, 116.

53 For example, see Denise M. Ackerman, *After the Locusts: Letters from a Landscape of Faith* (Grand Rapids, MI: Eerdmans, 2003).

54 For example, see Anne Streaty Wimberly, *Soul Stories: African American Christian Education* (Nashville, TN: Abingdon, 1994).

55 For example, see Mary Elizabeth Mullino Moore, "Dynamics of Religious Culture: Ethogenic Method," in *International Handbook of the Religious, Moral and Spiritual Dimensions in Education, Vol 1*, ed. M. de Souza et al. (Dordrecht, The Netherlands: Springer, 2006), 415–31.

56 For example, see James Newton Poling, *Rethinking Faith: A Constructive Practical Theology* (Minneapolis, MN: Fortress Press, 2011).

57 Chow, *Protestant Ethnic*, 112–13.

What makes confessing problematic for scholars of color, says Chow, is that confessing fulfills white expectations of ethnic availability to be seen and known as other.[58] "Confessing" is not my "native" style of speaking or what would be considered normative within my own Japanese American community. However, I write confessionally about race in conformity with a practice that is valued and intelligible to those in the center of the field, which suggests that I tacitly accept my captivity in the zoo. At the same time, because I seek not only to identify but also to unsettle coercive mimeticism, I must speak outside the bounds of what is expected, offering images that destabilize what is taken for granted so that we might try to take alternative steps together. If I do not, colleagues will remain unaware of my experience, and I aid the perpetuation of coercive mimeticism.

Confessing for white theorists is neither required, nor common, nor encouraged. Some white scholars situate themselves as authors; naming particulars such as gender, socio-economic background, racial heritage, and sometimes sexual orientation. This practice acknowledges that an author's context matters, affecting how scholarship is approached. However, white colleagues rarely write *confessionally* in terms of whiteness. As in other fields, white practical theologians are not expected to be articulate how their whiteness, their experience of it, and their formation in it affects their thinking, research, and writing.

Beaudoin and Turpin's chapter is a striking departure that challenges the practice of not writing about whiteness. Their writing is not confessional in the sense that they speak personally, but more in the sense that they address what is regarded as unnecessary and is uncomfortable for white scholars to discuss. By transgressing white privilege, it feels vulnerable and honest. If more white colleagues reflected critically about their whiteness, it would shift the practice of confession from being a coercive practice for those on the margins to a practice that involves "epistemic responsibility" in Code's words. One might argue that not all scholarly conversations require one to discuss one's race, but coercive mimeticism does not belong to study of race alone. Not accounting for one's race in scholarly writing perpetuates racializing practices in the rhetorical spaces of practical theology.

As the case of Beaudoin and Turpin's chapter demonstrates, the courage and wisdom to challenge coercive mimeticism comes from small groups where there is sufficient trust and support. Their chapter emerged within a small, face-to-face meeting of authors over the course of several days. To analyze the

58 Chow, *Protestant Ethnic*, 115.

situation using Chow and Berger's analogy, when Beaudoin and Turpin realized that the white authors in the book project were in the role of zookeepers, they refused to remain in that role. Their chapter was a gesture of empathy, in effect saying to the scholars of color on the project, "If your work is going to be subjected to racialization, we (white authors) can subject ourselves to it as well." By turning a critical gaze on themselves, they disturbed the privilege of whiteness not being scrutinized, giving others (including people of color) the "right to look."[59] The chapter was the result of a spontaneous, collective response to coercive mimeticism—perhaps not only for the purpose of filling an intellectual gap, which it did, but also to practice being a more just practical theology community.

My own writing that challenges power and privilege within practical theology emerges from working one-on-one and in small groups, where I felt heard and valued by white colleagues. I would not have dared to speak publicly or to write about coercive mimeticism without their encouragement, support, and feedback. White and minoritized colleagues underestimate their own capacity to give hope in taking on together what is hard—not only by writing critically but in being with and for one another.

Coercive mimeticism is a conundrum from which we will probably never be completely free, but I see pockets of hope for the field. When I participate in small breakthroughs, where colleagues engage in honest conversation about race and power, I take heart. When I read brave pieces of scholarship, like Beaudoin and Turpin's chapter on white practical theology or Dreyer's work on reflexivity, I feel that I am not alone. I am encouraged by a growing interest in postcolonial theory, which is being addressed by theorists in multiple subdisciplines of practical theology. There seems to be a willingness to look within, recognizing oppression not only in faith communities but also within our own ranks. Perhaps a young field like practical theology must reach a certain stage in its development to be able to tolerate and respond well to internal critiques of power and privilege within the field. Perhaps this essay, and this larger book, will serve to facilitate that constructive and collaborative movement.

Bibliography

Ackerman, Denise M. *After the Locusts: Letters from a Landscape of Faith.* Grand Rapids, MI: Eerdmans, 2003.

59 Mirzoeff, *The Right to Look.*

Andrews, Dale P. "African American Practical Theology." In *Opening the Field of Practical Theology: An Introduction*, edited by Kathleen A. Cahalan and Gordon S. Mikoski, 11–29. Lanham, MD: Rowman & Littlefield, 2014.

Arisaka, Yoko. "Asian Women: Invisibility, Locations, and Claims to Philosophy." In *Women of Color and Philosophy: A Critical Reader*, 209–34, edited by Naomi Zack. New York: Blackwell, 2000.

Beaudoin, Tom and Katherine Turpin. "White Practical Theology." In *Opening the Field of Practical Theology: An Introduction*, edited by Kathleen A. Cahalan and Gordon S. Mikoski, 251–69. Lanham, MD: Rowman & Littlefield, 2014.

Berger, John. *About Looking*. New York: Pantheon, 1980.

Cahalan, Kathleen A., and Gordon S. Mikoski, eds. *Opening the Field of Practical Theology: An Introduction*. Lanham, MD: Rowman & Littlefield, 2014.

Cheryan, S., & Bodenhausen, G.V. "Model Minority." In *Routledge Companion to Race & Ethnicity*. Edited by S.M. Caliendo and C.D. McIlwain, 173–76. New York: Routledge, 2011.

Chow, Rey. *The Protestant Ethnic and the Spirit of Capitalism*. New York: Columbia University Press, 2002.

Code, Lorraine. *Rhetorical Spaces: Essays on Gendered Locations*. New York: Routledge, 1995.

Cooley, Charles Horton. *Human Nature and the Social Order*. New York: Charles Scribner's Sons, 1902.

Du Bois, W.E.B. *The Souls of Black Folk*. Rockville, MD: Arc Manor, 2008.

Espiritu, Yen Le. "Asian American Panethnicity: Challenges and Possibilities." In *The State of Asian America: Trajectory of Civic and Political Engagement; A Public Policy Report*, edited by Paul M. Ong, 119–36. Los Angeles: LEAP Asian Pacific American Public Policy Institute, 2008.

Fulkerson, Mary McClintock. *Places of Redemption: Theology for a Worldly Church*. Oxford: Oxford University Press, 2010.

Gonzáles, Justo L. *The Changing Shape of Church History*. St. Louis, MO: Chalice, 2002.

Goto, Courtney T. "Asian American Practical Theologies." In *Opening the Field of Practical Theology: An Introduction*, edited by Kathleen A. Cahalan and Gordon S. Mikoski, 31–44. Lanham, MD: Rowman & Littlefield, 2014.

Jennings, Willie James. *The Christian Imagination: Theology and the Origins of Race*. New Haven, CT: Yale University Press, 2010.

Jones, Serene and Paul Lakeland, eds., *Consructive Theology: A Contemporary Approach to Classical Themes*. Minneapolis, MN: Fortress, 2005.

Kim, Nami. "The 'Indigestible' Asian: The Unifying Term 'Asian' in Theological Discourse." In *Off the Menu: Asian and Asian North American Women's Religion and Theology*, edited by Rita Nakashima Brock, Jung Ha Kim, Kwok Pui Lan, and Seung Ai Yang, 23–44. Louisville, KY: Westminster John Knox, 2007.

Kim-Cragg, HyeRan. "Between and Beyond Asian-ness: A Voice of a Postcolonial Hybrid Korean-Canadian Diaspora." In *What Young Asian Theologians Are Thinking*, edited by Leow Theng Huat, 90–102. Singapore: Trinity Theological College, 2015.

Kwok, Pui-lan. *Postcolonial Imagination and Feminist Theology*. Louisville, KY: Westminster John Knox, 2005.

Liew, Tat-siong Benny. *What is Asian American Hermeneutics? Reading the New Testament*. Honolulu: University of Hawaii Press, 2008.

Lowe, Lisa. *Immigrant Acts: On Asian American Cultural Politics*. Durham: Duke University Press, 1996.

Mead, George Herbert. *Mind, Self and Society*. Chicago: University of Chicago Press, 1934.

Memmi, Albert. *The Colonizer and the Colonized*. Translated by Howard Greenfeld. Expanded edition with an introduction by Jean-Paul Sartre and afterword Susan Gilson Miller. Boston: Beacon, 1991.

Mirzoeff, Nicholas. *The Right to Look: A Counterhistory of Visuality*. Durham, NC: Duke University, 2011.

Moore, Mary Elizabeth Mullino. "Dynamics of Religious Culture: Ethogenic Method." In *International Handbook of the Religious, Moral and Spiritual Dimensions in Education, Vol 1*, edited by Marian de Souza, Kathleen Engebretson, Gloria Durka, Robert Jackson and Andrew McGrady, 415–431. Dordrecht, The Netherlands: Springer, 2006.

Osajima, Keith. "Asian Americans as the Model Minority: An Analysis of the Popular Press Image in the 1960s and 1980s." In *Reflections on Shattered Windows: Promises and Prospects for Asian American Studies*, edited by Gary Okihiro, Shirley Hune, Arthur A. Hansen, and John M. Liu, 164–74. Pullman, WA: Washington State University Press, 1988.

Poling, James Newton *Rethinking Faith: A Constructive Practical Theology*. Minneapolis, MN: Fortress, 2011.

Robinson, Elaine A. *Race and Theology*. Nashville: Abingdon, 2012.

Rodríguez, Rubén Rosario. *Racism and God-Talk: A Latino/a Perspective*. New York: New York University Press, 2008.

Shaffer, Leigh S. "From Mirror to Self-Recognition to the Looking-Glass Self: Exploring the Justification Hypothesis." *Journal of Clinical Psychology* 61 (2005): 47–65.

Spivak, Gayri Chakravorty. "Subaltern Studies: Deconstructing Historiography." Chap. 12 in *In Other Worlds: Essays in Cultural Politics*. New York: Routledge, 1988.

Stanley, Damian A., Peter Sokol-Hessner, Mahzarin R. Banaji, and Elizabeth A. Phelps. "Implicit Race Attitudes Predict Trustworthiness Judgments and Economic Trust Decisions." *Proceedings of the National Academy of Sciences* 108, no. 19 (May 10, 2011): 7710–15. Accessed May 15, 2015. doi:10.1073/pnas.1014345108.

Thornton, Sharon G. "America of the Broken Heart." In *Realizing the America of Our Hearts: Theological Voices of Asian Americans*, edited by Fumitaka Matsuoka and Eleazar S. Fernandez, 200–13. St. Louis, MO: Chalice, 2003.

Visweswaran, Kamala. "Predicaments of the Hyphen." In *Our Feet Walk the Sky: Women of the South Asian Diaspora*. Edited by Women of South Asian Descent Collective, 301–12. San Francisco, CA: Aunt Lute, 1993.

Wimberly, Anne Streaty. *Soul Stories: African American Christian Education*. Nashville, TN: Abingdon, 1994.

Winnicott, D.W. *Home Is Where We Start From*, edited by Clare Winnicott, Ray Sheperd and Madeleine Davis. New York: Norton, 1986.

Winnicott, D.W. *The Maturational Processes and the Facilitating Environment; Studies in the Theory of Emotional Development*. New York: International Universities Press, 1965.

Winnicott, D.W. *Playing and Reality*. London; New York: Routledge, 2005.

CHAPTER 6

From the Outside, Within, or In Between? Normativity at Work in Empirical Practical Theological Research[1]

Tone Stangeland Kaufman

The relationship between the descriptive and normative is implicitly or explicitly addressed in numerous publications in the field of practical theology.[2] Furthermore, a tension between these terms appears on the agenda of various seminars, workshops, conferences, in conversations, and at doctoral defenses.[3] I hardly ever sit through a session where a paper presenting empirical research framed as practical theology is discussed without someone mentioning the relationship between the descriptive and the normative. Frequently, the author is accused of being too normative, which often means their normativity is implicit, tacit, off the page, or at least between the lines. However, the critique might also go the other way around: the text is considered to be "insufficiently theological" or "insufficiently normative," although the two are not identical. The former critique is often posed by one of the social scientists in the room, whereas the latter is usually voiced by one of the scholars inclined to systematic theology. The researcher is at one and the same time faulted if they do include normative assumptions *and* faulted if they do not. In order to make graduate students more aware of this dilemma, I have them write a paper trying to tease out their own normative values concerning the phenomenon or

1 I am indebted to Jonas Ideström for suggesting this title. Although he appears officially in the latter part of the chapter, Ideström has also been a conversation partner for me while working on this chapter.

2 Don S. Browning, *A Fundamental Practical Theology: Descriptive and Strategic Proposals* (Minneapolis: Fortress, 1991); Johannes A. van der Ven, *Practical Theology: An Empirical Approach* (Leuven, Belgium: Peeters Press, 1998); Elaine Graham, *Transforming Practice: Pastoral Theology in an Age of Uncertainty* (Eugene, OR: Wipf and Stock, 2002 [1996]); John Swinton and Harriet Mowat, *Practical Theology and Qualitative Research* (London: SCM, 2006).

3 For example, consider the AAR 2013 Pre-session "Normative and Empirical Modes in Fieldwork: A Conversation with a Theologian and a Social Scientist" sponsored by the Ecclesial Practices Group, the AAR 2014 Session "Beyond Description in Practical Theology: Analysis, Norms, and Revised Praxis" co-sponsored by the Practical Theology Group and Ecclesial Practices Group, and Ecclesiology and Ethnography conferences in Durham, 2012 and 2014.

 | DOI 10.1163/9789004324244_008

topic they are going to study. Most PhD and master's students I encounter experience this as something that they keep coming back to or struggle to move beyond; that is, they experience it as a conundrum, and so do I. In the spring of 2014, I was invited to give a paper on reflexivity and normativity at a conference. I basically argued that paying attention to reflexivity might turn out to be a crucial interpretive key for research and that it might also change a naïve and implicit normativity into an explicit normativity, contributing to a better understanding of the phenomenon under investigation.[4] However, there are certain areas in that paper that were neither satisfactorily resolved, nor sufficiently discussed, and in many ways the present chapter builds on that piece, seeking to extend it.

Thus, the conundrum for this chapter is *normativity* in what is often termed "descriptive work." More specifically, I would like to explore more in depth various normative dimensions at work in empirically oriented practical theological research.[5] The terms "descriptive" and "normative" are used in different ways both within practical theology and in other academic disciplines. I will elaborate on my understanding of these terms below, but for now they are used in a "common sense way" as opposite positions on a continuum where "normative" denotes an explicitly evaluative position making value claims, whereas the "descriptive" end of the continuum entails a minimum of explicit value claims. However, in the course of the chapter, my aim is to complexify the understanding of these notions. At this point, though, I should specify that "normative" does not equal "prescriptive," as I find the latter to be a narrower term.

I write this chapter as an ordained pastor in the Lutheran Church of Norway and as a practical theologian with interests in spirituality, youth ministry studies, ecclesiology, and homiletics. Hence, I am myself deeply embedded in a number of the practices studied within the field. As a master of divinity graduate in Norway, I have been trained in several theological subdisciplines. However, interdisciplinary doctoral courses with social scientists and the use of sociological methods and approaches in my master and PhD theses have also profoundly shaped me as a scholar.[6] Moreover, there are several different

4 A revised version of the paper was published in the journal *Ecclesial Practices* in the spring of 2015. Tone Stangeland Kaufman, "Normativity as Pitfall or Ally? Reflexivity as an Interpretive Resource in Ecclesiological and Ethnographic Research," *Ecclesial Practices. Journal of Ecclesiology and Ethnography* 2 (2015).

5 For "creative tensions" in practical theology, including that of description *and* prescription, see James Woodward and Stephen Pattison, eds., *The Blackwell Reader in Pastoral and Practical Theology* (Malden, MA: Wiley-Blackwell, 2000), 16.

6 See Joyce Ann Mercer's chapter 7 (pp. 164–189) on interdisciplinarity in this volume.

normative dimensions at play in various academic disciplines, not to mention different understandings of normativity, and for an interdisciplinary enterprise such as practical theology it is helpful to take a closer look at some of these dimensions.[7]

As an interdisciplinary discipline, then, practical theology often includes qualitative or ethnographic work, and the question I am grappling with in this chapter is: *What forms does the conundrum of relating normative and descriptive dimensions take in practical theological work, and how might scholars in the discipline best respond to it?* The chapter proceeds in the following way: I set out by describing the emergence of this conundrum in our field, seeking to show various positions as well as why this is such a dilemma for practical theologians. Second, I argue that we might respond to the conundrum by exploring how various normative dimensions at work in empirical practical theological research can be identified, understood, and negotiated. More specifically, I address this question by first offering some theoretical perspectives followed by an analysis of two empirical studies conducted in the Scandinavian context.[8] Since a conundrum is by definition an unresolvable puzzle or riddle, my aim is not to suggest solutions to this dilemma. Rather, in this chapter I offer some perspectives and resources for conducting empirically oriented practical theological research.

Various Forms of a Conundrum

Building on Don Browning's classic *A Fundamental Practical Theology* and various versions of the pastoral cycle, a number of recent contributions strongly emphasize the importance of *the empirical dimension* of practical theology and of ethnographic studies in ecclesiology.[9] However, in the aftermath of this

---

7 The terms "normative" and "theological" should not be regarded as synonyms. *Theological* is in one way or another related to truth claims as well as experiences and interpretations of divine action, yet the term "theological" might also entail a whole range of different meanings. However, *normative* is a much broader term, as all academic disciplines include more or less normative dimensions.

8 The theoretical lenses used in this analysis are introduced in the next main section.

9 Browning, *A Fundamental Practical Theology*. Recent contributions that emphasize the empirical dimension of practical theology include Pete Ward, ed. *Perspectives on Ecclesiology and Ethnography*, Studies in Ecclesiology and Ethnography (Grand Rapids, MI: Eerdmans Publishing Company, 2012); Christian B. Scharen, ed. *Explorations in Ecclesiology and Ethnography*, Studies in Ecclesiology and Ethnography (Grand Rapids, MI: Eerdmans Publishing

empirical turn, the question of the normative status of empirical research has become a matter of dispute. In most empirical practical theological works, there is similarly a call for practical theology to be something more than purely social science or empirical theology. Some scholars would like practical theology to become more theological and ministry oriented.[10] Others argue that the discipline should become less "churchy" and more interreligious as well as give due authority or weight to human experience as it is expressed in empirical data.[11] While the former group often adheres to "systematic theology," the latter (and others) tends to be influenced by interdisciplinary methodologies and epistemologies beyond academic theology. For many scholars in the field, this takes the shape of some kind of correlation or conversation, which ranges from being asymmetrical to being at least in principle mutual.[12]

However, a dilemma of any correlational approach is, as Paul Ballard and John Pritchard noted in 1996, "that it may lack criteria for giving adequate weighting to different sources of information in the conversation."[13] Thus, practical theologians face a difficult question. *What should be given priority* in a mutual, critical conversation *between* human experience—the empirical, the descriptive, practice,[14] or local knowledge[15] on the one hand—*and* the theological tradition or normative systematic theology on the other? While

---

Company, 2012); Mary McClintock Fulkerson, *Places of Redemption: Theology for a Worldly Church* (Oxford: Oxford University Press, 2007). Moreover, there has been an Empirical working group at several meetings of the International Academy of Practical Theology (IAPT) and an Empirical symposium at the 2013 IAPT conference. Furthermore, a number of practical theologians are involved in the *International Society for Empirical Research in Theology*. See http://www.isert.info/.

10 Andy Root, *Christopraxis: A Practical Theology of the Cross* (Minneapolis, MN: Fortress Press, 2014); Helen Cameron et al., *Talking about God in Practice: Theological Action Research and Practical Theology* (London: SCM Press, 2010).

11 Tom Beaudoin, *Witness to Dispossession* (Maryknoll, NY: Orbis Books, 2008); Stephen Pattison, "Some Straw for the Bricks: A Basic Introduction to Theological Reflection," in *The Blackwell Reader in Pastoral and Practical Theology*, ed. James Woodward and Stephen Pattison (Malden, MA: Blackwell Publishing, 2000), 140. See also Beaudoin's chapter 1 (pp. 1–32) on theological reflection on practice in this volume.

12 Bonnie J. Miller-McLemore, "Cognitive Neuroscience and the Question of Theological Method," *Journal of Pastoral Theology* 20, no. 2 (Winter 2011): 64–92.

13 Paul Ballard and John Pritchard, *Practical Theology in Action: Christian Thinking in the Service of Church and Society* (London: SPCK, 1996), 123.

14 See Bonnie Miller McLemore's chapter 8 (pp. 190–218) on theory-practice as a political binary in this volume.

15 See Katherine Turpin's chapter 10 (pp. 250–275) on local knowledge in this volume.

those practical theologians who adhere to systematic theology tend to understand "the normative" as equivalent with "the theological," often implying academic systematic theology or any ecclesial theological tradition, other practical theologians clearly favor or give precedence to experience as possessing normative claims.

On one hand, practical theologians are in trouble if they decide to give primacy to one of the conversation partners in advance, as this might downplay the voices of the others, not granting them a real chance to have an impact on the conversation. On the other hand, though, they are also in trouble if they do *not*, because then they might easily be critiqued for not being transparent of their evaluation or value claims, as no one is able to offer a value neutral description of the field studied. Furthermore, the theological tradition is not one single Tradition with a capital T. It is a conglomerate of various traditions, and the relationship between these can easily be an extensive discussion on its own.[16] Additionally, there are various understandings of how the Christian tradition should play a normative role in empirical practical theological studies. For example, is the tradition considered a once-and-for-all given entity available to us through Scripture and the various confessions of different faith traditions, or is the Tradition (often with a capital T) considered a dynamic, ongoing revelation? Hence, there are several layers of normativity at work, and practical theologians doing empirical research face a conundrum in terms of how to handle these normative dimensions and what role to give the theological tradition(s), whether that be a normative ecclesial tradition or the extant theoretical (and often normative) works of academic theologians.

To make this even more complex, Bonnie J. Miller-McLemore argues that practical theology cannot be reduced to simple formulas such as "the correlation between the Christian tradition and contemporary experience," although, as she remarks, "these are valid and helpful snapshots."[17] She further notes that practical theology differs from systematic theology in that it "is seldom a systematic enterprise, aimed at the ordering of beliefs about God, the church, or classic texts."[18] Hence, practical theology deals with messier material than

16 See the chapters by Turpin (pp. 250–275) and Beaudoin (pp. 1–32) in this volume. See also Elaine Graham, Heather Walton, and Frances Ward, *Theological Reflection: Methods* (London, UK: SCM Press, 2005), 169, 94–95.

17 Bonnie J. Miller-McLemore, "Introduction: The Contributions of Practical Theology," in *The Blackwell Companion to Practical Theology*, ed. Bonnie J. Miller-McLemore (Malden, MA: Wiley Blackwell, 2014), 17.

18 Miller-McLemore, "Introduction," 14.

most systematic theologies. Moreover, like Miller-McLemore, several contributors in the field increasingly find various models of correlation to be lacking in terms of *where* normative dimensions in such practical theological works are located.

In order to take a closer look at how some practical theologians handle this conundrum, I have made a grid (see Figure 6.1 below). The vertical axis runs from a position that explicitly privileges the theological tradition and divine revelation, whereas the position at the bottom end of the continuum gives more weight to human experience or practice in terms of revising or reshaping the received ecclesial tradition. The horizontal line runs from an understanding of correlation where empirical data and the normative theological tradition are correlated as two separate entities to a position where normativity cannot be cut out like a piece of the pie to be correlated with human experience or empirical data. Normativity is instead like the frosting which covers the entire pie. Or more precisely, various normative dimensions are inherent in the entire practical theological process or enterprise.

The conundrum of how to deal with normativity in what is often termed descriptive or empirical practical theological work, then, takes different shapes

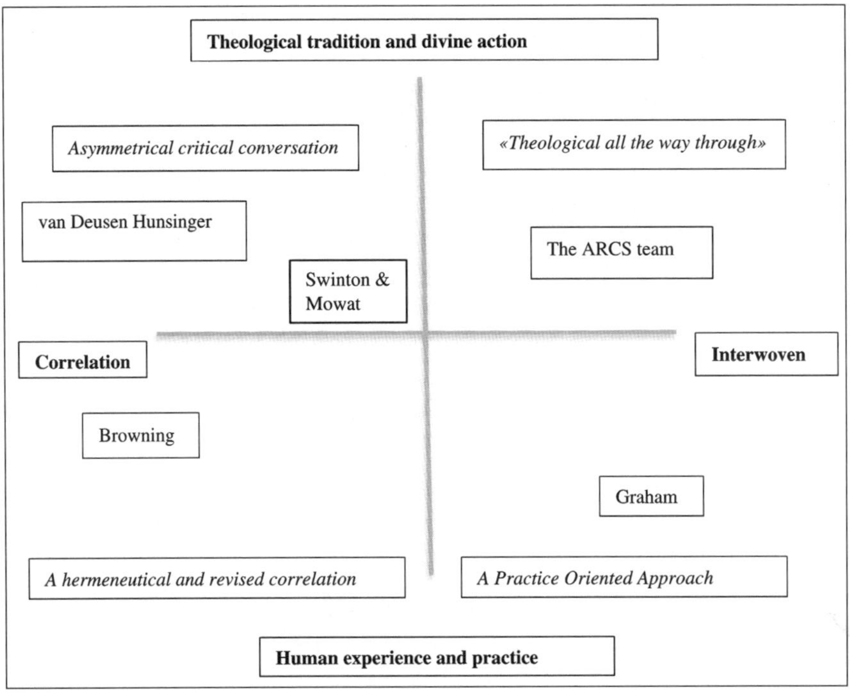

FIGURE 6.1 Grid of practical theological positions.

in the various types emerging from this grid. In the following, I seek to identify and discuss some of these shapes. As with any typology, these categories are simplifications of more nuanced positions, and I am aware that I am not able to do full justice to the complexity of these works.

An Asymmetrical, Critical Conversation: Primacy to Theological Tradition

In the top left corner of the grid, I place Deborah van Deusen Hunsinger, who has suggested a model of an asymmetrical, critical conversation. Here theology is explicitly given primacy over experience and psychology based on her Barthian approach to method, termed "the Chalcedonian pattern."[19] In short, the two natures of Christ as presented in the Chalcedonian creed can be seen as a pattern or a model for the relationship between theology and the social sciences in that there should be indissoluble differentiation (both disciplines have specific roles to play and should not be blended), inseparable unity (their unity should also be acknowledged), indestructible order (which is the crucial point for van Deusen Hunsinger, where "the voice of theology has logical precedence within the critical conversation"[20]), and logical priority of theology grounded in a realist ontological stance.[21]

Building on van Deusen Hunsinger's work and other models of critical correlation, John Swinton and Harriet Mowat offer an approach termed "a critical *mutual* conversation."[22] Although not buying into all aspects of van Deusen Hunsinger's model, they still "recognize and accept fully that theology has logical priority; qualitative research tells us nothing about the meaning of life, the nature of God, cross, resurrection or the purpose of the universe."[23] Yet, they acknowledge the hermeneutical dimension of doing theology and find it somewhat unclear how van Deusen Hunsinger's method relates to theological challenges emerging from communities of faith. They argue for listening to

---

19 Deborah van Deusen Hunsinger, *Theology and Pastoral Care: A New Interdisciplinary Approach* (Grand Rapids, MI: Eerdmans, 1995). This summary is also partly based on Swinton and Mowat, *Practical Theology*, 84–88.

20 Swinton and Mowat, *Practical Theology*, 86.

21 In his recent book *A Christopraxis Practical Theology*, Andy Root ends up with a neo-Barthian position similar to van Deusen Hunsinger. While acknowledging how practical theology in North America has positively incorporated human experience into the works of the discipline, he simultaneously critiques practical theology for not being "theological enough." See Root, *Christopraxis*, ix, 24, 26.

22 Swinton and Mowat, *Practical Theology*, 78.

23 Swinton and Mowat, *Practical Theology*, 89.

the theological voices of the practice field of empirical research in their mutual critical conversation model.[24] However, this is precisely where the conundrum presents itself because their approach nevertheless ends up privileging normative or ecclesial theology and is thus a model of a critical, *asymmetrical* conversation despite their use of the term "mutual."[25] In my grid, they can still be placed in the top left square, though more towards the center. Yet another part of the conundrum concerns *which* understanding of tradition should be granted such an authoritative role and *why*? This is not a normatively innocent question.

"Theological All the Way Through," but Primacy to Theological Tradition

Moving over to the top right square, I place Helen Cameron and colleagues, the Action Research Church and Society (often referred to as the ARCS team) with their project Theological Action Research (TAR) and the model *The Four Voices of Theology*.[26] Arguing that "the making of genuine and transformative connection with theology can often be rather weak or superficial,"[27] the ARCS team emphasizes that their own *Four Voices of Theology* model is "theological all the way through."[28] "This means that the practices participated in and observed are themselves bearers of theology," and *in principle* they seek to give voice to all conversation partners in the dialogue, including the research participants.[29]

Nevertheless, sympathetic to Swinton and Mowat's position,[30] the ARCS team ultimately uses a theology of fall and grace as a normative lens for facilitating this conversation.[31] Thus, whilst wanting to bring the various voices of the empirical field (in Cameron and colleagues' language: *operant* and *espoused*), church (*normative*), and academy (*formal*) into a theological conversation, and while acknowledging the empirical material as a theological text, they still end up giving primacy to the theological tradition.[32]

In more recent contributions, Clare Watkins, who is part of the ARCS team, has elaborated on issues of normativity and epistemology related to the *Four*

24 Swinton and Mowat, *Practical Theology*, 88ff.
25 Swinton and Mowat, *Practical Theology*, 88–98.
26 Cameron et al., *Talking about God*.
27 Cameron et al., *Talking about God*, 28.
28 Cameron et al., *Talking about God*, 51.
29 Cameron et al., *Talking about God*, 51, 59.
30 Cameron et al., *Talking about God*, 31; Swinton and Mowat, *Practical Theology*, 83.
31 Cameron et al., *Talking about God*, 31.
32 Cameron et al., *Talking about God*, 30–31, 60.

Voices of Theology methodology.[33] She understands TAR to have a commitment to "conversational methods," which is "an attempt to ensure that a space is kept open for the *mutual* engagement of these practical, normative and academic authorities."[34] Truth resides not only in what they term *the normative voice.* Rather, "theological disclosure" emerges "from within that conversation."[35] Despite this willingness to regard the espoused and operant voices of the field as theological voices, Watkins explicitly states: "There remains an intractable *asymmetry* between the 'four voices of theology,' given that the authority of the normative (notably magisterial) voices are already legitimated readings for tradition."[36] Thus, there is a *tension between* facilitating space for all the four voices of theology to encounter one another *and* wanting to grant the normative voice a privileged position. However, the ARCS team and Watkins do not seem to reflect explicitly on this tension, and, in my opinion, it actually illustrates the conundrum under investigation.

A Hermeneutical and "Revised Correlational Approach"

Crossing over to the lower part of the left side, I position Don Browning's *A Fundamental Practical Theology*. Like David Tracy, Browning describes his contribution as "a revised correlational approach."[37] Yet, as opposed to Swinton and Mowat and other contributions presented above, he is not relying on such a "high" theology of revelation, as Cameron and colleagues put it.[38] Still, Browning's practice-theory-practice model has been criticized for privileging systematic theology when it comes to making normative claims.[39] Crediting Browning for having reclaimed "the praxis-orientation for the whole

33 Clare Watkins, "Reflections on Particularity and Unity," in *Ecclesiology in the Trenches: Theory and Method under Construction*, ed. Sune Fahlgren and Jonas Ideström (Eugene, OR: Pickwick Publications, 2015); Clare Watkins, "Practicing Ecclesiology: From Product to Process: Developing Ecclesiology as a Non-Correlative Process and Practice through the Theological Action Research Framework of Theology in Four Voices," *Ecclesial Practices. Journal of Ecclesiology and Ethnography* 2 (2015).

34 Watkins, "Reflections" 146, emphasis added.

35 Watkins, "Reflections" 146.

36 Watkins, "Reflections" 147, emphasis added.

37 Browning, *A Fundamental Practical Theology*, 44.

38 Cameron et al., *Talking about God*, 30.

39 Graham, *Transforming Practice*; Ruard Ganzevoort, "What You See Is What You Get," in *Normativity and Empirical Research in Theology*, ed. Johannes A. van der Ven and Michael Scherer-Rath (Leiden: Brill, 2005). A previous version of this section was co-written with Tron Fagermoen as part of an idea for a different project, and bits and pieces of that text were published in Kaufman, "Normativity as Pitfall or Ally?," 93–95.

theological enterprise by stressing the descriptive and strategic phase,"[40] Ruard Ganzevoort nevertheless critiques him for allowing systematic theology to define the interpretive movement. Following Ganzevoort, then, I see a discrepancy in Browning between his emphasis on the tacit normativity inherent in our practices attended to in the descriptive task of practical theology *and* his insistence on locating the normative move in his model primarily in theological theory, i.e. in historical and systematic theology, which he terms normative–constructive theology. Surely, Browning acknowledges the theory-laden character of the religious practices,[41] just as he allows for a normative negotiation or encounter between the normative stances of the researcher team and the practitioners of the field.[42] Yet, despite his ability to show the complexity of the descriptive phase, this move in Browning remains first and foremost descriptive, leaving "descriptive theology" with the task of articulating adequate descriptions for later normative deliberation.

Furthermore, although acknowledging that there are normative and ecclesial traditions and practices *within the practice field itself* (what I will later term "the activity system of the field"), Browning does not elaborate how these are being negotiated and how these normative deliberations play a crucial role in the overall theological enterprise. Hence, we are left with unresolved questions regarding the conundrum investigated.

A Practice Oriented Approach

At the lower end of the vertical continuum, it is explicitly stated that no one voice is given primacy in advance. Here human experience and the practice encountered in the empirical field studied are granted the position of possibly revising or reshaping the received tradition. Furthermore, at the bottom right corner of my grid, neither normative dimensions nor "the theological" can be nicely located or placed in any one of the steps of a practice-theory-practice model or the pastoral cycle. Rather, these dimensions are embedded in the entire practical theological undertaking or the practice of practical theology.

Elaine Graham's postmodern and practice oriented contribution to practical theology locates the ultimate normative mandate neither in the received ecclesial tradition nor in extant theological theory, but rather in the ongoing

40 Ganzevoort, "What You See," 25.

41 Browning, *A Fundamental Practical Theology*, 5–6.

42 See Turpin in this volume, 251–252.

practices of the Christian community.[43] While acknowledging the invaluable contribution of Browning, she still problematizes his emphasis on "practical moral reasoning" and the lack of diversity, alterity, and embodiment in his work, as found, for example, in theories of gender and critical theory.[44] This approach considers "orthopraxis" a normative criterion and understands theory and practice to be deeply interwoven.

Graham offers an example of how feminist theology, grounded in women's experiences with church and theology, actually challenges certain traditional understandings of atonement, the cross, and the resurrection. Granting authority to the normative and theological dimensions inherent in the "empirical" voice based on human experience and practice, she states: "Yet a piece of action research might generate very novel forms of spirituality, or conclude that traditional ways of imagining God are in need of fundamental revision."[45]

Despite Graham's important point in allowing the practices of the faith community as a collaborative entity to be the criteria for normative value statements, the conundrum still presents itself. There is not one normative Christian community, but rather a vast array of different faith communities. Hence, there are as many practices of Christian communities as there are theological interpretations of the Christian tradition. When are women's experiences allowed to trump traditional theological positions and why? Which voices in the faith community are given priority if there are disagreements? Moreover, if one were to take Browning's understanding of the complexity of the descriptive move seriously, it is not sufficient to wait until the third move or step in his model to address this issue. Even if Graham gives authority to the complexity of lived experience and to the voices of the marginalized in particular, the conundrum is still not resolved. It remains in terms of how these faith communities negotiate the various bits and pieces of the received tradition and cultural and human practice embedded in the normative practices. Given her hermeneutic understanding of our field of study, self-reflexivity is crucial in order to deal responsibly with the conundrum.

---

43 Graham, *Transforming Practice*. See, for example, pp. 3, 6, and 10. A somewhat similar, though not identical approach is that of Ganzevoort, who also claims that *theological normativity* is located *not only* in theological *theory*, but is also to be found in the *ongoing practices of the church*, as they are analyzed by empirical practical theological studies. See Ganzevoort, "What You See."

44 Graham, *Transforming Practice*, 6.

45 Elaine Graham, "Research Report: Is Practical Theology a form of 'Action Research'?" *International Journal of Practical Theology* 17, no. 1 (2013): 160–61.

Still a Conundrum

Practical theologians, then, are in trouble if they decide to give primacy to one of the conversation partners in advance, such as those in the top left corner of the model, as this downplays the real impact other voices can make on the conversation. Yet, practical theologians are *also* in trouble if they do *not* give primacy to one of the conversation partners, because then they might easily be critiqued for not being transparent regarding her or his value judgments, as no one is able to offer a completely value neutral description of the field studied. This might be the case for those in the bottom parts of the grid. Additionally, these theologians might also be accused of not "being normative" or even "theological" enough[46] or not giving sufficient weight to the Christian tradition. For example, when are the experiences of any particular group allowed to trump traditional theological positions and based on which criteria? Which voices in the faith community are given priority if there are disagreements? Moreover, if we take Browning's understanding of the complexity of the descriptive move seriously, it is not sufficient to wait until the third move or step in his model to address normativity.

How, then, as practical theologians, do we respond to these dilemmas? In order to deal responsibly with the conundrum, it is neither helpful to place normativity solely in one of the steps of the pastoral cycle, whether in human experience/practice or in the theological tradition. Rather, normativity is inherent in both the theological tradition as offered by ecclesial traditions and academic works and in the experiences and practices of individuals and faith communities studied by empirical practical theology, as well as in the research process itself. I begin by introducing some theoretical perspectives as resources to deal with the conundrum in a constructive way before moving on to analyzing the two empirical cases.

Theoretical Lenses: Activity System and Normativity-from-Within

In *The Wiley-Blackwell Companion to Practical Theology*, Miller-McLemore distinguishes between "the ministerial practice at hand" and "the practice of the discipline that studies and teaches that practice."[47] Hence, her twofold use of practice in this introduction acknowledges the enterprise of studying practical

46 See for example Watkins's critique of three Swedish empirical and historical contributions in Watkins, "Reflections," 146.

47 Miller-McLemore, "Introduction," 13.

theology as a practice.[48] Similarly, Norwegian theologian and education theorist Geir Afdal argues that *researching religious education* can be considered a practice.[49] Following both Afdal and Miller-McLemore, I regard practical theological research as a practice. Moreover, the phenomenon or field under practical theological investigation can also be understood as a practice.

In order to better understand some of these dimensions of normativity, I find Yrjö Engeström's theory of practice as an *activity system* helpful.[50] Engeström's intention is to overcome the split between a theory of practice on the one hand and the actual social (or ecclesial) practices on the other.[51] Attempting to move beyond the reductionism of a simple correlation model, Engström's theory of activity systems emphasizes that both the field to be studied by the practical theological enterprise as well as the research process itself are theory-laden practices with inherent normative dimensions. The activity system thus acknowledges contradictions and seeks expansive transformation. Hence, it might help us see how the complex and partly contradictive normative practices taking place in the activity systems under investigation are deeply interwoven.

Building on cultural-historical psychologist Lev Vygotsky and his student Alexei Leontiev's work on mediation, *artifacts* (cultural signs and tools) are central to Engeström's approach.[52] Hence, learning or change is always mediated by various kinds of cultural signs and tools, including language. Thus, theology or theory too is mediated and negotiated by a number of artifacts, such as theological texts and books, liturgies, websites, workshops, paintings, hymnals, conversations, lectures, computers, etc. Furthermore, normative dimensions are deeply embedded in the artifacts and in the negotiation processes taking place *within* an activity system and *between* two or more activity systems. Following this theory, then, new knowledge is produced by reconceptualization *from within the collective of practice, as a sideways move*, rather than a vertical one:

---

48 For an elaboration on the conundrum of theory and practice, see Miller-McLemore's chapter 8 (pp. 190–218) in this volume.

49 Geir Afdal, *Researching Religious Education as Social Practice* (Münster: Waxmann, 2010).

50 Engeström is Professor of Adult Education and Director of the Center for Activity Theory and Developmental Work Research at University of Helsinki. He is also Professor of Communication at University of California, San Diego.

51 His version of activity system, Cultural-Historical Activity Theory (CHAT), acknowledges and underscores multi-voicedness, historicity, contradictions, and the move towards "the possibility of expansive transformations or cycles." See Yrjö Engeström, "Expansive Learning at Work: Toward an Activity Theoretical Reconceptualization," *Journal of Education and Work* 14 (2001): 136–37.

52 Afdal, *Researching Religious Education*, 50–53.

> Knowledge was not created "from above," from theory or management, and then implemented [or as the former, and much critiqued, paradigm of theology went: From theory to practice]. Nor was it a fusion of everyday and theoretical concepts [or various forms of correlational models where experience is correlated with theological theory]. If one conceives theory as above practice, there was never a vertical movement towards theory. It was a movement "within below," a constitution of new knowledge in practice. It is important to notice, however, that it was triggered by research, by theory. New knowledge.... consists in crossing the boundaries between two different activity systems.[53]

The quote emphasizes that knowledge creation or transformation is neither created in a single movement "from above," from theory to practice, nor "from below," from practice to theory. Rather, there is "a movement 'within below,'"[54] which, in the cases to be analyzed below, happens as a result of the researcher oscillating between the two activity systems during the research process, setting the activity systems in motion towards new objects. Hence, the theoretical perspectives brought into the field of research contribute to reconceptualization from within the collective of practice, *and consequently, to normative transformation*. Without going into all the details of Engeström's comprehensive model, I propose that (1) the practice of the field of study and (2) the practice of researching this field framed within practical theology may be considered two different activity systems. For convenience, I will call them the activity system of the *field* and the activity system of the *research*.

However, before moving on to an analysis of the two cases, I will add a few more theoretical perspectives that I find helpful in addressing issues of normativity in empirical research. In a volume on agency and normativity in Science, Technology, and Society (STS) studies,[55] German STS scholar Hans Harbers argues that STS does not recognize the dichotomy between facts and values, between *description* and *prescription*. He rather makes the case that both of these "options presuppose an outsider position, either as a detached analyst, or as an involved, but no less exclusive judge."[56] Instead, he suggests that a different kind of normativity is at stake here, which is no neutral undertaking, but rather

---

53 Afdal, *Researching Religious Education*, 63.

54 Afdal, *Researching Religious Education*, 63.

55 I am aware that STS and practical theology are situated in different epistemological positions and contexts. While the former has been accused of avoiding normativity by all means, the latter has traditionally carried a long tradition of theological normativity.

56 Hans Harbers, "Epilogue: Political Materials-Material Politics," in *Inside the Politics of Technology: Agency and Normativity in the Co-Production of Technology and Society*, ed. Hans Harbers (Amsterdam, NLD: Amsterdam University Press, 2005), 265.

a *rescription* or *re-construction*.[57] This rescription is more than a mere re-description, as it is also "a *remaking* of the situation.... Rescriptions do actively intervene into realities and therefore are not normatively neutral."[58] Hence, he distinguishes between *normativity-from-within* and *normativity-from-the-outside*. Whilst the former is a hermeneutical normativity, the latter is an evaluative normativity.

Seeking to move beyond the same dichotomy of descriptive and normative theories as addressed by Harbers, Geir Afdal expands this binary with a new continuum moving from *prescriptive* to what he terms *expressive*. He thus distinguishes between four different types of theories based on the issue of normativity: *Descriptive, normative, prescriptive,* and *expressive* theories.[59] In my view, though, these can more precisely be understood as *four dimensions of normativity*, and Afdal's point is that there is no clear-cut line between the descriptive and normative. Rather, the difference is one of degree.[60] Hence, both prescriptive and expressive theories include descriptive and normative dimensions, but to varying degrees.

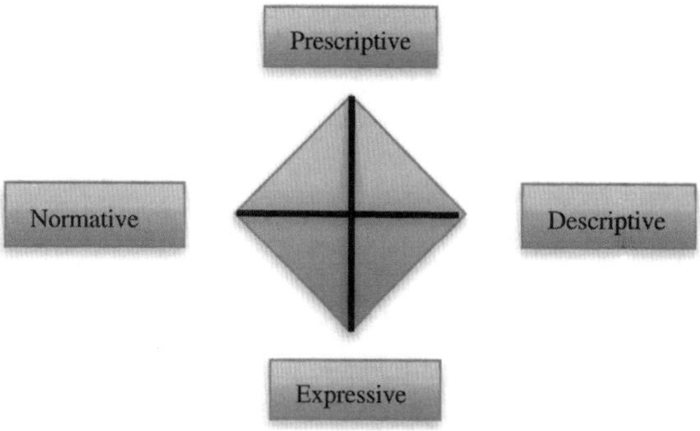

FIGURE 6.2 Afdal's four different types of theories.

---

57 Harbers, "Epilogue," 265, 70. Drawing on David Martin, Mark Cartledge also employs the concept of *rescription* in his study of ordinary Pentecostal theology. The metaphor of "rescription" entails the hermeneutical task of analysis and interpretation; of rescripting the *scripts* of the research participants. See Mark Cartledge, *Testimony in the Spirit: Rescripting Ordinary Pentecostal Theology* (Aldershot: Ashgate, 2010). As Harber explicitly relates rescription to a discussion of normativity, I have chosen to refer to his work in this chapter. Yet, it could also prove fruitful to take a closer look at Cartledge's use of this metaphor.

58 Harbers, "Epilogue," 270, note 13, emphasis added.

59 Afdal, *Researching Religious Education*, 72–75.

60 Afdal, *Researching Religious Education*, 73.

As Afdal puts it: "Change happens either by some experience that triggers expansion of language, or by an alternative and better account that opens up new ways of understanding" rather than through detailed prescriptions of a more faithful practice.[61] Expressive theories are more or less identical with Harber's rescriptive normativity-from-within, but I find it helpful to bring in this fourfold conceptualization of various theories, as it pinpoints *the blurring* of the descriptive and normative dimensions both within activity systems and between them. For that reason, I would like to revise slightly Afdal's model by exchanging his language of expressive theory for Harber's terminology of rescriptive normativity.

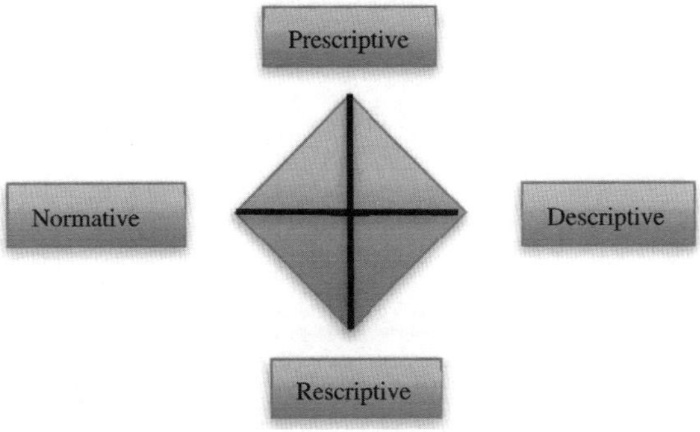

FIGURE 6.3 Afdal's four different types of theories, slightly revised by Kaufman.

Afdal's revised model shows some of the complexity of the normative dimensions at work in empirical practical theological research. Combining these theoretical perspectives, then, the activity system of the research contributes to the activity system of the field by rescripting these practices in a way that can create new knowledge in terms of an expanded understanding. Hence, I suggest that the normative dimensions at play within each activity system have to be negotiated prior to and simultaneously with the external negotiation between them. Normativity within each activity system will have to be negotiated prior to negotiations between them. This normativity-from-within will influence the normativity-from-the-outside, yet the two are also closely intertwined.

61 Afdal, *Researching Religious Education*, 73–75. See also Graham, *Transforming Practice*, 208–09.

From the Outside, Within, or In Between?

Having introduced some theoretical perspectives, my aim in this section is to address possible responses to the conundrum by exploring how various normative dimensions at work in empirical practical theological research can be identified, understood, and negotiated. I analyze two empirical studies where the kind of normativity-from-within introduced above is at play, albeit in different ways. The first case is my own doctoral work, an empirical study of clergy spirituality in the Church of Norway. The second case is Jonas Ideström's ethnographically oriented ecclesiological study, exploring what it entails to be church in a rural parish in Sweden. In both cases, the researcher can be situated within both activity systems, as well as between them, thus, negotiating normativity both *within* each of the activity systems and *between* them.

Normative Dimensions in a Study of Clergy Spirituality (*Case Kaufman*)

For my PhD work, I explored the spirituality of Norwegian Lutheran pastors based on twenty-one semi-structured, transcribed, open-ended interviews.[62] The qualitative data of this research was interpreted through an *abductive process*[63] moving between the empirical data and extant theory, which can be considered an oscillation between the two activity systems of the *field* (as described by the research participants) and the *research*. Proposing that it is precisely a normativity-from-within that is at play here, I suggest that paying attention to this kind of normativity is a constructive way of addressing the conundrum investigated in this chapter.

In order to show how important empirical discoveries or epiphanies expanded the understanding of participants and myself as a researcher, I will offer some examples of how this normativity-from-within also came to play a transformative role. During the process of analysis, a discrepancy between *descriptions* and *evaluations* of the spiritual practices of some interviewees caught my attention. These pastors expressed an image of themselves as "not very good at praying" or "not as spiritual as the previous pastor." Nevertheless,

---

62 The material in this first main part of the analysis is based on my doctoral dissertation. See Tone Stangeland Kaufman, "A New Old Spirituality: A Qualitative Study of Clergy Spirituality in the Church of Norway" (MF Norwegian School of Theology, 2011).

63 See Mats Alvesson and Kaj Sköldberg, Tolkning och reflektion: Vetenskapsfilosofi och kvalitativ metod (Lund: Studentlitteratur, 2008), 55–56.

they described their everyday lives both in ministry and privately as more or less enveloped by prayer and other spiritual practices.[64] Some of the participants realized this gap *as we were speaking*, in other words *within the activity system of the field*, and came to see their spiritual lives with new eyes. Olav, who was in his mid-fifties and serving in a rural area at the time of the interview, reflects on his prayer life in the following quote: "I find that it [my prayer life] is not much to cheer for. Because I am not the one praying the long prayers. But most of the time I do pray.... Prior to the service, I pray for the service. I mostly pray before things are going to take place. And then I feel... I mean, my prayer life is mine there and then.... There is much in that, I guess. There aren't many things we do around here that don't begin with a prayer."

Olav's comment that "a prayer life to cheer for" equals "praying the long prayers" could very well mean having a specific time set aside for prayer concurring with the pietistic ideal of having "a daily quiet time." In the Norwegian context, the spiritual tradition rooted in eighteenth-century Pietism has contributed to shaping ideals for the Christian life, which is part of the historicity of the activity system of the field. Such Christian backgrounds seemed to be the common denominator for the pastors in my study who considered their own spiritual lives or practices insufficient. This might be one reason why spiritual practices that did not exactly fit the pietistic ideal of a "spiritual life" could go unnoticed or unacknowledged by these pastors. Hence, the research process itself contributed to an expanded understanding of the ongoing practices of the activity system of the field. Furthermore, as a researcher and practitioner who discovered practices that had previously gone unnoticed, I argued that such practices should also be acknowledged as "the real thing," as "real spirituality."[65]

One way of dealing responsibly with the conundrum is to pay attention to researcher reflexivity. In my PhD work, I sought to make my implicit normative values explicit by playing the devil's advocate. Here I offer the example

64 Some of the material in this section has previously been published in a somewhat different shape in Tone Stangeland Kaufman, "Pastoral Spirituality in Everyday Life, in Ministry, and Beyond: Three Locations for a Pastoral Spirituality," *Journal of Religious Leadership* 12, no. 2 (2013).

65 See Tone Stangeland Kaufman, "The Real Thing? Practicing a Spirituality of Everyday Life," in *Between the State and the Eucharist: Free Church Theology in Conversation with William T. Cavanaugh*, ed. Joel Halldorf and Fredrik Wenell (Eugene, OR: Picwick Publications, 2014), 85–101.

of the pastors' attitudes to contemplative, silent retreats.[66] At first, it seemed like most of them benefitted from such retreats and really appreciated this kind of spiritual practice, as do I. Hence, it would have been easy to stop there and conclude that the majority of the interviewees embrace this contemplative practice. I could have easily labeled their spirituality as "contemplative," which is an existing category in spirituality studies. Yet, when being honest about my own deeply held notions and values, I knew that my tendency would be to highlight these findings and rejoice in them. How could I play the devil's advocate against my own initial normative values, seeking to reach an expanded understanding of clergy spirituality? How about the minority that did not prioritize or need the set frames of such a contemplative retreat? Having a hunch that there was something I had missed, I decided to dig deeper into the data from precisely these interviews. This proved to be important for the study as a whole. At a certain point, the pattern of a dialectic between spiritual practices *embedded in our daily lives privately and professionally*, on the one hand, and spiritual practices *located at the margins of daily life*, on the other, emerged, and these categories can bring novel perspectives into the study of Christian spirituality generally and to that of clergy spirituality more specifically.[67] Being attentive to what seemed important to the interviewees gave me access to numerous stories of their spiritual practices and experiences that actually contributed to widening and challenging my own normative understanding of clergy spirituality. As Engeström argues, "change must always happen from where the practices and practitioners are."[68] Hence, this can also be understood as a rescriptive normativity, and it was influenced by the literature (artifacts) that I as a researcher brought into dialogue with the data.

Coming to realize the significance of spiritual practices embedded in daily life, both professionally (in ministry) and privately (often in the context of family life), made me look for theoretical perspectives beyond my original idea, which had been to draw on Dietrich Bonhoeffer's, Henri Nouwen's, and Kenneth Leech's pastoral spirituality as theoretical frameworks and pos-

66 This point has previously been made in Kaufman, "Normativity as Pitfall or Ally?" However, the argument is further developed in the present chapter. Attending a contemplative, silent retreat, often in the Ignatian spiritual tradition, is a spiritual practice that has become quite common in Norway over the last few decades. Key is to spend some days, a week or (more seldom) several weeks in solitude and silence, to meditate on Scripture, and often also to see a spiritual director.

67 For further elaboration of this model, see Kaufman, "Pastoral Spirituality."

68 This quote is cited in Afdal, *Researching Religious Education*, 74.

sible conversations partners for my data. Instead, I ended up using Gordon Lathrop's liturgical spirituality and Elizabeth Dreyer's and Bonnie Miller-McLemore's spirituality of everyday life as helpful theoretical lenses for my research.[69] The decision to bring in other theological voices was clearly a normative move, but not in the sense of using this literature as a measuring rod for evaluating the spirituality of the interviewed pastors. Rather, by bringing these texts into conversation with my data, my horizon of understanding was expanded, and I was enabled to "see the more" of the activity system of the field. Accordingly, I could rescript these reported practices differently. When looking back, I realize how this oscillation between the activity systems of the field and research entails both a *descriptive* and *normative* dimension, and it contributed to transformation both in the lives of the research participants as well as in my own life. As a consequence, I was able to offer a normative account of clergy spirituality, which raises the conundrum in terms of which voices are allowed into the conversation and whose voices are considered representative for a given ecclesial tradition.

During the research process, it also struck me that the pastors placed a more positive value on self and the body than what has been the traditional theological anthropology emphasized in certain Lutheran circles, particularly those influenced by pietism. One example is Sophie, a mother of three, who goes swimming and sits in the hot tub and sauna once a week in order to clear her mind and to have her own little everyday retreat:

> I have made my own places of retreat.... [I] facilitate places to breathe in, or I feel that it is important to do so. Once a week I go swimming and sit in the sauna and hot tub. And then I specifically use that time to clear my mind and put aside stuff.... And I feel that it is important both for my body and my mind. And also to just sit down and be completely silent, as I try to do every day, but also occasionally go to the chapel.... And I do the various things to unwind, but also to concentrate, or to do away with busyness. Because I don't like to be an all too busy person. And I know that when meeting with other people, I need to have peace and be calm.

Like Sophie, the clergy I interviewed do not necessarily attend to self solely for the sake of self, as would perhaps be the case in fully subjectivized spiritualities. Rather, their attitudes resemble Elizabeth Dreyer's "asceticism of everyday

69 Elizabeth Dreyer, *Earth Crammed With Heaven: A Spirituality of Everyday Life* (New York: Paulist Press, 1994); Bonnie J. Miller-McLemore, *In the Midst of Chaos: Caring for Children as Spiritual Practice*, 1st ed., Practices of Faith (San Francisco, CA: Jossey-Bass, 2007).

life,"[70] where working on personal issues prepares one to be the best possible self for the sake of the other. Hence, the pastors in my research express a balanced focus on God, self, and other. Thus, it may be argued that subjective-life spiritualities, in critiquing a too pessimistic anthropology, have actually been a positive asset to traditional religion in encouraging a more balanced theological anthropology.

However, when I was recently giving a talk about my doctoral work to a group of Danish pastors, one of them asked if I, being a Lutheran theologian, did not find this anthropology to be deeply problematic. He found my approach severely lacking in critique of this kind of contemporary spirituality and anthropology. This raised the conundrum of the status granted the rescriptive normativity established through empirical research versus that of extant normative theology, that is, the activity system of the research, here in the shape of certain theological (or ecclesial) texts, such as Luther's writings. In my dissertation work, then, I did not employ a uni-directional normativity-from-the-outside as a measuring rod for the normativity-from-within established through the empirical research. I made the normative decision to consult Luther's theology of vocation and his everyday spirituality, allowing the empirical data to point to this theological reservoir that has to a large extent gone unnoticed by Lutheran pastoral theological literature. Moreover, the question of what is the "authoritative" or normative understanding of Lutheran theology is raised in this example, as part of the conundrum. Who is in the position of making such normative decisions? Not only are there a number of interpretations and positions within Lutheran theology in terms of what authority tradition is to be given and how this tradition should be interpreted. There are also different understandings of what normative status empirical data should be granted in practical theological work.

What ended up being normative in my own study on clergy spirituality? I first used the conceptual framework developed through analysis of the data and extant literature to analyze my findings. Hence, "the descriptive move" was not purely descriptive. It was also influenced by the theoretical perspectives that I used as a sensitizing device to help me "see the more" of the activity system of the field. Following this, it struck me that the way my data was rescripted challenged certain aspects of traditional Lutheran pastoral spirituality. Thus, I sought to nuance this understanding as well as expand the existing categories of clergy spirituality. As opposed to approaches oriented more toward systematic theology, though, this process of negotiation was messier,

70 Dreyer, *Earth Crammed*, 136–49.

following the abductive move of the study, going back and forth between the inherent normativity of both the activity systems of field and research. Looking back, I see more clearly how the normative is intertwined with the descriptive, which expanded my understanding of normativity in the empirical field.

Moreover, this normative rescription of clergy spirituality has been "fed back" to the activity system of the field, as I have given numerous talks about this topic to clergy and other employees in the Church of Norway, allowing for yet another cycle of transformation to take place in that activity system.

Normative Dimensions in a Study of Implicit Ecclesiology (*Case Ideström*)

A Swedish Lutheran theologian and ethnographically oriented researcher, Jonas Ideström aims at contributing to theological conversations about what it entails to be church in Northern Swedish rural parishes by employing philosopher and anthropologist Bruno Latour's principle of "following the actors" (research participants).[71] Drawing on Afdal and describing his approach as *expressive*,[72] Ideström is less concerned with the negotiation of normative voices between the various steps of the pastoral cycle, or normativity-from-the-outside. Instead, he facilitates a conversation between various theological voices *within the field itself*, in what has traditionally been considered the descriptive realm. Ideström reflects: "In the analysis that follows, the understanding of the ecclesiological implications of the content of the conversation is shaped by a conversation including *the voices of the practitioners*, *my voice as a researcher*, and *the voice of Scripture*."[73] By asking the research participants to engage in a dialogue with Gospel narratives, he, as a researcher, brings an artifact belonging to the Christian tradition with its historicity and multi-voicedness into the field of study, facilitating an ecclesial practice and a normative negotiation as part of his fieldwork. Reflecting on this, he writes: "It is interesting to see how *truth* and *normativity are expressed in a certain manner that refuses to be reduced to a plain descriptive or normative theory*. It is dependent on the situation and the relationships between the people engaged

---

71 Jonas Ideström, *Spåren i snön* (Skellefteå: Artos & Norma Bokförlag, 2015), 243. See also Bruno Latour, *Reassembling the Social: An Introduction to Actor-Network Theory* (Oxford: Oxford University Press, 2005); John Law, *Organizing Modernity* (Oxford: Blackwell Publishers, 1994). For my analysis I have primarily used Jonas Ideström, "It is that Loving Gaze," *Ecclesial Practices. Journal of Ecclesiology and Ethnography* 2 (2015). However, I have additionally consulted the more comprehensive Swedish book Ideström, *Spåren*.

72 Ideström, "Loving Gaze," 109ff emphasis in the original.

73 Ideström, "Loving Gaze," 111–12, emphasis added.

in the dialogue.... This was an *ecclesial context*, which, in a both direct and indirect manner, has an impact on the conversation and its content."[74]

The encounter between the field, the researcher, and the theological tradition takes place "immanently" *within the field itself, as part of establishing the data.* Furthermore, as Ideström notes, the dialogue is marked by *the ecclesial context* in which the conversation is situated. Yet, these Gospel texts are not used as a measuring rod in an evaluative way. Ideström makes the case, though, that the transcribed conversations taking place during his fieldwork should be considered *theological texts* in the same way academic theological literature or formal theological documents are regarded as such.

> The content of the expressive ecclesiologies is dependent on the actual people participating and their engagement. This is a creative process for them as well as for me. There is not a body of information simply waiting to be presented to me. In the act of talking and listening meaning and understanding is formed and translated. Another aspect has to do with the relations between them, me and *the Word of God.* From a theological perspective, in line with e.g. Gordon Lathrop's liturgical ecclesiology, the Gospel narratives are important conversational partners. In the church's tradition this is one significant mediator of the divine revelation in Jesus Christ and therefore a central voice in the ongoing interpretation and reflection concerning the mission and identity of the church.[75]

As Ideström argues, the data to be analysed in this study was not simply "lying around" waiting to be picked up by him as a researcher, like pieces of gold in a gold mine. Rather, meaning and understanding are formed and translated in the actual dialogue itself. Yet, as a researcher he played an active part in co-creating or establishing this material in conjunction with the people participating in the research. A baptized member and an ordained minister in the Church of Sweden, Ideström is clearly an insider participant in the activity system of the field.[76] Thus, he also brings along his own normative voice and lens, for example, in regarding the Gospel narratives as normative and an important conversation partner—the "Word of God" and "one significant mediator of the divine revelation of Jesus Christ."[77] Hence, a part of Scripture is

74 Ideström, "Loving Gaze," 115, emphasis added.
75 Ideström, "Loving Gaze," 118, emphasis added.
76 Ideström, *Spåren* 21.
77 Ideström, "Loving Gaze," 118.

brought in as a significant voice in the theological conversation facilitated by him as researcher. At the same time, though, this normative dimension of the Biblical texts chosen for the dialogue is already present in the activity system of the field. Scripture thus represents a normativity that is deeply embedded in the historicity of this activity system. As an insider in this activity system, Ideström's positionality as a researcher also plays a part in raising the conundrum under investigation, as his own interpretive repertoire and normative values allow him to see certain things, whereas other perspectives go unnoticed. Moreover, while allowing a real dialogue to take place, it still remains unclear what normative status the various voices are granted and on what criteria his interpretations and value judgments are based. Is it the dynamics of the dialogue itself that is granted the ultimate normative claim in his approach?

Another interesting part is how these Gospel narratives function in terms of negotiating normativity within the field. There is clearly a normative and transcendent dimension present in this encounter, as both the researched and the researcher believe in a transcendent God and divine action. Divine action is, in a paradoxical way, negotiated as normativity-from-within, as there is *a transcendent dimension within the immanent*, within the activity system of the field. This again raises the conundrum, as the practical theologian might decide to either share the interpretation of the research participants or to question them. Moreover, is it possible to make any transcendent normative claims of divine action based on what is rescripted as a normative theological text within the immanent realm of the field? And if possible, according to what criteria? This question is not easily answered, and, thus, points to the conundrum.

Furthermore, how will this normativity-from-within shape the next step when the researcher is to analyze, interpret, and discuss the material established during his fieldwork? Which voices are allowed into the dialogue?[78] In the case of Ideström's research, no one voice is given primacy *in advance*. This includes the voice of the researcher. Instead, it is a collaborative process where meaning is created, and the biblical text is corporately interpreted. Thus, Ideström argues that the theological reflections of the research participants are just as important as the voices and artifacts of the academy or the theological tradition. However, when moving into the activity system of the research and analyzing and interpreting the data as a next step, Ideström is in the position of choosing additional conversation partners. At this stage,

78 Ideström, "Loving Gaze," 119.

then, theological thinkers such as Rowan Williams, Mary McClintock Fulkerson, Gordon Lathrop, and William T. Cavanaugh are drawn into this ongoing theological conversation. Here normativity-from-the-outside is at play too, and there is a normative negotiation between the two activity systems: that of the *field* and that of the *research*. Nevertheless, the formal voices of the academy are not given the role of a measuring rod used to evaluate the voices of the research participants. Rather, the theoretical lenses brought about by the research process are used in order to expand the understanding of the activity system under investigation.

What Ideström ends up with as "normative claims" in the large overall study is the result of achieving a transformed or expanded understanding of the field. Hence, change must happen "from within below," from where the practices and practitioners are located.[79] Subsequently, this is the kind of normativity offered to the readers rather than a prescriptive normativity telling them how to run a church in a rural parish. His rescription is not purely descriptive, but has, in accordance with Afdal's model, both descriptive and normative dimensions.

A Remaining Conundrum

Having explored some of the forms the conundrum takes in practical theological works and briefly discussed two empirical cases where various dimensions of normativity are at play as the researcher oscillates between the activity systems of the field and that of the research, I hope to have shown some of the dynamics of the normative dimensions at work both within and between the activity systems. Furthermore, I have emphasized the significant role of the researcher in deciding which voices and artifacts are allowed into the negotiation process. When practical theologians conduct empirical research, they frequently find themselves wearing both the hat of the insider (practitioner of the phenomenon and field to be studied) and that of the outsider (researcher belonging to the academy). This gives practical theologians quite a different position than most social scientists studying the same field. Secular scientists are usually not part of the activity system of the field in the same way as practical theological scholars.[80] Additionally, the practical theologian has a different

79 Afdal, *Researching Religious Education*, 74.

80 Natalie Wigg-Stevenson reflects extensively on this in an essay presenting an extreme case of researcher proximity to the field under investigation. Natalie Wigg-Stevenson, "Reflexive Theology: A Preliminary Proposal," *Practical Matters*, no. 6 (2013). See also Eileen

"interpretive repertoire"[81] to draw from than most social scientists and will be able to pose different research questions and theoretical perspectives due to his or her training as a practical theologian.

When returning to the ongoing conversation on normativity within the field of practical theology, I side with Miller-McLemore in arguing that we need to move beyond "simple formulas such as 'the correlation between the Christian tradition and contemporary experience.'"[82] Privileging neither the theological tradition nor contemporary experience, I here make the case that we have to attend to experiences, practices, the theological and ecclesial tradition, and theological and sociological theories without giving primacy to any one in advance, as we move back and forth between the activity systems of field and research. Here I disagree with positions such as those of van Deusen Hunsinger as well as Swinton and Mowat in the upper left corner of the grid offered in this chapter. In my view, the normativity-from-within of the empirical field is not granted a fair chance to reshape or challenge existing theological traditions in these contributions. This also partly holds true for the Four Voices of Theology model despite a willingness in principle to facilitate a space for theological epiphanies to emerge.

Furthermore, I propose that distinguishing between a rescriptive normativity-from-within and an evaluative normativity-from-the-outside might prove helpful as an attempt to be more explicit about one's normative deliberations. Drawing on Afdal, I argue that the descriptive and normative dimensions are deeply interwoven and that the difference is one of degree. Hence, although I am in many ways deeply indebted to Browning, I find his practice-theory-practice model lacking in discerning normative dimensions that count for the overall practical theological enterprise in all of the steps. Albeit having a different epistemological point of departure than that of the approaches in the upper part of my grid, Browning too ends up granting systematic theology the ultimate normative position.

Not wanting to try to solve this conundrum with a prescriptive solution, I follow Elaine Graham in considering our discipline to be primarily interpretive, or more specifically, as previously argued, *rescriptive* rather than prescriptive.[83] Despite Graham's important point in allowing the practices of the faith

---

Campbell-Reed and Christian B. Scharen, "Ministry as Spiritual Practice: How Pastors Learn to See and Respond to the 'More' of a Situation," *Journal of Religious Leadership* 12, no. 2 (2013).

81 I use this term as described in Alvesson and Sköldberg, *Tolkning*, 55–56.

82 Miller-McLemore, "Introduction," 17.

83 Graham, *Transforming Practice*, 208–09.

community as a collaborative entity to be the criterion for normative value statements, the conundrum still remains somewhat unresolved, as there are as many different practices of faith communities as there are theological interpretations of the Christian tradition. Still, I support her point of placing this responsibility in the collaborative practices of the faith community instead of solely in normative doctrinal or academic texts.

In terms of practical theological research, I have emphasized the oscillation between the two activities systems as well as the significant role of the researcher. Nevertheless, the messy process of identifying, understanding, and negotiating these normative dimensions remains a conundrum. Acknowledging this messiness and complexity, I suggest, is not a way of escaping the conundrum, but a way of dealing with it in a constructive and responsible way.

Bibliography

Afdal, Geir. *Researching Religious Education as Social Practice.* Münster: Waxmann, 2010.

Alvesson, Mats and Kaj Sköldberg. *Tolkning och reflektion: Vetenskapsfilosofi och kvalitativ metod.* Lund: Studentlitteratur, 2008.

Ballard, Paul and John Pritchard. *Practical Theology in Action: Christian Thinking in the Service of Church and Society.* London: SPCK, 1996.

Beaudoin, Tom. *Witness to Dispossession.* Maryknoll, NY: Orbis Books, 2008.

Browning, Don S. *A Fundamental Practical Theology: Descriptive and Strategic Proposals.* Minneapolis: Fortress, 1991.

Cameron, Helen, Deborah Bhatti, Catherine Duce, James Sweeney, and Clare Watkins. *Talking about God in Practice: Theological Action Research and Practical Theology.* London: SCM Press, 2010.

Campbell-Reed, Eileen and Christian B. Scharen. "Ministry as Spiritual Practice: How Pastors Learn to See and Respond to the 'More' of a Situation." *Journal of Religious Leadership* 12, no. 2 (2013): 125–44.

Cartledge, Mark. *Testimony in the Spirit: Rescripting Ordinary Pentecostal Theology.* Aldershot: Ashgate, 2010.

Dreyer, Elizabeth. *Earth Crammed With Heaven: A Spirituality of Everyday Life.* New York: Paulist Press, 1994.

Engeström, Yrjö. "Expansive Learning at Work: Toward an Activity Theoretical Reconceptualization." *Journal of Education and Work* 14 (2001): 133–56.

Fulkerson, Mary McClintock. "Interpreting a Situation: When Is "Empirical" also "Theological"?" In *Perspectives on Ecclesiology and Ethnography*, edited by Pete Ward.

Studies in Ecclesiology and Ethnography, 124–44. Grand Rapids, MI: Eerdmans Publishing Company, 2012.
Fulkerson, Mary McClintock *Places of Redemption*. Oxford: Oxford University Press, 2007.
Ganzevoort, Ruard. "What You See Is What You Get." In *Normativity and Empirical Research in Theology*, edited by Johannes A. van der Ven and Michael Scherer-Rath, 17–34. Leiden: Brill, 2005.
Graham, Elaine. "Research Report: Is Practical Theology a form of 'Action Research'?". *International Journal of Practical Theology* 17, no. 1 (2013): 148–78.
Graham, Elaine. *Transforming Practice: Pastoral Theology in an Age of Uncertainty*. Eugene, OR: Wipf and Stock, 2002 [1996].
Graham, Elaine, Heather Walton, and Frances Ward. *Theological Reflection: Methods*. London, UK: SCM Press, 2005.
Harbers, Hans. "Epilogue: Political Materials-Material Politics." In *Inside the Politics of Technology: Agency and Normativity in the Co-Production of Technology and Society*, edited by Hans Harbers, 257–71. Amsterdam, NLD: Amsterdam University Press, 2005.
Ideström, Jonas. "It is that Loving Gaze." *Ecclesial Practices. Journal of Ecclesiology and Ethnography* 2 (2015): 108–19.
Ideström, Jonas. *Spåren i snön*. Skellefteå: Artos & Norma Bokförlag, 2015.
Kaufman, Tone Stangeland. "A New Old Spirituality: A Qualitative Study of Clergy Spirituality in the Church of Norway." MF Norwegian School of Theology, 2011.
Kaufman, Tone Stangeland. "Normativity as Pitfall or Ally? Reflexivity as an Interpretive Resource in Ecclesiological and Ethnographic Research." *Ecclesial Practices. Journal of Ecclesiology and Ethnography* 2 (2015): 91–107.
Kaufman, Tone Stangeland. "Pastoral Spirituality in Everyday Life, in Ministry, and Beyond: Three Locations for a Pastoral Spirituality." *Journal of Religious Leadership* 12, no. 2 (2013): 81–106.
Kaufman, Tone Stangeland. "The Real Thing? Practicing a Spirituality of Everyday Life." In *Between the State and the Eucharist: Free Church Theology in Conversation with William T. Cavanaugh*, edited by Joel Halldorf and Fredrik Wenell, 85–101. Eugene, OR: Picwick Publications, 2014.
Latour, Bruno. *Reassembling the Social: An Introduction to Actor-Network Theory*. Oxford: Oxford University Press, 2005.
Law, John. *Organizing Modernity*. Oxford: Blackwell Publishers, 1994.
Miller-McLemore, Bonnie J. *In the Midst of Chaos: Caring for Children as Spiritual Practice*. The practices of faith series. 1st ed. San Francisco, CA: Jossey-Bass, 2007.
Miller-McLemore, Bonnie J. "Cognitive Neuroscience and the Question of Theological Method." *Journal of Pastoral Theology* 20, no. 2 (Winter 2011): 64–92.
Miller-McLemore, Bonnie J. "Introduction: The Contributions of Practical Theology."

In *The Blackwell Companion to Practical Theology*, edited by Bonnie J. Miller-McLemore, 1–20. Malden, MA: Wiley Blackwell, 2014.

Pattison, Stephen. "Some Straw for the Bricks: A Basic Introduction to Theological Reflection." In *The Blackwell Reader in Pastoral and Practical Theology*, edited by James Woodward and Stephen Pattison, 135–48. Malden, MA: Blackwell Publishing, 2000.

Root, Andy. *Christopraxis: A Practical Theology of the Cross*. Minneapolis, MN: Fortress Press, 2014.

Scharen, Christian B., ed. *Explorations in Ecclesiology and Ethnography*. edited by Pete Ward and Christian B. Scharen, Studies in Ecclesiology and Ethnography, vol. 2. Grand Rapids, MI: Eerdmans Publishing Company, 2012.

Swinton, John and Harriet Mowat. *Practical Theology and Qualitative Research*. London: SCM, 2006.

van der Ven, Johannes A. *Practical Theology: An Empirical Approach*. Leuven, Belgium: Peeters Press, 1998.

van Deusen Hunsinger, Deborah. *Theology and Pastoral Care: A New Interdisciplinary Approach*. Grand Rapids, MI: Eerdmans, 1995.

Ward, Pete ed. *Perspectives on Ecclesiology and Ethnography*. edited by Pete Ward and Christian B. Scharen, Studies in Ecclesiology and Ethnography. Grand Rapids, MI: Eerdmans Publishing Company, 2012.

Watkins, Clare. "Practicing Ecclesiology: From Product to Process: Developing Ecclesiology as a Non-Correlative Process and Practice through the Theological Action Research Framework of Theology in Four Voices." *Ecclesial Practices. Journal of Ecclesiology and Ethnography* 2 (2015): 23–39.

Watkins, Clare. "Reflections on Particularity and Unity." In *Ecclesiology in the Trenches: Theory and Method under Construction*, edited by Sune Fahlgren and Jonas Ideström, 139–53. Eugene, OR: Pickwick Publications, 2015.

Wigg-Stevenson, Natalie. "Reflexive Theology: A Preliminary Proposal." *Practical Matters*, no. 6 (2013): 1–19.

Woodward, James and Stephen Pattison, eds. *The Blackwell Reader in Pastoral and Practical Theology*. Malden, MA: Wiley-Blackwell, 2000.

CHAPTER 7

Interdisciplinarity as a Practical Theological Conundrum[1]

Joyce Ann Mercer

Without exception, when practical theologians talk about what constitutes our work and how we define our field, the term *interdisciplinary* arises. Practical theology, with its focus on the lived practices of persons and communities within their social contexts, is inherently interdisciplinary, since this kind of work necessitates not only knowledge of theology but also of human personhood alongside social and contextual knowledge. As such, practical theology requires deft engagement of multiple fields of knowledge and methods of study to address the complexity of practical theology's aims. Interdisciplinary scholarship seeks to acknowledge, utilize, and integrate the resources of various disciplinary perspectives in order to create a systemic outcome that is more than the sum of its parts.[2] Working among diverse disciplines, practical theologians aim to transcend limitations conferred by single-disciplinary boundaries on what may be known and done with knowledge; to overcome discipline-based limits on the kinds of questions that may be asked legitimately; and to become open to a wider array of research methodologies. This scholarship is exciting in post-modernity's press for border crossings and the disruption of fixed identities within the academy and churches. It also is challenging, raising questions about researcher identities, the meanings of expertise in scholarship, and what constitutes appropriate use of academic fields into which one has not been apprenticed.

Interdisciplinarity is constitutive of practical theology. While many practical theologians continue to identify themselves in relation to one disciplinary

1 I wish to thank my co-editor, Bonnie Miller-McLemore, and other authors for this volume, for insightful suggestions and helpful conversation that improved this chapter immeasurably. I am also grateful to practical theology colleagues at Virginia Theological Seminary and at Yale Divinity School, who live with the tensions of border crossings between disciplines and grasp so well why it matters for our work in theological education.

2 Catherine Lyall, et al., *Interdisciplinary Research Journeys: Practical Strategies for Capturing Creativity* (New York: Bloomsbury Academic, 2011), 14.

 | DOI 10.1163/9789004324244_009

home, such as pastoral theology/care, religious education, popular culture studies, or womanist theology, in fact I do not know any practical theologians on the planet who "only do one thing." In a recent text introducing the field of practical theology, Kathleen Cahalan and Gordon Mikoski identify interdisciplinarity as one of the field's defining "elements and values," a key "point of convergence" amid the disciplinary diversity that exists among practical theologians themselves.[3] Pattison and Woodward likewise name interdisciplinarity as one of practical theology's "essential characteristics."[4]

Even though interdisciplinary is constitutive of practical theology, the commitment to interdisciplinary teaching, research, and scholarship creates a very real conundrum. A conundrum by definition is a confusing problem, riddle, or dilemma for which there exists no easy solution. So here are two riddles. The first asks, "What is both a constitutive, necessary element of the field of practical theology and yet at the same time impossible to accomplish?" The second riddle is, "What gives identity and erases it at the same time?" My answer to both riddles, of course, is interdisciplinary scholarship. Stating the quagmire in the form of riddles exposes how interdisciplinarity forms a conundrum in practical theology. First, even as it constitutes one of practical theology's most significant contributions within the academy, church, and society, interdisciplinarity renders our work too complex to achieve in the fullest sense of the term.[5] In a study of interdisciplinary research, Catherine Lyall and her colleagues note its multifaceted nature, concluding with the question, "How can a researcher cope constructively with this degree of complexity?"[6] In practical theology, complexity is not only a matter of volume or a function of the growing number of disciplines to which a scholar must attend, but also of effects. That is, the added labor that comes with the continual need to "get up to speed" in new areas of knowledge in order to utilize them credibly makes any research venture incredibly more complex.

Second, interdisciplinary scholarship interjects the work of practical theologians with identity-issues, functioning as a site for the performance of identities and the negotiation of power within the academy's hierarchies of knowledge. On the one hand, interdisciplinarity participates in the distinctive methods, values, and styles of discourse that make practical theology the kind of

3 Kathleen A. Cahalan and Gordon S. Mikoski, eds., *Opening the Field of Practical Theology: An Introduction* (Lanham, MD: Rowman and Littlefield, 2914), 1, 272.

4 James Woodward, Stephen Pattison and John Patton, eds., *The Blackwell Reader in Pastoral and Practical Theology* (Oxford, UK & Malden, Mass.: Blackwell Publishers, 2000), 15.

5 Lyall, et al, *Interdisciplinary Research Journeys*.

6 Lyall, et al., *Interdisciplinary Research Journeys*, 19.

discipline it is within the academy. On the other hand, interdisciplinary scholarship in its most radical, integrative forms can put practical theologians in the position of not being recognized as holding full membership within *any* particular site within the academy. In this essay, I explore these two riddles with an eye toward constructive ways to address the challenges that the interdisciplinary conundrum presents.

Complexities at the Borders of Knowledge and Practice

Multiple terms describe scholarly work with more than one discipline: interdisciplinary, multidisciplinary, cross-disciplinary, transdisciplinary.[7] Where these terms differ is in the relative degrees of integration expected within the process or the product of the work. Multidisciplinary research, for example, generally refers to the use of several disciplines side by side, each informing the other but without any fundamental alteration of any of the participating disciplines. Cross-disciplinary studies involve the use of several disciplines with relatively low levels of integration in either the work itself or the product. Transdisciplinary work, in contrast, seeks to work across the various disciplines to overcome their divisions toward the construction of a new and fully integrated knowledge. In this essay I use the term "interdisciplinary" as the general referent for these various forms along the continuum.

Truly interdisciplinary studies involve significant integration, as teachers and researchers invite two or more disciplines into mutual engagement, allowing these disciplines themselves to be informed and re-formed by their engagements with each other. Interdisciplinary scholarship and practice holds forth the possibility of creating methodologies of inquiry and constructing forms of knowledge, theory, and practice that move beyond the previous boundaries of any of the discreet partner disciplines. This kind of work seeks collaboration among disciplines, whether that takes place in the way an individual scholar utilizes them in relation to one another, or, less commonly, in actual face-to-face collaborative work with scholars from diverse fields.

---

7 Julie Thompson Klein, *Interdisciplinarity: History, Theory, and Practice* (Detroit: Wayne State University, 1990); Lisa R. Lattuca, *Creating Interdisciplinarity: Interdisciplinary Research and Teaching among College and University Faculty*, Vanderbilt Issues in Higher Education, 1st ed. (Nashville: Vanderbilt University Press, 2001); Lyall, et al., *Interdisciplinary Research Journeys*; Myra H. Strober, *Interdisciplinary Conversations: Challenging Habits of Thought* (Stanford, Calif.: Stanford University Press, 2011), http://site.ebrary.com/lib/yale/Doc?id=10459532.

When practical theologians talk about the palate of disciplines within which we work, most frame the relationship between these disciplines in a fairly integrated way, saying for example, "It is not possible to talk about human personhood theologically without at the same time using available social scientific understandings of personhood. I don't add theology to social science, nor do I add social science to theology. Both are present and interacting in a practical theological analysis of a person or a community."[8] The fact that multiple disciplines are always already in play from the very outset of a practical theologian's work underscores again the complexity of such an endeavor, because the scholar becomes responsible for competence across multiple frames of knowledge and practice.

Why then would scholars wish to engage in interdisciplinary scholarship? Pastoral theologian Homer U. Ashby, Jr., tells the story of team teaching a course in the early 1980's with another scholar: "Our sense was that theology needed psychological insights in order for it to address the human situation with any integrity and that pastoral care needed to be more closely aligned with theology than with psychology if it sought to honor its desire to care for the soul."[9] Their interdisciplinary foray thus came from a felt need to bring the resources of pastoral psychology and theology to bear on each other in ways that would transcend the limits of each discipline on its own. Scholars in religious education, pastoral care, and homiletics, to cite only a few examples, have been utilizing knowledge from other fields in addition to theology for many years. Since the 1990's and the "sociological turn" in practical theology, the number and types of disciplinary perspectives has multiplied, shifting from a fairly exclusive reliance upon those more individually focused cognate disciplines, such as psychology, to those which help explain persons-in-contexts, religious organizations, and complex systems. But the same impetus guiding Ashby's interdisciplinary team teaching in the 1980's remains salient now among practical theologians, namely, the pragmatic need to move beyond the inadequacies of a single discipline's construal of knowledge.

Going off of the adage that a field is most fertile at its edges,[10] many of us do this work because of the constructive creativity that such a positioning on the edges of multiple disciplines permits. It is not only a matter of working with

8 This is a paraphrase from a conversation among several practical theologians discussing the sources and norms of their work at the November 2014 meeting of the Association of Practical Theology.

9 Homer U. Ashby, Jr., "A Black Perspective on Interdisciplinary Work," *Currents in Mission* 31.3 (2004): 172.

10 Strober, *Interdisciplinary Conversations*, 23.

other fields, though: interdisciplinary conversation can open up new ways of perceiving one's own field, getting us out of what public opinion analyst Daniel Yankelovich terms, in reference to academic disciplines, "gated communities of the mind."[11]

Practical theologian Elaine Graham provides a helpful example. Confronted with the complexities of new technologies and what she calls "post/human futures," Graham explores intersections between human biology, technology's artificial intelligence and digital life forms, science fiction, and theology. Through these intersections she posits that the meaning of human personhood in the digital age is "not only the province of academic and scientific debate. It is also, crucially, addressed in the realms of popular culture and the creative arts, where a proliferation of representations of the 'posthuman' serve as *refractions* of what it might mean to be human, examining the possibilities–and the limits–of the relationship between humans, their tools and technologies."[12] As is the case in the work of other practical theologians, the intricacy of Graham's subject of inquiry makes requisite an engagement of other resources beyond theology alone in order to construct theological meanings adequate for the questions. This, in turn, acts back on the kind of theological anthropology she envisions. It is a daunting task, though, to bring together into a coherent argument so many divergent forms of knowledge. The necessary complexity of interdisciplinarity operates as a conundrum when practical theologians recognize our inability to ever fully and sufficiently engage all the frameworks truly necessary for our work.

The Necessary Impossibility: Problems with Interdisciplinarity's Complexity

The question of how to handle the complexity in practical theology's interdisciplinarity came home to me in a recent course with Master of Divinity students. Providing students with a case study about a low-income family's need for affordable housing in our high-cost mid-Atlantic, east coast city, I set them to work in small groups to initiate inquiry into various disciplines from which they might need to draw in order to come to a more adequate understanding of the various issues germane to this case study. Students used Internet resources, texts, and their own life experiences to explore the contributions a wide array of disciplines and practices might make to the problem of

11 In Strober, *Interdisciplinary Conversations*, 50.

12 Elaine L. Graham, *Words Made Flesh: Writings in Pastoral and Practical Theology* (London: SCM Press, 2009), 277, emphasis in original.

affordable housing, among them theology, economics, psychology, education, community organizing, political science and public policy, social work, urban geography, critical race studies, and history.

After several minutes of such work, a student timidly raised his hand, saying, "I'm overwhelmed! When is it enough? I can't possibly know about all of these things—it's just too complex. In fact, I'm probably not going to know much about *most* of these disciplines we've named, much less be competent in relation to them! But I see how they are all important for a wider, more holistic framing of the case study." Another student joined in, saying, "So how do practical theologians draw a line around the kind and number of disciplines they need to use? What do you do when you can't be an expert in everything? I know just enough about most of these fields to be dangerous! How can we become 'fluent enough' in all these different areas to use them well? And how do you decide what to leave out?"

My students' alarm at the complexity of the task posed by practical theology's interdisciplinarity expresses the same dilemma faced by many practical theology faculty advising doctoral students on the appropriate breadth and boundaries around their dissertation research. The contexts and problems we and our students investigate are generally multidimensional, requiring multi-axial frameworks to interpret them well. We practical theologians study child poverty, middle class males suffering from depression in North American, spiritual practices in relation to time, Indonesian women's peacebuilding practices, racial profiling as violence, rock music, congregational conflict, consumerism and teens, and women's educational experiences in religious schools, to name just a few examples. Such complex foci beg for an equally complex engagement of diverse bodies of knowledge to help make sense of them because they all involve the interplay between lived experience theorized by many diverse fields and theological inquiry. In fact, in the complex, global reality in which practical theologians do our work, we cannot do competent scholarship *without* interdisciplinary engagements that are equal to the task.

But given human finitude in the face of the seemingly infinite variety of disciplinary approaches that could relate to practical theological research, how can we really do justice to the demands of good scholarship? How do faculty credibly advise students working with other disciplines that lie outside the faculty members' expertise, much less outside the bounds of our students' most rigorously concentrated areas of study? What disciplines need to be used and which are optional for a given project? What level of competence constitutes responsible scholarship when dealing with a discipline beyond one's so-called primary location in the academy? What should faculty and our graduate students do with the methodological inconsistencies between the different disciplines they engage toward new forms of knowledge and practice? How do we help these students negotiate the expansiveness and limitations of their own identity-boundaries within the field—not to mention those we must negotiate ourselves as practical theologians?

Such questions are not easily answered because there is no singular path to addressing these issues. One place to look for assistance is in the experience many practical theologians already have negotiating these kinds of questions in relation to specific projects. When researching and writing my practical theology of childhood, *Welcoming Children*,[13] for example, I experienced both the joy and the terror of interdisciplinary work's complexity. *Welcoming Children* works with perspectives on childhood from the Gospel of Mark as a counter-narrative to the imperial regime of late modern consumer capitalism's constructions of childhood in North America. In this work, I look at the possibilities in religious education and liturgy for nurturing an alternative Christian identity in children and for congregational life and mission that privileges the welcome of children. The empirical research underlying the project was a congregational study of three churches in the San Francisco Bay area that "do good church with children."

In other words, this single book project involved me in the mind-expanding experience of encounters with postmodern urban geographers and economists working with the meaning of time-space compression for the U.S. economy and consumer culture, while also consulting with sociologists and anthropologists toward rethinking ethnographic practices in relation to particular communities (such as churches and children). I read and re-read systematic theologians. I read and talked with biblical scholars engaging a socio-cultural hermeneutic in their work and asked them to check my translations of biblical texts. I studied educational theorists and socio-biologists retrieving the work of Lev Vygotsky for understanding apprenticeship in practices; liturgical and ritual theorists on how liturgies shape identities; and marketing experts and economic historians addressing the rise of children as a niche market group in American commerce.

At the same time, I was trying to talk about these extremely complex, multidimensional realities without benefit of long-term exposure to and study within every thought world I had cause to enter. More than once I "got stuck" in the problem of how to understand deeply enough myself, much less com-

13 Joyce Ann Mercer, *Welcoming Children: A Practical Theology of Childhood* (St. Louis, Mo.: Chalice Press, 2005).

municate clearly enough to readers, the interplay of these many strands of knowledge. I experienced the limits of my own resources and of time: sometimes I simply had to made decisions either to proceed with the degree of immersion I had acquired in a new body of literature or to leave something out of the analysis even when I felt it could be beneficial, for fear of insufficient competency in that discipline to use it responsibly.

An example of this concerns a portion of *Welcoming Children* that depends heavily on economic theory and history as "background perspectives" to my discussion of the construction of children as consumers. I am not an economist nor do I have much background in this theoretical universe, but I nevertheless find the history and theory of economic movements essential for making sense of children's situations in consumer societies. In this case, I reached a certain level of depth in my own studies in these areas, at which point I assessed that I was at the limit of my capacity, mostly through noticing a level of saturation in the concepts I already understood, alongside a kind of disinterest in some of the more complex material which relied upon theoretical constructs foreign to me. I took that to be a clue that I had reached the limits of my ability to "read my way into" these fields. I therefore decided to rely heavily on some other thinkers who are more fluent in these areas and whose work I trust (e.g., in this case, David Harvey). In addition to noticing signals about limitations, a working principle used by me and many other practical theologians I know in making such determinations is "follow your instincts—and then get lots of feedback from other people in case your instincts are misguided!"

In my research, I determined which disciplines to engage as conversation partners and sources in part through an internal negotiation between what the research called for and my own interests and inclinations. I did not start out in this study of children in the church, for instance, with the intention of becoming conversant in the history and organizational psychology of niche marketing to children. The foray into business and marketing happened on an "as needed" basis, when the empirical work of exploring concrete realities of particular children surfaced the need to better understand how consumerist practices come to inhabit children's lives. It is likely that if this research had called me toward the need to know theoretical physics or organic chemistry to make sense of children in the church, however, I would not have taken on the burden of becoming conversant there: I lack interest and aptitude. With this example from my own work, I recognize that I am guided in making choices in interdisciplinary research not only by the demands of a particular project but also by my own interests, limitations, and dispositions toward certain bodies of knowledge.

Reframing Expertise

One byproduct of practical theology's interdisciplinary work that is salient for the "complexity" aspect of this conundrum is its drawing into question certain notions of expertise that tend to operate as a priori facts, largely uninterrogated within the academy. For example, one common understanding of an expert is a person who knows more than others about a subject. This definition of expertise, when situated in the academy, frequently leaves out practical knowing. Increasing specialization within fields over the past half-century only serves to heighten the sense that knowledge can be produced and managed properly only by persons at the pinnacle of the meritocracy academia is widely believed to be. Such a world divides into experts and lay people. Any engagement with a field's body of knowledge at a less-specialized level, or one that starts with practices themselves, may be deemed inadequate for credible scholarly use. The expert-layperson dualism created thereby participates in the establishment of certain kinds of expert knowledge as a form of capital only available to the most elite in a field of study, but nevertheless needed by the rest of us to do our work.

I have no quarrels with the notion that it is possible to achieve greater and lesser standards of excellence in academic work. Nor do I object to the idea that some persons with particularly deep wells of accumulated knowledge about a subject can make singularly significant contributions to their fields. It is the case that sometimes scholars do make less-than-credible use of disciplinary knowledge beyond our fields, a reality that simply needs to be acknowledged. Credibility and depth of knowledge do matter. If I need brain surgery, in fact, I hope that my surgeon knows about the workings of the brain in more nuanced and better ways than I do!

The problem I raise here concerns unwarranted assumptions that *all* engagements with a field of study require such a level of high specialization in order to be legitimate. This is a critique about definitions of expertise that only allow it to mean one thing, namely, positioning at the top of a (historically and socially constructed) knowledge hierarchy, in which higher levels of abstraction from practice signal greater expertise.[14]

There are varieties of expertise to consider in relation to interdisciplinarity, some of which take the form of a more utilitarian level of engagement of outside fields that, while not completely comprehensive, are "good enough" (to borrow from D.W. Winnicott) to do the work of interdisciplinary scholarship

14 See Bonnie Miller-McLemore's chapter 8 in this volume on "The Politics of Knowledge" (pp. 190–218).

well for the purposes of such work.[15] In this sense, expertise is constituted as much by the ability to scan for and select the appropriate portion of a particular subject area to handle the pragmatic demands of a concrete situation, as it is by the capacity to walk through an entire body of literature in depth. This suggests that scholars do not always need maximum depth-immersion in a field of study to have a kind of expert knowledge of it adequate for their purposes. We can know some fields well and others at a level of competence that grants us borrowing privileges.

Philosopher William M. Sullivan gives credence to the ability to make pragmatic choices based on practical reason as its own form of expertise, when he writes that expertise evolves through practice, "the gradually developing ability to see analogies, to recognize new situations as similar to whole remembered patterns. Expertise means a learned ability to grasp what is important in a situation without proceeding through a long process of formal reasoning. Sometimes called expert 'intuition; or 'judgment,' it is the goal of training for practice in the mode of apprenticeship."[16] This kind of experience frequently is discounted in academic contexts, however, even in professional programs ostensibly organized to prepare people for professional practice.

Note that Sullivan refers to expert judgment as a *gradually developing ability*, meaning that it takes time and experience to acquire the skill of recognizing what forms of knowledge and disciplinary expertise are important. How can a student of ministry, a new graduate student in practical theology, or even a newly minted faculty colleague gain this ability, short of waiting out the passage of time? One valuable strategy involves intentional creation of opportunities for reflection on practice with colleagues of different "generations" in this developmental process. When I was a newly ordained minister and hospital chaplain in Minnesota, I belonged to two groups that met every month. One was a group of women clergy of our presbytery. The other group

---

15 Strober seems to have this "good enough" notion of expertise in mind with what she names instrumental interdisciplinarity, in which scholars "use another discipline at a certain stage in a project because they realize they need its tools." She contrasts this with radical interdisciplinarity or the "turn to multiple disciplines at the very beginning of their work, at the conceptual stage." See Strober, *Interdisciplinary Conversations*, 146. Winnicott introduced his notion of "good enough" mothers/objects for attachment in 1953. See Donald W. Winnicott, "Transitional Objects and Transitional Phenomena; a Study of the First Not-Me Possession," *International Journal of Psychoanalysis* 34, no. 2 (1953).

16 William M. Sullivan and Carnegie Foundation for the Advancement of Teaching, *Work and Integrity: The Crisis and Promise of Professionalism in America*, 2nd ed. (San Francisco, CA: Jossey-Bass, 2005), 247.

included chaplains of various denominations working in hospitals across the Twin Cities. Both of these groups gave personal support, but they also became places to offer up experiences in ministry for reflection on practice by people with different degrees of "seasoning" in the arts of employing expert judgment and recognizing limits. Later, as a graduate student and then as a new scholar, I participated in writing groups in which more seasoned scholar-colleagues helped to apprentice me in these ways of working, not only by sharing their own work and looking at mine, but also by making their processes of scholarship transparent. Such collaborations were invaluably formative of intuition around "good enough" knowledge. It takes time to grow into the habitus of interdisciplinarity whether in ministry or in academia, and the process involves a journey of "guided participation in practice."[17]

Another way to redefine expertise is through the concept of improvisation. One meaning of improvisation is the ability, in the words of my mother's Great Depression-era generation, to "make do with what you've got." "If you don't have something, well, improvise," was the watchword of many in her generation, for whom such improvisation was both artful skill and necessity. This older generation's tales of everyday life are replete with examples of improvising in response to a problem: making a tasty meal using only what is left in the pantry; creating a new party dress by adding fancy lace from a pillowcase to an existing piece of clothing. One does not need to become a top chef conversant in the molecular structure of flavor composition, or a professional fashion designer to do these things. Improvisational expertise is the kind of expert practical knowledge adequate to address a specific, pragmatic problem or need.

Jazz Musicians and Practical Theologians as Improvisational Experts

Many writers working in the study of expertise cite jazz music as the quintessential example of improvisation as a highly sophisticated practice. Musicologists, for instance, have studied how jazz players create improvisational music that is "made up on the spot" as a one-off rendering rather than fixed in a written score that is practiced and reproduced time and time again. The improvised music generally remains recognizable to both the musician and the audience as jazz and generally has a kind of effortless aura around its

17 Jean Lave and Etienne Wenger, *Situated Learning: Legitimate Peripheral Participation*, Learning in Doing (Cambridge [England]; New York: Cambridge University Press, 1991); Barbara Rogoff and Jean Lave, *Everyday Cognition: Its Development in Social Context* (Cambridge, Mass.: Harvard University Press, 1984).

production. But behind these musicians' apparently casual ease of composition lie hours and hours of practice that leads to their deep internalizing of musical forms and a musical "culture." The spontaneous variations comprising improvisation are simultaneously made up in the moment yet also are formed within the boundaries of shared and well-practiced norms for jazz composition. Once a player has this deeply internalized knowledge, she has the freedom to improvise because the basic framework of the "rules" for jazz provide a broad yet loosely bounded landscape on which to play, recognizable amid its creativity because it draws on the musical culture of which it is a part.[18] At the same time, the very act of improvisation brings with it the possibility of altering the rules, by virtue of the absence of fixed forms. Sociologist Pierre Bourdieu makes a similar claim about how practices, taking shape within a broader cultural habitus that provides actors with an implicitly held, bounded "sense of the game," also are continually undergoing transformation.[19]

Like jazz musicians, practical theologians employ what I am calling improvisational expertise in the ways we engage various fields of study in our work.[20] This expertise involves high attunement to persons and contexts, employing skills of listening and observing the particular context or case before us to discern what types of knowledge will be helpful in its analysis, and making judgments as to which other possible fields of knowledge should recede to the background in a particular instance. It includes the ability to find, selectively engage, and play with unconventional combinations of theory from diverse fields, akin to the unconventional combinations of notes played by improvisational jazz musicians that, while unusual, still constitute jazz music. Finally, the improvisational expertise of practical theologians, like that of jazz musicians shaped by a largely implicit culture of music that informs their improvisations, optimally takes place within a deeply internalized scholarly habitus that sets out the broad parameters for such experiments while maintaining

18 Aaron Berkowitz, *The Improvising Mind: Cognition and Creativity in the Musical Moment* (New York: Oxford University Press, 2010), 2.

19 Pierre Bourdieu, *The Logic of Practice* (Cambridge: Polity, 1990).

20 Others talking about this idea in relation to practical theology include Bonnie J. Miller-McLemore, "Practical Theological Pedagogy: Embodying Theological Know-How," in *For Life Abundant: Practical Theology, Theological Education, and Christian Ministry*, ed. Craig Dykstra and Dorothy C. Bass (Grand Rapids, MI: Wm. B. Eerdmans Publishing Co., 2008); Katherine Turpin, "Teaching Practical Theologies: Distinctive Pedagogies in Religious Education," *International Journal of Practical Theology* 12, no. 1 (2008); John D. Witvuliet, "Teaching Worship as a Christian Practice," in *For Life Abundant: Practical Theology, Theological Education, and Christian Ministry*, ed. Craig Dykstra and Dorothy C. Bass (Grand Rapids, MI: Wm. B. Eerdmans Publishing Co., 2008).

openness to unforeseen variations. In general terms, the scholarly habitus of practical theologians within which improvisational engagement of other fields occurs involves the conceptual privileging of practice and methods oriented toward interpretation of theology as it arises out of practice. Upon this habitus of practical theological scholarship, significant variations play out.

Not everyone is well suited to playing improvisational jazz. Improvisation is difficult, and some musicians prefer symphonic scores. Like the musician who veers too far from the parameters that allow her sound to be recognizable as music, much less a particular genre such as jazz, or who overshoots his own technical ability to spontaneously riff on a theme, sometimes practical theologians may overextend our reach in the way we use theory from other disciplines. We risk getting it wrong or engaging the other fields beyond our "habitual" areas of knowledge in superficial ways. Part of the reason interdisciplinarity is a conundrum for practical theology, thus, is that the field may well attract people who prefer the risks and ambiguities of improvisational forms of expertise more than the security and certainty of content-mastery types of expertise—but such forms of scholarship remain challenging to carry out on an ongoing basis.

The Shaping Power of a Conundrum

Over time, the continual scholarly practice of interdisciplinarity with all its inherent possibilities and dangers forms practical theologians in a set of capacities that come to mark our work. Practical theologians become quite adept, even expert, at scanning and selecting the "usable" elements from a much larger canon of literature. We become skilled in the art of collaborating with others who can assist us toward a more adequate level of knowledge in a new field we need to employ, and in the process many of us are shaped by the kind of humility that comes from continual reminders that we cannot do our work without the aid of multiple others.[21] Given that humility often is in short supply in academia, a certain level of expertise in its practice actually may constitute an important contribution to the wider academy! In short, the conundrum that comes from practical theology's interdisciplinary complexity forms

21 The flip side of this can be seen in some scholars who bring an over-inflated sense of their own capacities to their work. I do not mean to suggest that all practical theologians are humble people! What I mean here is that the very act of continually needing to rely on colleagues within and outside of the field for assistance, and the continual posture of being a new learner, has the capacity to shape this characteristic—and practical theologians appear to have more opportunities than scholars in some other fields to be so shaped.

its scholars in particular and unconventional kinds of expertise. These forms of expertise may not be measured with fixed markers such as the granting of academic degrees. The standards by which "good enough knowing" or suitable improvisation can be measured in interdisciplinary work must instead be continually negotiated by scholarly communities because they remain relatively unfixed.

The above exploration of practical theology's complexity does not yield a solution. It does, however, suggest a way to deal constructively with the interdisciplinary conundrum's problem of seemingly infinite choices about which or how many disciplines to engage. This includes: (1) Taking on a grounded-theory approach to interdisciplinarity, selecting those areas most strongly arising out of the research situation itself; (2) Allowing these selections to be tempered by an awareness of one's own interests and limits and by the norms of the community of practical theologians for the appropriate use of fields outside one's training; (3) Remaining in a continual learning mode that is open to being educated in new fields and perspectives as a requisite part of practical theological scholarship; (4) Permitting notions of "good enough" and improvisational expertise to critique regnant understandings of academic expertise that work to paralyze interdisciplinary forays into new knowledge construction; and (5) Developing scholarly- and spiritual-practices that increase one's ability to tolerate some discomfort, heightened vulnerability, and ambiguity for the sake of one's larger academic or ministerial endeavors. While this position is admittedly uncomfortable and does not ultimately resolve the conundrum's problem of being in over one's head in the complexity of multiple disciplines, it does offer a provisional path for embracing the valuable possibilities the conundrum presents that can ultimately add to our work.

The pathway I name here underscores interdisciplinarity's positive possibilities. Even so, as I have suggested above, the dangers of interdisciplinary work are very real to me. There is the risk of engaging in a kind of scholarship that is "ten miles wide but only one inch deep" and of conceptual muddiness or methodological sloppiness that comes from borrowing tools and ideas outside the intellectual habitus of one's own formation. When one must continually engage in new learning across diverse disciplines, research and writing become rather inefficient. And collaborative interdisciplinary work may require participation in multiple guilds, which can be an expensive enterprise in time and money. But perhaps one of the greatest risks in this work is the possibility of being so completely committed to it as to become a "scholar without a country," not recognized as belonging anywhere in particular. This is an issue of professional identity that takes us to the second part of the interdisciplinary conundrum.

Interdisciplinary Scholarship and Identity

Education professor Myra Strober, in her study of interdisciplinary faculty seminars, speaks of the boundary-work performed by disciplines. Disciplines set boundaries around the types and methods of work conducted and "police the territory from incursions by others,"[22] thus becoming sites for the performance of academic identities. She highlights the formative role of apprenticeship in a discipline in terms of the structuring of habits of mind and ways of perceiving reality. What is most difficult in interdisciplinary conversation is not the inability to understand the concepts of another area of study. It is the ability to recognize and value the alternative ways of thinking and knowing utilized by other disciplines.

To put it plainly, disciplinary identities are only partially about the content of knowledge. Strober found that the experience of talking to a colleague outside of one's disciplinary home often was the functional equivalent of a conversation across cultures. The principle difficulty came not with the ability to understand what colleagues in other disciplines know about, but rather in understanding *how they think*: "not that they did not understand one another's language; it was that they did not accept one another's fundamental beliefs about how to ascertain knowledge."[23] This means that for serious interdisciplinary collaboration between scholars to happen, scholars must "become ethnographers of their own disciplines, encouraging one another to understand how their disciplines' habits of mind and cultural practices structure their thinking."[24]

What makes this so difficult, of course, are the power relations between different disciplinary groups within the academy.[25] Disciplines function as "institutionally structured epistemic and social practices, with specific culture, professional identities, histories and teaching practices. As such, disciplines are always 'fields of power,'"[26] and their institutional arrangements express status distinctions. Practical theology's interdisciplinary work in the current century

---

22 Strober, *Interdisciplinary Conversations*, 60.

23 Strober, *Interdisciplinary Conversations*, 4.

24 Strober, *Interdisciplinary Conversations*, 162.

25 See Bonnie Miller-McLemore's chapter 8 in this volume on "The Politics of Knowledge" (pp. 190–218).

26 Jaco S. Dreyer, "Practical Theology and Intradisciplinary Diversity: A Response to Miller-McLemore's Five Misunderstandings About Practical Theology," *International Journal of Practical Theology* 16.1 (2012): 39.

converges with postmodern re-formations of the academy whereby boundaries between disciplines are increasingly problematized and challenged. But even in this convergence, interdisciplinary work can threaten identities protected by still existing disciplinary boundaries when the need to utilize resources of other disciplines to do practical theological work situates us outside of the academic- and social-positioning that adjudicate our "rights" to do so. What makes me competent to use this discipline's knowledge, approach, or method in my own work, if I have not been apprenticed, educated, and socialized specifically into that particular field?

I recognize why persons from other disciplines might have this question about practical theologians' engagements with their work. A parallel experience happens with my own negative reaction to scholars from other fields who recently have "jumped on the practices bandwagon," whether out of genuine interest or in relation to availability of funding. In the same way that mere interest in sociology or economics does not provide me with the habits of mind and scholarly worldview held by those internal to these disciplines, a casual interest in practice as a fashionable concept, coupled with the use of some of the vocabulary of practical theology, does not provide automatic access to the more complex layers of understanding that come from disciplinary apprenticeship of scholars in practical theology. I and other practical theologians have at times felt ill-at-ease when a scholar from an "outside" discipline such as systematic theology lands an appointment as a practical theologian. Such is the conundrum: we can value acts of interdisciplinary border crossings at the same time that we assert the sometimes-competing good of respect for focused, deep disciplinary expertise. There is no escape from the discomfort created by inhabiting these two seemingly irreconcilable positions.

Such discomfort, whether on my part as a practical theologian concerned about how others engage my field, or on the part of another scholar whose disciplinary boundaries I am stepping over in my interdisciplinary endeavors, is a protectionist instinct by those wanting to insure that the academic issues, methods, and processes at the heart of their passions will be well-represented by others. But it also concerns power in the form of the symbolic capital represented by disciplinary discourse. What power relations and status positionings are at stake when persons from outside of, or on the edge of, a discipline's boundaries begin to claim a place and a voice in relation to that field? If anyone can be a practical theologian by self-declaration, the symbolic capital vested in such an identity declines in direct proportion to the erasure of distinction.[27] For scholars in disciplines that typically possess higher symbolic

27 Pierre Bourdieu, *Distinction: A Social Critique of the Judgement of Taste* (Cambridge, Mass.: Harvard University Press, 1984).

capital within the academy than practical theology, the sense that they are losing something important with the incursions of others into their territories can promote hardening of the boundaries that define and/or exclude one from membership in the discipline. In concrete terms, careers may be at stake here in such protectionist moves, as promotion and tenure decisions in the academy may be made by scholars in other disciplines who do not understand or value how practical theologians engage these other fields. Given such political realities with their material consequences, practical theologians may need to make strategic decisions to (1) recruit reliable interpreters of practical theology's interdisciplinarity among colleagues who can provide a bridge to others who are more concerned with protecting their territory; (2) temporarily "mute" the use of certain outside disciplines for the sake of political expediency; or, (3) risk misunderstanding or censure for the sake of one's scholarship. Any or all of these choices can be legitimate in a given circumstance within the academy.

There is yet another strategy that practical theologians may need to adopt around matters of hiring and remaining employed. Given that most academic positions still use titles expressing single-disciplinarity, practical theologians must learn to "speak within the language" of particular constitutive disciplines in order to be understood by others. This is not a matter of being deceptive or confused: we are not trying to "sound like" experts in a discipline we cannot claim knowledge of within our practical theological work. Rather, this strategy is akin to what biblical theologian Walter Brueggemann names in his interpretation of I Kings 18, the story of the dramatic encounter between Israel and Judah taking place at the wall of the city. In front of the wall, the king of Israel uses the language of international diplomacy (here, Aramaic) to talk with Assyrian negotiators. Behind the wall, however, the king utilizes the community's language, Hebrew, to express his grief and talk with his own people.[28] To communicate well requires different languages depending upon the context and audience. In a similar way, practical theologians may need to distinguish between occasions in which it is more appropriate to use insider, interdisciplinary language to depict our work and those times when a "language beyond the wall" that can communicate well to people outside of practical theology is more helpful.

For practical theologians, not all difficulties concerning complexity and power relations with interdisciplinary scholarship take place in relation to the engagement of fields outside of practical theology. Practical theology also involves scholars in doing interdisciplinary work internal to its own borders:

28 Walter Brueggemann, "2 Kings 18–19: The Legitimacy of a Sectarian Hermeneutic," *Horizons in Biblical Theology* 7, no. 1 (1985).

within the diversity comprising practical theology itself, multiple subdisciplines operate side by side, and no scholar possesses expertise across all of them. Yet the very enterprise of practical theology assumes at least some basic familiarity and facility across these *intra*disciplinary conversation areas, as well as with disciplines beyond the scope of the theological curriculum.

The flip-side of this openness to intradisciplinary identity fluidity is a defensive policing of internal boundaries between subdisciplines that sometimes goes on within practical theology. I continue to experience a certain suspicion, and even professional snubbing, from some colleagues in one subdisciplinary area because my scholarly work does not reside exclusively within that area. Over the years, as a practical theologian I have worked in faculty positions with a primary portfolio teaching pastoral theology and pastoral care in some institutions, and then religious education in others, largely because the job categories of most academic institutions maintain such divisions between subspecialties. Fortunately, in most cases I have experienced the freedom to work and teach both within and across subfields in practical theology. At the same time, though, I observe that the strong policing of subspecialty boundaries from within practical theology can pose real problems around employment, when search committees wonder if a job candidate is "really" a pastoral theologian or religious educator or homiletician. Interdisciplinary competencies means making choices about guild participation that unsettles traditional understandings of what it means to belong to a professional group, felt even more acutely if one's employment record shows frequent border crossings between practical theological subdisciplines (often coupled with an unconventional path of training).

As the field of practical theology has undergone redevelopment and growth over the past few decades, some scholars most fully identified with at least one of its so-called subdisciplines balk at what they experience as the colonizing desires of the field of practical theology. As one colleague put it, "Religious education has been its own discipline for ages. Now practical theology comes along and decides to make religious education a subdiscipline of practical theology. Says who? My discipline is religious education." Others, however, claim dual citizenship in one or more subdisciplines and practical theology: Bonnie Miller-McLemore, widely known as a practical theologian, in her 2011 presidential address to the International Academy of Practical Theology, reasserted the distinction between practical and pastoral theologies, and declared herself "a pastoral theologian at heart."[29] Practical theologians are people with multiple identities.

29 Bonnie J. Miller-McLemore, "Five Misunderstandings About Practical Theology," *International Journal of Practical Theology* 16.1 (2012): 17.

Negotiating Distinctive Identities Amid Indistinct Borders

For several years, I have been part of a group of scholars bound together by a shared interest in the research practices of congregational studies as a way to learn about religious organizations. Congregational studies as a research methodology generally has its main disciplinary home within the sociology of religion, although scholars from many other fields make use of it in research and practice. The strongest voices in the scholars' group of which I am a part are its sociologists who were the group's founding members and who also make up a majority of its membership. The group administers a fellowship for newer scholars across diverse disciplines, all of whom conduct some kind of research in their fields that involves the study of congregations or other religious organizations. And each year in the process of vetting new research proposals, I hear someone in the group, usually a sociologist, comment on a proposal as "another one of those practical theology-type proposals," code language for a project that lacks conceptual clarity or methodological sophistication in the eyes of the sociologist-speaker.

My experience is that in that moment, such a remark can be made with impunity in my presence because as a member of the group I am granted implicit, temporary status as an "honorary sociologist" of sorts, and my tribal affiliation as a practical theologian becomes invisible. Because I (ostensibly unlike those *other people* identified with practical theology in such comments) have some training in the field and somewhat understand, make use of, and value the particular ways of thinking and methods of inquiry that constitute the *habitus* of sociology as an academic discipline, in this context my identity as a practical theologian is temporarily subsumed under the congregational studies mantle, a border-land that intersects sociology and practical theology.

And yet, it also remains clear that just because I have training in and utilize resources from the discipline of sociology strongly in my work—just because I have a deep appreciation for and understanding of the worldviews that inform the sociological imagination—I am *not* a sociologist nor do I claim to be so. My professional identity is shaped by interests in a kind of scholarly and pastoral work that engages communities in strengthening their ministries of compassion and justice, not just in learning *about* these ministries. I am committed to a kind of research, for instance, that can be of practical significance for a church sorting out how to improve upon the relative adequacy of their theological claims for the kind of communal life they seek to embody. Such a commitment is different from scholarship that simply describes and analyzes the gaps between what a faith community wants to be and the kinds of faith commitments they actually embody in their practices, without theological reflection on those claims.

As a practical theologian engaged in congregational studies, I am as interested in the theological claims (implicit or explicit) that these congregations express, for example, as I am in the other factors (social and organizational) that make up congregational life and that are visible through the ways they go about assembling for worship, making decisions, structuring their life together, dealing with material resources, and dealing with conflicts. For me, the theologies arising out of such practices constitute a primary focus for research. Such normative *theological* interests in the wellbeing of these faith communities and in their transformation mark me as a practical theologian who holds other goals for scholarship and research than some of my sociological colleagues, whose work is differently valuable and productive. This goes beyond having different styles or methodologies for research. In fact, we hold different professional identities and aims.

When colleagues from other fields label a research proposal "another one of those practical theology proposals," they may be genuinely responding to a poorly conceived research proposal that adopts the trappings of social science research without an adequate understanding of how to use these overlapping methods well for their own purposes. But sometimes I as a practical theologian see strengths in a practical theology study that go unnoticed by colleagues who claim their professional identities in other disciplines. This underscores the way disciplinary distinctions form scholars to attend to certain kinds of questions, use similar methods in different ways, and construct arguments out of dissimilar logics, shaping particular identities out of academic practices. Contrasting habits of mind and patterns of action make it hard for scholars to understand and converse with one another across disciplines. Strober notes that "not only do participants [in interdisciplinary conversations] have to learn one another's disciplinary language, they have to learn one another' approaches to knowledge acquisition and truth claims, as well as one another's styles of intellectual interaction.... Disciplines train people to see quite different realities."[30]

I sometimes can recognize strengths in the research proposals from practical theologians that sociologists may not see because I have an intuitive understanding of how those who write these proposals think about their projects. I call this the "field logic" of practical theology, referring to the particular ways of approaching questions that many persons apprenticed in practical theology utilize. This involves a process of attending to a complicated dance between a particular context and situation in the here-and-now, using whatever forms of knowledge are needed to help make sense of it.[31] These features

30 Strober, *Interdisciplinary Conversations*, 155.

31 See Katherine Turpin's chapter 10 in this volume (pp. 250–275) on "The Complexity of Local Knowledge."

occur alongside the use of knowledge of religious traditions/religious experience that allows practical theologians to name and theorize the kinds of theological meaning-making that arises out of lived practices themselves, toward strategically chosen actions that can make a difference in lives/practices/persons/communities/policies.

In practice, this work may well involve practical theologians in using a skill set very similar to that engaged by social anthropologists, sociologists, social workers, scholars engaged in educational research, and psychologists (among others) who also are inquiring into a human situation or context with the goal of making sense of it. But practical theologians do so in a way that may be unrecognizable to persons from overlapping fields, particularly because we are especially attentive to the theological features of the lives and contexts we investigate, which causes us to see, hear, and write about things somewhat differently.

No Place Like Home?

Interdisciplinarity in practical theology involves yet another identity challenge beyond the difficulty of having one's identity valued and understood by colleagues formed in alternative epistemologies and scholarly practices. When I leave my congregational studies colleague group and my temporary status as an honorary-though-odd quasi-sociologist behind, I do not necessarily go "home" to a land called the Practical Theology Discipline where my identity is automatically recognized, accepted, and unproblematically understood. In fact, my experience as a practical theologian deeply engaged with other fields such as sociology, and working at times in close collaboration with sociologists, means that the way I perform my identity *as a practical theologian* also shifts. I do not "do practical theology" in the same way as I did before these deep intersections with other disciplines. Deep interdisciplinary collaboration works not only to provide "value added" new ways of thinking and acting from the so-called outside discipline for any one specific scholarly project, but also re-shapes ways of engaging one's *own* disciplinary identity and work. Collaborations with sociologists and others have changed the way I do my own practical theological work and evaluate that of others, to be more critical of the conclusions drawn from qualitative research, for example, or to take a harder look at how methods of study line up with a researcher's central questions. Such input from other fields unsettles scholarly identities back at home. In interdisciplinary scholarship, disciplinary homes are not entirely stable spaces.

Historian Catherine Manathunga speaks to this phenomenon when she borrows three themes from post-colonial theory to describe the identity positions of interdisciplinary scholars in the academy. Interdisciplinary research, she says, locates scholars in "liminal space between and across diverse disciplinary cultures. The disciplinary identity that [researchers] may have originally formed becomes challenged and changed by [their] engagement with different disciplinary discourses and practices."[32] Such spaces, while uncomfortable at times, also can be generative and highly creative. In fact, Manathunga's point, taking her cue from post-colonial theory's inversion of the dynamics of oppression into spaces of creative resistance and feminist epistemological claims of the "epistemological privilege of the oppressed," is that a place of liminality in between disciplines is more insightful and opportune for scholarship. Interdisciplinarity disrupts static identities, and while such disruptions complicate many professional relationships, these disruptions have positive features as well. Sometimes the transgressive act of border crossing between academic fields entailed in interdisciplinary work also creates small moments of scholarly coherence akin to other complex identity positionings some of us experience related to gender, race, sexuality, immigration status, religion, and nationality.

Manathunga names two additional concepts from post-colonial theory that further underscore the identity issues at work in practical theology. The first is Homi Bhabha's term of "unhomeliness," describing the estrangement and dislocation experienced by people like refugees and cultural minorities, which Manathunga parallels to the scholarly dislocation of interdisciplinary work. A practical theologian focusing on religious education, for example, might find herself unwelcome in her school's theology division, but equally lacking credentials (even with a Ph.D. in an educational discipline) in its school of education. The second concept, transculturation, as used in post-colonial theory refers to changes that take place in convergences between cultures. Manathunga contends that in the play of power relations between groups in (colonialist) convergences, subordinated groups maintain agency as they still make choices about what from the dominant culture they use and how they will use it. As an analogy to interdisciplinary scholarship, Manathunga sees this position as one of hopeful possibility:

> Interdisciplinary researchers have power and agency in their interactions with the different disciplines they work between to adopt certain practices and knowledge. For example, researchers may decide to adopt aspects of ways of thinking and being common in the other disciplines they

---

32 Catherine Manathunga, "Post-Colonial Perspectives on Interdisciplinary Identities," in *Academic Research and Researchers*, ed. Angela Brew and Lisa Lucas (Maidenhead: McGraw Hill Education, 2009), 133.

> are engaging with on interdisciplinary projects and may return to their own disciplines with the goal of incorporating some of these new practices, changing disciplinary cultures in the process. The impact of transculturation on interdisciplinary researchers' identities is more than an issue of temporary accommodation or resistance to certain disciplinary cultural practices: it is also a form of adaptation that may create new cultural possibilities.[33]

As I understand her intentions in mapping onto interdisciplinary scholarship the politics of subordination and domination, Manathunga poses interdisciplinary scholars in a minoritized position because they so often remain situated as outsiders to some or all of the fields in which they work. Such comparisons to post-colonial perspectives express why interdisciplinarity poses such a conundrum for practical theology: it is simultaneously a space of rich opportunity and also of potential painful identity exclusion.

Concept Migration and Practical Theological Politics

In this essay's earlier discussions around complexity, I reference the possibility that scholars in other fields may view practical theologians as people whose reach exceeds their grasp when we borrow ideas and theories from other disciplines and then use them for very different purposes. The concern in terms of identity is whether a scholar must actually have studied within a particular field and thereby be schooled in the identity of that field at some level in order to have the ability to make use of certain concepts associated with it. Dutch cultural theorist Mieke Bal writes about the phenomenon of "traveling concepts," or what happens when interdisciplinary inquiry allows a concept having a core place or long intellectual history in one field to "travel" into another field where it comes to be used by scholars with a somewhat different meaning. On the one hand, Bal argues against what she refers to as the "diffusion" of concepts, in which particular concepts rendered portable between disciplines are used in a manner akin to casually applying a label, a phenomenon that happens when a concept becomes fashionable. In such an instance, the concept only names but does not theorize its object, says Bal. It is a careless employment of a label apart from the search for new meanings that would make such traveling productive.

Bal points to the ability of traveling concepts to bring life into the academy by evoking new meanings when their travel includes a new engagement in the

33 Manathunga, "Post-Colonial Perspectives," 133.

development of meanings salient and generative for the new field of study. She offers "hybridity," a concept that traveled from its origins in nineteenth century biology where it had racist overtones, to its location in post-colonial discourse where it has "come to indicate an idealized state of postcolonial diversity... because it traveled.... All of these forms of travel render concepts flexible. It is this change-ability that becomes part of their usefulness for a new methodology that is neither stultifying and rigid nor arbitrary or 'sloppy.'... The travelling nature of concepts is an asset rather than a liability."[34]

Against those whose "primary concern is the 'correct' philosophical understanding of concepts," Bal thus suggests that concepts traveling between historical times and across disciplines can be constructive when "the primary concern is not 'correct' but 'meaningful' use."[35] She advocates therefore for a space that is neither the mere labeling diffusion described above, nor the rigidly bound assertion of a single legitimate way to use a concept, opting instead for "a kind of productive confusion rather than a precision of concepts."[36] For practical theologians, Bal's thinking offers a reason for shaking off overly fastidious concerns of our own, or the critiques of others, that we cannot speak at all about "x" concept because, having not read everything ever written on "y," we will not use it correctly.

Left with Riddles

By definition, a conundrum cannot be solved easily or in only one way. So I will not attempt here to write a conclusion that somehow solves the riddles posed at the beginning of this essay or fixes all the difficulties inherent in interdisciplinary scholarship among practical theologians. Instead, I will summarize what I see as some of the most significant implications for our discipline of working through this conundrum. First, I expect that increasingly our scholarship will be formed in ways that do not require allegiance to a subdiscipline. Scholars will continue to have greater and lesser interests in different subject areas within the field and will develop competencies pertaining to that area more than others. If, as I suggest earlier, interdisciplinarity itself is constitutive, then scholars formed in this way of thinking increasingly are socialized into practices and processes of scholarship that always already include

34 Bal and Marx-MacDonald, *Travelling Concepts*, 23–24.

35 Bal and Marx-MacDonald, *Travelling Concepts*, 17.

36 Bal and Marx-MacDonald, *Travelling Concepts*, 16–17.

these cross interrogations between disciplines. This is already the current direction: scholars of practical theology start out formed in interdisciplinarity itself, where the various subdisciplines are sites of specific enactment/embodiment of scholarly practice rather than anchors of identity within a larger arena of practical theology. With practical theologian Aaron Ghiloni I am saying that such interdisciplinarity is not just a 'style change': "To write theology that is interdisciplinary, pragmatic, practical and aesthetic is to write a different sort of theology."[37]

Second, embedded with the claim that interdisciplinarity's complexity invites humility is the implication that our work needs to make room for more consultation with scholars whose disciplinary home is in other fields from which we draw. This includes making time for conversations or asking colleagues to read our writing before it goes to press. At the same time that such collaborative endeavors attempt to ensure responsible use of other disciplines, Bal's notion of seeing meaningful uses of "traveling concepts" in interdisciplinary work rather than correct ones points to the breaking down of the unnecessary sense of proprietary rights to knowledge embedded in current disciplinary divides and in intellectual production more generally. Such work foregrounds the public good and the communal context for scholarship ahead of negatively possessive forms of individualism. Living into more fluid identities and borders means having more opportunities to gain skills in collaboration with others across disciplinary boundaries and more chances to practice graciousness in offering our best practices to one another for the larger good of all scholarship.

Finally, since power and its negotiations comprise a continuous feature of social life, practical theologians will continue to need constructive strategies for navigating these dynamics in interdisciplinary endeavors. Even though practical theology does not universally exist in the minoritized position it once held in the academy, it remains the case that interdisciplinary conversations are as much about establishing and reestablishing power arrangements and status positions as they are about content differences. This reality underscores the importance of continuing to strengthen sites for "in-house" conversations with other practical theologians that build solidarity and support for continuing the work. Interdisciplinarity, with its accompanying complexity and identity difficulties for practical theologians, is indeed a conundrum. It also can be a gift for the field of practical theology to steward and offer generously as a part of our contribution to theological knowledge and practice.

37 Aaron J. Ghiloni, "On Writing Interdisciplinary Theology," *Practical Theology* 6, no. 1 (2013): 12.

Bibliography

Ashby, Homer U. "A Black Perspective on Interdisciplinary Work." *Currents in Mission* 31, no. 3 (2004): 172–78.

Bal, Mieke, and Sherry Marx-MacDonald. *Travelling Concepts in the Humanities: A Rough Guide*. Green College Lectures. Toronto: University of Toronto Press, 2002.

Berkowitz, Aaron. *The Improvising Mind: Cognition and Creativity in the Musical Moment*. New York: Oxford University Press, 2010.

Bourdieu, Pierre. *Distinction: A Social Critique of the Judgement of Taste*. Cambridge, Mass.: Harvard University Press, 1984.

Bourdieu, Pierre. *The Logic of Practice*. Cambridge: Polity, 1990.

Brueggemann, Walter. "2 Kings 18–19: The Legitimacy of a Sectarian Hermeneutic." *Horizons in Biblical Theology* 7, no. 1 (June 1985): 1–42.

Cahalan, Kathleen A., and Gordon S. Mikoski, eds. *Opening the Field of Practical Theology: An Introduction*. Lanham, MD: Rowman and Littlefield, 2014.

Dreyer, Jaco S. "Practical Theology and Intradisciplinary Diversity: A Response to Miller-Mclemore's Five Misunderstandings About Practical Theology." *International Journal of Practical Theology* 16, no. 1 (2012): 34–54.

Ghiloni, Aaron J. "On Writing Interdisciplinary Theology." *Practical Theology* 6, no. 1 (2013): 9–33.

Graham, Elaine L. *Words Made Flesh: Writings in Pastoral and Practical Theology*. London: SCM Press, 2009.

Klein, Julie Thompson. *Interdisciplinarity: History, Theory, and Practice*. Detroit: Wayne State University, 1990.

Lattuca, Lisa R. *Creating Interdisciplinarity: Interdisciplinary Research and Teaching among College and University Faculty*. Vanderbilt Issues in Higher Education. 1st ed. Nashville: Vanderbilt University Press, 2001.

Lave, Jean, and Etienne Wenger. *Situated Learning: Legitimate Peripheral Participation*. Learning in Doing. Cambridge [England]; New York: Cambridge University Press, 1991.

Lyall, Catherine, Ann Bruce, Joyce Tate, and Laura Meagher. *Interdisciplinary Research Journeys: Practical Strategies for Capturing Creativity*. New York: Bloomsbury Academic, 2011.

Manathunga, Catherine. "Post-Colonial Perspectives on Interdisciplinary Identities." In *Academic Research and Researchers*, edited by Angela Brew and Lisa Lucas, 133–145. Maidenhead: McGraw Hill Education, 2009.

Mercer, Joyce Ann. *Welcoming Children: A Practical Theology of Childhood*. St. Louis, Mo.: Chalice Press, 2005.

Miller-McLemore, Bonnie J. "Five Misunderstandings About Practical Theology." *International Journal of Practical Theology* 16, no. 1 (2012): 5–26.

Miller-McLemore, Bonnie J. "Practical Theological Pedagogy: Embodying Theological Know-How." In *For Life Abundant: Practical Theology, Theological Education, and Christian Ministry*, edited by Craig Dykstra and Dorothy C. Bass, 170–190. Grand Rapids, MI: Wm. B. Eerdmans Publishing Co., 2008.

Rogoff, Barbara, and Jean Lave. *Everyday Cognition: Its Development in Social Context.* Cambridge, Mass.: Harvard University Press, 1984.

Strober, Myra H. *Interdisciplinary Conversations Challenging Habits of Thought.* 2011. http://site.ebrary.com/lib/yale/Doc?id=10459532%3E.

Sullivan, William M., and Carnegie Foundation for the Advancement of Teaching. *Work and Integrity: The Crisis and Promise of Professionalism in America.* 2nd ed. San Francisco, CA: Jossey-Bass, 2005.

Turpin, Katherine. "Teaching Practical Theologies: Distinctive Pedagogies in Religious Education." *International Journal of Practical Theology* 12, no. 1 (2008): 37–44.

Witvuliet, John D. "Teaching Worship as a Christian Practice." In *For Life Abundant: Practical Theology, Theological Education, and Christian Ministry*, edited by Craig Dykstra and Dorothy C. Bass, 117–48. Grand Rapids, MI: Wm. B. Eerdmans Publishing Co., 2008.

Winnicott, Donald W. "Transitional Objects and Transitional Phenomena; a Study of the First Not-Me Possession." *International Journal of Psychoanalysis* 34, no. 2 (1953): 89–97.

Woodward, James, Stephen Pattison, and John Patton, eds. *The Blackwell Reader in Pastoral and Practical Theology.* Oxford, UK & Malden, Mass.: Blackwell Publishers, 2000.

CHAPTER 8

The Theory-Practice Binary and the Politics of Practical Knowledge[1]

Bonnie J. Miller-McLemore

A few years ago I co-taught a course for first- and second-year doctoral students from different academic areas in our graduate department of religion. As they rotated responsibility for presenting, I noticed a subtle but clear posturing, running just below the surface, written into body postures, gestures, and speaking habits. More credibility and status surrounded those in certain disciplines. For those familiar with theological education, I hardly need say: the more theoretically-focused areas garnered more esteem.

Why did those closer to practice (e.g., homiletics, pastoral theology) question their knowledge, while those who foreground theory (e.g., historical studies, systematic theology) assume an air of greater confidence? Since I served on the committee that oversaw their matriculation, I knew that on paper there was little discrepancy in their credentials. Their behavior was even more peculiar because these students had entered a funded program designed precisely around teaching for the practice of ministry. By the program's standards at least, those closer to pastoral and religious practice should even have had an advantage. What most surprised me was how early in the students' careers such patterns set in and became established. How did people fresh to the academy so readily absorb its unspoken values about theory's dominance?

This moment in time encapsulates a conundrum in relating theory and practice that persists within the theological academy and its constituencies despite ourselves. Despite all that practical theologians have accomplished in advancing the cause of practice—and one of my central points in a 2011 presidential address to the International Academy of Practical Theology stressed the need to quit lamenting our sorry state—the very categories we seek to unsettle, those of theory and practice, continue to entrap us.[2] The terms

---

1 In addition to my appreciation for suggestions from other authors in the volume and my co-editor, I am grateful to Don Ottenhoff, Dorothy Bass, and Kathleen Cahalan for their constructive feedback on drafts of this chapter.

2 Bonnie J. Miller-McLemore, "Five Misunderstandings About Practical Theology," *International Journal of Practical Theology* 16, no. 1 (2012): 5–26.

 | DOI 10.1163/9789004324244_010

theory, *practice*, and *praxis* appear repeatedly in our literature, more frequently than other terms, precisely because a primary disciplinary aim has been to address the modern divorce between academic theology and everyday life.[3] Yet those closer to the ground—those with practical knowledge and those who study it—still struggle to validate our particular kind of knowledge. We claim knowledge in practice but struggle to put that knowledge and its value into words and institutional practice. What exactly is going on here?

Several dynamics intensify the persistent academic devaluation of practical knowledge and practice and make the conundrum difficult to tackle. How theory relates to practice is actually a problem that has evaded satisfactory resolution for centuries, all the way back to Aristotle.[4] As this suggests, epistemology or how we know what we know is in many ways a highly speculative subject, especially for those invested in theology as practical. The categories themselves reflect the hegemony of Western constructs. Why has practical theology's story been told through this terminology anyway? Have we reinforced the very dualism we are critiquing through our obsession with it? And does pursuit of this conjectural matter simply enact the opposite of what practical theologians recommend—attention to the concrete, immediate, and grounded? Theory/practice is simply not a key concern for those in underrepresented communities, as one colleague pointed out.[5] Or, as another colleague objected, "haven't we gotten beyond this?" Finally and possibly most troubling, how do we talk about our own devaluation without sounding like complainers, simply furthering alienation and stymieing progress? Do we further reify the hegemony by talking about it? "It is wise," I remark in my presidential address, "to know the politics out of which our discipline emerged.... But it is no longer necessary to start here or bemoan our status."[6]

---

3 Duncan Forrester, a leading Scottish scholar in the 1990s, claimed that the question of the "proper relationship" between practice and theory "must bulk large in any discussion of the nature of practical theology" in "Can Theology be Practical?" in *Practical Theology: International Perspectives*, ed. Friedrich Schweitzer and Johannes A. van der Ven (Frankfurt am Main: Peter Lang, 1999), p. 22.

4 Systematic theologian Matthew L. Lamb says dissecting the relationship between theory and practice "goes right to the core of the entire philosophical enterprise," and he makes exactly the same claim about systematic theology at the end of his own survey in "The Theory-Praxis Relationship in Contemporary Christian Theologies," *CTSA Proceedings* 31 (1976): 149, 178.

5 See Courtney Goto's chapter 5 in this book where she discusses the demand that she conform to a "template" of key issues that are "taken for granted as neutral" (p. 117).

6 Miller-McLemore, "Five Misunderstandings," 10.

Despite or perhaps because of these intellectual and practical entanglements, the troubled relationship between theory and practice is a problem to which I think we need to return. While repeated negative disciplinary self-portraiture is problematic, gaining greater understanding of the dynamics behind demotion of practical knowledge is needed, even if the historical, conceptual, and political complexities cannot be fully addressed or resolved in one chapter. Questions about how we know what we know in theology and the connections between theoretical and practical knowledge have not gone away and even comprise, I would argue, the heart of practical theology's most valuable contribution. In this chapter, I want to explore why the relationship between theory and practice remains such a stumbling block—that quintessential idiomatic Biblical term for an impediment that leads to human transgression. Why does the dominance of theory remain, despite all the efforts to disrupt it in Marxism, pragmatism, hermeneutics, liberationism, post-structuralism, and practical theology? By examining the enduring influence of the modern theory-practice hierarchy and mixed efforts to undo it, I hope to show that unique perspectives arise precisely when we approach this question from a practical angle. For, as my opening story and many others like it reveal, the question of the proper relationship between theory and practice is more than a theoretical puzzle. It involves us almost immediately in troubled, contested political and institutional tensions and patterns—curricula, habits of learning and speaking, practices of entitlement and non-recognition, naming of disciplines and doctoral areas—that sustain systemic hierarchies and make it difficult to prize practical knowledge. One way to respond to the problem, I argue, is to gain greater consciousness of the power dynamics that surround it. Ultimately, resolution lies not in better theories alone but in changed practices.

The Relentlessness of the Modern Split

It is difficult to think outside the modern epistemological box in which theology is so separate from everyday life, although sometimes we catch a glimpse of times when the disjuncture was less stark. In an eloquent public address, Anglican Bishop Rowan Williams describes a period in the fourteenth and fifteenth centuries when the university was considered a "cell of the Body of Christ" and Christianity was not seen as a series of truth claims for professing or debate but as an "action that created a form of human life" or "instruction for shaping and ordering holy lives" in divine image. So, education was not about "abstract argument... for abstract persons" but about equipping honest and astute guides and interpreters for the Christian life.[7]

This seemingly cohesive medieval worldview seems so utterly foreign today that it is nearly impossible to fathom. Fortunately, Williams does not pine nostalgically for a return to an idyllic pre-divided time but instead deftly makes a case for Christianity's contribution to forming wise citizens capable of making reasonable and just decisions previously given over to the monarchy. I wonder, however, if he is idealistic about our ability to reform education so it fosters a kind of "mediaeval practicality" that avoids the "false polarity between disinterested research and the world of target setting," especially for those in theological education.[8] It seems that the divide that severs theory and practice runs right through those of us in the modern theological academy.

A Swedish colleague states the problem bluntly when he explains the situation in Lund. He says his own context "can only fully be understood against the background of the Lundensian School of Theology," which shaped Swedish theology between 1925 and 1960. For the school's most important representatives and internationally famous theologians, such as Anders Nygren, a "strong division between theory and practice was necessary in order for theology to remain a subject among the sciences." Nygren and his colleagues "believed that the strong connection Schleiermacher made between academic theology and church practices was a mistake."[9] By contrast to Schleiermacher, they wanted to "make theology scientific, and therefore to keep theory and praxis and facts and values apart." In the words of another commentator, the "Lundensian theologians strongly maintained that they did not do normative or constructive theology. They only provided a rigorously objective description of the distinctively and authentically Christian."[10] They sought to make clear to the university that theology was not connected in any way with the confessional church and its (emotional irrational) biases. Theology analyzes but refrains from influencing—or worse, converting—the world.

7 Rowan Williams, "Oxford University Commemoration Day Sermon," *TAO* XLV, no. 1 (Winter 2007), 26, 28–29.

8 Williams, "Commemoration Day Sermon," 27, 30.

9 Thomas Girmalm, "Perspectives on Practical Theology: Searching Tools and Arenas in Modern Swedish Theology Up to the Present Day," p. 1, paper presented at the International Academy of Practical Theology, Amsterdam, July 25, 2011.

10 Arne Rasmusson, "A Century of Swedish Theology," *Lutheran Quarterly* 21, no. 2 (2007): 135, cited by Girmalm, "Perspectives on Practical Theology," 2. See Tone Kaufman's chapter 6 in this volume on persistent questions about normativity in empirical research (pp. 134–162)

Prejudice against practice lingers not just in Sweden, however, but also in others places partly because the bias is built right into institutional infrastructures. In leading Catholic universities, for example, the university theology department does theory (e.g., systematics and history) and farms out practice to separate graduate programs in ministry (e.g., religious education, counseling).[11] In U.S. Protestant seminaries, the term "fourth area" has served for decades to demarcate and segregate "arts" of ministry from so-called classical areas of bible, history, and doctrine. A similar hierarchy characterizes many European contexts where ministerial education occurs in two sites—study of theory in the university followed by time in a seminary focused on practice.

During a 2013 American Academy of Religion (AAR) panel on human senses and religious experience, a religion and psychology colleague observed: "Nowhere has the separation of theory and practice done more damage than in the study of religion and theology."[12] A hyperbole perhaps, and his rationale for the assertion was buried within a paper on embodied cognition that only implicitly challenged the division. But others, such as revisionist theologian David Tracy, have elaborated the point. In several places in the last decade, he distinguishes the "three great separations of modern Western culture"—feeling and thought, form and content, and theory and practice—as devastating for theology and theological education. In an interview, he credits French philosopher Pierre Hadot's *Spiritual Exercises in Ancient Philosophy* for his own change of heart. His description of Hadot's thesis captures the problem well:

> [Hadot] claims that the reason we moderns have such a difficult time reading ancient and non-Western texts stems from the fact that in modernity we've lost a link that was once present in our own culture—and still endures in other contemporary cultures. We generally phrase it as a link "between theory and practice," but I think a more exact way to say what's weak for us is the link "between theological and philosophical theories and spiritual exercises." If you were an ancient Stoic, every day you would practice certain exercises that would heighten awareness of "my" logos and "the" Logos.... There is a need, of course, for a genuine *dis-*

11 See Claire Wolfteich's chapter 11 in this volume on Catholic practical theology (pp. 276–304)

12 James W. Jones, informal panel comment during a session on "Religious Experience Through the Senses," paper presented at the American Academy of Religion, Baltimore, November 24, 2013.

> *tinction* between theory and practice, as the scholastics used to say, but not for separation.[13]

According to Tracy, practical theologians are among those who best understand this disjunction, and they have the means, he says, to recover the "classic link" between theoretical reflection and spiritual exercise. But he himself pictures the recovery as a personal, spiritual, and intellectual enterprise more than an institutional and political matter, and this misperception is partly due to his failure to recognize that the separation is not simply a disconnection but also a hegemony.

Even though many "hope for reform"—as Tracy's interview is titled—there is an institutional and political intractability to the problem. The Association of Practical Theology hosted a panel at another AAR in which institutional leaders were invited to reflect on the accomplishments, challenges, and implications of new initiatives in practical theology. Social ethicist Elizabeth Bounds, then coordinator of a Lilly-funded doctoral program on religious practices and practical theology at Emory (comparable to Vanderbilt's program with which I opened this chapter), identified "theory vs. practice" as one of four dichotomies that have impeded a cohesive institutional identity for their program. Her conversations with faculty members led her to conclude:

> The most pervasive and distorting dichotomy comes from the difficulty Western academic or intellectual culture has had in grappling with the connections between theory and practice. Understanding practice as an application of theory is virtually hardwired into the Western academic mind. While there have been challenges to this assumption: Marx's notion of praxis, the tradition of American pragmatism, and more recently MacIntyre's revival of an Aristotelian account of practical reason, I often find that even when we claim to be working with one or more of these heritages, we academics still have theory lead and practice follow.[14]

---

13 William R. Burrows, "Reasons to Hope for Reform: An Interview with David Tracy," *America* 173 (October 14, 1995), 15–16, emphasis in the original. See also David Tracy, "Traditions of Spiritual Practice and the Practice of Theology," *Theology Today* 55, no. 2 (1998): 235–241 and "A Correlational Model of Practical Theology Revisited," in *Religion, Diversity, and Conflict*, ed. Edward Foley (Berlin: Lit Verlag, 2011), 49–61.

14 Elizabeth Bounds, "Border Crossings: Some Thoughts on the Initiative in Religious Practices and Practical Theology at Emory University," paper presented at the American Academy of Religion, Atlanta, Georgia, November 22, 2003, 3. The other dichotomies include objective vs. engaged study, religious vs. theological, and specialization vs. interdisciplinary approaches.

Like Tracy, Bounds sees practical theology as a resource for correction, and she hopes the Emory initiative will explore approaches that overcome the dualism. But how will the hardwiring be changed, especially if programs like Emory's and Vanderbilt's stand at loggerheads with unexamined powers that be?

An Evasion of Theory-Practice as Political

An evasion of the politics surrounding theory-practice characterizes the longer philosophical discussion. This obfuscation is especially evident in surveys of the theory-practice relationship. Two philosophically trained theologians, Matthew Lamb and Francis Schüssler Fiorenza, wrote articles in 1976 and 1987 respectively offering useful theory-practice typologies that, nonetheless, completely ignore practical biases and inequities. Since people look to such overviews as useful resources in understanding the problem, noting this shortcoming is important. Lamb names five theory-practice positions: primacy of theory (e.g., Catholic scholasticism, orthodoxy), primacy of practice (e.g., liberal Protestantism), primacy of faith-love (e.g., neo-orthodoxy, which eschews the theory-practice question); critical theoretic correlations (e.g., revisionist theology); and critical-praxis correlations (e.g., political and liberation theology). However, because Lamb's analysis equates *practice* with *experience* and *theory* with the Christian *tradition*, he essentially reduces the discussion to a debate in systematic theology over where religious truth or revelation resides (experience or tradition). Consequently, rather than explore how theory-practice relate to one another, his essay turns into a review of twentieth-century schools of systematic thought as a whole, similar to Tracy's "five basic models" (to which he makes frequent reference) and modernist taxonomies such as those of H. Richard Niebuhr and Avery Dulles (which he footnotes).[15] Although Lamb provides a helpful comparative analysis of doctrinal positions from orthodox to progressive, he skirts questions about the complexity of practical knowledge and its academic marginalization regardless of where scholars and schools of thought fall on his continuum.

A decade later, Fiorenza's aims are more practical because he writes for a theological education journal and audience. However, his account of four models for relating theory and practice—hermeneutical, linguistic, liberation, and pragmatic—is quite brief; it is organized around theoretical differences

15 David Tracy's *Blessed Rage for Order: The New Pluralism in Theology* (New York: Seabury, 1975), 22–42; H. Richard Niebuhr, *Christ and Culture* (New York: Harper, 1951); and Avery Dulles's *Models of the Church* (New York: Doubleday, 1974), cited by Lamb, "The Theory-Praxis Relationships," 149.

in university theologies; and the bulk of the essay examines how theological education stands up to science, pluralism, and secularization, returning only peripherally to theory-practice.[16] The anxiety that drives both Fiorenza and Lamb is how to make an intellectual case for Christian truth in modernity, not how theology matters for people in practical contexts. Hence, both focus on non-material issues in one narrow sphere where theology occurs—among systematic theologians. Presented in this fashion, the theory-practice problem is largely speculative. Neither scholar considers its implications for how one teaches, does ministry, or practices faith. In short, the theory-practice problem is a problem in theory, not in practice.

This evasion does not mean that these treatments are without value. Beyond offering categorical distinctions, they provoke critical consciousness about the categories themselves. German political theologian Johann Baptist Metz, Lamb's and Fiorenza's teacher and a pivotal figure in the revitalization of lived theologies of all kinds, credits Lamb's "penetrating" article as significant in his own emerging awareness of the "practical limitations of a purely theoretical critical theology."[17] Key to the development of his own "practical fundamental theology," whose oddity he admits is apparent in its very title, is the need to recognize the limitations of the "standardized subjects… (professors, teachers and specialists in theological studies), places (universities, seminaries colleges), the normal forms of communication (books, lectures, discussions) and interests (the Church's teaching mission)."[18] The professional theologian is not theology's sole executer, a theme that arises again and again in liberation, practical, and contextual theologies influenced by his work. Nevertheless, however admirable Metz's effort to moderate the distinction between laity and professional and to forge a genuine dialectic between theory and practice, his effort is for naught without further institutional analysis of the very sort his own political theology invites.

A Well-Funded Yet Unsuccessful Attempt to Overthrow the Split: A Case Study

The desire to repair the rife between theory and practice is apparent in almost every book on practical theology and theological education from the

16 Francis Schüssler Fiorenza, "Theory and Practice: Theological Education as a Reconstructive, Hermeneutical, and Practical Task," *Theological Education* 23, no. 3 (1987): 113–141.

17 Johan Baptist Metz, *Faith in History and Society: Toward a Practical Fundamental Theology*, trans. David Smith (New York: Seabury, 1980), 50–51, and 79, note 3.

18 Metz, *Faith in History and Society*, 59.

1980s and 1990s. It is helpful to return to this literature because it gives such a pristine picture of an early and not wholly successful attempt to right distorted theory-practice relationships at the beginning of practical theology's twentieth-century revitalization. A constantly repeated refrain throughout the scholarship is criticism of education designed around the application of theory to practice. "Theological schooling is not a movement from theory to the application of theory in practical techniques," contends Yale theologian David Kelsey in a 1997 summary in *Christian Century*. When education is understood purely as the acquisition of ideas, bodies of theory become the "ultimate subject matter," the "curriculum becomes a clutch of unrelated courses," and students focus on becoming "skilled in certain professional techniques" rather than attending to what scholars at this time identified as the real subject matter—"deeper understanding of God."[19]

It is clear from these remarks that Kelsey spent time talking extensively with theological educators such as Edward Farley, Barbara Wheeler, and Joseph Hough about the one-way movement of theory to practice as part of an Association of Theological Schools "Basic Issues Research" in theological education.[20] Introductions to two edited volumes supported by this program tell the same story. As Hough and Wheeler argue in introducing *Beyond Clericalism*, faculty members can do the research they enjoy while absolving their responsibility for its practical implications by seeing their endeavors as providing a "'theory' for the profession" or the "'theory' necessary to undergird the 'practice' of ministry."[21] So, scholars have little motivation to mend their ways.

The next logical step in Hough and Wheeler's description of the problem comes straight from Farley's classic treatise on theological education, *Theologia*, which they identify as a central influence: "Complaints about the irrelevance of academic theory… encourage a focus on practical skills," and ministry becomes captive to the "modern professional model" or what Farley christened the *clerical paradigm*, "with its focus on managing and counseling at the expense of genuine theological reflection."[22] When Wheeler teams up again two

19 David Kelsey, "What's Theological about a Theological School?" *Christian Century*, February 5–12, 1997, 132. See also his book, *To Understand God Truly: What's Theological about a Theological School* (Louisville: Westminster John Knox, 1992).

20 Hereafter, referred to simply as "Issues" literature or discussion. For a bibliography, see W. Clark Gilpin, "Basic Issues in Theological Education: A Selected Bibliography, 1980–1988," *Theological Education* 25 (Spring 1989): 115–121.

21 Joseph C. Hough, Jr. and Barbara G. Wheeler, "Foreword" to Hough and Wheeler, eds., *Beyond Clericalism: The Congregation as a Focus for Theological Education* (Atlanta: Scholars Press, 1988), xxi.

22 Hough and Wheeler, "Foreword," xxi. See also Edward Farley, *Theologia: The Fragmentation and Unity of Theological Education* (Philadelphia: Fortress, 1983), 127–135.

years later with Farley, his voice also comes through in her introduction to their edited book, *Shifting Boundaries*. She applauds the theological turn, a move Farley calls for in *Theologia*. We must disrupt an assumption, "so widely held that it is often taken to be self-evident," she writes, "that theological education is best conceived as the preparation of clergy for their tasks."[23]

Here, I find myself saying somewhat irreverently, "Imagine that—preparing clergy for ministry." In the margin next to Wheeler's dismissal of clergy tasks, I have written: "something really right *and* wrong about this." I recognize that by "tasks" she actually means a truncated focus on techniques, and I understand and even agree with the need for a renewed "theological focus." *Theologia*, Farley's term for sapiential understanding of God, is meant to get beyond theology as mere theory. But if theology is not theory, what is it and how does it function? The answer to this question is less clear, and this problem has not received the attention it deserves. In a sense, the entire case for change in theological education is placed on the return to *theology*, an unstable, unwieldy term for something everyone can favor but few can pin down.

Instead, these accounts share a fixation on the demise of education into "technique." As I argue elsewhere, the "clerical paradigm" becomes the final whipping boy in a long string of historical events troubling theological education—an emphasis that I see as misplaced when it is not accompanied by concern about academic theology that barely touches the ground of everyday life (the "academic paradigm").[24] But only now do I see more clearly that despite a deep desire at the heart of this work to subvert the theory/practice polarity, the standard storyline that runs through this literature still perpetuates a dualism, now reinstated as *thinking theologically* versus *developing practical skills*. That is, despite all good intentions, a theory-practice division and hierarchy rise up once again in the tension between *theologia* and the clerical paradigm.

The persistence of this hierarchical dichotomy actually runs counter to the original intention of the 1980s and 1990s "Issues" literature. The point is not a "matter of the 'academic' side... dumping on the 'practical side,'" Kelsey underscores.[25] In identical fashion, Wheeler clarifies, the proposal that theological education become more theological is not meant "to privilege any current

23 Barbara G. Wheeler, "Introduction" to Wheeler and Edward Farley, eds., *Shifting Boundaries: Contextual Approaches to the Structure of Theological Education* (Louisville: Westminster John Knox, 1991), 9.

24 Bonnie J. Miller-McLemore, *Christian Theology in Practice: Discovering a Discipline* (Grand Rapids: Eerdmans, 2012), Ch. 7, "The Clerical *and* the Academic Paradigm"; and "Five Misunderstandings," 13–15.

25 Kelsey, "What's Theological," 132.

field or area of study" but to question curricular divisions themselves.[26] A few years later, when Wheeler co-writes again, this time with Kelsey for a Farley festschrift, we hear the same refrain. They laud Farley and then explore why his work and the "Issues" literature as a whole had so little effect, and we hear once again: People have misinterpreted the call for a more theological orientation as a "plot to privilege academic theology" and take over the less "theoretical" fields. According to Kelsey and Wheeler, people also fear that the turn to practice will not be intellectually credible, that the "kinds of intellectual rigor traditionally linked with studies in the 'theoretical' fields of the curriculum will be slighted."[27] Uttered twenty years ago, these words could have been said yesterday. These recurrent worries about privilege and rigor actually reveal the persistence of deep institutional fissures by which the theory-practice hierarchy gets reinstantiated in unexamined educational practices.

This divisive way of organizing knowledge, in other words, will not give up the ghost so easily. Why not? Why does Tracy's "great separation" continue to resurface even in places where people genuinely wish to subvert it? Why is it so entrenched? This question plagues the discussion and goes to the heart of my argument. My hunch is that answering this question will require further study of two important dynamics: first, political power within the theological academy; and second, the distinction between theoretical and practical knowledge. Although this chapter focuses primarily on the first dynamic, the overarching question remains: Can the difference between theory and practice be understood in a way that yields respect for each rather than hierarchy and disregard?

A Sociology of Theological Knowledge

In his 1985 book *Constructing Local Theologies*, now in its tenth printing, Robert Schreiter sketches a sociology of theological knowledge that begs for further elaboration. He is among the few then and now who extend the political analysis suggested by Latin American liberation theology to the theological school itself. He is also singular in questioning the modern sovereignty within academy and church alike of one kind of theology—theology as sure

26 Wheeler, "Introduction," 10.

27 David H. Kelsey and Barbara G. Wheeler, "New Ground: The Foundations and Future of the Theological Education Debate," in *Theology and the Interhuman: Essays in the Honor of Edward Farley*, ed. Robert R. Williams (Valley Forge, Pennsylvania: Trinity Press International, 1995), 189–190.

knowledge. Almost all other attempts to classify types of theology ignore such politics.

A sociology of knowledge traces cultural dynamics and political pressures behind the construction of human concepts. In Schreiter's words, it asks how "certain ideas or ways of thinking become prevalent at a particular point in time."[28] Its roots go back to Marx and later German sociologists, such as Karl Mannheim and Max Scheler, who shared the conviction that knowledge is driven or at least powerfully shaped by class interests and ideology. A sociology of theological knowledge therefore investigates theological reflection as a practice shaped by cultural conditions.

There is nothing new today, of course, about the idea that Christian theology is shaped by politics and social context. Over the last several decades, people have argued convincingly from a number of angles that class, race, ethnicity, gender, orientation, ability, age, and other factors shape how one imagines God, faith, Christian community, human sin, and salvation. In the three decades since Schreiter's work, scholars have found other resources in post-colonial theory, for example, and in Michel Foucault's corpus to extend even further the analysis of power and knowledge. In fact, Schreiter recognizes his own debt to liberation theologians who were among the first to raise questions in 1960s about theology as the property of a bourgeois class. Along Marxist lines, they sought to return theological authority to the poor. Theology comprises far more than words, they insisted, and is most fundamentally embodied in actions that liberate the captive and free the oppressed.

What was new in Schreiter was his intimation that the theological school is itself a culture worth investigating. To be clear, this is my reading of what he accomplishes; he himself puts this forward more by implication than by direct assertion. But his argument leads inescapably to this conclusion. The entire Christian scholarly corpus is merely a "series of local theologies" to use his words.[29] More important, academic theology is just one cultural instantiation among others, not the superlative or only such happening. "What has counted for theology since the thirteenth century in Western Christianity," he observes, is no longer the whole of theology, if it ever was. This form extols a university model of knowledge, "with its emphasis on clarity, precision, and relation to

28 Robert J. Schreiter, *Constructing Local Theologies* (Maryknoll, NY: Orbis, 1985, 2002, Tenth printing), 78. He cites Karl Mannheim, *Ideology and Utopia: An Introduction to the Sociology of Knowledge* (New York: Harcourt, Brace and World, 1955 [1936]) and *Essays on the Sociology of Knowledge* (Oxford: Oxford University Press, 1952).

29 Schreiter, *Constructing Local Theologies*, 32.

other bodies of knowledge."[30] Its proponents assume that this universally-valid theology should be applied to local communities and that the professionally trained theologian plays *the* key role in doing so.

Most Christians have bought wholeheartedly into this construction. Indeed, most people in congregations feel "they do not have 'real' theology until they have theology as sure knowledge."[31] They seldom see their own words and actions in the church and their lives as theological. The word *theology* is associated with an endeavor removed from daily encounter and located in theological schools and ecclesial doctrines. This model of theology as sure knowledge or *scientia* has loomed "so large in the West, and is so often held up as the theological ideal elsewhere," Schreiter says, "that it is hard to think of it as one form of theology alongside others" even though it is itself embedded within its own particular culture.[32] A kind of false consciousness covers over its material location and elevates this form over other forms.

Schreiter makes two moves here that challenge the politics of theological knowing. First, he explores local theologies that relativize the authority of the professional theologian, recognizing complimentary roles of lay leaders in the Christian community as well as what he calls prophets, poets, insiders, and outsiders, all of whom contribute to the development of theology. Second, in identifying "theology as sure knowledge" as only one of many kinds, he exposes ways in which its dominance has slighted three other forms, which he names as theology as *variations on sacred texts*, theology as *wisdom*, and theology as *praxis*. In a word, he questions the "very paradigms of [theological] thought themselves."[33] Mapping local theologies offers fresh categories, language, and grids by which people might better discern theologies in context. Moreover, naming the multiple forms of theology underscores the plurality and power dynamics.

It is important to note that in a sociology of knowledge a typology is valuable not just for its specific content (e.g., these four forms of theology) but also for the ideological work that it accomplishes. That is, a typology is more than a classificatory tool that sorts out kinds of theology; it is a political tool that reveals systems of power. Broadening our awareness of the "range of possible forms of theological expression" is "especially important," Schreiter insists, because of the temptation for one group to "judge another group's theology as

30 Schreiter, *Constructing Local Theologies*, 4.
31 Schreiter, *Constructing Local Theologies*, 91.
32 Schreiter, *Constructing Local Theologies*, 89.
33 Schreiter, *Constructing Local Theologies*, 77.

not being 'real' theology, or as being more or less sophisticated." Such dynamics are "odious," he says, and based on an unjust "comparison of qualitatively different entities."[34] Although he does not say so explicitly at this point, those inclined toward theology as a science—that is, most or all of us in academe—bear the heaviest burden of guilt for the competition deeply woven into university infrastructures and the patterns of dominance that spill over into religious communities. Typically, we judge other forms of knowledge "by sure-knowledge standards" and find them wanting, leading "to the situation today where it is now a struggle to relearn how a community engages in theological reflection."[35] In other words, a typology not only describes modes of theology; it uncovers and challenges hierarchies of knowledge, affirms suppressed knowledge, and calls for a repositioning of alternative forms.

Of course, Schreiter has his blinders, more easily seen in hindsight. He understood culture as a cohesive holistic way of life, a view that postmodern anthropologists now question.[36] But, if anything, today's redefinition of culture as plural, fluid, fragmentary, and eclectic only furthers his challenge to theology as conventionally understood in distilled holistic doctrinal and academic forms. He also seems oblivious of a parallel interest in "local theologizing" in the pastoral and practical theologies that were developing largely in Protestant institutions from mid-century into the 1980s, none of which appear in his text.[37] Nor does he imagine further implications of the liberationist theory on which he draws. As a Catholic theologian, practical and liberation theologies likely had ambiguous, perhaps even unwelcome, connotations when he wrote the book, which predated much of the 1980s practical theology discussion and the growing acceptance of liberation theology. More important for my purposes than these deficiencies, however, his book significantly advances insight into how theological institutions deform theology. Merely recognizing theologies as plural raises significant question about justice among the diverse forms. In turning from philosophy to the social sciences, naming the disdain for the "religion of the people" in colonial theology, and questioning the property ownership of theological construction by an elite, *Constructing*

34 Schreiter, *Constructing Local Theologies*, 80.

35 Schreiter, *Constructing Local Theologies*, 90.

36 See Kathryn Tanner, *Theories of Culture: A New Agenda for Theology* (Minneapolis: Augsburg Fortress, 1997). However, she tends to reduce theology's complexity to a two-fold binary—academic and everyday theology—even though she recognizes theology as itself a "material social practice" (p. 72).

37 Schreiter lists five new forms of theologizing, including local and contextual, but does not include pastoral and practical theologies (pp. 5–6).

Local Theologies was a daring book for its time, perhaps even incendiary in certain circles. No doubt Schreiter was keenly aware of the power relationships he was challenging within his own context and beyond.

Interrogating Theory-Practice as a Political Binary

In the last decade, religion scholars have interrogated the intellectual category of *religion* as an artificial Western construct, fabricated as a colonialist category to contain "other" cultures.[38] But few have asked how the category of *theology* itself has functioned in similar ways to sustain power and control knowledge in the academy itself.

This oversight is astonishing when one thinks about it. Early liberation leaders and political theologians certainly raised questions about the hegemony of professional Western theologians. But once the academy absorbed the critique of oppression of the poor and applied it to multiple venues such as race and sex, few people extended the inquiry to theological schools themselves and the stratified relationship between theory and practice in the organization of disciplines and curriculum, perhaps because we would be indicting ourselves. *Theology* as a freighted term somehow rises above the fray within its own academic institutions. We analyze hegemony and hierarchies of knowledge almost everywhere else but in our own backyard. The "praxis" needing investigation, in other words, is that of the production of theological knowledge, a kind of ethnography of our own academic habits and behaviors.[39]

A closer look at 1980s and 1990s publications, however, reveals ways in which the "Issues" literature actually began to disrupt previously unquestioned power structures by naming what anthropologist Pierre Bourdieu describes as the *habitus* or deeply embedded habits and practices of theological education. The organizers of *Beyond Clericalism*, for example, question the "almost automatic tendency" of those in the "so-called classical fields" of assigning "anything to do with ministry to the practical or ministry field," inevitably turning curricular review into a battle over "theory" and "practice."

38 See, for example, early Marxist liberation texts, such as Georges Casalis, *Correct Ideas Don't Fall from the Skies: Elements for an Inductive Theology*, trans. from the French by Sister Jeanne Marie Lyons and Michael John (Maryknoll, NY: Orbis, 1984, originally published 1977), and more recent postcolonialist work, such as Richard King, *Orientalism and Religion: Postcolonial Theory, India, and 'the Mystic East'* (London and New York: Routledge, 1999).

39 See also Joyce Mercer's chapter 7 in this volume and her reference to Myra Strober (p. 177).

They name the "vested interests" of faculties in sustaining the status quo and identify the organization of theological studies into discrete disciplines as the "most critical *political fact* of life" in seminaries.[40] A few years later, Wheeler contends that a theory-to-practice movement is "codified and continuously re-presented" by the "structure of studies," a phrase she repeats throughout her essay. The "presuppositional package" that orders the disciplines is "more than a pedagogical arrangement; it is also a *socioeconomic reality*." It is "rarely scrutinized"; it is "simply taken for granted, and its power to shape perceptions and behavior goes unnoticed."[41] Finally, in a culminating assessment of the 1980s and 1990s "Issues" literature, Kelsey and Wheeler imply that the failure to understand how educational institutions operate on the ground is one reason for the literature's limited impact. They gleaned this insight from feminist and Latin American theologies, translated through Rebecca Chopp who criticizes the discussion as highly ideational, removed from the concrete "historical, cultural and symbolic factors at work." The analysis is "unrealistic and distant from the way things actually are."[42] In response, Kelsey and Wheeler call for ethnographic studies of institutional cultures—"studies that describe the practices of schools in thick detail." A few years later, Wheeler spearheads a project contrasting a mainline and an evangelical seminary.[43] However, although the study captures well student experience and school environment, it remains entirely on the surface in terms of academic politics.

Wheeler and company are on the right track; they just do not go far enough in spelling out the stratification that haunts hallowed halls and sanctuaries. In some ways, they are not that far removed from two leaders of the discussion—Kelsey and Farley—who confess that they refrain in their major works from comment on the actual "institutionality" of theological education and focus instead on the conceptual or the "ironically utopian," as Kelsey says.[44] In *Theologia*, Farley quotes Foucault and promises an "archaeology of the theological

40 Hough and Wheeler, "Foreword," x, xxi–xxii, emphasis added.

41 Wheeler, "Introduction," 11–14, emphasis added.

42 Kelsey and Wheeler, "New Ground," 192. They cite Rebecca Chopp's book, *Saving Work: Feminist Practices of Theological Education* (Louisville: Westminster John Knox, 1995), 9–11. See also Chopp, "Practical Theology and Liberation," in *Formation and Reflection: The Promise of Practical Theology*, ed. Lewis S. Mudge and James N. Poling (Philadelphia: Fortress, 1987), 120–138.

43 Kelsey and Wheeler, "New Ground," 193. See Jackson W. Carrollet et al., *Being There: Culture and Formation in Two Theological Schools* (New York: Oxford University Press, 1997).

44 Farley, *Theologia*, xi–xii; 22–23; Kelsey, *To Understand God*, 15–16, 111.

school" rather than a "straightforward" history.[45] But his analysis falls short despite its historical erudition because it ultimately does not take seriously disciplinary regimes and practices internal to the academy of religion.

Some people, such as Dale Andrews, decry the chasm between academic theology and folk religion in religious communities, and others, such as Michel Andraos, study how classroom pedagogy replicates colonialist imposition of Western epistemology.[46] But among the few scholars who have looked more closely at the production of theological knowledge, Schreiter and Mary McClintock Fulkerson are unique in urging closer inspection of the "social location of theologians" as "members of the professional managerial class" in Fulkerson's words. They come at this problem from different angles and for different purposes—Fulkerson as a Protestant feminist postmodern theologian interested in deconstructing narrow views of theology in feminist and doctrinal circles and Schreiter as a Catholic theologian and missiologist invested in reclaiming local theologies. But they reach similar conclusions about the politics. Fulkerson, however, identifies only one instance of the misuse of managerial power. Those who rely on a "MacIntyrean definition of practice," such as her own Duke colleague Stanley Hauerwas, ignore the "work of the so-called 'practical' field," thereby reinstating the power of certain preferred academic guilds.[47] Schreiter looks beyond postliberal theologians to a longer history of discrimination. For centuries and well before the advent of modernity and science, a university model of theology discounted common theologies as lacking theoretical clarity and precision.

Feminist and critical theorists provide resources to extend the interrogation. Black feminists in particular have distinctive insights precisely because they find themselves confronting diverse but interlocking systems of oppression (race, gender, class, etc.) and have found it useful to focus on commonalities among the injustices. In particular, sociologist Patricia Hill Collins characterizes the "either/or dualistic thinking" or what she calls the "construct of dichotomous oppositional difference" as a basic tenet of domination that cuts across multiple sites. She quotes author and activist bell hooks who depicts dichotomies as the "central ideological component of all systems of domina-

45 Farley, *Theologia*, 30.

46 Dale Andrews, *Practical Theology for Black Churches: Bridging Black Theology and African American Folk Religion* (Louisville: Westminster John Knox, 2002); Michel Elias Andraos, "Engaging Diversity in Teaching Religion and Theology: An Intercultural, De-colonial Epistemic Perspective," *Teaching Theology and Religion* 15, no. 1 (2012): 3–15.

47 Mary McClintock Fulkerson, "Theology and the Lure of the Practical: An Overview," *Religion Compass* 1, no. 2 (2007): 300.

tion in Western society."[48] In Collins's analysis, binaries such as black/white and male/female share three basic characteristics: stark difference from one another, inherent opposition, and, most important for understanding the conundrum of theory's recurrent dominance, intrinsic instability. This instability is often resolved, she observes, "by subordinating one half of each pair to the other." So terms are understood "only in *relation* to their difference from their oppositional counterparts."[49] Each pole is inherently opposed to the other, they do not enhance each other, and, most significant, they devolve into patterns of disempowerment. She summarizes: "Thus, whites rule Blacks, males dominate females, reason is touted as superior to emotion in ascertaining truth, facts supercede opinion in evaluating knowledge, and subjects rule objects. Dichotomous oppositional differences invariably imply relationships of superiority and inferiority, hierarchical relationships that mesh with political economies of domination and subordination."[50] Similar ideas have arisen among poststructuralists. As captured well by political theorist and philosopher Seyla Benhabib, the "logic of binary oppositions is also a logic of subordination and domination."[51] Or, in the words of a peer in the philosophy of religion Grace Jantzen who studies gender and the theism/atheism binary, "wherever there is a binary distinction, we need to ask whose interest does such logic serve."[52]

Of course, the scale of the binaries foregrounded by Benhabib, Jantzen, Collins, and hooks is formidable compared to that of theory-practice. As Benhabib puts it, "The Orient is there to enable the Occident, Africa is there to enable western civilization to fulfill its mission, the woman is there to help man actualize himself."[53] So I hesitate to draw analogies. But it is still important to

48 bell hooks, *From Margin to Center* (Boston: South End Press, 1984), 29, cited by Patricia Hill Collins, "Learning from the Outsider Within: The Sociological Significance of Black Feminist Thought," in *Beyond Methodology: Feminist Scholarship as Lived Research*, ed. Mary Margaret Fonow and Judith A. Cook (Bloomington: Indiana University Press, 1991), 42.

49 Collins, "Learning from the Outsider Within," 42, emphasis in the original.

50 Collins, "Learning from the Outsider Within," 42.

51 Seyla Benhabib, *Situating the Self: Gender, Community, and Postmodernism in Contemporary Ethics* (New York: Routledge, 1992), 15.

52 Jacob A. Belzen, "Back to Cultural Psychology of Religion" in *Religion and Psychology: Mapping the Terrain: Contemporary Dialogues, Future Prospects*, ed. Diane Jonte-Pace and William B. Parsons (London and New York: Routledge, 2001), 118, referring to Grace M. Jantzen, *Becoming Divine: Toward a Feminist Philosophy of Religion* (Bloomington: Indiana University Press, 1998), 66.

53 Benhabib, *Situating the Self*, 15.

note the hegemonic dynamic within the theory-practice binary, especially because it is so seldom noted. The theory-practice dichotomy functions in ways similar to more commonly recognized dualisms, operating to suppress and control knowledge, turning those who stand closer to material practice into the "other" to stabilize dominant structures of knowledge, and assigning positions of inferiority and superiority that harm theology's potential to flourish in diverse places within and beyond the academy. This dynamic breeds competition over who does "real" theology that cannot be resolved within the limitations of the schema itself because the underside is often rendered invisible or unseen, and inferior placement becomes a means for further domination. So, for example, academics do not "know" about scholarship in pastoral and practical theology despite a sixty-year history. Moreover, people are assigned a "group inferior status," in Collins's words, and then that status is used as "proof of the group's inferiority." Black women are denied literacy and then accused of lacking necessary information for sound judgment.[54] Practical theologians are expected to teach arts of ministry and then said to lack rigor and precision.

When Jeremy Carrette, a critical theorist in religion and psychology, draws on Foucault to examine the knowledge economy behind the construction of modern psychology, he also analyzes how binary knowledge functions and a second concept with implications for our analysis, *disciplinary amnesia* or the "art of suppressing those features of a discipline that undermine" its logic and practice.[55] Maintaining divisions "as fixed rather than temporary" is a way of wielding power in the construction of knowledge, he argues.[56] The creation of modern psychology rests on just such an unexamined, fixed bifurcation of the individual and the social that assigns psychology to the individual and artificially brackets the social. But because disciplinary amnesia suppresses recognition of how this division has ordered and controlled knowledge, few people notice how much economics shape psychology and how individually-oriented psychology sustains a market economy, selling products for the self. Subtly, quietly, binaries become epistemological linchpins, controlling what is recognized as knowledge and insulating the recognized knowledge from political scrutiny. That binaries seem so irresolvable actually reveals that they are hiding certain values and material realities behind their surface patina.

Has the theory-practice binary functioned in similar ways in theology? Although I cannot answer this question to the extent that Carrette does in his

---

54 Collins, "Learning from the Outsider Within," 42.

55 Jeremy Carrette, *Religion and Critical Psychology: Religious Experience in the Knowledge Economy* (London/New York: Routledge, 2007), 23.

56 Carrette, *Religion and Critical Psychology*, 22.

book-length treatment of economics and the production of specialist psychological knowledge, his pursuit of a *critical psychology*, exposing the "fault lines" in the formation of a discipline, remains suggestive for a comparable *critical theology*.[57] How has theological knowledge, constructed around a stark and unbalanced theory-practice division that privileges only one kind of intelligence, been wed, for example, to the exploitations of certain peoples or to the cost-benefit values of an efficient profitable market economy, values that go against the grain of many religious communities and traditions? Or, as another example, how has the hegemony of theory over practice insulated theology from political critique and obscured its wider ethical responsibilities? The take-away here, as he suggests, is the reminder that binaries are always "value-motivated and, consequently, politically fuelled." Hence, they cannot be resolved without reassessing the values we hold "about being human."[58] In the end, he argues for an ethic of not-knowing that challenges totalitarian forms of knowledge and redefines knowing as a more open-ended and evolving relationship, which allows more room than an owned and controlled canon for what William James called the "More."

When narrative therapists Michael White and David Epston turn to Foucault to reconstruct counseling as a political process, they also describe a kind of epistemological amnesia that arises around two kinds of subjugated knowledges: "One class is constituted by those previously established or 'erudite' knowledges that have been written out of the record by the revision of history achieved through the ascendance of a more global and unitary knowledge."[59] In theology, one can think of the tensions between speculative and practical theology in Bonaventure and Aquinas in the thirteenth century, Luther's not entirely successful protest against speculative theology in the Reformation, and even Farley's own attempt to "restore unity" across specialized disciplines by recovering *theologia*, "'theology' [as] a single thing.... the one ground of the one thing." In each case, the eruption of new theological knowledges is submerged or controlled through formal systematization designed to "mask the ruptural effects" in Foucault's words.[60]

57 Carrette, *Religion and Critical Psychology*, 26.

58 Carrette, *Religion and Critical Psychology*, 98.

59 Michael White and David Epston, *Narrative Means to Therapeutic Ends* (New York: W.W. Norton, 1990), 25.

60 Farley, *Theologia*, 142, 151. For an overview of this submerged history, see Farley himself, *Theologia*, 34–39, and Randy L. Maddox, "The Recovery of Theology as a Practical Discipline," *Theological Studies* 51 (1990): 650–72, especially 652–653, 654–655.

Practical theological knowledge also resembles a second kind of subjugated knowledge that Schreiter's work touches on—"local popular" or "indigenous" knowledges that are operative but "denied or deprived of the space in which they could be adequately performed." These knowledges "survive only at the margins of society and are lowly ranked—considered insufficient and exiled from the legitimate domain of the formal knowledges and the accepted sciences" or, in Foucault's words, "beneath the required level of cognition or scientificity."[61] In general, lost knowledges can be resurrected "only by careful and meticulous scholarship" that challenges the claims for a unitary and uniquely scientific truth, as White and Epston suggest.[62]

Of course, as any reading of Foucault would suggest, power is continuously under negotiation, and there are few innocent parties. People occupy varying positions of relative power and disempowerment, perpetuating discriminations to which they are subject. Given the "ambiguity of all power-knowledge practices within even the most seemingly liberative" efforts in practical theologian Tom Beaudoin's words, we should recognize the new knowledge production in practical theology as both disorienting earlier power relations *and* establishing new regimes.[63] So, for example, people rank some practical disciplines over others or disregard the knowledge of students, ministers, or certain types of Christianity or other religions. However, the constant renegotiation of power does not dispel the persistence of imbalances and inequities. Even Foucault evidences what Beaudoin describes as a "preferential option" for the repeatedly marginalized.

Raising Consciousness: Practical Theologians as Outsiders Within

Around the edges of their writing, scholars have put into print their concern about academic prejudice against those proximate to practice. Several decades ago, Juan Luis Segundo said the effort to liberate theology is threatened by what he described as an "academic disdain" for a "theology rising out of the urgent problems of real life" as "naïve and uncritical."[64] Twenty years later, in one of the first international volumes in practical theology in the 1990s, a

61 White and Epston, *Narrative Means*, p. 26, citing Michel Foucault, *Power/knowledge: Selected Interviews and Other Writings* (New York: Pantheon Books, 1980), 82.

62 White and Epston, *Narrative Means*, 25–26.

63 Tom Beaudoin, *Witness to Dispossession: The Vocation of a Post-Modern Theologian* (Maryknoll, NY: Orbis, 2008), 68.

64 Juan Luis Segundo, *The Liberation of Theology* (Maryknoll, N.Y.: Orbis Books, 1976), 5.

United Methodist scholar best known for research on faith stages, James W. Fowler, describes the "revolution" in the discipline as a move from the "basement" of departments housed "as though they were afterthoughts." The "more academically prestigious the school of theology," he continues, "the greater the status difference."[65] Bernard Lee, whose investment in practical theology grew when he assumed directorship of the Institute of Ministry at Loyola University in New Orleans in 1989, declares his eagerness "to reject the epithet of 'soft theology' made by many who remember an older form of pastoral theology as what you did after you learned theology and *then* need to apply it."[66] Long before these folks, Seward Hiltner himself, heralded as a founder of the turn to the study of living human documents in theological schools, hid his frustration in a string of testy footnotes about the deep "antipractical bias" in academe that views pastoral theology as "merely practical without the ability to make genuinely theological contributions."[67] More recently and not surprisingly, Carmen Nanko-Fernandez names "academic second-class citizenship" as one reason why so few Latino/a scholars identify themselves with practical and pastoral theologies. Those who "already experience marginalization" find little advantage in affiliating with practical theology, she remarks, "especially when others seek to classify our theologies as practical as a means of dismissing" their value.[68]

In many ways, practical theologians find themselves as "outsiders within," to borrow Collins's phrase, only partially belonging but also understanding a great deal from the margins about the complexities of theological knowledge. She coins the phrase to capture the more pernicious discrimination she experiences as a black woman sociologist "caught between groups of unequal power," privy to deep internal secrets, as with domestic workers or support staff, but never fully belonging. Whereas early figures in the sociology of knowledge, such as Georg Simmel and Alfred Schütz, identified the *stranger* or the *insider* and *outsider* as valid positions for obtaining knowledge, she draws on Mannheim who saw "marginal intellectuals" in academia as capable of bringing a "critical posture" to the "creative development of academic disciplines

65 James W. Fowler, "The Merging New Shape of Practical Theology," in *Practical Theology: International Perspectives*, ed. Friedrich Schweitzer and Johannes A. van der Ven (Frankfurt am Main: Peter Lang, 1999), 75.

66 Bernard J. Lee, "Practical Theology: Its Character and Possible Implications for Higher Education," *Current Issues in Higher Education* 14, no. 2 (1994): 25, emphasis in the original.

67 Seward Hiltner, *Preface to Pastoral Theology* (Nashville: Abingdon, 1958), 217–218, note 11; 218–219, note 14; and 220–221, note 16.

68 Carmen Nanko-Fernandez, *Theologizing en Espanglish: Context, Community, and Ministry* (Maryknoll, NY: Orbis, 2010), 22.

themselves."[69] Life on the edge fosters "a particular way of seeing reality," as bell hooks says, from both the "outside in" and the "inside out."[70] Although Collins later protests the personalized and depoliticized overuse of her phrase, black women's experience of marginalization exposes dynamics faced by "any group of less powerful outsiders encountering the paradigmatic thought of a more powerful insider community."[71] In a sense, practical theologians who strive to understand theological knowledge within practice join feminists and postmodernists who criticize Western rationality, in Benhabib's words, "from the standpoint of what and whom it excludes, suppresses, delegitimizes, renders mad, imbecilic or childish."[72]

Professors who teach in the so-called practical areas are accustomed to careless aspersions or even well intended but distorted characterizations of our "madness."[73] Some of my Vanderbilt peers have harbored an assumption similar to that of the students with whom I began this essay—that those admitted in the practical areas have lower entrance exam scores, a misperception I accepted uncritically myself until I noticed that the facts proved otherwise. One colleague in systematic theology also evidenced surprise that I could actually find fifty-some established or credible authors to contribute to *The Wiley-Blackwell Companion to Practical Theology*. On a fairly regular basis, I have heard graduates and faculty members from another top U.S. divinity school announce proudly that their institution discourages students from taking practical courses as simply less valuable. A graduate from a prestigious religion department told me recently she had "gotten away" with including "practice" and "theology" in her dissertation in a department that frowns on both terms because they are regarded negatively within the wider university. When I was a doctoral student at a university divinity school surrounded by a plethora of religiously-affiliated seminaries whose primary aim was education in the practice of ministry, I absorbed from the air we breathed a quiet condescension toward these "lesser" institutions, one of which later hired me. When I left this school for my current appointment, my stronger publication record earned me a lower rank than a colleague coming from an Ivy League college in a more "classical" discipline. Another colleague accepted a demotion in rank in

69 Mannheim, *Ideology and Utopia*, in Collins, "Learning from the Outsider Within," 36.

70 bell hooks, *From Margin to Center*, vii.

71 Patricia Hill Collins, "Reflections on the Outsider Within," *Journal of Career Development* 26, no. 1 (Fall 1999): 85; Collins, "Learning from the Outsider Within," 53.

72 Benhabib, *Situating the Self*, 14.

73 See Ryan LaMothe, "Method and Madness: A Pastoral Theological Reflection," *Pastoral Psychology*, June 2016, doi: 10.1007/s11089-016-0709-1.

moving from seminary to university divinity school because book publications for church audiences were perceived as less demanding. Late in his career, my own mentor, ethicist and practical theologian Don Browning, spent half of each year at another institution on research leave at least in part because of the lesser regard for his work in his otherwise leading home institution. In another school, as faculty members of a professional ministry program discussed whether to allow students who would likely serve Catholic parishes to take more than one ministerial arts course, one classically-trained faculty turned to his practical theology colleague and asked quite sincerely, "But aren't these classes *just* hands-on?"

How does one reply in such situations? How would one explain in a soundbite the actual value and intricacy of hands-on knowledge? If I had written down every prejudice since I began thinking about the latent politics, I would have amassed a large database. Those in practical theology tell these stories to each other but seldom put them out there for analysis. Perhaps to do so is impolite, ungracious, and counterproductive; perhaps it inflates the magnitude of the harm done. Over the years, however, I have begun to see a resemblance between these comments and "microagressions" now recognized as sexist, racist, heterosexist, and so forth. It has taken time to see this. Psychologist and Chicano/a Studies professor Aída Hurtado describes the different experiences with sexism of women of color and white women. Women of color have a clearer view of oppression because they do "battle every day," encountering overt racial discrimination as early as they can remember. Hence, they learn survival skills at the beginning of their lives. By contrast, many white women are oblivious, "seduced" into subordination because they occupy "more contradictory positions vis-à-vis white male power," often unknowingly coopted into their own oppression. Consequently, they fail to acquire "political consciousness of gender oppression until they become adults."[74] So also are many academics like white women—lulled into our prejudices and lacking in political consciousness by the conflicting positions we occupy with regard to power.

The disciplinary amnesia that prevents discussion of power politics also characterizes conversations about the very terms *practical theology* and *theology*. The quizzical expressions of those who persist in asking, "What is practical theology *anyway*?" remind me of questions asked in 1980s about feminism that constantly put the burden of explanation back on women, just as similar requests to explain racism continue to be foisted on people of color. Sometimes it is hard not to hear the question as willed ignorance on the part of a

74 Collins, "Learning from the Outsider Within," 41.

dominant group that is as interested in subjecting practical theology to suspicion as understanding it.[75] A parallel query, sometimes said with a smile of self-satisfaction, as if the inquirer has just scored a match point, runs like this: "Is there such a thing as *impractical* theology?" The last time someone asked me this I unloaded years of pent up frustration not deserved by the questioner. Would anyone ask a systematic or biblical theologian if there is such a thing as *unsystematic* or *unbiblical* theology, as if the pursuit is inevitably illogical or always in tension with its opposite? Not often, because the validity of these subjects is automatically assumed. The question also presumes that theology *is* practical, all the while obscuring the reality of a modern *impractical theology* removed from life. So those interested in how theology gets embodied in practice find themselves once again explaining themselves on the downside of an unexamined hegemony of theory-practice. The power of naming; the confusion around the very term *theology* and its conflicted institutional meanings for a denomination's beliefs, an entire faculty or school, *and* a solitary discipline reserved for only a select few; the admitted ambiguities of *practical* as a qualifier for *theology*; and questions about when and why doctrinal theologians switched identifiers to terms like *systematic* and *constructive* (as opposed to unsystematic or unconstructive?) or why they introduce themselves simply as *theologians* while others in theological education must use qualifiers, such as *biblical* or *pastoral*—all these matters go largely unexamined. And thus, we academics agree to ignore the political and ideological dimensions of our definitional and institutional maneuvering.

To be clear, my aim in recounting these experiences and making these claims is not to gain more respect for an academic discipline that still has work to do in establishing its distinct knowledge and methods. Rather, without awareness of how the hegemony of theory-practice is embedded in educational habits, definitions, nomenclature, and who has access to producing and maintaining knowledge, progress in understanding practical theological knowledge will be slow. We can talk all we want about the dialectic between theory-practice and the value of practical knowledge, but if these ideas are not embodied in actual institutional structures and actions, the dialectic is largely cosmetic and conceptual. In short, there is a reality that few name in their theoretical analyses of the theory-practice relationship: When one has a binary, it is hard to keep it from becoming institutionalized as a hierarchy.

75 See Bonnie J. Miller-McLemore, "The Hubris and Folly of Defining a Discipline: Reflections on the Evolution of *The Wiley-Blackwell Companion to Practical Theology*," *Toronto Journal of Theology* 29, no. 1 (2013): 152–153.

Years ago, when our family brought a chocolate Lab home from its litter, a friend loaned me a book on raising puppies by the monks of New Skete. One insight lingers because it proved useful in helping our five-year-old son establish authority with a dog about his size. Dogs are pack animals, and from birth they fall into rank from dominant to weakest. Owners of the mother dog had in fact handpicked our puppy because she stood in the middle of the pack and would blend well into our family clan. Our son simply had to stand his ground and make the dog believe she was smaller, weaker. Academic politics, I thought at the time, are not all that far removed. Establishing rank and supremacy comes with the territory of our mammalian nature. So, the relationship between theory and practice is a stumbling block—that scriptural phrase for a circumstance that leads to sin—precisely because it incites a striving for status and domination. Practical theologians exemplify this tension: The revival of practical theology as one more disciplinary science within the academic study of theology in the 20th century emerged directly out of the establishment of theology as sure knowledge, a development that was certainly about power and status; yet the discipline has made representation of underrepresented and undervalued modes of practical theological knowing its mission.

When it comes to Christian theology scriptural mandates turn power structures upside down, and we find an appeal to a different relationship among those who seek the truths and best practices of the tradition. To acknowledge power dynamics, therefore, is not about turning the tables and installing practical theology as kingpin "within this lack, this negative, even by denouncing it," to use the words of French psychoanalyst and philosopher Luce Iragaray on the male-female polarity. Rather, naming the politics is meant to destablize the terms and make way for a "different, multi-faceted strategy" that hears other voices in the wake of such binaries.[76] The important question then becomes how to reconceive the relationship of theory and practice in less stratified, hierarchical, and institutionally repressive ways.

Bibliography

Andraos, Michel Elias. "Engaging Diversity in Teaching Religion and Theology: An Intercultural, De-colonial Epistemic Perspective." *Teaching Theology and Religion* 15, no. 1 (2012): 3–15.

76 Jantzen, *Becoming Divine*, p. 11, quoting Luce Iragaray, *This Sex Which is Not One*, trans. Catherine Porter (Ithaca, NY: Cornell University Press, 1977), 159.

Andrews, Dale. *Practical Theology for Black Churches: Bridging Black Theology and African American Folk Religion.* Louisville: Westminster John Knox, 2002.

Beaudoin, Tom. *Witness to Dispossession: The Vocation of a Post-Modern Theologian.* Maryknoll, NY: Orbis, 2008.

Belzen, Jacob A. "Back to Cultural Psychology of Religion" in *Religion and Psychology: Mapping the Terrain: Contemporary Dialogues, Future Prospects,* edited by Diane Jonte-Pace and William B. Parsons, 43–56. London and New York: Routledge, 2001.

Benhabib, Seyla. *Situating the Self: Gender, Community, and Postmodernism in Contemporary Ethics.* New York: Routledge, 1992.

Bounds, Elizabeth. "Border Crossings: Some Thoughts on the Initiative in Religious Practices and Practical Theology at Emory University." Paper presented at the American Academy of Religion, Atlanta, Georgia, November 22, 2003.

Burrows, William R. "Reasons to Hope for Reform: An Interview with David Tracy." *America* 173 (October 14, 1995), 12–18.

Carrette, Jeremy R. *Religion and Critical Psychology: Religious Experience in the Knowledge Economy.* London/New York: Routledge, 2007.

Carroll, Jackson W., Barbara G. Wheeler, Daniel O. Alshire, and Penny Long Mabler. *Being There: Culture and Formation in Two Theological Schools.* New York: Oxford University Press, 1997.

Casalis, Georges. *Correct Ideas Don't Fall from the Skies: Elements for an Inductive Theology.* Translated by Sister Jeanne Marie Lyons and Michael John. Maryknoll, NY: Orbis, 1984, originally published 1977.

Chopp, Rebecca S. "Practical Theology and Liberation." In *Formation and Reflection: The Promise of Practical Theology,* edited by Lewis S. Mudge and James N. Poling, 120–138. Philadelphia: Fortress, 1987.

Chopp, Rebecca S. *Saving Work: Feminist Practices of Theological Education* Louisville: Westminster John Knox, 1995.

Collins, Patricia Hill. "Learning from the Outsider Within: The Sociological Significance of Black Feminist Thought." In *Beyond Methodology: Feminist Scholarship as Lived Research,* edited by Mary Margaret Fonow and Judith A. Cook, 35–59. Bloomington: Indiana University Press, 1991.

Collins, Patricia Hill. "Reflections on the Outsider Within." *Journal of Career Development* 26, no. 1 (Fall 1999): 85–88.

Dulles, Avery. *Models of the Church.* New York: Doubleday, 1974.

Farley, Edward. *Theologia: The Fragmentation and Unity of Theological Education* Philadelphia: Fortress, 1983.

Fiorenza, Francis Schüssler. "Theory and Practice: Theological Education as a Reconstructive, Hermeneutical, and Practical Task." *Theological Education* 23, no. 3 (1987): 113–141.

Forrester, Duncan B. "Can Theology be Practical?" In *Practical Theology: International*

Perspectives, edited by Friedrich Schweitzer and Johannes A. van der Ven, 15–27. Frankfurt am Main: Peter Lang, 1999).

Foucault, Michel. *Power/knowledge: Selected Interviews and Other Writings*. New York: Pantheon Books, 1980.

Fowler, James W. "The Emerging New Shape of Practical Theology. In *Practical Theology: International Perspectives*, edited by Friedrich Schweitzer and Johannes A. van der Ven, 75–92. Frankfurt am Main: Peter Lang, 1999.

Fulkerson, Mary McClintock. "Theology and the Lure of the Practical: An Overview." *Religion Compass* 1, no. 2 (2007): 294–304.

Gilpin, W. Clark. "Basic Issues in Theological Education: A Selected Bibliogrphy, 1980–1988." *Theological Education* 25 (Spring 1989): 115–121.

Girmalm, Thomas. "Perspectives on Practical Theology: Searching Tools and Arenas in Modern Swedish Theology Up to the Present Day." Paper presented at the International Academy of Practical Theology, Amsterdam, July 25, 2011.

Hiltner, Seward. *Preface to Pastoral Theology*. Nashville: Abingdon, 1958.

hooks, bell. *From Margin to Center*. Boston: South End Press, 1984.

Hough, Joseph C., Jr. and Barbara G. Wheeler, eds. *Beyond Clericalism: The Congregation as a Focus for Theological Education*. Atlanta: Scholars Press, 1988.

Iragaray, Luce. *This Sex Which is Not One*. Translated by Catherine Porter. Ithaca, NY: Cornell University Press, 1977.

Jantzen, Grace M. *Becoming Divine: Toward a Feminist Philosophy of Religion*. Bloomington: Indiana University Press, 1998.

Kelsey, David. *To Understand God Truly: What's Theological about a Theological School*. Louisville: Westminster John Knox, 1992.

Kelsey, David. "What's Theological about a Theological School?" *Christian Century*, February 5–12, 1997, 131–132.

Kelsey, David. and Barbara G. Wheeler. "New Ground: The Foundations and Future of the Theological Education Debate." In *Theology and the Interhuman: Essays in the Honor of Edward Farley*, edited by Robert R. Williams, 181–201. Valley Forge, Pennsylvania: Trinity Press International, 1995.

King, Richard. *Orientalism and Religion: Postcolonial Theory, India, and 'the Mystic East.'* London and New York: Routledge, 1999.

Lamb, Matthew L. "The Theory-Praxis Relationship in Contemporary Christian Theologies." *CTSA Proceedings* 31 (1976): 149–178.

LaMothe, Ryan. "Method and Madness: A Pastoral Theological Reflection." *Pastoral Psychology*, June 2016, doi: 10.1007/s11089-016-0709-1.

Lee, Bernard J. "Practical Theology: Its Character and Possible Implications for Higher Education." *Current Issues in Higher Education* 14, no. 2 (1994): 25–36.

Maddox, Randy L. "The Recovery of Theology as a Practical Discipline." *Theological Studies* 51 (1990): 650–72.

Mannheim, Karl. *Essays on the Sociology of Knowledge*. Oxford: Oxford University Press, 1952.

Mannheim, Karl. *Ideology and Utopia: An Introduction to the Sociology of Knowledge*. New York: Harcourt, Brace and World, 1955 [1936].

Metz, Johan Baptist. *Faith in History and Society: Toward a Practical Fundamental Theology*, trans. David Smith. New York: Seabury, 1980.

Miller-McLemore, Bonnie J. *Christian Theology in Practice: Discovering a Discipline*. Grand Rapids: Eerdmans, 2012.

Miller-McLemore, Bonnie J. "Five Misunderstandings About Practical Theology." *International Journal of Practical Theology* 16, no. 1 (2012): 5–26.

Miller-McLemore, Bonnie J. "The Hubris and Folly of Defining a Discipline: Reflections on the Evolution of *The Wiley-Blackwell Companion to Practical Theology*." *Toronto Journal of Theology* 29, no. 1 (2013): 143–174.

Nanko-Fernandez, Carmen. *Theologizing en Espanglish: Context, Community, and Ministry*. Maryknoll, NY: Orbis, 2010.

Niebuhr, H. RIchard. *Christ and Culture*. New York: Harper, 1951.

Schreiter, Robert J. *Constructing Local Theologies*. Maryknoll, NY: Orbis, 1985, 2002, Tenth printing.

Segundo, Juan Luis. *The Liberation of Theology*. Maryknoll, NY: Orbis Books, 1976.

Tanner, Kathryn. *Theories of Culture: A New Agenda for Theology*. Minneapolis: Augsburg Fortress, 1997.

Tracy, David. *Blessed Rage for Order: The New Pluralism in Theology*. New York: Seabury, 1975.

Tracy, David. "Traditions of Spiritual Practice and the Practice of Theology." *Theology Today* 55, no. 2 (1998): 235–241.

Tracy, David. "A Correlational Model of Practical Theology Revisited. In *Religion, Diversity, and Conflict*, edited by Edward Foley, 49–61. Berlin: Lit Verlag, 2011.

Wheeler, Barbara G. and Edward Farley, eds. *Shifting Boundaries: Contextual Approaches to the Structure of Theological Education*. Louisville: Westminster John Knox, 1991.

White, Michael and David Epston. *Narrative Means to Therapeutic Ends*. New York: W.W. Norton, 1990.

Williams, Rowan. "Oxford University Commemoration Day Sermon." *TAO* XLV, no. 1 (Winter 2007): 25–31.

CHAPTER 9

Raced Bodies: Portraying Bodies, Reifying Racism

Phillis Isabella Sheppard

Conundrum:
a: a question or problem having only a conjectural answer
b: an intricate and difficult problem[1]

The anthropologist Zora Neale Hurston proclaimed, "Research is formalized curiosity. It is poking and prying with a purpose." In this chapter, I poke and pry and problematize the near absence of raced bodies in practical theology. Even though race is wedged into the crevices of the United States cultural imagination and in day-to-day practices of research, actual raced bodies seldom confront us in our critical texts. The poking and prodding, however, exposes a conundrum closely connected to the problem of appropriation and reciprocity with which womanist and feminist ethicists have grappled. Womanist ethicist Emilie M. Townes admonished that there are dangers in exercising a "hegemonic control" when we take up other peoples' experiences and incorporate them "into a mundane and unnuanced analysis."[2] In the case of the hegemonic appropriation of raced bodies in research, the aims of the researcher—to publish and raise questions for the discipline—can be privileged such that the negative cultural depictions of raced bodies are reinforced. In other words, raced bodies do not exist in a vacuum. They can be appropriated but not without also giving form to the racist ideologies attached to those bodies. Herein lies the conundrum: if practical theology commits to a robust analysis of raced bodies and, in essence, critiques current discourses on bodies, it will do so with an ingrained bias that reads raced bodies through the lens of racist imaginaries. In other words, the researchers and readers alike are already predisposed to read through the lens of cultural misrepresentations.

Racist depictions of raced bodies within disciplines form the very individuals who shape those disciplines. This is just one indication of the pervasiveness of our malformation. Due to the increased numbers of previously underrepre-

1 "Definition of Conundrum," accessed November 20, 2014, http://www.merriam-webster.com/dictionary/conundrum.

2 Emilie M. Townes, Introduction to Katie Geneva Cannon and Kristine A. Culp, "Appropriation and Reciprocity in the Doing of Womanist Ethics," *The Annual of the Society of Christian Ethics* 13 (1993): 187.

 | DOI 10.1163/9789004324244_011

sented groups, practical theologians are discussing race in a variety of ways. Most often the literature is focused on particularity and written by people whose bodies are the sites for racing. In this chapter, I return to a longstanding concern: the place of bodies in practical theological discourse and practices. The struggle to take bodies' experience seriously, on their own terms, has been documented.[3] The problem is twofold: those doing the theorizing have tended to be those in the majority and, despite all our theorizing, scholars who are the subject of that theorizing often remain absent. They are not represented, and they are not speaking about their own bodies. It is a challenge and maybe impossible to reserve a place for the lived bodily experiences when we rely so much on text rather than embodied experience in our scholarship. This is even more problematic when we are reduced to discourse that considers "the body" as if we all experience the same bodily experiences. In the absence of non-white academic bodies doing the talking, we are left with theories of the body where race is acknowledged but quickly relegated to the footnote and reference sections, and where the text advises the reader to consult scholars of color rather than actually including their voices.

Two questions shed light on the conundrum: First, how are practical theological scholarship and practice implicated in the invisibility of lived raced bodies? Second, can practical theology prioritize the lived experience of raced bodies without exploiting or reproducing the negative cultural productions of raced experiences? All too frequently practical theology fails to theorize the experiences and therefore perpetuates the invisibility. In addition, practical theology is sometimes appropriated to reinforce negative cultural images of some raced bodies. In this chapter, I intersperse pictures, personal narrative, and pedagogical practices with the goal of rethinking and at times undermining the ways in which raced bodies are represented, ignored, or exploited.

Race as a Social and Historical Construct

In recent years, the highly contested dialogue around race has been critiqued for its reliance on the U.S. context of structural oppression of black people who

3 Phillis Isabella Sheppard, "Mourning the Loss of Cultural Selfobjects: Black Embodiment and Religious Experience after Trauma," *Practical Theology* 1, no. 2 (2008): 233–257; Phillis Isabella Sheppard, *Self, Culture, and Others in Womanist Practical Theology* (London, UK: Palgrave Macmillan, 2011); Bonnie Miller-McLemore, "Embodied Knowing, Embodied Theology: What Happened to the Body?" *Journal of Pastoral Psychology* 62 (2013): 743–758; Stephanie Crumpton, *A Womanist Pastoral Theology Against Intimate and Cultural Violence* (New York: Palgrave Macmillan, 2013).

are the descendants of enslaved Africans. The limitation of these discussions is that the complexity of the history of race as a category is lost. Also lost is the history and practice of defining and appointing racial classification onto groups of people. This specialized grouping included black Americans, Asian Americans, Native Americans, Indigenous peoples, multi-racial/ethnic categories, such as mulatto, and white Americans. In this process of categorization, each group was granted varying degrees of legal rights and opportunities based on the group's proximity to whiteness. Each group was also subject to various forms of discrimination based on proximity to blackness. The construction of social, economic, and political relations between "raced groups" in the U.S. remains contested, as is the more recent "racing" of groups new to the U.S. Racing groups of people remains a social, structural, and legal process reserved for those wielding political and economic power—those claiming white as the normative designation.

Obviously critical race studies and whiteness studies have shed a small, direct light in this direction, but in practical theology we suffer even more from the lack of a robust and sustained engagement with the complexity of whiteness, race, and power as race is lived in our field. While practical theologians consider "social analysis" crucial to our work, the intersections that frame race are frequently tangential to our actual thinking.

Practical theologians are still grappling with race as a social construct. Put more bluntly, many practical theologians still act as if race is an ontological reality, something unchangeable and set in stone, rather than a social inscription and therefore eminently changeable. But the idea of race and the attributes assigned to "the races" is a part of the early DNA of the U.S. The effect of the idea of race cannot be ignored and is patently obvious in societally pervasive choreographed acts of racism. People in power use the category of race to define others in order to regulate and indeed diminish their access to certain cultural goods, such as education, jobs, and sexual self-determination. Race structures our relationship to each other, to our surroundings, and to language. For instance, depending on the racial identity of the speaker and listener, one may live in a suburb or "ethnic enclave" or "the ghetto."

The category of race, while often thought of as solely based on color, has a more complex history. Race is a legal category and a legal designation that has been contested in the U.S., and, for some groups, has changed over time.[4] In cases where groups were redefined and moved from white to non-white status,

4 "For example, Asian Indians were determined by the courts to be non-white in 1909, white in 1910 and 1913, non-white in 1917, white again in 1919 and 1920, but non-white after 1923." Brian K. Obach, "Demonstrating The Social Construction of Race," (1999), http://www.asanet.org/introtosociology/Documents/TSObach1999.pdf. Also see Noel Ignatiev, *How the Irish Became*

the consequences were legal, economic, and social. Thus, the category of race should be viewed in terms of its history and its effect rather than as a fixed biological reality. Racial categories evolve over time and ultimately re-produce the ideology of racial superiority, generally that of whiteness.

In addition, racial categories structure professional and relational dynamics, as we can see in practical theology. I have already mentioned that practical theology rarely considers the perspective of those who are not white, and even more rarely allows such persons to speak for themselves. In addition, we see the negative work of racial categories by looking at citation practices across the discipline: we rarely include the work of people of color. Instead, we cite certain field-defining scholars and mentors over and over again. The result is that we reproduce particular perspectives and particular selves and avoid the challenge of grounding and expanding our knowledge in the experiences of raced bodies. This leaves (the unacknowledged) white bodies in the driver's seat of practical theology as in so many other fields.

When Raced Bodies Appear

Womanist practical theologians are among those who have increasingly paid attention to black women's bodies. Evelyn Parker describes the womanist methodology of practical theology as "an analytical and reflexive process focused on the experiences and practices of African and African American diasporic… people of faith" with girls and women. She notes that black women's bodies are the sites where the discourse on and the lived realities at the core of black life are inscribed. Even so, "the corpus of womanist practical theology on embodiment is small,"[5] and this lack of attention to black female embodiment has implications for the trajectory of womanist practical theology and beyond. For when we consider the practices and impact of racism, we need to ask ourselves what bodies we see in our texts and which ones are missing.

White (NY: Routledge, 1995); Ian F. Haney-Lopez, "The Social Construction of Race: Some Observations on Illusion, Fabrication, and Choice," *Harvard Civil Rights-Civil Liberties Law Review* 29, no. 1 (1994), http://scholarship.law.berkeley.edu/cgi/viewcontent.cgi?article=2815&context=facpubs; Ruth Frankenberg, *White Women, Race Matters: The Social Construction of Whiteness* (Minneapolis: University of Minnesota Press, 1993).

5 Evelyn L. Parker, "Womanist Theory" in *The Wiley-Blackwell Companion to Practical Theology*, ed. Bonnie J. Miller-McLemore (Oxford: Blackwell Publishing, 2012), accessed August 30, 2015, http://www.blackwellreference.com/subscriber/tocnode.html?id=g9781444330823_chunk_g978144433082320.

For those of us who appropriate psychoanalytic perspectives in our work, we often find that bodies of any color are absent in the theories we employ, and post-Freudian constructions give even Freud's emphasis on the nexus between biological (body) and psyche scant attention. Contemporary clinical theory and practice leans toward an emphasis on the intersubjective, relational, and the constructive—usually without explicitly theorizing the body's or bodies' position in theory or practice. Two noteworthy exceptions are Joyce McDougall and Janine Chasseguet-Smirgel. In their work, both reconfigure the body's place in the psyche and consider classical psychoanalytic views concerning gender and sexuality. McDougall considers bodily illness as psychosomatic—as signs and symptoms of her patients' wrestling with their sexuality, perversions, and episodic physical problems.[6] Likewise, Chasseguet-Smirge argues that the body is intertwined with the psyche and is the site, either in reality as in physical illness or in perverse fantasies, for intrapsychic conflict often arising out of pregenital difficulties. These difficulties, in her view, involve the body and are indicative of the person's processing of psychosexual dynamics. A failure during this developmental process can result in a perverse relationship to bodily-psychical experiences.[7] These psychoanalytic perspectives are helpful in the recovery of the body, but the body they recover is generic, not only theoretically but also culturally and racially. Thus, for our purposes, the theoretical conclusions are not without problems. Though McDoughall and Chasseguet-Smirgel practiced in France and Britain, and though race as a construct has a different history and reality in those contexts, race is nonetheless a feature of social interaction in those countries too. Yet even here raced bodies are invisible.

We do, however, see a psychoanalytic concern with the relationship between race, gender, and culture in womanist practical theology. My own book as well as works by Markeva Hill and Stephanie Crumpton are evidence of this.[8] In these texts, the primary aims are to re-situate black women's experiences in practical and pastoral theology by critiquing their absence and to

6 Joyce McDougall, *Theatre of the Body: A Psychoanalytic Approach to Psychosomatic Illness* (New York: W.W. Norton, 1989).

7 Janine Chasseguet-Smirgel, *Sexuality and Mind: The Role of the Father and the Motehr in the Psyche* (London: Kamac, 1989). See also Chasseguet-Smirgel, *Female Sexuality: New Psychoanalytic Views* (London: Kamac, 1992).

8 Phillis Isabella Sheppard, *Self Culture and Others in Womanist Practical Theology* (New York: Palgrave Macmillan, 2011); Markeva Hill, *Womanism Against Socially-Constructed Matriarchal Images: A Theoretical Model Towards a Therapeutic Goal* (New York: Palgrave Macmillan, 2012); and Stephanie Crumpton, *A Womanist Pastoral Theology Against Intimate and Cultural Violence* (Basingstoke: Palgrave Macmillan, 2014).

articulate a womanist practical theology informed by psychoanalytic theory. Some of them appropriate self psychology and object relations, revised in light of black culture and black women's experience of culture, religion, and embodiment. These authors pay particular attention to persons who have experienced bodily violations, such as sexual abuse, domestic violence, and social violence in religious, intimate, and cultural contexts. They depict black female embodiment most powerfully when they make ethnography integral. Significant effort is given to black women as readers of culture and interpreters of their own experience. These works must be read as advancing the black female body in theological and psychoanalytic discourse, and close readings also suggest that black female bodies are, to some degree, represented as black bodies in distress. I would add that despite the clear commitment to addressing black bodies, the texts often privilege theories over bodies to scaffold the work. The absence of the raced body in practical theology and its place in womanist practical theology also shines a light on the conundrum of raced bodies: black bodies can be central to theorizing and simultaneously reproduce raced social dynamics. In my own consideration of this conundrum, I make raced bodies the fulcrum and observe in vivo this dynamic of reproduction. I also expand the reading of whose bodies are raced, and, finally, I consider the ethical demand that raced bodies place on our discipline.

We must ask how and why raced social dynamics are reproduced in the attempt to resituate bodies in our work. The "how" is related to practices of cultural production. Cultural theorists Elisabeth Klaus and Elke Zobl describe how we use "cultural material and imaginary resources in a unique way to serve our purposes. … Our daily routines seem natural and self-evident to us and we don't usually think about the fact, that while carrying them out exactly in the way we do, we appropriate and articulate culture."[9] We re-reproduce in our everyday patterns of scholarship raced dynamics that in turn shape our discipline and criteria for advancement. However, while the manifest practices—in this case, publishing—seem self evident in their intent, the relationship to previous and seemingly unrelated cultural productions and their effects may not be as readily evident. Therefore, "this productive side of our everyday routines… is often hidden from view."[10] The insidious aspect of the reproduction culture is due to the experience of normalness in our surround that sustains and re-insinuates culture socially, relationally, and internally. Fur-

9 Elisabeth Klaus and Elke Zobl, "Cultural Production in Theory and Practice: 'Doing Culture'" in *P/art/icipate: Kultur Aktiv Gestalten* 1 (2012), accessed August 18, 2015, http://www.p-art-icipate.net/cms/cultural-production-in-theory-and-practice/.

10 Klaus and Elke Zobl, "Cultural Production."

thermore, this state of affairs appears so natural that we fail to reflect on our operative processes.[11]

Zobl and Siglinde Lang expand this line of reasoning. They argue that we are cultural producers who "operate within a matrix of cultural production" in which the "meaning of cultural artifacts is never fixed, but always remains tentative and contested; meanings are being worked on and continuously being reworked."[12] The relationship of raced bodies to the "why" of reproduction is partly economics: the negative reproduction of negative cultural images and artifacts of raced bodies is economically advantageous and effectively imposes control beyond the artifact's representation. Townes captures this well in her pioneering *The Cultural Reproduction of Evil* when she analyses the permutations of the image of Aunt Jemima. Not only did the image help the company turn a profit, it also expressed what whites thought the appropriate attitude and behavior of black women should be—that is, smiling, cooking, and serving the white-controlled economy.[13] The dilemma for practical theology then is a lack of analysis around cultural artifacts. The effects of such negative cultural representation are part of the skeletal framework of lived experience, but their meaning and effects depend on whether one is the object of representation or the viewer engaged in objectification.

In a bible study on the text the Charleston nine were reading the night they were murdered, Townes raised the question, "Why does our daily existence depend on racist/sexist/classist/ heterosexist/ageist structures so evident to the marginalized but invisible to the powerful?"[14] For the practical theologian, this means that the invisibility of the social dimension of raced bodies seems normal if one is not situated at the margins. The disavowed yet operative ideologies and values of those closest to the center of power, along with the lack of sustained reflection, results in the internalization of ideological positions and cultural artifacts of oppression that shape the questions and solutions of the discipline. The psychologies and ideologies of privilege are entrenched in the scholarly production and constructive efforts of practical theology. With rare exception, the lived realities of raced bodies generally fail to materialize or to

11 Klaus and Elke Zobl, "Cultural Production."

12 Elke Zobl and Siglinde Lang, "Investigating the Matrix of Cultural Production" in *P/art/icipate: Kultur Aktiv Gestalten* 1 (2012), accessed August 18, 2015, http://www.p-art-icipate.net/cms/investigating-the-matrix-of-cultural-production/.

13 Emilie M. Townes, *Womanist Ethics and the Cultural Production of Evil* (New York: Palgrave Macmillan, 2006).

14 Emilie M. Townes, "The Ground We Choose," Fearless Bible Study Series, Benton Chapel, Vanderbilt University Divinity School. Jun 24, 2016. Unpublished. Bible Study using the same text, Mark 4: 16–20 the Charleston Nine were studying before they were massacred.

become the basis for the discussion. Thus, discussing racism and the body relies on the listeners' and the presenters' preexisting internalized images. And the conundrum arises: when racial bodies do "show up," we must ask if the words and images of raced bodies in scholarship mirror negative images and ideas that reside in the psyches of some readers. Thus, unless practical theologians engage in critical social analysis, their professional advancement will occur at the expense and exploitation of raced bodies.

Given the commitment to describing lived experience, practical theology will more thoroughly inhabit its identity and aims when it pays attention to raced bodies. This effort is not without complication as is evident in cultural historian Sandar Gilman's treatment of Saartie Baartman, a black South African woman whose body was displayed publically as part of the raced medical discourse of the early 1800s. In the medical and scientific literature of the day, Baartman is referred to as the Hottentot Venus and described as having a "hideous form" with a "horribly flattened nose," large and primitive genitalia, and protruding buttocks. Gilman notes that in addition to being on display in South Africa, she was exhibited in London and Paris. Under the guise of science and medicine, she served as an example of a primitive, different (from white European), and apelike female. Her body and the medical discourse surrounding it undergirded negative views of black female sexuality. Even after her death, Baartman was exhibited. However, in his critique of the exploitation of black women's bodies to satisfy European sexualized fantasies, Gilman perpetuates such exploitation by including in his book photos from the medical journals. Thus, Baartman was yet again displayed and discussed in the service of white scientific discourse. He sought to reveal the ways in which medical iconography expresses racial and gender ideologies. Yet, his unnecessary and unnecessarily frequent display of Baartman's naked body reproduced the sexualized content of the medical iconography he sought to challenge and, just as the medical journals of the 1800s, made the reader complicit in the process.[15] Practical theology will have to combat such practices too.

Pedagogical Mirrors: Racing White Bodies

Some years ago, in a class on "African American Spirituality and Religion," I had the class view the website www.withoutsanctuary.org created by James Allen.

15 Sander Gilman, "Black Bodies, White Bodies: Toward an Iconography of Female Sexuality in Late Nineteenth-Century Art, Medicine and Literature," *Critical Inquiry* 12, no. 10 (1985): 204–242.

It is a gallery of photos turned into postcards depicting lynchings between 1882–1968 in the U.S. My primary aim for the class was to wrench "spirituality" out of the hegemonic grasp of white Christian western perspectives.

The class was comprised of five or six black African Americans, one woman from Puerto Rico and one from Argentina, and five white students of Swedish-American background. Prior to viewing the website, the discussions had been robust, sometimes a little loud, but deeply engaged. As the class became less vocal and after a period of silence, I asked what was happening. All of them were angry—with me. Some were angry that I had exposed this horrible past; others, mostly white students, were angry that now I had created gulf between them and black students in the class. The Latina women were angry that they "felt horrible" and no longer knew how to participate in the conversation. The visuals were too much. Bodies hanging and displayed on a large screen was too much.

As I reflected on their intense responses, and my own, I knew there was more that I needed to include in this discussion of terrorized raced bodies. Over time, I realized that for all my focus on embodiment and the black/brown body, I had theorized the black body, ignored white bodies, and presumed only adult bodies as engaged in the act of lynching. As a consequence, I was surprised by the amount of anger directed toward me. It was evident that I had internalized a message that lynching was a one-dimensional bodily production where only black bodies were to perform race.

Yet the truth is that the photos of the lynchings can be viewed from a variety of perspectives, including one that focuses on the participation of white bodies, as Allen himself suggests in his own work. In a postcard chronicling the 1935 lynching of Rubin Stacy, a young white girl of about 10 is shown among the crowd of white observers. She is smiling. Her face stands out in the crowd of whiteness: she is the only one smiling.[16]

Generally, we have focused on the black bodies being lynched and not on the entertainment-seeking white bodies. Allen, in his narration, repeatedly makes clear that lynching was a public, social, and socially acceptable ritual event for whites to attend. And, as is evident in Allen's photos, the intended audience included white children. It can be argued that these ritual events were a means of socialization designed to sustain community and power dynamics. Lynching is a ritual practice, practical theologian Emmanuel Lartey reminds

16 James Allen, *Without Sanctuary: Lynching Photography in America* (New Mexico: Twin Palms Publishers, 1999), plate 57. To comprehend my argument, I encourage readers to view the photos.

us in a discussion of healing ritual: "Ritual is engaged in to effect transformation in the physical and material circumstances of the living community. Ritual action powerfully changes things… The ritual activity has to knowingly and symbolically reverse the evil that has been done or ritually performed."[17] In communal acts of lynching, the ritual was for incarnation of a cultural artifact and enactment of evil.

Materialization is the process of creating and reenacting the artifact in which latent and manifest meanings are evoked to serve particular ends. The living community, as Lartey suggests, is comprised of those who are the physical and symbolic targets and those who are agents of evil. Ritual action makes demands on the living, exploits the dead, and requires the process to be embodied by all parties—the whole community—and, for good or evil, functions as religious practice and lived religion. Historian Amy Louise Woods apprehends the religious features of lynching in its linguistic justification: those whose rhetoric spoke of the rightness of lynching used evangelical revival language of sin, salvation, and redemption, as well as holy retribution. Advocates "borrowed the language of evangelical moral crusades to justify—and sanctify" their actions. The rituals themselves "also uncannily reenacted evangelical church practices… (and) imbued lynching with the sacred meaning and even consecrated it as God's vengeance… the presence of witnesses linked individual members of the crowd to a larger community of believers."[18] Thus, lynching performed a major interior and social aspect of religion of the time; it distinguished the righteous from the unrighteous, the saved from the damned. Lynching made it clear that the base line was predicated on raced bodies.

Whereas ritual that is liturgy is sometimes defined as the work of the people of God and aimed at the transformation of the individual and community, the ritual of lynching worked to transform the (predominantly male) black body into the grotesque and subjugated. Lynching enforced conformity to racialized asymmetrical social positions: white bodies as enforcers and black bodies as the subjugated. Thus, lynching as ritual formed and socialized blacks *and* whites in relation to one another over a lifetime and across communities. Lynching was part and parcel of lived bodies' racialized and ritual experience. Pastoral theologian Lee H. Butler traces the "orchestrated" and even choreographed terroristic nature of lynchings. He sees a link between lynching and

17 Emmanuel Lartey, "Postcolonial African Practical Theology: Rituals of Remembrance, Cleansing, Healing and Re-Connection," *The Journal of Pastoral Theology* 21, no. 2 (2011): 1–17; 4.

18 Amy Louise Wood, *Lynching and Spectacle: Witnessing Racial Violence in America, 1890–1940* (North Carolina: University of North Carolina Press, 2009), 59–67.

the care of souls—and I concur. Lynching as a social symbol of oppression and arbitrary and lethal violence primarily directed toward black Americans is socially and psychologically powerful. It leaves what Butler calls a "psychic imprint,"[19] what Jay-Paul Hinds metaphorically describes as "Traces on the Blackboard" and "vestiges of racism on the African American psyche."[20] Its legacy is psychological but it is also social in that it is internalized in the collective cultural identifications of black Americans as well as in white Americans. This is why a picture, an effigy, or linguistic reference to the possibility of lynching evokes rage, terror, and protest and why white Americans can still draw on it as a symbol of white power and a threat reminding black men and families of the potential for violence, retribution, and murder. These vestiges are not just imprinted on the psyches of black Americans but also on the psyches of white Americans who make use of the history to signify violent intent readily directed toward black people. Lynching then is clearly a concern for the care of souls despite the great resistance to seeing it as such. Butler found that the resistance is often expressed as confusion. He reports:

> When I gave an address on the subject, the audience was not just horrified… they also seemed to be confused about why pastoral theology should take this up as a topic. One person kept asking, "How do you teach that in pastoral care?" Although the question was "how," the person's concern was really, "What does the history of lynched African Americans have to do with the care of souls?"[21]

How can lynching not have everything to do with the care of souls in a country where effigies of lynching show up on major university campuses as well as "Christian" colleges? The disruptive nature of a violent effigy is its immediate threat to one's psychic peace of mind. The bodies hanging from the tress are not silent. This is not a distanced museum experience. Neither are other experiences, such as the rape of black women in the Midwest described by historian Darlene Clarke Hine.[22] The prevailing ideology held that black women could

19 Lee H. Butler, "Lynching: A Post-Traumatic Stressor in a Protracted-Traumatic World," *Sacred Spaces: The e-Journal of the American Association of Pastoral Counselors* 4 (2012): 8.

20 Jay-Paul Hinds, "Traces on the Blackboard: The Vestiges of Racism on the African American Psyche," *Pastoral Psychology* 59 (2010): 783–798.

21 Butler, "Lynching," 8.

22 Darlene Clark Hine, "Rape and the Inner Lives of Black Women in the Middle West: Preliminary Thoughts on the Culture of Dissemblance," *Signs* 14, no. 4 (Summer 1989): 912–920.

not be raped and were, in fact, illicit and sexually available; rather than take responsibility for raping black women, white men blamed the black women themselves. White society's apparent acceptance of such inhumane treatment rests on a highly developed and long-standing ideology of denial, violence, and, deafness to intense intergenerational pain.

Whereas lynching postcards primarily produced the disfigured black male body, colonialist photography and postcards of the African and African American women, often in various stages of nakedness, gained their own social capital by proliferating dehumanized and uncivilized views of black femaleness. Cultural anthropologist Christraud Geary notes that "in the heyday of postcard production before the First World War (1914–1918), postcards were akin to newspapers and covered all kinds of topics."[23] Black women's bodies, often half clothed and sometimes naked, were readily available. These postcards were touted as a form of ethnographic research and claimed to represent "Africans' daily life" while actually revealing ideologies of race, gender, and culture of "Western photographers' and consumers' imagination"—thus creating, reproducing, and sustaining a static imaginary of tribal Africa.[24] Moreover, they marketed black women's images as forms of erotica and pornography. The texts that accompanied the postcards and the notes written on the blank side fueled the colonial racialized sexual fetishes of African black life. The images and the photographs intertwined a faux scientific approach and language to construct the race, gender, and sexuality of African women.[25] Geary uncovers the veiled sexual nature of many of the postcards, and especially those where the pose or positioning of the "model" is clearly designed to present "a crass erotic depiction. Inspired by Orientalist imagery, Fortier (the photographer) had young nubile women pose—often in pairs—and accentuated their availability and sexuality."[26] Thus, postcards of black bodies, and in this case, black women's bodies, reveal and shape western imagination and notions of the manipulability of black bodies by and for the gratification of white sexualized and racialized appetites. So, unlike the aim of lynching postcards of inscribing murderous terror and entertainment, many of these postcards inscribe a text of sexual "primitivity," availability, and exploitability at will. The black female's body is used to prove her need for civilizing influence and appropriated for

23 Christraud M. Geary, "The Black Female Body, The Postcard and the Archives," in *Black Womanhood: Images, Icons, and Ideologies of the African Body*, ed. Barbara Thompson (Seattle, Washington: University of Washington Press, 2008), 144.

24 Geary, "The Black Female Body," 148.

25 Geary, "The Black Female Body," 151.

26 Geary, "The Black Female Body," 151.

the aggressive sexual gaze. Exposing the veiled perverted desires of the photographers and consumers, however, does not free us from the conundrum that runs through this essay: "the critic may become the expository agent and contribute to this legacies' continuous impact and exploitation" regardless of intent.[27] The wrestling, however, must continue in order for practical theology to take raced bodies seriously.

Speaking Bodies

In the streets

beauty, love and horror
surround us in the cities called
Baltimore and Ferguson
and beyond.

Brothers, sisters
our children

slain in a rhythmic
2/4 cadence
rituals of horror

mothers, sisters, fathers and brothers
wailing in the street

resistance is the beauty
we claim
that we grasp
with tear
caressed hands

our psyches traumatized
horror
as blood flows from bodies
battered bruised
to death

27 Geary, "The Black Female Body," 158.

I see too in the streets
love survives
for the lost and struggling

Beauty calls
for change
change: justice
where are you?

Still. Silent. Moaning. Calling.

Beauty can be heard crying in the streets:
Where are you justice and liberty?

Heart break as bodies remember:
this steady methodical terror
is not a new thing:
old hatreds must not prevail.

Love demands more
Love emboldens
Love requires
eyes wide open courage

love and beauty
survive to protest
another day.[28]

Like writer and activist Darnell Moore, I am interested in the ways in which religious scholars have theorized or failed to theorize the "Black body." More specifically, I am interested in the places and ways our theorizing has dislocated the actual body from our discourse. More broadly, I am interested in how some bodies—black bodies—are allowed into the discourse as more "raced" than other bodies. In other words, black bodies, it seems to me, represent race and racism. Moore is helpful because he describes a communicating body that expresses its own discreet experiences. Thus, he argues for the body's subjectivity:

28 Phillis Isabella Sheppard, "Speaking Bodies," Author's unpublished poem, April 30, 2015.

> Bodies speak. And if we attentively listen, we may perceive enchanting utterances or terrible articulations: deep bewailing; faded susurrations; or divine musings. Bodies emote. Every moment when tears spill from our eyes, cold chills race across the skin, and the heart thumps with the chest cavity, we bear witness to an emotive performance. Bodies remember. They are recorders of histories: recalling life's journeys, capturing ethereal groanings, calling forth blissful memories, summoning joys and pains, the hurts and the healings, that which we choose to remember and even that which we will to forget.[29]

Thus bodies have linguistic and evocative qualities; that is, bodies communicate subjectivity and produce responses that are context-specific and ripe with meanings. As a consequence of this communicative, evocative, and meaning producing ability, bodies' subjectivities can be altered and transformed, and they in turn affect the subjectivity of surrounding communicating bodies. Thus bodies engender subjectivities.

Shortly after the Ferguson killing of Michael Brown, two doctoral students at Vanderbilt Divinity School organized an exhibit and forum, "Nightmare On ~~Elm~~ Our Street." Courtney Bryant created a "Living Memorial" that my class on womanism attended. We struggled to take in the battered black and brown bodies. We made a slow meditation walk through the memorial of large sculptures of those who had been beaten or murdered by police. The walk was disruptive. Pictures and posters filled with quotations that most of us had heard before were now jarring when paired with sculptures. Some of the quotations are listed below.

> *Sign 4: Nearly two times every week in the United States, a police officer killed a black civilian, 2007–2012*
>
> *Sign 5: Black males aged 15 to 19 are eight times as likely as white males to be gun homicide victims, 2009*
>
> *Sign 6: "The idea of calling this poor young man [Michael Brown] unarmed when he was 6′4″, 300 pounds, full of muscles, apparently, according to what I read in the* New York Times, *on marijuana. To call him unarmed is like calling Sonny Liston unarmed or Cassius Clay unarmed. He wasn't unarmed. He was armed with his incredibly strong, scary self."* ~ Ben Stein, Aug. 27, 2014
>
> *Sign 7: What does this mean for me?*

29 Darnell L. Moore, "Theorizing the 'Black Body' as a Site of Trauma: Implications for Theologies of Embodiment," *Theology and Sexuality* 15, no. 2 (2009): 175–188.

Sign 8: Police are "barometers of the society in which they operate." Hubert Williams, former police director of Newark, N.J., and Patrick V. Murphy, former commissioner of the New York City Police Department, 1990

Sign 9: Black people are almost three times more likely than white people to be subjected to force or threatened with force by the police, 2008[30]

One person noted that initially she thought the experience would be like going to a museum, but instead the memorial "invaded" the space and forced a response. In a museum, one has time to ward off despair, anger, and hopelessness. The memorial had no "trigger warning."[31] The "nightmare on our streets" requires mourning and grieving. Bodies on display surrounded by quotations and statistics disrupted our sense of *knowing*. No longer could brown and black bodies under attack be an intellectual discussion of abstract methodologies, thought, and aims. Bodies displayed in the center of academic discourse—dead—were here made visible, visceral, animated. They became speaking bodies. What do dead but speaking bodies say to us? What are their demands? As a panelist for a discussion of the Nightmare on ~~Elm~~ Our Street Living Memorial, I asked the audience to think about the need for specific rituals during this time mourning:

Rituals Required

What kinds of rituals of mourning, lamentations, and grief need to
accompany—maybe even evoke, our scholarship and activism?
As I considered the highly publicized "event" of Michael Brown's
funeral, I lamented that it seemed to me that his family had little
time or space to grieve and mourn his death; to cradle his black
loved body. As in the murder of so many black and brown
people—whose bodies are publically displayed in the streets—
the loving tender care of transition from life to death is denied.
I dream of water rites, washing of bodies by loved ones, holy water,
blessed oil lavishly, lovingly applied.[32]

30 Curated by Courtney Bryant (2014), Vanderbilt Divinity School doctoral student in Ethics and Society as part of the "Nightmare on ~~Elm~~ Our Street."

31 Trigger warnings are statements appearing on some syllabi that inform students that they may be affected by the class content. There is considerable debate around their usefulness and their impact on the learning and teaching environment.

32 Phillis Isabella Sheppard, "Mourning Reflections for Nightmare on ~~Elm~~ Our Street Panel," Vanderbilt Divinity School (2014). I am grateful to Emmanuel Lartey's work on ritual and healing for inspiration.

Remembering, Mourning and Acting

I think one of the hardest things we have to do
as black folk is to remember
the terrors running like lightning
through all of our lives,
and, then, to mourn the deep losses;
the repetitive evils levied against bodies—
ours and those toward whom we must clasp arms with
in the struggle.
We sometimes think the burying of desecrated black and brown
bodies is the
mourning *phase*; it is not.
Mourning,
the life changing kind,
takes time; takes courage; and it takes a change in us.
The kind of change that happens when we go there, go deep,
and then go out
activists—even in mourning.[33]

Bodies Formed to Speak

In 1994 I experienced a blatant form of racially based housing discrimination. As a Sister of Providence in my third year, I moved into an apartment with another sister—a white woman—with the landlord's agreement. Though he had not met me, he liked renting to nuns. He also assumed I was white. One week after moving in, his son met me, and that evening the owner called to say he needed us to move in a week because a family member needed the apartment. As it turned out, no family member was seeking housing; he simply did not want a black person living in the apartment. My body spoke in stammering communiqué. Slowly over a three-year period, beginning with a mediation process, and finally litigation, I went completely bald. I lost all the hair on my body except my eyebrows and lashes. Truthfully, I did not *think* about *going* bald; rather, I felt pangs of loss and rage as my hair was stolen from me. My dermatologist, an expert on alopecia areata, determined, after several forms of treatment, that I would probably remain bald for the rest of my life. At one point, when I had one round mound of hair about two inches wide and long

33 Phillis Isabella Sheppard, "Remembering, Mourning, and Acting," Author's unpublished poem, 2015.

left, he suggested we "just shave it off. The rest is not coming back." I refused, not because I thought that he was wrong but because I did not want to participate in the theft. He was quite "curious" because he had not seen such a case of alopecia areata from someone not experiencing some other form of medical illness.

Psychiatrist Laurence J. Kirmayer argues that "there are two orders of experience: the order of the body and the order of the text."[34] He argues that our aching bodies remind us of this, that "if the text stands for a hard-won rational order, imposed on thought through the careful composition of writing, the body provides a structure to thought that is, in part, extra-rational and disorderly. This extra-rational dimension to thought carries important information about emotional, aesthetic, and moral value."[35] His work is both a corrective to the absence of the body (especially in psychiatric and medical illness discourse) and further problematizes the body in relation to illness and society. In locating the body's "insistence on meaning" in the realm of the extra-rational, bodies that express the experiences related to or resulting from racism, sexism, heterosexism, or colorism subtly become marked as irrational. This problem is, of course, an old one that specifically and more readily marks black and brown bodies, women's bodies, transgendered bodies, and all bodies that do not reflect the bodies assumed to be white/male/heterosexual/body.

In a brief treatment on the Wall Street Journal's 2007 blogsite, Robin Moroney reveals a dire but not too surprising connection between experiences of racism and health issues. Cited in the piece is Jules Harrell, a psychology professor at Howard University: "The expressions on their faces. All I could think was, 'Good God, I'd hate to see their cortisol levels."[36] Harrell is referring to the Rutgers women's basketball team which was the target of sportscaster Don Imus' sexist and racist rant. Imus and two of his colleagues continued their ranting as the team won their game. A search of "2007 Rutgers women's basketball team" offers a plethora of images of these women's faces revealing various emotional responses.

I, on the other hand, would have hated to see their cortisol levels the day radio talk show host Don Imus offered his apology for his racist remarks (etc.) to the team, and the coach announced that the team had accepted his apology. She announced, "We, the Rutgers University Scarlet Knight basketball team,

34 Laurence J. Kirmayers, "The Body's Insistence on Meaning: Metaphor as Presentation and Representation in Illness Experience" *Medical Anthropology Quarterly* 6, no. 4 (1992): 323.

35 Kirmayers, "The Body's Insistence," 325.

36 Robin Moroney, "How Racism Hurts the Body," http://blogs.wsj.com/informedreader/2007/07/15/652/.

accept—accept—Mr. Imus' apology, and we are in the process of forgiving."[37] Imus' comments were focused on his fantasy of their bodies and made clear that he thought of them as appropriate and safe for the projection of fantasies. In the moment that Imus made his comments, it was clear, or should have been, that he was exploiting these young women for the purposes of his sexualized and racialized craving for humiliation. That his wife attended the ceremonial apology only further revealed his perverted psychology. Following the choreographed apology, Deidre Imus went on air to say, as she co-hosted a fundraiser for children's charities, "They gave us the opportunity to listen to what they had to say and why they're hurting and how awful this is." "He feels awful," she said. "He asked them, 'I want to know the pain I caused, and I want to know how to fix this and change this.' I have to say that these women are unbelievably courageous and beautiful women."[38] My reading—and it is one fueled by exhaustion and anger at the repeated mis-representation and exploitation of black and brown bodies—is that the Imus couple gratified their own needs, beyond the obvious financial ones, in the exchanges directed toward these women. The Imus couple obviously needed to absolve themselves in order to regain their social standing—so they "confessed." But they also voyeuristically reproduced the young women's pain, and re-insinuated their position of power by calling for the team to listen to their confession. The Imus's responses re-exerted their white social power by declaring, these women are "courageous and beautiful." Their courage and beauty is defined on the Imus's terms: the team members, while not offering forgiveness, have agreed to work toward forgiving them—publically, verbally, and on command.

Racing Transgender Bodies

I am persuaded to consider transgender experience at this point as a further example of the conundrum concerning raced bodies because I have been interested in how the news outlets have covered Bruce Jenner's transition to being a transgender woman. His expensive and highly choreographed entrance on the Hollywood stage of "reality TV," touted as a generic transition process, is obviously problematic when viewed through the lens of race, gender, class, and sexuality. His photograph on *Vanity Fair* reproduces fantasies, mostly men's, of femininity, gender, and sexuality. Caitlyn's gender non-conformity and trans-

37 Vivian Stringer, "Rutgers Team Accepts Imus' Apology," CBS News, 2007, accessed May 1, 2015, http://www.cbsnews.com/news/rutgers-team-accepts-imus-apology/.

38 Stringer, "Rutgers Team."

formation is presented in stark contrast to the narrative of most transgender women of color. Sakia Gunn, a black fifteen year-old lesbian who identified as aggressive (very male identified), was murdered in 2003 when she rejected the sexual advances of a group of black men who attempted to 'pick-up' Gunn and her friends. Her murder was a hate crime that barely made the local news.

I am not suggesting that these two women—one senior-aged and one still a teenager—did not both struggle mightily with expressing their identities. I am pointing out the obvious: Sakia Gunn, a black woman, was brutally murdered on the street, yet her murder was barely reported, and Caitlyn Jenner, a white transgender woman, is glamorized, making money, and experiencing considerable fame. A young black woman is unknown to many. A very privileged white woman is photographed and reported on multiple times a day. We are told her body is what women strive for—and in her transformation, and with a lot of money and social capital, she has achieved it.

Kelly Cogswell and Ana Simo offer a reason for Sakia's murder and its minimal coverage. It is not just white racism that renders Sakia invisible and unimportant as a black lesbian who resists oppressive notions of femininity and gender; it is the deeply hostile view that both blacks and whites hold toward black queers that reproduces violence against queer bodies: "The reason why Sakia Gunn was killed, and why her murder has faded from the headlines, is that both whites and blacks wish young black queers would disappear. Until things change, they will, thanks to violence, and AIDS, and hate."[39] What is apparent is that some nonconforming gendered raced bodies, black and brown, remain targets of violence and hate while other white raced bodies with financial and social standing are given a space of public acceptance. The conundrum emerges in recognizing the racism and classism present in the public dismissal of Sakia Gunn's murder and the racial, sexist, and classist privilege afforded Caitlyn Jenner. Their lived experiences may be read by some as a morality tale, namely that resistance to regulated gender norms is death dealing.

In 2009, 17 percent of all reported violent hate crimes against LGBTQ people were directed against those who identified themselves as transgender, with most (11 percent of all hate crimes) identifying as transgender women. The remainder identified as transgender men, genderqueer, gender questioning, or intersex.[40] Consider the *New York Times* report on a black transgender woman's death in what police identified as a "suspicious" fire:

39 Kelly Cogswell and Ana Simo, "Erasing Sakia Who's to Blame?" *The Gully Online Magazine*, 2003, accessed May 3, 2015, https://web.archive.org/web/20130509035706/, http://www.thegully.com/essays/gaymundo/030606_sakia_gunn_murder.html.

40 http://www.ovc.gov/pubs/forge/sexual_numbers.html.

> She was 25 and curvaceous, and she often drew admiring glances in the gritty Brooklyn neighborhood where she was known to invite men for visits to her apartment, her neighbors and the authorities said.
>
> Called Lorena, she brought two men to her apartment, at 43 Furman Avenue in Bushwick, either late Friday night or in the early hours of Saturday, the police said. About 4 a.m., a fire broke out in the apartment. A passer-by ran into the four-story building and began banging on doors... everyone seemed to emerge from the building—except Lorena.
>
> When the blaze was extinguished, at 4:37 a.m., Lorena was discovered, "unconscious and unresponsive," the police said, and paramedics declared her dead at the scene.[41]

There is a problem with this picture. While the police are "authorities" on crime, and news outlets "authorities" on newsworthiness, in this case they represent themselves as moral authorities and commentators on this woman's life. What is the newspaper account reporting—a suspicious fire, murder, or a black transgender woman's body? Why is Lorena identified as "curvaceous" and a target of "admiring glances in the gritty Brooklyn neighborhood"? Furthermore, the article states she was "called Lorena." Does this mean she was actually someone else? A fake? In so describing her, old highly sexualized tropes of black women are imposed on the news account. A transgender black woman then is immediately appropriated to fit into already existing racial stereotypes. She is murdered, and this is the best we can expect of the New York Times and police investigators?

Malformed White Bodies' Lived Experience

Contrary to the common ideation that the racing of bodies is predominantly a phenomena limited to brown and black bodies, every one and every group is subject to racing in the U.S. context. However, there is variation and variety in the life of the raced body. Some of the variation and variety is due to color, gender, racial classification, class, ethnicity, sexual orientation, and education. What might these bodies be telling us?

The photo of the very young child wearing KKK attire and staring at his reflection in a black state trooper's guard shield was taken by Todd Robertson in 1992. We cannot know but are compelled to ask, what might this child experi-

41 http://www.nytimes.com/2012/05/13/nyregion/woman-in-group-of-transgender-performers-dies-in-brooklyn-fire.html?_r=5.

FIGURE 9.1 Todd Robertson photo of toddler in Klan uniform. 1992.

ence, and how might it influence his formation as a white child to see such a reflection of himself? We might also ask, what might the black officer experience during this occasion of protecting the KKK's right to march? And finally, the child's mother, whose back is to the viewer of the photo is almost on the periphery, dressed in black. We cannot see her expression.

FIGURE 9.2 Little Rock Nine protesters. 1959. GETTY IMAGES.

In the 1959 picture above are two Little Rock, Arkansas, white children during the integration of the school system by the "Little Rock Nine." The angry adults and the mob festering with rage immediately draw our attention. But note the two children: a white girl to the viewer's left, with her face turned away from the crowd and their line of gaze, and the boy to the right behind the flag, his hands clasped together on top of his forehead. Unlike the adults, these children seem to be experiencing something very different from the adults. Is the girl being formed or forced to turn away from white mob behavior or to not notice or to experience her own full affective experience? How are hers, and the boy's, white bodily responses relevant or represented in the work of practical theology? How is their bodily presence integral to their formation?

In the photograph below, the black reporter, L. Alex Wilson, who was then editor of the Memphis, Tennessee-based office of *The Defender*, covered the Little Rock story. While there, he was repeatedly attacked.[42] Will Counts, who

42 Will Counts' Photograph, taken September 23, 1957 Indiana University Bloomington Archives Photograph Collection, image number P0026614 http://webapp1.dlib.indiana.edu/archivesphotos/results/item.do?itemId=P0026614&searchId=1&searchResultIndex=4.

FIGURE 9.3 Will Counts' photo of L. Alex Wilson, journalist for *The Chicago Defender* being attacked. INDIAN UNIVERSITY ARCHIVES, 1957.

also took many photographs we have come to associate with that crisis, took the photograph. The white crowd behind Wilson and the unnamed white man who is 'riding' Wilson's back all reproduce various representations of raced bodies: Wilson is straddled like a horse and resists being ridden. The crowd, some adjacent with the bulk following have an investment in Wilson's submission. I ask of the photograph(er): what are you telling us about white and black bodies? And, are you seeking to reveal, transform, or solely represent the power dynamics between white and black raced bodies? Or is the photographer a disinterested, objective conveyor of images? While I may be employing what Ayo Abletou Coty describes as a "postcolonial response to colonial representations"[43] of white and black bodies, I must also ask: have I only reproduced raced bodies in an already culturally embedded and socially established asymmetrical power relation? These kinds of quandaries and questions about raced

43 Ayo Abletou Coly, "Housing and Homing the Black Female Body in France: Calixthe Beyala and the Legacy of Sarah Baartman and Josephine Baker," in *Black Womanhood: Images, Icons, and Ideologies of the African Body*, ed. Barbara Thompson (Seattle, WA: University of Washington Press, 2008), 275.

bodies in society and in practical theology have given me pause, and at times lead me to despair.

What then is the conundrum with which I struggle? Can we take up raced bodies in our work as practical theologians? Will these images of white racism in action, while generally invisible as a daily dynamic, reveal, transform, or reproduce stereotypes and icons of terror? Although in practical theology we are able to analyze race, gender, and sexuality, I wonder whether we are able to represent fully lived raced bodies in our scholarship—our texts—without benefiting from the underside of "images, icons, and ideologies" in the name of research. The academy demands texts but we are faced with profound limits. One limit is that the "ideology of whiteness becomes actualized and normalized to the point of invisibility by way of language, media culture, and schooling."[44] Strangely enough, it is not just whiteness that becomes actualized and normalized into invisibility: black bodily experiences are conscripted into maintaining the invisibility of whiteness. This conscription occurs through the calculated establishment of norms that reflect an unacknowledged culture of whiteness. And this culture of whiteness moves among us in bodily forms and cultural practices.

This is not a new conundrum for me: Over fifteen years ago, I wrote a dissertation entitled *Fleshing the Theory: A Critical Analysis of Select Theories of the Body in Light of Black Women's Experience*. The generally understood task of scholarship—theological and otherwise—replaces the body's experience of race and of being a raced body with text, words, and a certain distance. It is not lost on me that in most of the news stories, YouTube videos of protesters and police responses, and 'on the street' interviews concerning Michael Brown and his death, so very little was said about his body, riddled with bullets bleeding lying in the street. However, after the grand jury failed to indict the officer, his mother said, "this could be your child. This could be anybody's child."[45] What as practical theologians do we hear being said to our field when we join Mrs. Brown staring at her black teenaged son riddled with bullets on a street in Ferguson, Missouri? Do we replace violated bodies with abstract theological questions and categories "appropriate" for and required by the scholarly guilds that claim our allegiance? Yes, it may be that our academic settings

44 Monica Beatriz deMello Patterson, "America's Racial Unconscious: The Invisibility of Whiteness," in *White Reign: Deploying Whiteness in America*, ed. Joe L. Kincheloe, Shirley Steinberg, and Ronald Chennault (New York: St. Martin's Press, 1998).

45 Dana Ford and Josh Levs, "Michael Brown's Mother: This Could be Your Child," *CNN News*, 2014, accessed November 27, 2014, http://www.cnn.com/2014/11/26/justice/ferguson-grand-jury-reaction/.

demand this of us. However, sometimes, it is a truth-telling act if we do not comply with that demand. The specter of raced bodies looms over practical theology—powerfully felt but unseen—and demands critical responses.

The Ethical Demands of Raced Bodies for Practical Theology Liturgy of Terror

Liturgy: the work of the people; public work; public practices with intention[46]
The Word: Black bodies

What if we were to admit we are living in exile from God—?
What if we were to confess that violence, the wielding of guns, and bloodshed—
the liturgy of terror—is sin?
What if we were to examine the liturgy of terror as is it used
for sadistic pleasure,
[*Why was he licking his lips?*],
psychic relief—through domination—
to escape the ethical demands of the day—and admit: It is evil?
What kind of people would we know our selves to be—
living among?[47]

The metaethical: The fact of the lived experience of raced bodies demands both a metaethical and normative turn in practical theology. Such shifts are not easy to make. Rather than pursue the epistemological question (what can we know from the body?) or a theological one (how do actual physical bodies shape religious and theological knowledge?[48]), I am making an ethical inquiry:

46 See William T. Cavanaugh, "The Work of the People as Public Work: The Social Significance of the Liturgy," *Institute of Liturgical Studies Occasional Papers*, 2008, accessed May 1, 2015, http://scholar.valpo.edu/cgi/viewcontent.cgi?article=1003&context=ils_papers; Delores S. Williams, "Rituals of Resistance in Womanist Worship," in *Women at Worship: Interpretations of North American Diversity*, ed. Marjorie Procter-Smith and Janet R. Walton (Louisville, KY: Westminster/John Knox Press, 1993), 215–223; and http://www.allsoulscville.com/sites/default/files/web/Liturgy_Drama%20and%20Work%20of%20Worship.pdf accessed 5/1/15.

47 Phillis Isabella Sheppard, "Liturgy of Terror," Author's unpublished poem, 2015.

48 Bonnie Miller-McLemore, "Embodied Knowing, Embodied Theology: What Happened to the Body?" *Journal of Pastoral Psychology* 62 (2013): 743.

what do raced bodies require *of* us as individuals and communities? Bodies formed to speak surely make ethical claims. The ethical turn is to include the reality of raced bodies while not reproducing the widespread stereotypes. But this ethical demand also insists that practical theology's scholarship more fully represent and engage scholars whose experiences and scholarship is not white and situated in other dominant categories. Moral theologian and womanist M. Shawn Copeland is helpful in her discussion of "racism and the vocation of the Christian theologian." The vocation of the Christian theologian is to hold tightly the

> spirit-filled, prophetic, critical, and creative edge... our theology must stand with society's most abject, despised, and oppressed... In the twilight of American culture, telling the truth about white racist supremacy is a theological obligation, no matter how cauterizing those truths may be. To speak about theology as truth-telling is to accentuate its core responsibility..."[49]

The question for practical theologians is: what do raced bodies require of our practical theology? The struggle to take on this inquiry, and how to do it, brings to mind womanist ethicist Katie Cannon's description of her task as an ethicist: The work of the black womanist ethicist is to "debunk, unmask, and disentangle the historically conditioned value judgments and power relations that undergird the particularities of race, sex, and class oppression."[50]

Furthermore, Cannon questions "an unspoken informal code within the guild that the Black woman academician must engage in... abstract moral discourse or else she runs the risk of being misunderstood, misinterpreted, and frequently devalued."[51] A similar concern grabs my attention; that is, is there a code within practical theology that demands that we treat raced bodies as invisible and, as a consequence, as having no moral agency? Invisible raced bodies without moral agency cannot make moral demands of our discipline or of lived raced bodies. Thus, raced bodies are rendered morally neutral, lacking moral action and lacking moral value. Such a rendering of raced bodies then means they can be missed or mistreated in our scholarship in whatever way

49 "M. Shawn Copeland, "Racism and the Vocation of the Christian Theologian," *Spiritus* 2 (2002): 21.

50 Katie G. Cannon, "Hitting a Straight Lick with a Crooked Stick: The Womanist Dilemma in the Development of a Black Liberation Ethic," *The Annual of the Society of Christian Ethics* 7 (1987): 165.

51 Cannon, "Hitting a Straight Lick," 166.

serves our disciplinary and professional purposes. Cannon is of further assistance when she notes that, "When ethical discourse provides truncated and distorted pictures of Black women, the society at large uses these oppressive stereotypes to define what it is to be Black and female in America."[52] She highlights our dilemma—a practical theology that ignores raced bodies is morally defunct and supplies society with a means to reproduce negative images that buttress oppressive structural (legal, religious, and relational) practices. Practical theology is complicit in silence and the failure to recognize moral agency of raced bodies. The other side of the conundrum is how should practical theology engage raced bodies and be accountable to their ethical demands while contending with the reality that such efforts can be exploited to reinforce racial cultural dynamics? The conundrum notwithstanding, a practical theology emerging from ethical commitments to articulating lived experience and the transformation of practices of oppression must turn to raced bodies as a central feature of our work.

The ethical turn here is very much connected to the conundrum of this chapter. The explicit question, 'what do raced bodies require *of* practical theology?,' is new and reiterates the conundrum. Practical theology requires an architecture that takes raced bodies seriously and makes raced bodies visible; however, in making raced bodies visible, dynamic, and powerful enough to evoke the transformation of communities, individuals, and religious and spiritual practices, it risks reproducing the very raced and racist ideologies it seeks to eradicate in the service of justice.

The resistance to recognizing the ethical demands of black bodies is significant. Most recently, for instance, resistance is evident in the linguistic culture wars between the Black Lives Matter movement and the counter messages of the All Lives Matter movement. Black Lives Matter, a movement that insists that black bodies matter and have moral value and agency, is a response to police violence against black children, men, and women. It claims that murdered black bodies should make ethical demands on society and the justice system. The shift to All Lives Matter seeks to undo the ethical demands by ignoring and erasing the larger social context that perpetuates the message that black lives do not matter and may be subjected to arbitrary and lethal violence. Thus, the All Lives Matter response actually reproduces white moral norms that are ineffectual for articulating a vision of the world where black lives really do matter. In actuality, All Lives Matter reinvigorates practices that are ultimately designed to protect white bodies by ignoring the broad social context of police

52 Cannon, "Hitting a Straight Lick," 167.

brutality against black and brown bodies. The social location, and therefore the very different experiences, of lived raced bodies are rendered ethically irrelevant. If we are to turn toward the ethical task in this conundrum, we have to ask on the front end of our work what difference raced bodies make for/in practical theology, certainly in the scholarship on the body and embodiment, but also on the whole enterprise called practical theology. We will not be freed from the conundrum of raced bodies on display in our work but we will bear witness to the lived experiences of dismissed raced bodies and the discipline's history of complicity. In the process, we just may transform the scholarship, membership, and practices of the discipline.

Bibliography

Allen, James. *Without Sanctuary: Lynching Photography in America.* Santa Fe: Twin Palms Publishers, 1999.

Baker, Al, and Nate Schweber. "Woman Dies in a Brooklyn Fire That Is Deemed Suspicious." *The New York Times.* May 12, 2012. Accessed September 12, 2015.

Butler, Lee H. "Lynching: A Post-Traumatic Stressor in a Protracted-Traumatic World." *Sacred Spaces: The e-Journal of the American Association of Pastoral Counselors* 4 (2012): 8–34.

Cannon, Katie G. "Hitting a Straight Lick with a Crooked Stick: The Womanist Dilemma in the Development of a Black Liberation Ethic." *The Annual of the Society of Christian Ethics* 7 (1987): 165–77.

Cavanaugh, William T. "The Work of the People as Public Work: The Social Significance of the Liturgy." (2008). http://scholar.valpo.edu/cgi/viewcontent.cgi?article=1003&context=ils_papers accessed 7/27/2016.

Chasseguet-Smirgel, Janine. *Sexuality and Mind: The Role of the Father and the Motehr in the Psyche.* London: Kamac, 1989.

Chasseguet-Smirgel, Janine. *Female Sexuality: New Psychoanalytic Views.* London: Kamac, 1992.

Cogswell, Kelly and Ana Simo. "Erasing Sakia Who's to Blame?" The GULLY | Gay Mundo | Erasing Sakia. 2003. Accessed May 3, 2015.

Coly, Ayo Abiétou. "Housing and Homing the Black Female Body in France: Calixthe Beyala and the Legacy of Sarah Baartman and Josephine Baker." *Black Womanhood: Images, Icons, and Ideologies of the African Body* (2008): 259–277.

Copeland, M. Shawn. "Racism and the Vocation of the Theologian." *Spiritus: A Journal of Christian Spirituality* 2, no. 1 (2002): 15–29.

Crumpton, Stephanie M. *A Womanist Pastoral Theology against Intimate and Cultural Violence.* Basingstoke: Palgrave Macmillan, 2014.

Ford, Dana and Josh Levs. "Michael Brown's Mother: 'This Could Be Your Child'—CNN.com." CNN. 2014. Accessed November 27, 2014.

Frankenberg, Ruth. *White Women, Race Matters: The Social Construction of Whiteness*. Minneapolis: University of Minnesota Press, 1993.

Geary, Christaud. "The Black Female Body, the Postcard, and the Archives." *Black Womanhood: Images, Icons, and Ideologies of the African Body* (2008): 142–61.

Gilman, Sander L. "Black Bodies, White Bodies: Toward an Iconography of Female Sexuality in Late Nineteenth-Century Art, Medicine, and Literature." *Critical Inquiry* (1985): 204–242.

Haney-Lopez, Ian F. "The Social Construction of Race: Some Observations on Illusion, Fabrication, and Choice." *Harvard Civil Rights-Civil Liberties Law Review*, 29 (1994).

Hill, Markeva. *Womanism Against Socially-Constructed Matriarchal Images: A Theoretical Model Towards a Therapeutic Goal*. New York: Palgrave Macmillan, 2012.

Hinds, Jay-Paul. "Traces on the Blackboard: The Vestiges of Racism on the African American Psyche." *Pastoral Psychology* 59, no. 6 (2010): 783–798.

Hine, Darlene Clark. "Rape and the Inner Lives of Black Women in the Middle West: Preliminary Thoughts on the Culture of Dissemblance," *Signs* 14, no. 4 (Summer 1989): 912–920.

Ignatiev, Noel. *How the Irish Became White*. New York: Routledge, 1995.

Kirmayer, Laurence J. "The Body's Insistence on Meaning: Metaphor as Presentation and Representation in Illness Experience." *Medical Anthropology Quarterly* 6, no. 4 (1992): 323–346.

Klaus, Elisabeth, and Elke Zohl. "Cultural Production in Theory and Practice: 'Doing Culture,'" *P/art/icipate: Kultur Aktiv Gestalten* 1 (2012).

Lartey, Emmanuel Yartekwei. "Postcolonial African Practical Theology: Rituals of Remembrance, Cleansing, Healing and Re-connection." *The Journal of Pastoral Theology* 21, no. 2 (2012): 1–1.

McDougall, Joyce. *Theatre of the Body: A Psychoanalytic Approach to Psychosomatic Illness*. New York: W.W. Norton, 1989.

Merriam-Webster. Accessed September 12, 2015.

Miller-McLemore, Bonnie J. "Embodied Knowing, Embodied Theology: What Happened to the Body?" *Pastoral Psychology* 62, no. 5 (2013): 743–758.

Moore, Darnell. "Theorizing the 'Black Body' as a Site of Trauma: Implications for Theologies of Embodiment." *Theology & Sexuality* 15, no. 2 (2009): 175–188.

Moroney, Robin. "How Racism Hurts the Body" http://blogs.wsj.com/informedreader/2007/07/15/652/.

Obach, Brian K. "Demonstrating The Social Construction of Race," *Teaching Sociology* 27, no. 3 (July 1999): 252–257.

Parker, Evelyn L. "Womanist Theory." *The Wiley-Blackwell Companion to Practical Theology Miller-McLemore/The Wiley-Blackwell Companion to Practical Theology*, 2011,

204–13. Accessed August 30, 2015. http://www.blackwellreference.com/subscriber/tocnode.html?id=g9781444330823_chunk_g978144433082320.

Patterson, Monica Beatriz Demello. "America's Racial Unconscious: The Invisibility of Whiteness." In *White Reign: Deploying Whiteness in America*, edited by Joe Kincheloe, Shirley Steinberg, Nelson Rodriguez, and Rodney Chennault, 103–122. New York: St. Martin's Press, 1998.

"Sexual Assault: The Numbers | Responding to Transgender Victims of Sexual Assault." Sexual Assault: The Numbers | Responding to Transgender Victims of Sexual Assault. Accessed September 12, 2015. http://www.ovc.gov/pubs/forge/sexual_numbers.html.

Sheppard, Phillis. "Mourning the Loss of Cultural Selfobjects: Black Embodiment and Religious Experience after Trauma." *Practical Theology* 1, no. 2 (2008): 233–257.

Sheppard, Phillis. *Self, Culture, and Others in Womanist Practical Theology*. New York: Palgrave Macmillan, 2011.

Sheppard, Phillis Isabella. "Liturgy of Terror." 2015.

Sheppard, Phillis Isabella. "Rituals Required." 2015.

Sheppard, Phillis Isabella. "Remembering, Mourning and Acting." 2015.

Stringer, Vivian. "Rutgers Team Accepts Imus' Apology." CBSNews. 2007. Accessed May 1, 2015.

Townes, Emilie Maureen. *Womanist Ethics and the Cultural Production of Evi*l. New York: Palgrave Macmillan, 2006.

Townes, Emilie M., Introduction to Katie Geneva Cannon and Kristine A. Culp. "Appropriation and Reciprocity in the Doing of Feminist and Womanist Ethics." *The Annual of the Society of Christian Ethics* (1993): 187–203.

Townes, Emilie M., "The Ground We Choose," Fearless Bible Study Series, Benton Chapel, Vanderbilt University Divinity School. June 24, 2016. Unpublished.

Wood, Amy Louise. *Lynching and Spectacle: Witnessing Racial Violence in America, 1890–1940: Witnessing Racial Violence in America, 1890–1940*. University of North Carolina Press, 2009.

Williams, Delores S. "Rituals of Resistance in Womanist Worship." *Women at Worship: Interpretations of North American Diversity*, edited by Marjorie Procter-Smith and Janet R. Walton, 215–223. Louisville, KY: Westminster/John Knox Press, 1993.

Zohl, Elke and Siglinde Lang. "Investigating the Matrix of Cultural Production," *P/art/icipate: Kultur Aktiv Gestalten* 1 (2012).

CHAPTER 10

The Complexity of Local Knowledge

Katherine Turpin

I recently attended an academic conference where practical theologian Denise Thorpe presented a fascinating paper on the practice of cemetery visitation on All Saints Day (*Velines*) in Lithuania.[1] Fully fifteen minutes of her presentation involved describing the history of the area through fifty years of political repression, warfare, displacement, and genocide. Thorpe described the role of religious space for political resistance under Communist rule, and she addressed the psychological trauma and deep silencing that this violent history caused in the people of Lithuania. The paper also included a few stories of representative individuals and their family histories within the broader context. All of this thick description was necessary for an audience half a world away to begin to understand the practice she was analyzing. After briefly outlining the contours of the particular religious practice and reflecting on its meaning, she noted that this meaning was so contextualized to the history of that particular community in place and time that it was difficult to imagine whether it might be translated or related to similar practices elsewhere. The audience engaged in a brief time for questions and answers, and we moved on.

Listening to this paper highlighted a conundrum in practical theology: How do we adequately account for and incorporate the complexity of local knowledge in the work of practical theology? While Thorpe's paper, written for an often ahistorical U.S. audience far from Lithuania, was particularly telling with its intense focus on the complexity of the local context that shaped the ritual practice on which she focused, the struggle to give an accurate or even good-enough account of all that comes together in any given moment of religious practice or human experience arises any time we want to engage in the work of practical theology. To attend to the complexity of local knowledge requires practical theologians to let go of the hope for orderly description and enter the murky, swirling waters of lived human experience.

1 The paper was a part of a panel entitled "The Materiality of Practical Theology" at the biennial meeting of the Association of Practical Theology, presented March 29, 2014 in Nashville, TN. Thorpe's fuller work on the practice is available in her dissertation: Denise Elaine Thorpe, "Memory on Fire: The Re-Membering of the Lithuanian Body (Politic)" (PhD diss., Duke University, 2013).

 | DOI 10.1163/9789004324244_012

Describing the full extent of what is going on in any moment of human experience or religious practice requires much more than we can hold in our minds, much less articulate clearly. The complexity of how experience comes together at the intrapersonal level of the individual, the interpersonal dynamics in relationships, the shared life of the congregation or local community, the local context and its history, and the broader cultural contexts and ideologies that interact with all of these levels of experience can become overwhelming. When we give nuanced accounts of the contradictions, unconscious influences, and embodied knowledges captured at each of these levels of interaction, the insurmountable complexity of local knowledge becomes painfully evident. All of our attention may be required just to get a handle on what is happening, and we may struggle to proceed to other important and necessary tasks. Careful attention to this level of nuance and detail in the engagement with living religious persons is a hallmark of practical theology; making decisions about which of these layers of complexity matter and must be accounted for in professional ministerial practice or practical theological work presents a conundrum to the practical theologian.

In this chapter I will articulate the layers of complexity in shaping an account of local knowledge and describe why this complexity matters both in the context of professional practice and in the production of the Christian tradition. After some attention to the ethical and pragmatic challenges such complexity poses to the practitioner or academic practical theologian, I argue that skilled attention to the irreducible complexity is a hallmark of the practical wisdom necessary for the discipline. Provisional claims about the salient features of a context lead to a range of possibilities for constructive engagement and response in the midst of the dynamic quality of lived religious experience.

Shaping an Account: the Descriptive Work of Practical Theology

The first task of practical theology is descriptive because in practical theology our reflections arise from and return to the concrete particularities of lived human experience and religious practice. In *A Fundamental Practical Theology*, Don Browning said the descriptive task goes beyond general grounding in the features of a situation (an introductory task common to many theological works outside of practical theology) and requires questioning the concrete particularities of people and their communities in detail. Understanding the concrete situation "consists of the special histories, commitments, and needs of the agents in the situation. It consists of the interplay of institutional systems and how they converge on the situation. And it includes an analysis of the various religio-cultural narratives and histories that compete to define and give meaning to the situation."[2] Even in this basic definitional moment, Browning hints at the competing and conflictual nature of these particularities, their complexity at multiple levels of descriptive engagement, and the multiple cultural logics at play. He names this work a combined social scientific and hermeneutical task, with attention to the "thickness of practice" in all of its visional, obligational, environmental-social, and psychological dimensions.[3] Browning also notes the hidden normativity embedded in the kinds of descriptions that we offer, calling out his congregational study colleagues on the way that their normative theologies impact the kinds of descriptive questions and data they report.

Like Browning, Richard R. Osmer affirms the function of good descriptive work by naming the descriptive-empirical task "priestly listening," a term that points to the potentially holy and transformative act of such deep attention to a context.[4] He focuses on the informal, semi-formal, and formal processes of attending to personal relationships, circumstances, and cultural contexts of others as the first task of practical theology. He recommends methods of qualitative research such as case study and participant observation to understand what is happening in concrete detail in the lives of people in congregational settings. While such expertise in depth research methods may be beyond the time commitments of what most ministers can actually manage in their settings, Osmer's overview provides a helpful sense of the range of complex inquiry required to discover "What is going on?" before engaging in pastoral intervention or leadership. He focuses primarily on the work of practitioners, including this kind of careful attention to local knowledge as part of the priestly task.

Similarly, when Thomas Groome describes his practical theological method of "shared Christian praxis," readers begin to develop an overwhelming sense of the complexity of a descriptive task that may initially seem fairly straightforward. His first movement, Naming/Expressing "Present Praxis," is more participatory and collaborative than the task of description undertaken by an individual practical theological scholar or practitioner as in Browning and Osmer. Like the Brazilian educator Paulo Freire who informs his work, Groome understands that the key to discovering "What is going on?" lies in the interac-

2 Don S. Browning, *A Fundamental Practical Theology: Descriptive and Strategic Proposals* (Minneapolis: Fortress Press, 1991), 55.

3 Browning, *A Fundamental Practical Theology*, 110.

4 Richard R. Osmer, *Practical Theology: An Introduction* (Grand Rapids: Eerdmans, 2008), 31–78.

tion between the forces at work in lived experience and the meaning people make of them. In order to access this knowledge held by participants about the situation under investigation, what Groome calls the "generative theme" that is motivating the shared theological reflection, I will give you his description in full: "With regard to content, participants can depict how the theme is being lived or produced, dealt with or realized, 'going on' or 'being done' in their own or in society's praxis; they can express their sentiments, attitudes, intuitions, or feelings toward it, the operative values, meanings, and beliefs they see in present praxis of the theme, their perceptions and assessments of it, their commitment regarding it, and so on."[5] If this task does not sound complex enough, it is followed by a second movement, which involves critical reflection on that praxis and requires attention to: "its reasons, interests, assumptions, prejudices, and ideologies (reason); its sociohistorical and biographical sources (memory); its intended, likely, and preferred consequences (imagination)."[6] Groome's attention to the complexity of local knowledge indicates that this knowledge is mediated in relationships between people and the context in which they are situated. His work also draws attention to the power-laden and aspirational qualities of local knowledge for the future identity and commitments of the community.

My gut response to the work of these first two movements in Groome's method is Psalmic: "Such knowledge is too wonderful for me; it is so high that I cannot attain it."[7] Any descriptive moment in practical theology is going to give an account of only part of what is going on, eliding the full complexity of that knowledge. But what elements of that knowledge are necessary to take into account in engaging a given practical theological project? Developing the practical wisdom to sort lived experience for the salient elements of local knowledge at play in a given situation is one of the key, and yet challenging and slippery, tasks of practical theological reflection and the initial framing moment of its constructive work.

Let me ground this complexity in a particular example. When I teach religious education, I often share a story about the formative power of liturgical language. Here is how I usually tell it:

> I once served a congregation where for fourteen years the pastor's invitation to the communion table each month had been: "This table does

5 Thomas H. Groome, *Sharing Faith: A Comprehensive Approach to Religious Education & Pastoral Ministry* (San Francisco: Harper Collins, 1991), 146.

6 Groome, *Sharing Faith*, 147.

7 Ps. 139: 6, New Revised Standard Version.

> not belong to me. The table does not belong to this congregation or the United Methodist Church. The table belongs to Jesus Christ. Whether or not you are even a Christian, if you hear the invitation from Jesus today, then come and eat." When a new pastor was appointed to the congregation, we warned him that the congregation was accustomed to a radically open communion table. "I understand," he replied. The first Sunday of the month he offered an open invitation to the communion table: "In the United Methodist tradition, we have an open table. All baptized Christians are welcome to partake." The congregation was deeply offended by his exclusivist invitation limiting the table to the baptized, and this example was repeatedly lifted up by lay persons over the next year as the congregation lamented the bad theological match between the pastor and the congregation.

In one sense, this story gives accurate and helpful insight into why the pastor's invitation was problematic in the local context. The account provides a strong example of the formative power of the repeated verbal forms of the liturgy.[8] The story rests in the particular experience of a local congregation, and it accounts for local practice in some detail.

At the same time, this story conceals many important details of what was happening in this interaction that could influence practical theological analysis of the situation, details I rarely mention when I tell this particular stock story to teach about the formative power of liturgy. For example, this new pastor was the first duly appointed minister of African descent to the congregation which, despite having been interracial for decades, had always been led by a white pastor appointed by its denominational bishop. Many of the African-American parishioners later wondered if the uproar over this statement had more to do with white resistance to a black pastor than anything about the theology of an open Eucharistic table. These parishioners wondered if deeply embedded white supremacy contributed to the revulsion at this pastor's presence at the altar rather than the explicit theological language of the spoken invitation to the table.

I could also share that the invitation to communion came after an entire service in which this pastor had exclusively referred to God and humanity in masculine pronouns in a congregation that had been intentionally using inclusive language for over two decades. This jarring shift caused much angst

8 I use this story as my teaching example for the concept of inscribing practice from Paul Connerton, *How Societies Remember* (Cambridge: Cambridge University Press, 1989), 73.

amongst the older generation of women of both races who had fought the battle for inclusive language as second wave feminists. Their sense of the pastor's exclusivity moved beyond the language of the invitation to the table to include all the ways that God and humans had been named throughout the service in male terms.

Or, I could tell you that because this congregation was located in the southeastern United States, many of the congregants were Southern Baptist by upbringing. Involvement in racial reconciliation through alternative service during the Vietnam era had also brought a significant Mennonite subpopulation to the congregation because of its social justice commitments. Coming from believers' baptism traditions, many of these congregants had unbaptized children who had been participating in communion for years who were suddenly excluded from participation in the ritual by this statement. So, denominational traditions and understandings were also at play in the reaction to this statement.

I could also explain that the pastor was Liberian and had been raised in congregations deeply informed by hierarchical relations between clergy and lay people. These missionized congregations tend to be more orthodox theologically than many mainline congregations in the United States. Class and cultural tensions between African immigrant and African-American persons were also playing out in the congregation's resistance to the pastor. His mannerisms of interaction were much more formal and his expectations for the respect of the congregation for the pastor more in line with the Liberian and African-American churches he had been serving than for this mixed-race congregation that leaned white liberal in its embodied culture of pastor/parishioner interaction. The congregants misread his embodied expectations for respectful deference in the pastoral role as his support of elitism and hierarchy, and this contributed to the tensions.

Finally, I could tell you that after this congregation had chosen to align itself with the Reconciling Movement of the United Methodist Church, as the first non-house church to name itself fully welcoming to LGBT persons in all aspects of church life in its region, the presiding bishop had sent a conservative pastor to bring this apostate congregation back into line. In the appointment process, the bishop had been clear that he thought the next pastor needed to "fix" the congregation and bring it back into orthodoxy on issues of sexual orientation, and many members of the congregation knew this situation and feared whom the bishop was going to send before this pastor ever arrived. Since much of the congregation came from congregational rather than episcopal traditions, suspicion of the authority of the bishop went beyond the interpersonal concerns about the particular bishop as a bad actor to include deeper formation that understood a congregational call process as the proper way to acquire a pastor.

Although I could go on, you get the picture. My stock practical theological story about the formative power of liturgical language is revealed to have elided realms of information about the local knowledges at play in this seemingly simple interaction. Instead of being a five sentence example grounded in actual contextual congregational practice, the example requires two full pages to even begin to explain, even though I have only spoken in gross shorthand about all that was at play. As you were reading these pages, you probably began to forget what my original point was for telling the story, and each level of information I shared began to elicit layers of questions, connections with personal experience, and doubts about my reliability as the narrator of the story. This kind of complexity makes telling a compelling story or giving an incisive analysis about a practice, an experience, or a situation that could translate beyond the immediate context difficult. All of the forces at play make leadership decisions about what matters the most in beginning to address the situation complicated and renders theological reflection about the situation by congregation members fractured and multiple. As professional practical theologians and practitioners, we make choices concerning which level of information about which kinds of knowledges we are going to attend in our own analyses, and in doing so, we often hide information that is contradictory or difficult to explain easily.

Why Complexity Matters, and Why We Don't Always Attend to It

One reason to make the complexity of local knowledge less vivid is to feel some control over the situation in order to respond with a sense of professional competence. Those contested and painful knowledges that make human religious experiences complicated and messy sometimes get eliminated to give the impression of expert knowledge and command of what is going on, a mastery that is built into the norms of academic discourse and professional practice. This elision of difficult and contradictory details also occurs in the case examples in care and counseling books, where the ambiguities and complexities of particular lives are often simplified in order to make assessment and decisions for intervention easier for student readers. Attending to all of the levels of local knowledge at play moment by moment can be overwhelming as part of the practical wisdom necessary to act, especially for beginners.

This sense of desire for control in the practice of description may go back to the origins of cultural analysis in Eurowestern culture. When systematic theologian Kathryn Tanner describes the origins of the term "culture" in theological discourse, she includes a telling description of the motivations for truncating local traditions and customs in early French understandings of culture: "Instead, the very objectification of local traditions and customs in the interest of social control prompted a totalizing vision of them, an effort to comprehend them as a whole. A sort of 'functionalism of the erroneous and the abhorrent' sprang up as a backdrop to the possibility of rational progress. How local customs and traditions hang together had to be investigated systematically if they were to be taken apart effectively."[9] If the purpose of description in the beginning of practical theological analysis is to get a sense of what is going on in order to create an intervention, this need for a description that allows control over the situation in order to stage a response and make it better may lead us to reduce complexity.

A second reason that the complexity of local knowledge poses a challenge to practical theology is that some local knowledges are seen as relevant and significant, and other knowledges have less status and legitimacy for theological knowing and professional practice. Talking about the historical experiences of colonialism and their effect on the reception of a pastor could be dismissed as nonessential to the theological explication of this case. While few would challenge my story about the formative power of liturgical language, when I introduce controversial ideological and political realities at play, my description of the theological situation becomes much more difficult to articulate and defend, especially which parts of all the contextual information could and should be considered properly theological.

The question of what counts as religious or theological knowledge in the context of living human communities is not unique to practical theology. Robert Orsi ponders the question in his work as a scholar of lived religion studying devotional practices to St. Jude. In one particular passage, he describes sitting in a service and trying to decide what elements to include as part of his description:

> What matters—the sermon or the range of interactions and exchanges taking place among the congregation in the interval of the sermon's time? My attention was inevitably drawn away from the official words and postures occurring on the main altar and toward the secret, subtle, but persistent interpersonal connections—nudges, glances, thighs

9 Kathryn Tanner, *Theories of Culture: A New Agenda for Theology* (Minneapolis: Fortress Press, 1997), 8.

> pressed against one another, hands held or withheld—going on all around me during the service. I noticed that women kept their prayer books in their purses, tucked in among their other private things. What relationship did this indicate between the shrine, with all its powers to heal and to comfort, and the intimate spaces of a woman's life?[10]

Orsi goes on to consider the editing out of "dirt, noise, children, the psychotic, animals, the smells of perfume" and other elements in order to represent an environment as sacred and begins to ask what this removal of the mundane and the difficult from the religious says about our own anxieties and desires to limit the sacred.[11] I would add to Orsi's list of characteristics many dominant culture persons have been taught to revise out of sacred experiences elements such as recognition of unequal power, class privilege, racial tensions and aversions, embodiment, and other tender subjects. To include too much of this kind of description marks theological work as ideological or politically interested, and this label challenges its validity as properly theological knowledge.

A third reason the complexity of local knowledge presents a conundrum to the practical theologian is that local knowledges move between micro and the macro levels of influence in intricate and sometimes confusing ways. The ideological impacts the personal, and communal histories link to both national and family histories in surprising ways. Accounting for this telescoping reality of interlocking forces at work can lead to halting and complex prose that can be difficult to follow. An example of a helpful multilayered description of this interlocking social ecology occurs in Pamela D. Couture's pastoral theological work mapping children's poverty, where she analyzes micro, meso, and macrosystems that affect children's socioeconomic realities.[12] By attending to the multiple levels of forces impacting local knowledges, connections between these levels may emerge and decisions about interventions may include attention to the broader realities contributing to the local context.

Individual Knowledges

At an individual level, people bring countless personal and relational histories, linked to social and communal histories, which create filters through which a particular religious ritual or experience is encountered. At the extreme micro

10 Robert Orsi, *Between Heaven and Earth: The Religious Worlds People Make and the Scholars Who Study Them* (Princeton: Princeton University Press, 2006), 165.

11 Orsi, *Between Heaven and Earth*, 165.

12 Pamela D. Couture, *Seeing Children, Seeing God: A Practical Theology of Children and Poverty* (Nashville: Abingdon Press, 2000), 43.

level, there are individual variances in the phenomenological level of sensory perception and dispositional reactions to sensory input, at the same time that these sensory experiences are already interpreted as they occur by the social categories and linguistic systems available to the person having the bodily experience. As psychoanalytic theorists would have us remember, some individual knowledge is below the level of consciousness, denied or repressed. To move to critical theory and gender and cultural studies, some local knowledges are made unthinkable to the individual by the social context, but are no less real and active in the experience of meaning-making even as the person would be unable to articulate them. Individual persons are contradictory: sometimes their espoused beliefs are quite different from their embodied behaviors. There are the things that people know they should believe, the things they are desperate to believe, the things they cannot bear to see as true, and the things they intuit but cannot articulate. Sometimes their cognitive understanding and their emotional responses are contradictory.[13] All of these experiences at the individual level are embedded in histories of power, normalization, language, and other social forms of knowing.

Interpersonal and Local Community or Congregational Knowledges

The pre-existing relationships between the players in the actual moment and their history of interaction play a role in religious experience, whether life-giving, abusive, loving, or benign. The habituated patterns of interaction between persons, drawing on cultural codes, gender norms, performances of sexuality, and other metasystems from the broader "field of play," inform contact between persons and what kinds of knowledge are generated from them.[14] These basic interpersonal interactions become systemic at the level of the family or the congregation or subcommunities within it, a phenomenon described in detail by the family systems work on congregations done by Edwin Friedman.[15] The dynamics of patterned responses over time influence how any given experience happens and is understood interpersonally.

When religious experience is embedded in the habituated religious practice of a particular congregation or local community, other factors come into

---

13 For a discussion of the relationship of feeling, bodies, and knowing in theology, see Bonnie J. Miller-McLemore, "Coming to Our Senses: Feeling and Knowledge in Theology" *Pastoral Psychology* 63 (2014): 689–704.

14 Pierre Bourdieu, *Practical Reason: On the Theory of Action*, trans. Randall Johnson (Stanford: Stanford University Press, 1998).

15 Edwin H. Friedman, *Generation to Generation: Family Process in Church and Synagogue* (New York: Guilford Press, 1985).

play: How has any particular practice happened here in recent memory? What are the norms of behavior that are enforced in this particular locale? Who is a part of the community who has a stake in this practice? What do they bring in terms of experiences, expectations, bodily formation and practice, and understandings? What are the meanings, both articulated and embodied, that emerge from the regular shared practice?

In their description of what they call "Corporate Theological Reflection," practical theologians Elaine Graham, Heather Walton, and Frances Ward note: "We examine how the faith community can construct a sense of corporate identity through the use of a central metaphor, or symbolic practices such as prayer, eating and working together, or by creating a narrative that tells the story of its ongoing life. Such metaphors, practices and narratives provide symbolic and theological power to enable a faith community to develop an idea of itself that sustains it through time and enables it to engage with and express its distinction from its culture."[16] Such corporate identity narratives are almost always contested and in motion. They are not repeated ad nauseam like branding in the corporate world, but emerge with more nuance and fragility in real life communities, even as they still contribute to local knowledge.

While the religious language or vocabulary common to the community may have one way of framing this sense of shared identity, the religious idiom is always in conversation with the cultural context. As Orsi observes, "Religious idioms are neither sufficient nor discrete. They interact with other competing, alternative, or complementary configurations of experience that are available outside the religious world."[17] One important question is how strong and vibrant the religious idiom in the congregation is compared to competing narratives and how well does the congregation know it?

While we might like to assert a collective identity within the family or the congregation, these systems are never uniform, and they become even more complex and negotiated in markedly multicultural communities where multiple socioeconomic class locations, racial/ethnic backgrounds, sexual orientations, and cognitive and physical abilities are present. In her study of Good Samaritan United Methodist Church, Mary McClintock Fulkerson works closely with the concepts of habitus in Pierre Bordieu and incorporating practice in Paul Connerton to assert: "Because practice refers to bodily as well as cognitive shaping, habituation into Christian faith is always accompanied by

16 Elaine Graham, Heather Walton, and Frances Ward, *Theological Reflection: Methods* (London: SCM Press, 2005), 109.

17 Orsi, *Between Heaven and Earth*, 169.

bodily habituations, from the proprieties of 'proper' body movement in a culture to its techniques and rituals."[18] This bodily shaping may reinforce the espoused theology of the community, or it may contradict it directly. She gives the example of the "tipping point" where whites feel uncomfortable because of the presence of "too many" black bodies as a bodily formation that directly contradicts the espoused beliefs of racial inclusion in the congregation she describes.[19] These formative norms are saturated with politicized social and ideological knowledges. They are more than individual quirkiness or how certain people consciously feel about race or gender, but instead these norms often follow in predictable patterns along the histories of racial inequality, embodied colonial practice, gendered, and/or classed norms. While there can be a congregational sense of these things, the individual variations and inflections matter: Was there a favored black uncle or explicit, derogatory racist language in the home of origin? Has there been a history of violence that amplifies more generic cultural fears and aversions related to race? How have these experiences been explicitly or subtly connected to the religious tradition?

Ideological, Historical, and Cultural Knowledges: Christian Traditions as Situated Knowledge

This complex descriptive task of local knowledges continues at the level of the broader context: How is this religious community positioned in its broader community? When was this community established and in response to what forces, such as economic growth, white flight, and urban redevelopment? To what extent does it define itself in congruence with its local community and where does it define itself in opposition to its local community? These local dynamics filter macro-level systemic knowledges such as histories, ideologies, regional cultures, national cultures, and media representations that are at work in the production of local knowledge.

In practical theology, the most commonly invoked macro-level elements are the theological beliefs and religious practices from Christian traditions. Philosopher of religion Mark C. Taylor describes the ways that an adequate understanding of religion requires recognition of its inextricable relationship to cultural, social, and natural networks as well. Each of these networks continue to be dynamic rather than static: "Each particular network must, therefore, be analyzed not only synchronically, i.e. in relation to other particular

18 Mary McClintock Fulkerson, *Places of Redemption: Theology for a Worldly Church* (New York: Oxford University Press, 2007), 49.

19 Mary McClintock Fulkerson, *Places of Redemption*, 82.

networks at a given moment, but also diachronically, i.e. in relation to its own development over time."[20] As an example, in Dale P. Andrews' *Practical Theology for Black Churches* we witness an extended contextual description of the relationships between the contemporary Black Church and a number of shaping factors, including African American folk religion, the historical context of racism and enslavement, the work of academic black theology, the ideology of American individualism, class displacement within the African American community, and the trajectory of black power movements. His nuanced account takes nearly an entire book to trace and understand what is going on in the relationship between the faith community and the broader historical and social forces impacting it before he can say something important about the role of black practical theology in bridging the gap between churches and academic theology.[21] His work models the effort to trace the synchronic and diachronic forces at work in black churches.

An additional complication is that the Christian tradition invoked in Christian practical theology is truly a set of Christian *traditions*, plural, that are themselves embedded in local knowledge generated out of particular contextual constructions, expressions, and retrievals in liturgies, artifacts, documents, texts, and histories of practice. At times, we fail to take the contextualized complexity of the tradition into account when we are connecting it with human experience for similar reasons that we reduce the complexity of local knowledge in the descriptive moment. In other words, the Christian tradition is as bound up in the complexity of local knowledge as the contemporary situations we engage. As Graham, Walton, and Ward conclude in their analysis of "local theologies" as one mode of theological reflection: "The articulation of 'local theologies' always involves a degree of tension between the immediacy of experience and cultural context and the claims of tradition that transcend any particular, specific geographical or temporal setting. Yet much of the argument of this chapter has been that no timeless essence of the gospel exists without its embodied expression in a particular time or place. Theology always addresses specific human dilemmas; and its continuing incarnation in the midst of different circumstances will of itself contribute to the continuing unfolding of revelation."[22] To wrestle with the complexity of the tradition as

20 Mark C. Taylor, "Refiguring Religion," *Journal of the American Academy of Religion* 77, no. 1 (2009): 113.

21 Dale P. Andrews, *Practical Theology for Black Churches: Bridging Black Theology and African American Folk Religion* (Louisville: Westminster John Knox, 2002).

22 Graham, et al., *Theological Reflection: Methods*, 226–227.

it emerges from local contexts as conflicted and intricate as the ones we experience requires an additional layer of reflection on the part of the practical theologian.

Additionally, the concerns of the local context drive our choices of what to invoke as normative from the breadth of the Christian traditions. As an example, in *Sharing Faith* Groome's description of what it means to make the Christian Story/Vision accessible with an awareness of its contextual specificity is instructive. He recognizes the way that any invoking of the tradition is always already embedded in the complex contextual particularity of that community. He names the following guidelines for interpreting the tradition before putting it into dialogue with the current praxis of the community:

> (1) Place the reign of God at the center of your consciousness as the constant "first criterion" that guides all interpretation and explanation. Then ask (2) Where am I coming from, and what am I bringing to this text? (3) How do I take account of the stories/visions of participants in my interpretation? (4) What life-giving truths and values does this expression of Christian faith mediate to our lives? (5) Are there possible distortions in the "dominant" interpretation and use of this text? Does it hold "dangerous memories" that can call in question and offer new life to the present? (6) What new and creative possibilities can or should I propose from the text to this context to encourage Christian commitment? *For explanation/application:* (7) Is my explanation in continuity with what is central to and constitutive of Christian Story? (8) Is my explanation likely to encourage these participants to live for God's reign? (9) Does my explanation reflect the teaching/learning of the "church" and respond adequately to the stories/visions of participants in this learning event?[23]

In this set of guidelines, we can also see how concern for the faithful practice of the local community in its particularity drives the choices of interaction with the tradition. Practical theological reflection emphasizes a formational and sustaining intent that allows the particularity of the local community and their desire for faithfulness to drive the interaction with the Christian tradition. There may be a reason that *Sharing Faith* went out of print almost immediately: such a posture of attention toward the complexity of the tradition in relation to the local community would be exhausting and likely impossible to achieve in practice when many of these layers are conflicted and hidden,

23 Groome, *Sharing Faith*, 240.

either by the power structures that inform knowledge or more intimate psychological processes of repression and denial.

Rather than this complex, ethically bound dialogical process between local knowledge and the Christian traditions, practical theologians may instead invoke major theologians such as Karl Barth, Catherine LaCugna, Karl Rahner, or James Cone as presumably valid dialogue partners with a particular situation without parsing the contextual realities that create both a particular theologian's knowledge and our desires to count it as authoritative. Sometimes in academic projects we see a scholar give an account for why a particular theologian is a good conversation partner for a particular situation, attending to translation possibilities between the local context of a theological figure and the current context. Other practical theologians will invoke someone like Bonhoeffer as authoritative as if he is automatically linked to any situation even if it does not involve the immediate crisis of genocide and imperial occupation. Thinking carefully about the complexity of local knowledge in the construction of a religious tradition begins to call into question whether there are shared traditions over time and across cultures and who decides what expressions of the tradition rise to the level of authoritative or normative knowledge cross-contextually. Careful practical theology attends to the particularity of both the context that produced the elements of the tradition that we are engaging and the complexity of the local context we are putting into dialogue with it and decides whether there is enough of a translation possible for a constructive conversation to take place.

Challenges to Practical Theology Raised by This Conundrum

All of this complexity of local knowledge is legitimately at play in any given human experience, religious practice, or life pattern about which we are concerned in practical theology. And yet, simply to describe them adequately takes loads of time, reams of paper, and people outside of the local context still would not quite understand the nuance available to someone immersed in the experience. Persons immersed in the experience would miss other distinctive elements that are obvious to outsiders. And so we shorthand, we make decisions about what to focus on and what to avoid, and those decisions have consequences for the kind of practical theology we do.

Practical theologians want to be able to speak across communities to say something useful to someone else about what we are learning in any particular circumstance, but speaking across different contexts requires the reduction of complex local knowledge into what we consider the most salient or compelling features of the experience we are exploring for the project at hand. As Tom Beaudoin and I argue in a critical examination of white practical theology, our willingness to engage that reduction, our deep trust in the value of the universal over the particular, may belie some of the roots of this discipline in a white supremacist project of controlling and reducing cultural difference and complexity for improved faith performance according to white standards.[24] At times, this impulse toward cross-contextual knowing should not be trusted. The over-valuing of the universal and trans-contextual as the crucial part of disciplined knowing may cause us to say more than we know about certain things. We may trust that our own localized knowledge, wisdom, and legitimized authorities can speak into other situations more than they should. These decisions necessarily reduce the complexity into a neater story. In that shorthand, like in my story of the pastor at the Eucharistic table, we may be eliminating important factors that inform local knowledge.

Practical theological researchers, teachers, and practitioners will inevitably pay attention to some of these levels of local knowledge, but not all of them, in their theological analyses and proposals for strategic action. The chosen knowledges and layers of experience that are attended to, either in simply "reading" the situation as a practitioner or in the descriptive moment in written practical theological accounts, begin to affect what counts as normative in practical theological discourse. For example, when I tell the story about the Liberian pastor and his exclusive invitation as a story about the inscribing power of liturgical language, I implicitly cast a vote in favor of liturgical language as the most important theological factor at play in that interaction rather than the intricacies of African immigrant, African American, and white liberal congregants and their racialized knowing. If I were to keep all of the knowledges I named at play in my analysis, I would be hard pressed to make one clear arguable thesis in a short piece. As a lay leader in the congregation, the bishop called to deal with this relationship, or the pastor reflecting on what is happening, I would be a little conflicted about which layer of interaction and knowing to begin to address within the situation as a ministry professional who engages in practical theological reflection. But we have to come down somewhere to start, so we make decisions about which elements are most salient.

The decisions practical theologians must make about which parts of this complexity to include in their work are not neutral. They are political, in that

24 Tom Beaudoin and Katherine Turpin "White Practical Theology" in *Opening the Field of Practical Theology*, ed. Kathleen Cahalan and Gordon Mikoski (Lanham, MD: Rowman and Littlefield, 2014), 251–269.

they are laden with the identity of groups and power relations that predate the current descriptive moment. They are ethical, in that they contain powerful judgments about the good, the just, and the beautiful that affect other people's experience. They are normative, in that the elements of local experience that gain attention generate a sense of the tradition and what matters within it through repetition and reinforcement. By focusing on certain elements over and over in time, the tradition begins to have weight and stability, and some knowledges count as part of the tradition and others are considered unimportant.

For example, within traditional Christian ritual practice, Eucharist has gained some measure of legitimacy in practical theological discourse for ethical behavior while hymn-singing has not. Outside traditional theological categories, experiences or practices deemed non-religious such as exclusion, body-shame, or infertility struggle to gain theological attention, even though these kinds of human religious experience occur in biblical texts and in historic and contemporary religious communities and are matters of grave importance in human experience. Because they have not been included as part of knowledge that is considered religiously important, they sometimes do not gain credence as "theological" experiences worthy of reflection without serious intervention.

Good practical theologians miscommunicate and get into conflicts because elements of the local complexity matter differently to different people, often by training or community of discourse. Some practical theologians focus more on the historical complexities of the production of the tradition, but do not attend as carefully to the multifaceted power dynamics of its contemporary practice. Others attend to the intricacy of the local community in practice, but fail to attend as much to the complexity of the religious tradition. I spent six chapters in a book on youth ministry amid difference, for example, exploring privilege and power, respect, class status as well as different understandings of being adult mentors to youth in different racial and class communities, and colleagues perhaps legitimately ask what is theological in the book.[25] Meanwhile, Kenda Creasy Dean, Chap Clark, and Dave Rahm's edited volume on youth ministry has five chapters about the context of youth ministry that do not name any of the dynamics I find so compelling and that focus instead on subjects such as owning up to our theological commitments and advocating for the global poor as a part of youth ministry.[26] Which parts of the complexity

25 Katherine Turpin and Anne Carter Walker, *Nurturing Different Dreams: Youth Ministry Across Lines of Difference* (Eugene, Oregon: Pickwick Press, 2014).

26 Kenda Creasy Dean, Chap Clark, and Dave Rahn, *Starting Right: Thinking Theologically About Youth Ministry* (Grand Rapids: Zondervan Academic, 2001).

of local knowledge we describe as our starting point influence the theological questions and categories we entertain, and sometimes make it difficult to recognize other people's work in the field as legitimate because their starting questions and concerns are so different from our own.

Failure to make wise decisions about which elements of the local knowledge are most salient to a project can run the risk of missing key factors for an audience and rendering either pastoral leadership or practical theological work unhelpful to them. As an example, I teach Thomas Long and Thomas Lynch's fine book *The Good Funeral* in a praxis course on rituals at the end of life. My students find it frustrating because it does not deal with contemporary realities in their own ministerial practices, namely funerals in interfaith families and the economic complexity that leads to geographically-scattered loved ones who cannot afford to gather quickly when the body is able to be present. While the authors engage contextual description, giving many reasons for the lack of bodies at funerals, such as modern squeamishness about bodies and distancing from daily care of the dying, they fail to address the contextual realities regularly experienced by my students.

In the book, Long's "perfect parable of the new religious pluralism" involves having to wait until the Wiccans finish their dance at a funeral at a different gravesite before he quietly starts the Christian funeral he is leading. For Long, religious pluralism was something that happens outside or on the fringes, rather than being an integral part of the religiously plural and Christian families involved in the ritual.[27] This description of contextual reality fails to connect with my students, many of whom are in religiously plural families, and whose ministerial experience more closely match the reflections of practical theologian Kathleen Greider in her work on religious pluralism: "However, [these vignettes] foreground a reality that has remained in the background in Christian practical theology: the persons, families, and communities practical theologians seek to serve have identities that are religiously multifaceted, and the webs of connection in which they interact are weighted by histories, futures, meanings, commitments, joys, and suffering shaped by religious multiplicity."[28] Would Long have been able to do the interesting work within the Christian tradition if he had wrestled with the contextual realities of interfaith, geographically dispersed, economically challenged families? His close

27 Thomas G. Long and Thomas Lynch, *The Good Funeral: Death, Grief, and the Community of Care* (Louisville: Westminster John Knox, 2013), 34–38.

28 Kathleen J. Greider, "Religious Pluralism and Christian-Centrism," in *Wiley-Blackwell Companion to Practical Theology*, ed. Bonnie J. Miller-McLemore (Malden, NJ: Blackwell Publishing, 2012), 452.

focus on the wisdom of the tradition and what it can offer was probably only possible by not being particularly engaged by these contextual realities that matter to my students. But his decision renders his account of the good Christian funeral suspect to my students, whose local knowledges are minimized in the text.

Paying attention to the complexity of local knowledge raises issues very similar to the problem of comparison in the study of religion more broadly. When can one legitimately speak across the complexity and embeddedness of particular communities of practice to compare them to other communities of practice? Scholars of comparative religion who address similar practices in wildly differing contexts and distinct religious traditions write about the difficulty of comparison when taking into account the complexity of local knowledge. In her work reflecting on comparativists Jonathan Smith, Robert Orsi, and Francis Clooney, Elizabeth McKeown notes that all three "insist that being in-between in the study of religion is the place to be, even though it entails personal risk, vulnerability, surprise and danger, as well as promise."[29] Instead of a stance of control of all the details characteristic of the modernist task of description, comparison starts from a place of humility and tentativeness. This need for modesty in what can be said across contexts may be one reason why attention to practice lacks legitimacy in the academy. Such a starting point conflicts with the performance of authoritative knowing that the academic voice of expertise demands.

Each of these layers of local knowing have entire disciplines (psychology, sociology, cultural anthropology, congregational studies, critical race theory, gender theory, historical theology) associated with being able to analyze and understand them. Developing the skills to "read" any experience or practice at each of these levels requires conceptual handles, characteristic questions, and modes of attention from these disciplines, as well as the ability to integrate them seamlessly in the description of what is happening. As a professional practical theologian, writing about all of these layers requires knowledge of vast literatures and histories of conversation beyond the capacity of any single scholar, so drawing across all of these disciplines becomes an issue of scholarly integrity when performed by an individual.[30] In their hermeneutical social scientific work on the family, *From Culture Wars to Common Ground*, Browning

29 Elizabeth McKeown, "Inside Out and In Between: Comparing the Comparativists," *Method and Theory in the Study of Religion* 20 (2008): 268.

30 Joyce Ann Mercer's chapter 7 (pp. 163–189) in the current volume addresses this related conundrum more fully, see pp. 162–181.

et al. described their strategy of working as a team of five authors as required by the demands of the discipline: “The complexity of this task takes insights from various disciplines and probably requires multiple authors, as was the case with this book. But such collaborative work is what is needed for good practical theology and is, we believe, a sign of what theology must become in the future.”[31]

When I used to help lead field education seminars at my school, one of the assignments that we regularly gave students to complete was a “social and theological analysis” of their internship site. Students were given instructions that included nearly two pages of questions about their site, meant to generate a thick description of it. These questions, like many given to novice participant observers, included everything from the use of space, to a theological analysis of language and symbol used in ritual, to questions about the distribution of power and relational patterns in the congregation. Students found this assignment both fascinating to complete and head-spinningly intricate. The curiosity it engendered was helpful in prompting them to begin to notice all kinds of information that previously was either taken for granted as “ordinary church stuff” or simply went unnoticed. The head-spinning came when we asked them to try to keep all of the complexity together in their minds as they thought about their work in the congregation, particularly in subsequent case study reflections and theology of ministry papers. Trying to account for the complexity of what was going on proved immensely difficult, at least for these novices, and they would often default to statements from their site supervisors, such as “The senior pastor says that if I just love on the congregation and show up when they are hurting, I don’t have to worry too much about all that is going on. They’ll give me a lot of grace.”

This kind of advice encouraged students to let go of the nuanced complexity of the organism that was their site and to focus merely on the primary demands of their gospel ministry: to love. For novices, this may not be terrible advice, but it certainly is not strong practical theological or pastoral leadership practice in the long run. More nefariously, it may also signal that love can happen without attention to particularity and sanction all kinds of patronizing and ignorant behavior in the name of the gospel (e.g., reducing persons with disabilities to objects of pity or charity rather than engaging their complex realities). This lack of attention to particularity is often compounded by faculty colleagues who dismissively or romantically talk about “the church”

31 Browning, et al., *From Culture Wars to Common Ground*, Second Edition (Louisville, KY: Westminster John Knox, 2000), 341.

as an abstract entity that functions the same way across space and time rather than paying careful attention to the complexity of local contexts, histories, and relational dynamics.

This complexity is also at the heart of the question of integration in theological education. Often we ask students to deal with the complexity of local knowledge by dragging all of these disciplines they have learned separately throughout their education into play in some magic integrational moment without ever telling them that keeping all of them in play at any given moment is impossible. They will always be making choices about the focus of their attention that have political and ethical implications. The emerging skill to do this kind of integration without blithely ignoring local complexity, but rather with an informed intuitive sorting of what is essential in the given moment, is part of the development of practical wisdom. This wisdom takes a long time and lots of experience in a given community to emerge.

What, Then, Shall We Do?

Holding all of the complexity of local knowledge of both lived human experience and the contextualized Christian traditions we engage in the pastoral and academic work of practical theology is impossible. And yet, I have claimed that such careful attention to the nuance and detail of local knowledge, its contradictions and complexity, is a hallmark of practical theology. As Joyce Ann Mercer notes in her practical theological research on children, "To be a credible account, such theological work must be recognizable both in terms of the adequacy of its description of a particular context or situation of human experience, and in terms of its description of God and God's activity."[32] So how do practical theologians address this conundrum?

To retain the attention to the complexity of local knowledge and to be able to speak across situations is a little like longing for God's perspective, a desire to pay attention simultaneously to the hairs on each head and the fate of nations. As academic practical theologians and ministry professionals who want to appear competent and in control, we seek a sweet spot: not too much complexity that it becomes only reflection on a very particular situation, but also not a universal perspective that ignores the complexity of local experience. Unfortunately, such a sweet spot does not exist. As practical theologians

32 Joyce Ann Mercer, *Welcoming Children: A Practical Theology of Childhood* (St. Louis, MO: Chalice Press, 2005), 11.

we always do violence in one direction or the other. This reality may call for practitioners and practical theologians to be more gentle with each other, to recognize the incomplete nature of any given project, and to imagine a range into which various projects and interventions fit, always partial and in need of revision, but contributions nonetheless.

When scholars take the time to analyze the complexity of experiences at multiple levels with attention to the contradictions, unconscious forces, and unexamined ideologies therein, they may produce papers or reflections that simply describe what is going on, without taking up its interaction with the shared claims of a faith tradition, how these inherited wisdoms might interact with the complex dynamic of the on-the-ground situation or the dialogical question about what to do in the face of this complex situation. In some cases, just completing a thorough description of what is going on may be an important achievement. Sorting out what is happening may allow later practitioners and theologians to do the dialogical work with the Christian tradition or make constructive claims about practice. However, paying careful attention to the complexity of local knowledge does not require that we become a discipline that only describes, because the constructive and praxical nature of the work of practical theology is essential to the task. So, as practical theologians we make constructive theological claims and recommendations for practice even in the face of this irreducible complexity, while recognizing with humility that these claims and recommendations are provisional at best.

Even after honing the ability to attend to the variety of dynamics and factors at play in any situation, even with careful observation and reflective thinking, the complexity of local knowledge assures that there is always something that remains unknowable. The realities we study are not stable; the emergent dynamic inherent to contemporary religious communities and lived human experience means they are always in motion. In practical theology, accounting for that remainder, the extent to which we do not know what is going on in any given practice or human experience, is often only tentatively mentioned rather than thematized as a normative part of working at the intersection of theology and lived human experience. Rather than approaching this unknowable remainder as a failure of the discipline, we might understand it as a marker of adequacy in attending to the uncontrollable multivocality of the local knowledges. We are responding reasonably to Orsi's challenge in the face of this complexity: "This is a call, then, for attention to religious messiness, to multiplicities, to seeing religious spaces as always, inevitably, and profoundly intersected by things brought into them from outside, things that bear their own histories, complexities, meanings different from those offered within the religious space. It is also a call to surrender dreams of religious order and singleness or of being able to organize descriptions and interpretations of religious worlds around sets of publicly shared and efficiently summarized meanings and practices."[33] This willingness to wrestle with the full complexity of local knowledge without reducing it to what we can control for the sake of appearing expert is a marker of practical theology's skilled provisional and improvisational quality as a discipline.

We might think of the different layers of local knowledge, its individual, interpersonal, communal, institutional, and ideological components, as different lenses on a camera that we look through to see what the image of the local situation looks like when framed through that lens. By noting which lens has been put on the camera, we can help readers and colleagues follow our trajectory in the task of description. Practicing going deep and going wide in our own thinking while changing the lenses through which we frame the situation frequently will improve our ability to navigate this complexity. We know that each intentional change of lens will produce a different picture and bear different risks in what it crops out. By trying to signal what we are framing and what we are cropping out, we risk speaking in the kind of qualified discourse that can make academic writing difficult to traverse, but we can also help our reader or our professional colleagues attend to the knowledges we ignore. As a model from the discipline, Mercer does precisely this kind of signaling in the beginning of her book *Welcoming Children:* "Instead, in my construction of a feminist practical theology of childhood I will start small. I will focus on a particular situation and problem, the welcome and flourishing of children in North American mainline congregations, who simultaneously participate in the church's education in Christian practices and in the culture's education in consumer practices… This work, then, represents an admittedly partial perspective, a specific topic and voice within the whole conversation, and not the whole of Christian theology itself."[34] Mercer declares her lens and its partial nature to her readers at the outset.

The strategic decision about where to focus may have something to do with the signs of the times or the pressing need of the moment for a given community. The descriptive account given of local knowledge always informs and frames the intervention that is the outcome of practical theological reflection. Like the photographer, the work of choosing lenses is somewhat intuitive in the writing of practical theology and in the practice of ministry more broadly. Through the development of practical wisdom, we develop antennae for the

33 Orsi, *Between Heaven and Earth*, 167.

34 Mercer, *Welcoming Children*, 6.

various layers and frames of lived human experience and develop our capacity to attend to what feels out of whack, contradictory, oppressive, or not resonant in a given moment.

As practical theologians, we also must ask to whom we are accountable in our various accounts of local knowledge. What is at stake for the community I am describing? Who will be implicated in my descriptive work? Who will benefit and suffer in the way I frame this account? By developing both the reflexivity in framing our choices to signal the range of forces at work and by honing the responsibility to the communities impacted by our work, we do the best we can with the messiness of living human religious experience. We begin to trust that perhaps practical theological attention to local knowledge ought to be more about comportment than completion. We come to understand that the local context is never the comprehensive and fully integrated description of a phenomenon, person, or community, but a disciplined attentiveness to who or what is studied that emphasizes where and how to look in this moment. We give up on the assumption that saying something significant is ultimately dependent on the possibility of someday being able to say everything significant about the topic under consideration. Like different retellings of the same legend, scholarly accounts of the complexity of local knowledge may engender positive connections through insights only possible through each author's distinctive methodological and analytical choices.

Practical theologians dealing with congregational uproars over Eucharistic invitations or trying to account for unique contextualized practices such as All Saints Day cemetery visitation in Lithuania will always be required to make strategic choices in their accounting for the complexity of local knowledge. These choices have ethical and normative implications for the forms of practice that they enable and the character of the traditions that they produce and reproduce. Recognizing with humility the strength of a provisional stance in the face of irreducible complexity in local knowledge requires letting go of desires for control and expertise typical of tidy accounts of context and claims about "best practices" across contexts. Developing practiced attention to multiple layers of interaction and practical wisdom regarding the most salient features operating in this moment allows for the improvisational response that is a hallmark of the skilled practical theologian.

Bibliography

Andrews, Dale P. *Practical Theology for Black Churches: Bridging Black Theology and African American Folk Religion*. Louisville: Westminster John Knox, 2002.

Beaudoin, Tom and Katherine Turpin. "White Practical Theology." In *Opening the Field of Practical Theology*, edited by Kathleen Cahalan and Gordon Mikoski, 251–269. Lanham, MD: Rowman and Littlefield, 2014.

Bourdieu, Pierre. *Practical Reason: On the Theory of Action*. Translated by Randall Johnson. Stanford: Stanford University Press, 1998.

Browning, Don S. *A Fundamental Practical Theology: Descriptive and Strategic Proposals*. Minneapolis: Fortress Press, 1991.

Browning, Don S., Bonnie J. Miller-McLemore, Pamela D. Couture, K. Brynolf Lyon, and Robert M. Franklin. *From Culture Wars to Common Ground*, Second Edition. Louisville, KY: Westminster John Knox, 2000,

Connerton, Paul. *How Societies Remember*. Cambridge: Cambridge University Press, 1989.

Couture, Pamela D. *Seeing Children, Seeing God: A Practical Theology of Children and Poverty*. Nashville: Abingdon, 2000.

Dean, Kenda Creasy, Clark, Chap and Rahn, Dave. *Starting Right: Thinking Theologically About Youth Ministry*. Grand Rapids: Zondervan Academic, 2001.

Friedman, Edwin H. *Generation to Generation: Family Process in Church and Synagogue*. New York: Guilford Press, 1985.

Fulkerson, Mary McClintock. *Places of Redemption: Theology for a Worldly Church*. New York: Oxford University Press, 2007.

Graham, Elaine, Heather Walton, and Frances Ward. *Theological Reflection: Methods*. London: SCM Press, 2005.

Greider, Kathleen J. "Religious Pluralism and Christian-Centrism." In *Wiley-Blackwell Companion to Practical Theology*, edited by Bonnie J. Miller-McLemore, 452–461. Malden, NJ: Blackwell Publishing, 2012.

Groome, Thomas H. *Sharing Faith: A Comprehensive Approach to Religious Education and Pastoral Ministry*. San Francisco: Harper Collins, 1991.

Long, Thomas and Thomas Lynch. *The Good Funeral: Death, Grief, and the Community of Care*. Louisville: Westminster John Knox, 2013.

Mercer, Joyce Ann. *Welcoming Children: A Practical Theology of Childhood*. St. Louis: Chalice Press, 2005.

Miller-McLemore, Bonnie J. "Coming to Our Senses: Feeling and Knowledge in Theology." *Pastoral Psychology* 63 (2014): 689–704.

McKeown, Elizabeth. "Inside Out and In Between: Comparing the Comparativists." *Method and Theory in the Study of Religion* 20 (2008), 259–269.

Orsi, Robert. *Between Heaven and Earth: The Religious Worlds People Make and the Scholars Who Study Them*. Princeton: Princeton University Press, 2006.

Osmer, Richard R. *Practical Theology: An Introduction*. Grand Rapids: Eerdmans, 2008.

Tanner, Kathryn. *Theories of Culture: A New Agenda for Theology*. Minneapolis: Fortress Press, 1997.

Taylor, Mark C. "Refiguring Religion." *Journal of the American Academy of Religion* 77 (2009): 105–119.

Thorpe, Denise Elaine. "Memory on Fire: The Re-Membering of the Lithuanian Body (Politic)." PhD diss., Duke University, 2013.

Turpin, Katherine and Walker, Anne Carter. *Nurturing Different Dreams: Youth Ministry Across Lines of Difference*. Eugene, Oregon: Pickwick Press, 2014.

CHAPTER 11

Reframing Practical Theology: Catholic Contributions and Conundrums

Claire E. Wolfteich

I have published two books with Paulist Press, the oldest and largest Catholic publisher in the United States. When I peruse the current academic catalog of Paulist Press, I notice that there is no category labeled "practical theology." Rather, under "theology" one finds: "Christian anthropology," "liturgical theology," "sacramental theology," "moral theology," "fundamental theology," "pneumatology" as well as a category for "papacy"—but no "practical theology." This takes a few minutes to sink in. Papacy or practical theology: the contrast between what is represented and what is not included here unsettles me. Must one choose? I resist the dichotomy. After all, Paulist has just published my edited volume, *Invitation to Practical Theology: Catholic Voices and Visions.*[1] Yet, there is no natural place to locate the book within the theological categories that structure the catalog. This dislocation stands at the heart of the conundrum I address in this chapter: how can I circumnavigate as a Catholic practical theologian within a discourse that is largely Protestant? The more disconcerting question underlies this: is there a fundamental disconnect between practical theology, the discipline in which I have been trained and which I have taught for nearly two decades, and Catholicism, my own tradition and spiritual home?

The conundrum of how to be a Catholic practical theologian is double-sided. Practical theology does not have a clear institutional home in Catholic structures—thus, the dislocation described above. In addition, where practical theology is vibrant, the discipline often is dominated by Protestant discourse and traditions of scholarship. The latter side of the conundrum can be illustrated by an anecdote from my own doctoral training. Like several other U.S. Catholic practical theologians, I completed my doctoral work at the University of Chicago Divinity School, an ecumenical, university-based school of theology. My first exposure to practical theology at the University of Chicago

1 Claire E. Wolfteich., ed., *Invitation to Practical Theology: Catholic Voices and Visions* (New York: Paulist Press, 2014).

 | DOI 10.1163/9789004324244_013

occurred during my Master of Divinity program, when I also did a field education placement at a local, progressive Catholic parish on the South Side of Chicago. Don Browning's masters-level practical theology course included a final project that involved the study of a concrete issue and context, working through the four movements of his fundamental practical theology, a method he had just recently developed in his 1991 book *A Fundamental Practical Theology: Descriptive and Strategic Proposals*.[2]

I was hooked. This was a way of studying that seemed to integrate and deepen my ministerial work rather than separating theology off in a disconnected academic vacuum. As a lay Catholic woman with uncertain prospects for a lifetime of ministry, I was thrilled at the opportunity to bring together teaching and scholarship in an intellectual/spiritual/pastoral vocation. I applied to the PhD program in Practical Theology, with a concentration in Spirituality, sure that this was the right fit. During my time in the doctoral program, I was able to spend a year doing a certificate in Pastoral Studies at St. Patrick's College, Maynooth, a pontifical university and national seminary in Ireland, thus deepening the integration of spirituality, ministry, and scholarship that I had sought. Alongside twenty-five Irish men preparing for ordination and two other laywomen, I learned to give retreats and studied moral theology, spiritual direction, and canon law. I did an internship in the marriage tribunal in Dublin. Every evening the seminarians sang the daily office. I remember the sound of Mary's Magnificat drifting through the chapel. When I told an American colleague where I was doing my work in pastoral studies, he remarked that the place must be "dripping in spirituality."

Back at the University of Chicago, spirituality was different, less visible. I worked on my doctorate in practical theology alongside a concentration in spirituality/mysticism, studying with Protestant faculty such as Professor Browning and Martin Marty and Catholic scholars such as Bernard McGinn, Anne Carr, and David Tracy. I asked Professor Browning once where to find spirituality in his book *A Fundamental Practical Theology*. Always generous, he grinned and said that he was a liberal Protestant and did not "do spirituality." Perhaps he "did spirituality" in his own way; more to the point, the term "spirituality" likely would not have resonated with a Disciple of Christ.[3] In any case, the conversation planted early seeds of a question that grew over time, one

2 Don S. Browning, *A Fundamental Practical Theology: Descriptive and Strategic Proposals* (Minneapolis, MN: Fortress Press, 1991).

3 See Joseph D. Driskill and Bonnie J. Miller-McLemore, "Spirituality and the Disciples of Christ: Sanctifying the Ordinary," in *The Chalice Introduction to Theology*, ed. Peter Goodwin Heltzel (St. Louis, MO: Chalice, 2008), pp. 227–237.

that I now can express in this way: how can scholars bring distinctive Catholic traditions of practice and language to practical theology when the predominant discourse and centers of power within the discipline are Protestant?

I feel a bit guilty naming this conundrum, for it has been those predominantly Protestant institutions—first, University of Chicago, now Boston University, where I have taught since 1997—that have nurtured my vocation as a practical theologian. In fact, I found at historically United Methodist Boston University School of Theology a position that explicitly charged me to teach and research both practical theology and spirituality and gave me a primary role in the pastoral and spiritual formation of students. This is perhaps the part of my work that is most meaningful to me.

Thus, I would note several qualifications as I explore the conundrum of Catholic practical theology. First, Protestant scholarship and centers of theological education have made major strides in advancing practical theology as a discipline. This is an important gift that offers potential models and dialogue partners for other traditions, even while the conundrum of how to make space for Catholic and other approaches must be addressed.

Second, there have been significant examples of dialogue between Catholic and Protestant theologians that have influenced practical theology to date. For example, it should be noted as well that Browning is highly dialogical and draws heavily on David Tracy's critical correlational method, as well as Aquinas and other pre-Reformation thinkers. Tracy in turn dedicates one of his few explicit essays on practical theology to the memory of his close colleague, Don S. Browning. Such exchanges of thought and friendship have influenced the discipline of practical theology. In my view, a dialogical approach in practical theology is both appropriate and generative in developing Catholic practical theology and in advancing the field as a whole.

Third, the conundrum cannot be generalized to all contexts. While I explore it here primarily in the U.S. context, and while British authors note this conundrum as well,[4] practical theology in continental Europe is more established within Catholic structures of theological education and research. Further research would need to explore the contours of the conundrum in diverse global contexts of theological inquiry. Finally, while the conundrum needs to be named and addressed constructively, and while it reflects some problematic realities within both the discipline and American theological education, navigating within the conundrum also can be a creative theological space. Thus, I prefer to name a conundrum not as entirely negative but rather as a

4 See James Sweeney, Gemma Simmonds, and David Lonsdale, eds., *Keeping Faith in Practice: Aspects of Catholic Pastoral Theology* (London: SCM Press, 2010).

complex question that requires attention in particular contexts; a conundrum may prove to be both frustrating and a site of creativity and growth.

That said, the conundrum of Catholic practical theology merits serious attention. Difficulties in establishing practical theology as a discipline in American Catholic theology and the separation of pastoral theology and university-based theology in Catholic educational contexts weaken the formation of an educated laity and the training of religious leaders for Catholic communities. This is no minor issue; Catholics are the single largest Christian group worldwide and the demands for leadership at this time in the life of the church can hardly be understated. Yet the conundrum is not simply resolved by transposing existing models of practical theology in Protestant seminaries and divinity schools into Catholic institutions. Rather, as will be discussed below, we need to critically engage and develop practical theological research and teaching in Catholic contexts, working in partnership with the predominant disciplines and distinctive discourses and concerns already operative within Catholic theology. As will be shown, this is a complicated task, requiring partnerships across disciplines and institutions that function as loci of theological work as well as complex negotiations of academic and ecclesial politics. The question of how to locate practical theology in Catholic contexts is difficult and even perplexing. For example, Catholic contextual theologies, such as Latino/a theologies, are quite robust and may be considered an organic form of Catholic practical theology, a natural inroad to fuller development of practical theology as a discipline in Catholic contexts. Yet, few Latino/a Catholic theologians identify as practical theologians, and one must consider whether introducing the discipline of practical theology would complement their work or impose an unnecessary or alien discourse on existing Catholic praxis-oriented theology. Below I will elaborate on the complexities and possibilities of doing Catholic practical theology given such thorny questions and negotiations.

At the same time, this is not just a Catholic issue. Many Catholic scholars are involved now in academic institutions such as the International Academy of Practical Theology, doing significant research and teaching in the field. For the continued development of the discipline, it is necessary to address more explicitly underlying differences of theology, discourse, and power that lie just below the surface of our work. Here the conundrum of Catholic practical theology may well have something in common with other burgeoning and/or marginalized trajectories of practical theology, including womanist and feminist practical theologies, Pentecostal and evangelical practical theologies, and interfaith practical theologies. In short, as will be discussed below, the conundrum of Catholic practical theology raises larger questions about the scope and future of the discipline. Will practical theology as a discipline be able to move beyond its historic Protestant roots to seriously engage other traditions? Will practical theology find institutional homes in diverse contexts of theological education? How should one best encourage those developments, which may well entail different discourses, conversation partners, and methods for practical theology, while retaining disciplinary identity and scholarly advances hard-won over the past three decades?

Practical Theology as a Mainline Protestant Discipline and Discourse

As an academic discipline, practical theology has been predominantly rooted in a liberal Protestant framework and discourse, often traced to Friedrich Schleiermacher as the prime apologist for the place of practical theology in the modern university. To recount a history of the discipline of practical theology would take far too much space here, and other texts establish well the location of the discipline in mainline Protestantism.[5] I will give just selected examples here. Edward Farley's influential book *Theologia: The Fragmentation and Unity of Theological Education* describes the rise of the theological encyclopedia movement in Germany and Friedrich Schleiermacher's defense of practical theology as a "positive science" in the university, akin to law or medicine. Farley bemoans the subsequent entrenchment of a functionalist "clerical paradigm" for theology and a hardening of the fourfold Protestant theological curriculum (biblical studies, church history, theology, and practical theology). According to Farley: "the pre-Schleiermacher fourfold pattern became virtually universal for Protestant schools throughout the nineteenth century and for theological education in Europe and America."[6] Practical theology was validated in terms of its role in the formation of Protestant clergy; this "clerical paradigm" dominated in the U.S. context until the move to a more public paradigm in the resurgence of practical theology in the United States

5 See, for example, Gordon S. Mikoski, "Mainline Protestantism," pp. 557–566 in *The Wiley-Blackwell Companion to Practical Theology*, ed. Bonnie J. Miler-McLemore (Malden, MA: Blackwell Publishing, 2012) and Sally A. Brown, "Hermeneutics in Protestant Practical Theology," pp. 115–132 in *Opening the Field of Practical Theology: An Introduction*, ed. Kathleen A. Cahalan and Gordon S. Mikoski (Lanham, MD: Rowman & Littlefield, 2014). Note also Friedrich Schweitzer's discussion of Schleiermacher in his chapter on "Continental Europe" in *The Wiley-Blackwell Companion to Practical Theology*.

6 Edward Farley, *Theologia: The Fragmentation and Unity of Theological Education* (Philadelphia, PA: Fortress Press, 1983), 101.

in the 1980s. Again, Farley references the Protestant context: "this expression, *clerical paradigm*, will be used to refer to the prevailing (post-Schleiermacher) Protestant way of understanding the unity of theological education."[7] Farley's text became influential in discussions about theological education and practical theology, and scholarship on this subject tended to replicate his focus on Protestant theological education and church life. In the introduction to *Shifting Boundaries: Contextual Approaches to the Structure of Theological Education*, Barbara Wheeler describes the growing attention in the 1980s to theological education as a Christian practice, what Wheeler calls "a nascent practical theology of theological education."[8] Most authors in the book focused on theological education in Protestant contexts. Even as recent as 2008, Craig Dykstra and Dorothy Bass's important edited volume *For Life Abundant: Practical Theology, Theological Education, and Christian Ministry* references predominantly Protestant contexts; note that Kathleen Cahalan is the only Catholic author in the volume.[9] In another recent publication, Gordon Mikoski and Richard Osmer document the centrality of pastoral and practical theology at Princeton Theological Seminary (PTS), a Reformed seminary, over the past two centuries.[10] They demonstrate the significant role of PTS in the development of the discipline and the importance of practical theology for the formation of Protestant ministers (though they also note that while practical theology at PTS serves pastoral formation, it also now extends beyond the clerical paradigm). Mikoski and Osmer provide a rich, detailed history that illustrates a larger point: practical theology in the United States has flourished largely at historically mainline Protestant seminaries and schools of theology such as Vanderbilt Divinity School, Candler School of Theology at Emory University, Princeton Theological Seminary, and Boston University School of Theology. And, indeed, many key texts in the field assume a mainline Protestant audience, work implicitly with liberal Protestant theological assumptions, and reference Protestant contexts of theological education and church life.

Evangelical and Pentecostal scholars have begun to push back on the dominance of mainline Protestant lenses. Charles Scalise notes that while main-

---

7 Farley, *Theologia*, 98, note 37.

8 Barbara Wheeler and Edward Farley, eds. *Shifting Boundaries: Contextual Approaches to the Structure of Theological Education* (Louisville, KY: Westminster John Knox Press, 1991), 9.

9 Dorothy C. Bass and Craig R. Dykstra, eds., *For Life Abundant. Practical Theology and the Education and Formation of Ministers* (Grand Rapids: Michigan, 2008).

10 Gordon S. Mikoski and Richard Osmer, *With Piety and Learning: The History of Practical Theology at Princeton Theological Seminary 1812–2012* (Münster, Germany: LIT Verlag 2011).

line and evangelical practical theologians were not in dialogue during the resurgence of practical theology in the 1980s, doctoral programs in practical theology grew in evangelical institutions such as Fuller Theological Seminary in California. Scalise calls for a broadened view of practical theology: "Mainstream practical theologians who claim a method of Christian emancipative praxis are called to find ways to broaden and rethink their understandings of the liberation of the gospel to encourage full participation of evangelicals."[11] So too Andrew Root seeks to unpack distinctive evangelical approaches to practical theology, most notably with a focus on their missional, biblical, and Christopraxical foci. Root describes evangelical involvement in the academic discipline of practical theology as episodic, and he writes: "Evangelicals have never found a solid footing within the established guilds of practical theology."[12] He urges both more sustained evangelical work in practical theology and more engagement of practical theologians in evangelical approaches. Mark Cartledge analyzes distinctive Pentecostal forms of practical theology while noting that few Pentecostal scholars participate in international practical theology societies. Pentecostal forms of practical theology tend to adopt a theory-to-practice application model, grounded in Biblical sources. Given this application model and the global character of Pentecostalism, Cartledge argues: "Pentecostal practical theology offers a critique of Western-oriented practical theology."[13] The inclusion of chapters by Scalise, Root, and Cartledge in significant, recently published resources in the field of practical theology indicates a growing attention to internal diversity within practical theology. At the same time, these authors highlight limitations in the discipline as currently construed. Such emerging evangelical and Pentecostal critiques provide another kind of mirror reflecting the circumscribed parameters of mainline Protestant practical theological discourse. While this chapter focuses on the conundrum of Catholic practical theology, such explorations can be fruitfully expanded by evangelical, Pentecostal, and Orthodox Christians—as well as scholars of other religious traditions—to enhance the scholarly range of practical theology.

---

11 Charles J. Scalise, "Protestant Evangelicalism," in *The Wiley-Blackwell Companion to Practical Theology*, ed. Bonnie J. Miller-McLemore (Malden, MA: Blackwell Publishing, 2012), 584.

12 Andrew Root, "Evangelical Practical Theology," in *Opening the Field of Practical Theology: An Introduction*, ed. Kathleen A. Cahalan and Gordon S. Mikoski (Lanham, MD: Rowman & Littlefield, 2014), 95.

13 Mark J. Cartledge, "Pentecostalism," in *The Wiley-Blackwell Companion to Practical Theology*, ed. Bonnie J. Miller-McLemore (Malden, MA: Blackwell Publishing, 2012), 594.

Catholic Complexities in Practical Theology

Practical theology has emerged as an academic discipline with international scope, including an international journal, university doctoral programs, and an international academy that meets regularly.[14] Catholics now are a significant presence in the field. At the 2013 conference of the International Academy of Practical Theology, for example, a working group on Catholic practical theologies drew roughly a quarter of the attending members from contexts that include the Netherlands, Germany, Belgium, Spain, Italy, Canada, the United States, India, and Australia. Explicit attention to Catholic contributions in practical theology is a burgeoning area of research. While just a decade ago, few English-language resources explicitly addressed the Catholic conversation in pastoral or practical theology, recent scholarship shows an encouraging uptick. A series of conversations among a small group of Catholic practical theologians resulted in several articles published in a 2011 issue of the *International Journal of Practical Theology*.[15] The new collection *Opening the Field of Practical Theology: An Introduction*, edited by Cahalan and Mikoski, includes chapters on "Roman Catholic Pastoral Theology" and "Hermeneutics in Roman Catholic Practical Theology" as well as additional chapters by Catholic authors on contextual theology and U.S. Latino/a practical theology. *The Wiley-Blackwell Companion to Practical Theology*, edited by Bonnie Miller-McLemore, includes a contribution by Lynn Bridgers that outlines diverse de-

14 Note, for example, the International Academy of Practical Theology, the *International Journal of Practical Theology*, the French-speaking Société Internationale de Théologie Pratique, and the American-based Association of Practical Theology. There also is a Practical Theology group at the American Academy of Religion Annual Meeting. Several major resources in practical theology have been published in recent years, including the *Wiley-Blackwell Companion in Practical Theology*, which includes chapters on practical theology in Europe, the United States, Asia, Africa, Oceania. See too Bonnie Miller McLemore's introduction to the volume, "The Contributions of Practical Theology," which makes the argument for practical theology as an international discipline, and her article, "Five Misunderstandings about Practical Theology," *International Journal of Practical Theology* 16, no. 1 (2012): 5–26.

15 Kathleen Cahalan, "Locating Practical Theology in Catholic Theological Discourse and Practice," *International Journal of Practical Theology* 15 (2011): 4. See also articles by Tom Beaudoin, Lynn Bridgers, Edward Foley, and Bryan Froehle in the *International Journal of Practical Theology* 15:1 (2011). James Sweeney, Gemma Simmonds, and David Lonsdale, eds., *Keeping Faith in Practice: Aspects of Catholic Pastoral Theology* (London: SCM Press, 2010).

velopments and dimensions of Roman Catholic practical theology.[16] I have designed and edited two volumes on Catholic work in practical theology, to be discussed further below. Such scholarship reflects the growing presence of Catholics in practical theology circles and lays a foundation for further development of Catholic practical theologies. However, perplexing issues persist in locating and advancing practical theology within the structures of Catholic theology and theological education and in advancing Catholic contributions to the discipline of practical theology. As distinct Catholic histories and traditions of pastoral and practical theology have been sketched in several recent publications,[17] I will not repeat those historical accounts here. Rather, I build upon this scholarship in addressing some of the puzzling angles of the current situation of Catholic practical theology, with particular focus on the U.S. context. The final section of this chapter will summarize what is at stake for practical theology and for Catholic theology as I also propose constructive ways forward in negotiating the conundrum of Catholic practical theology.

Confusion of Terminology: Pastoral and Practical Theologies

While practical theology as a discipline in the United States has taken hold in mainline Protestant contexts, many aspects of practical theology are deeply resonant in Catholicism and have roots that well precede the German encyclopedias or Schleiermacher's apology for practical theology in the modern university. Practical theology's concern with practice, praxis, experience, performance, engagement, transformation, formation, church, the everyday: this all resonates deeply with Catholicism. As liturgical scholar and Catholic practical theologian Edward Foley notes, for example, practice is more central than explicit theologizing to the early Christian community: "The liturgical equivalent to a formula of correlation between theory and practices is a celebrated maxim from Prosper of Aquitaine (d. 475): *legem credendi lex statuat suplicandi* ('the law of praying established the law of believing'), sometimes abbreviated *lex orandi, lex credendi* ('law of praying, law of believing')… the early community was more concerned with practice than theory, more about *orandi* than

16 Lynn Bridgers, "Roman Catholicism," pp. 565–576 in *The Wiley-Blackwell Companion to Practical Theology*, ed. Bonnie J. Miller-McLemore (Malden, MA: Blackwell Publishing, 2012).

17 See Wolfteich, *Invitation to Practical Theology: Catholic Voices and Visions*, particularly Kathleen A. Cahalan and Bryan Froehle, "A Developing Discipline: The Catholic Voice in Practical Theology." See also aforementioned article by Cahalan, "Locating Practical Theology in Catholic Theological Discourse and Practice," *International Journal of Practical Theology* 15 (2011): 1–21 and the chapter by Bridgers, "Roman Catholicism."

credendi."[18] Kathleen Cahalan outlines various forms of pastoral theology that can be identified in Catholic theological traditions, including the teaching of moral casuistry that was part of clergy formation for centuries. She notes the strong "application" model and the clerical paradigm that framed Catholic pastoral theology from the rise of scholasticism up until the Second Vatican Council (1962–1965). Pastoral theology applied the principles of doctrinal theology to pastoral practice and was located primarily within seminaries, focused on the formation of ordained clergy.[19] Obviously, such history makes it difficult to reconcile some Catholic traditions of practical theology with current assumptions in the field that reject both the so-called clerical paradigm and an application model of practical theology.[20]

The Second Vatican Council profoundly shifted Catholic theological orientations, opening to serious engagement with the modern world; attention to the particularities of context and culture; attention to the vocation and mission of the whole Church, and not simply the ordained clergy; and endorsement of ecumenism. As several authors have noted, and as I have argued elsewhere,[21] Vatican II accorded high value to the "pastoral" as it also expanded the term's meaning beyond a focus on the activities of ordained pastors. Indeed, Catholicism stands to offer to practical theology a distinctive history and vision of the "pastoral." The "Pastoral Constitution on the Church in the Modern World" (*Gaudium et Spes*), one of the most important documents of the council, fundamentally reorients the ecclesial stance from a guarded triumphalism to a church-world engagement seen as the heart of the ecclesial mission.

18 Edward Foley, "Eucharistic Practice-Eucharistic Theology: The Fount and Summit of the Church's Life," in *Invitation to Practical Theology*, ed. Claire E. Wolfteich (New York: Paulist Press, 2014), 114. In this quotation, Foley refers to the *Patrologia Latina* 51: 209.

19 Kathleen Cahalan, "Roman Catholic Pastoral Theology," pp. 217–232 in *Opening the Field of Practical Theology*, ed. Kathleen Cahalan and Gordon Mikoski (Lanham, MD: Rowman & Littlefield, 2014).

20 See Bonnie Miller McLemore's description of these current biases in the field and her own critique of their excesses, in "Five Misunderstandings," *International Journal of Practical Theology* 16, no. 1 (2012): 5–26.

21 For arguments along these lines in my own work, see Wolfteich, "Hermeneutical Approaches in Practical Theology: Catholic Perspectives," in *Opening the Field of Practical Theology*, ed. Kathleen Cahalan and Gordon Mikoski (Lanham, MD: Rowman & Littlefield, 2014), 133–152 and Wolfteich, "Time Poverty, Women's Labor, and Catholic Social Teaching: A Practical Theological Exploration," *Journal of Moral Theology* 2, no. 2 (June 2013): 40–59.

The meaning of "pastoral" in Catholic theology and the status of "pastoral theology" are part of the conundrum of Catholic practical theology. Cahalan writes: "Despite the explosion of 'pastoral' activity in the wake of the Council, however, pastoral theology never became a serious, well-developed academic discipline.... In many ways pastoral theology was left behind since it had no real place in Catholic university-based theology."[22] Cahalan's assessment cannot be generalized to all contexts, as will be noted below. Yet it does point to a persistent marginalization of pastoral theology in American Catholic theology that must be addressed. Bridgers also notes confusion within Catholic circles regarding the use of the terms "pastoral theology" and "practical theology": "The term *practical theology* itself is amorphous in Roman Catholicism, shifting in shape historically and in contemporary thought. Theologians debate whether it is a self-standing discipline or merely a method. Some use *pastoral* and *practical* as interchangeable."[23] Cahalan observes that the term "pastoral theology" is still a more common term than "practical theology" in many Catholic contexts of theological education, including seminaries and Latino/a pastoral formation programs, despite the fact that pastoral theology has not developed into a robust discipline: "There is little evidence of pastoral theology as a theological discipline in Catholic discourse: there are no academic journals for pastoral theology, no professional organizations... and few theologians would identify with pastoral theology."[24] Thus, we are in something of a catch-22: pastoral theology remains a common term in Catholic theology, making the introduction of the language of practical theology somewhat confusing, yet pastoral theology carries little academic weight in Catholic theology circles.

Although "pastoral theology" has lost the opportunity to develop as a rigorous scholarly discipline within American Catholic contexts, still the distinctive conciliar vision for the "pastoral" should be sustained because it offers a more expansive use of the term than typically used in Protestant discourse around "pastoral care," understood as a practice of ministry, or "pastoral theology," understood as a subdiscipline of practical theology. The "Pastoral Constitution" *Gaudium et Spes*, in my view, presents an important grounding for contempo-

22 Kathleen Cahalan, "Locating Practical Theology in Catholic Theological Discourse and Practice," *International Journal of Practical Theology* 15 (2011): 6.

23 Lynn Bridgers, "Roman Catholicism," in *The Wiley-Blackwell Companion to Practical Theology*, ed. Bonnie J. Miller-McLemore (Malden, MA: Blackwell Publishing, 2012), 567.

24 Kathleen Cahalan, "Roman Catholic Pastoral Theology," in *Opening the Field of Practical Theology: An Introduction*, ed. Kathleen A. Cahalan and Gordon S. Mikoski (Lanham, MD: Rowman & Littlefield, 2014), 230.

rary Catholic practical theology. It reads: "the Church seeks but a solitary goal: to carry forward the work of Christ under the lead of the befriending Spirit.... To carry out such a task, the Church has always had the duty of scrutinizing the signs of the times and of interpreting them in the light of the Gospel" (nos. 3–4). This conciliar vision resonates with practical theology as a dynamic interpretive task grounded in the gospel and attentive to the particularities of culture and context. It also positions theology as an ecclesial and spiritual task, two dimensions of practical theology that I see as integral to a Catholic approach. The conundrum is how to carry forward this rich conciliar meaning of the "pastoral" into practical theology, which in Protestant contexts links the "pastoral" to a "subdiscipline" and in Catholic contexts relegates "pastoral theology" to ministerial formation, often in pastoral institutes separated from university-based theology.

Practical Theology as Critical Discipline: Issues of Authority, Power, and Risk

One of the foremost Catholic theologians of the twentieth century, German Catholic theologian Karl Rahner explicitly embraced "practical theology" over "pastoral theology" (though he also collaborated on the *Manual of Pastoral Theology*, published in 1964[25]). Rahner calls pastoral theology (understood more narrowly as related to issues of pastoral ministry) a "false conscription" of the scope of the discipline.[26] In his essay "Practical Theology within the Totality of Theological Disciplines" within *Theological Investigations*, Rahner defines practical theology as "that theological discipline which is concerned with the Church's self-actualisation here and now... This it does by means of theological illumination of the particular situation in which the Church must realise itself in all its dimensions."[27] Rahner situates practical theology squarely in service of the Church's ecclesial task. He offers a way to affirm the ecclesial dimension of practical theology while advancing its place in the university—thus presenting what could be a Catholic alternative to Schleiermacher. In other words, Rahner's conception of practical theology aptly makes an argument for practical theology as a rigorous discipline in the Catholic university. The fact that practical theology for Rahner is intrinsically ecclesial

---

25 Franz Arnold, Karl Rahner, Viktor Schurr, and Leonard Weber, eds., *Handbuch der Pastoraltheologie. Praktische Theologie der Kirche in ihrer Gegenwart. Band I* (Freiburg: Herder, 1964).

26 Karl Rahner, "Practical Theology within the Totality of Theological Disciplines," *Theological Investigations IX* (New York: Herder & Herder, 1972), 102.

27 Karl Rahner, "Practical Theology within the Totality of Theological Disciplines," 102.

does not undermine its status as an autonomous scientific discipline; rather, its role in proffering critical scientific interpretations of situations oriented toward "committal" with the aim of ecclesial self-realization cannot be replicated by other disciplines, nor is practical theology simply the application of doctrine. Practical theology is an independent, fundamental discipline that must be in reciprocal relationship with other theological disciplines. This is an apt vision for practical theology—dialogical yet autonomous, scientific while committed, and retaining always "an element of creativity and prophecy."[28] Rahner's embrace of practical theology stalled, perhaps in part due to the critical, creative, and prophetic function of practical theology. Herbert Haslinger describes the critical function of practical theology according to Rahner and the context of ecclesiastical resistance:

> If now practical theology has been assigned to reflect on both, the actually given self-realization of the Church and the one meant to be, then there is an obligation of practical theology to not simply accept the things she perceives as given in the self-realization of the Church. She always has to critically question everything given by the Church—and this means the entire spectrum of Church-related truths, from the activities of individual believers via the institutional structures to exercising the Magisterium—as to what extent it complies with the respective valid standards and criteria and how it can be changed into a better, more suitable model. Unfortunately critical questioning is still defamed as a destructive, anti-ecclesiastical act, especially by ministers. Such a reflex of defense and prevention of criticism neglects the character and the value of critical thinking in theology and Church.[29]

For practical theology to expand beyond mainline Protestant concerns, it must comprehend and address such issues related to authority, power, and the risks of ecclesial critique, which are vital concerns in current Catholic theology circles. Such issues deeply shape the context in which Catholic practical theologians operate. I have elsewhere described the rise of Catholic hermeneutical models of pastoral and practical theology in the decades after Vatican II—including prominent figures such as David Tracy, Thomas Groome, Evelyn

---

28 Karl Rahner, "Practical Theology within the Totality of Theological Disciplines," 105.

29 Herbert Haslinger, "Vatican II, the Legacy of Rahner, and Catholic Distinctives in Practical Theology," in *Catholic Approaches in Practical Theology: International and Interdisciplinary Perspectives*, ed. Claire E. Wolfteich and Annemie Dillen (Leuven: Peeters Publishing, forthcoming 2016).

and James Whitehead, Robert Kinast, and Patricia Killen. Such authors developed models of theological reflection that emphasize the interpretive task and value experience, a theological source minimized in preconciliar Catholic theology.[30] Texts, such as Groome's *Christian Religious Education: Sharing Our Story and Vision* and the Whiteheads's *Method in Ministry: Theological Reflection and Christian Ministry*, were widely used in the formation of lay and ordained ecclesial ministers in the 1980s and 1990s. Certainly the emphasis on the hermeneutical nature of the theological task in postconciliar writings resonates with strong currents in the discipline of practical theology. For example, while Groome did not use the term "practical theology" in describing his "shared praxis" method, Browning early on pointed to Groome's work as "a powerful practical theology of Christian education."[31] What is less obvious perhaps to an outside observer, though, is the tensive context within which "interpretation" is practiced in postconciliar Catholicism. Part of the tension revolves around the question of how to interpret Vatican II itself. The "battle for meaning"[32]—to use a phrase of historian Massimo Faggioli—has exposed deep fault lines in the Catholic community. For Catholic theologians, work with hermeneutical theories and methods inevitably entails complex questions about the norms of "authentic interpretation"—and related issues of the criteria for authenticity, the definition and authority of the magisterium, and the role of the Spirit in communal processes of interpretation. The stakes of hermeneutics are high, as has been made abundantly clear by recent moves of the Congregation for the Doctrine of the Faith to interpret, correct, censure, and silence Catholic theologians.[33]

Catholic practical theologians operate within these hermeneutical debates. As they draw upon hermeneutical theories, which have been quite important to the work of practical theology in recent decades, Catholic practical theologians must address questions such as: How do we adjudicate among conflicting interpretations of Scripture, tradition, and culture? How does the Holy

30 See James D. and Evelyn Eaton Whitehead, *Method in Ministry: Theological Reflection and Christian Ministry*. Rev. ed. (Chicago: Sheed and Ward, 1995); Patricia O'Connell Killen and John de Beer, *The Art of Theological Reflection* (New York: Crossroad, 1994); Robert Kinast, *Let Ministry Teach: A Guide to Theological Reflection* (Collegeville, MN: Liturgical Press, 1996).

31 Don Browning, "The Revival of Practical Theology," *Christian Century*, February 1–8, 1984, 134.

32 Massimo Faggioli, *Vatican II: The Battle for Meaning* (Mahwah, NJ: Paulist Press, 2012).

33 Richard R. Gaillardetz, ed., *When the Magisterium Intervenes: The Magisterium and Theologians in Today's Church* (Collegeville, MN: Liturgical, 2012).

Spirit guide interpretation and understanding—through what channels, institutions, and charisms? What is or should be the magisterium's role in the hermeneutical process? What is the relationship between practical theology and doctrine? These are simply critical, contested questions in contemporary Catholicism and certainly issues that Catholic practical theologians encounter. Yet they are inadequately or rarely addressed in influential texts in the field of practical theology. Catholic practical theologians are left with insufficient resources to situate their work vis-à-vis these important issues, and the discipline is not pressed to confront these challenging questions.

Partnership or Colonization: Catholic Contextual Theologies

The conundrum of locating and cultivating Catholic practical theology arises also in considering Catholic contextual theologies. One of the most promising grounds for Catholic practical theology would appear to be the growing body of U.S. Latino/a, Black, and Asian Catholic scholarship. Here "praxis," "experience," and "context" are key categories, and the transformative aims of theology as itself praxis are advanced. Building upon the praxis-oriented scholarship of Catholic contextual theologies would seem an obvious route for practical theology to make inroads in Catholic theology.

An example of the potential cross-pollination between Catholic contextual theologies and practical theology can be seen in the work of M. Shawn Copeland, whom I invited to write for the volume *Invitation to Practical Theology*. In her chapter, Copeland brings a contextual theological analysis of the ritual practices, symbols, and narratives of African American popular religion with particular attention to the practice of commemorating the ancestors. She looks specifically at how the practice, which she describes as a "critical cultural intervention," is enacted at one center of theological education and ministerial formation, the Institute of Black Catholic Studies at Xavier University of Louisiana in New Orleans. Copeland understands the practice as a "creative practical theological response to the ongoing need for ebonization in the Catholic Church in the United States." Moreover, she argues that a goal of theological education is the "formation of practical theological agency," which, among black Catholic laity is an intellectual, ethical, aesthetic, and worshipful process. This process is a key component of the legacy of black Catholic *traditio*, handing on the faith.[34] Copeland embraces the language of practical theology here and situates it as a key aspect of ecclesial work.

34 M. Shawn Copeland, "Weaving Memory, Structuring Ritual, Evoking Mythos: Commemoration of the Ancestors," in *Invitation to Practical Theology*, 126, 130.

And yet, the relationship between Catholic contextual theologies and practical theology is unclear or even contested. Copeland, who teaches in the department of theology at Boston College, is known as a systematic theologian. So too, most U.S. Latino/a Catholic theologians identify with systematic theology, and their work is fostered by professional networks such as the Academy of Catholic Hispanic Theologians of the United States (ACHTUS). I will refer here to two Latino/a authors to illustrate both the potential and the complexity of situating practical theology vis-à-vis Catholic contextual theologies. In *Caminemos Con Jesús: Toward a Hispanic/Latino Theology of Accompaniment*, Roberto Goizueta highlights the aesthetic dimension of liberative praxis as he also grounds theology in a praxis of solidarity and accompaniment.[35] He builds upon Latin American liberation theologies to draw the "hermeneutical circle" of theological inquiry—beginning in experience (particularly popular U.S. Hispanic experience), moving to analysis of the experience, and returning to experience in a new light.

Recognizing the relevance of his work for practical theology, I invited Goizueta, who like Copeland teaches in the Department of Theology of Boston College, to write a chapter for *Invitation to Practical Theology: Catholic Voices and Visions*. In this chapter, he made an important contribution to practical theology, analyzing liberative and aesthetic dimensions of praxis in popular devotion to Our Lady of Guadalupe. At the same time, Goizueta's chapter points to the conundrum of scholarly identity and terminology. He writes: "we Latino/a scholars have been inspired and informed by the ground-breaking insights of our Latin American colleagues who have argued for the foundational methodological import of a 'preferential option for the poor,' thereby locating Christian praxis at the very heart of the theological task—not as this latter's consequence but as its very source. Latin American and U.S. Latino/a theologies are thus intrinsically 'practical' theologies, even if the term itself is not often found in the literature of either."[36]

Carmen Nanko-Fernandez more strongly critiques the Euro-American bias of practical theology and resists affiliation with practical theology. Nanko-Fernandez teaches at the Catholic Theological Union (CTU), which was founded in 1968 in the wake of Vatican II, inspired by conciliar visions of church renewal and an ecumenical spirit. CTU is now one of the largest Ro-

35 Roberto Goizueta, *Caminemos Con Jesús: Toward a Hispanic/Latino Theology of Accompaniment* (Maryknoll, NY: Orbis, 1995).

36 Roberto S. Goizueta, "Practicing Beauty: Aesthetic Praxis, Justice, and U.S. Latino/a Popular Religion," in *Invitation to Practical Theology*, 149.

man Catholic graduate schools of theology and ministry in the United States. Among other degrees, CTU offers the Master of Arts in Pastoral Studies and the Ecumenical Doctor of Ministry degree, which according to the CTU website is "grounded in the principles of practical theology."[37] Yet, Nanko-Fernandez sharply critiques practical theology, arguing for "decolonizing practical and pastoral theologies." She notes that "Latin@ theologians are virtually absent, as partners and resources, in shaping agendas, strategies, and discourse in the scholarship of both pastoral and practical theologies." She attributes this absence to both what Gilberto Cavazos-González calls a "racism of omission"—ignorance and neglect by Euro-American scholars—and to a strategic choice of Latin@ scholars who cannot risk further marginalization. "To claim identity as either a pastoral or a practical theologian often conveys a degree of academic second-class citizenship. For Latin@s, whose scholarship already experiences marginalization, this is not an advantage."[38]

Can U.S. Latino/a theology be called a site for Catholic practical theology, an "intrinsic" practical theology, or does this risk attempting to "colonize" an already flourishing body of theology under a Protestant rubric? Would the language of practical theology simply be redundant, adding little to the Latino/a conversation? Worse, would identification with practical theology contribute to the further marginalization of scholarship by racial/ethnic minorities?

Casting a Wide Net: Disciplinary Bridging and (Loss of?) Scholarly Identity

Questions of disciplinary identity are not limited to Catholic contextual theology but more broadly are integral to the conundrum of Catholic practical theology. Can the gap between Catholic pastoral theology and Catholic university-based theology be bridged? Can practical theology serve as that bridge? How might one locate forms of practical theology already at work in the dominant disciplines of more recognizable Catholic powerhouse fields of systematics and moral theology? Such questions were significant in my thinking about the design of two recent edited book projects. The first book, *Invitation to Practical Theology: Catholic Voices and Visions*, includes primarily American Catholic theologians. The second volume, *Catholic Perspectives in Practical Theology: International and Interdisciplinary Perspectives*, which I co-edited with a Belgian practical theologian, Annemie Dillen, encompasses a larger international

37 http://www.ctu.edu/academics/general-information, accessed July 31, 2015.

38 Carmen Nanko-Fernandez, *Theologizing en Espanglish: Context, Community, and Ministry* (Maryknoll, NY: Orbis, 2010), 22. See Bonnie Miller-McLemore's chapter 8 in this volume for further discussion of the politics surrounding practical knowledge (pp. 190–218).

range, including scholars from the Netherlands, Belgium, Germany, Canada, Nigeria, Australia, Croatia, Austria, the Philippines, and the United States. Both volumes explore, query, and advance Catholic practical theological scholarship. These two book projects reflect the dilemma of disciplinary identity in locating and advancing Catholic contributions to practical theology.

Admittedly, I embarked on these projects with a fairly optimistic perspective about the consonance between Catholicism and practical theology. I wanted to introduce practical theology more prominently as a discipline to Catholic scholars and communities while also making visible and advancing Catholic contributions to the predominantly Protestant academic discipline of practical theology. In short, I have not shaken my initial instinct, back from my time in Chicago, that practical theology and Catholic theology and community have distinctive contributions to offer each other. I also embarked on the book projects with confidence in practical theology as a rigorous academic discipline appropriate to university-based teaching and research due to my own location in two university-based practical theology programs and my involvement in highly academic professional organizations such as the International Academy of Practical Theology.

Invitation to Practical Theology sets out these dual aims: to make a substantial Catholic contribution to the discipline of practical theology and to explore the import of practical theology for Catholic theology and theological education. Questions that emerged in the book project included typical issues with any edited volume: who should be included? How to represent a diverse range of scholarship? A key question for this volume concerned how to navigate disciplinary boundaries and identities. Should contributors be limited to self-identified practical theologians? Because practical theology is not as common a discipline in Catholic contexts of theological education, and because some groups such as Latino/a scholars may choose for strategic reasons to identify with more widely recognized and powerful disciplines such as systematic theology, to limit the contributors to self-identified practical theologians would narrow the book in ways I decided unwise. As Cahalan and Bryan Froehle write, practical theology in Catholic contexts is "both concentrated in a discipline of 'practical theology' and simultaneously diffused throughout the theological disciplines."[39]

The book thus brings together self-identified practical theologians with well-known systematic, philosophical, and moral theologians whose work intersects interestingly with practical theology. I looked for authors who brought

39 Kathleen A. Cahalan and Bryan Froehle, "A Developing Discipline: The Catholic Voice in Practical Theology," in *Invitation to Practical Theology*, 27.

a focus on the category of "practice" or "popular religion"; those with theological expertise about a particular practice deeply rooted in Catholicism such as spiritual direction, mission, liturgy, or education; and those who linked practice with systematic theological categories such as "tradition," "Trinity," and "ecclesiology." What emerged in the volume, aided by several in-person meetings among authors, is an unusual collaboration between self-identified practical theologians and significant philosophical, systematic, and moral theologians. I remain convinced that this sort of bridging is critical to the development of Catholic practical theologies, given the importance of such disciplines to traditional understandings of theology in Catholic contexts. And yet, casting such a wide net for practical theology raises important questions for those who have worked hard to establish practical theology as its own academic discipline. Do we risk losing hard-won gains in delineating practical theology as a discipline with its own scholarly literature, research foci and methods, and aims? Will systematic theologians assume or reinforce an "application model" whereby practical theology simply applies the findings of other theological disciplines? How do theologians draw disciplinary lines to secure the future of a discipline and yet not neglect the richness of practical theology beyond such boundaries?

I am convinced that despite these continuing conundrums, partnership with systematic and moral theologians is critical given the current structures of theology and the need to address key contested Catholic questions such as the nature of tradition and the church. In *Invitation to Practical Theology*, for example, leading systematic and philosophical theologian Terrence Tilley frames tradition—of course a key concept in Catholic theology—as an "enduring, complex communal" practice or set of practices. He gives particular attention to the practice of celebrating Eucharist and to practices of reconciliation. Undercutting the idea that tradition is simply a collection of unchanging beliefs (*tradita*), Tilley focuses on *traditio*, the dynamic *practice* of handing on the faith, without which traditions have no life. As practices are the context in which theory arises, argues Tilley, so "practical theology is construed as the context in which systematic theology arises."[40] In effect, Tilley, who has not been known as a practical theologian, offers a powerful rationale for including practical theology as a constitutive part of theological study and teaching. Strategically, the inclusion of such systematic theologians in practical theological conversation and research is important to gain visibility and "legitimacy"

40 Terrence W. Tilley, "Practicing the Faith: Tradition in a Practical Theology" in *Invitation to Practical Theology*, 89.

in Catholic contexts of theological education. So too, this collaboration with systematic theologians lends theological weight to a discipline that is struggling to identify/reclaim the place of the normative, given practical theology's eager embrace of the social sciences and descriptive tasks. Yet the questions remain: will such bridging blur the disciplinary boundaries of practical theology, which for any emerging discipline may be important to secure? Will the conversation advance in bi-directional ways, such that systematic and moral theologies are informed and transformed by practical theology as well as the reverse?

The second volume, *Catholic Approaches in Practical Theology: International and Interdisciplinary Perspectives*, extends the work with broader international reach. Here it was easier to locate Catholic scholars who self-identify as practical theologians and invest in the discipline as members of professional organizations such as the International Academy of Practical Theology and the French-speaking Société Internationale de Théologie Pratique. As Friedrich Schweitzer has noted, it is not advisable to generalize across the multiple traditions and discourses of practical theology in Europe. However, one can observe with Schweitzer that practical theology now is widely embraced by both Protestant and Catholic European scholars: "In line with different ecclesial understandings of the church, practical theology tended to be a Protestant endeavor while Catholics preferred pastoral theology.... In Europe today, however, *practical theology* has become the term used most often in Protestantism as well as in Catholicism."[41] Practical theology is an established discipline in the theological curriculum at both Protestant and Catholic European universities, with leading Catholic practical theologians emerging particularly from the Netherlands, Germany, Belgium, and Switzerland. Contributors to *Catholic Approaches in Practical Theology: International and Interdisciplinary Perspectives* show the range of geographic contexts and disciplines from which Catholic practical theologians emerge as well as the public significance of their research foci. For example, Klaus Kiessling, a German scholar, outlines fundamental issues in relating psychology, pastoral care, and practical theology. Annemie Dillen analyzes important moves in empirical theology and practical theology, particularly in Dutch, Belgian, and German contexts. Solange LeFevre analyzes secularization and public theology in Quebec. Gerard Hall, well known Australian practical theologian, teams up with a more junior scholar, Michael Muonwe of Nigeria, in a cross-cultural exploration of

41 Friedrich Schweitzer, "Continental Europe," in *The Wiley-Blackwell Companion to Practical Theology*, ed. Bonnie J. Miller-McLemore (Malden, MA: Blackwell Publishing, 2012), 468.

missiology, inculturation, and practical theology in the contexts of Africa and Oceania. Because we sought global diversity and analyses of the relationship between practical theology and other related disciplines or subdisciplines, we also included several scholars whose disciplinary affiliations are ethics, religious studies, or systematic theology. One example: ethicist Agnes Brazal of the Philippines analyses the role of praxis/practice in practical, moral, and contextual theologies. Thus, the question of disciplinary boundaries is not absent from this volume—it is indeed an issue we address—yet it is not as acute as in the first volume due to larger numbers of Catholic scholars across disciplines who identify as practical theologians.

In comparing the two book projects, it is clear that it is important to avoid generalizations about the conundrum of Catholic practical theology. Due to differences in the histories and organization of theological education, Catholic practical theology is differently located in particular global contexts. Catholic scholars in continental Europe and French-speaking Canada have been important leaders in the discipline and claim scholarly identities in practical theology with more ease. Yet certainly in the U.S. context, part of the conundrum of Catholic practical theology involves the question of whom to include, where to draw the disciplinary boundaries (if at all), how to invite students and colleagues into a discipline where none exists in the structures of many Catholic undergraduate and graduate departments of theology. The following section, on stakes and constructive responses to the conundrum, will focus on the U.S. context, leaving for further research a more detailed assessment of the relevance of the conundrum in other contexts.

What is at Stake: Practices of Teaching, Research, and Formation

Why is there a need for work in Catholic practical theology? Catholics are the single largest Christian denomination in the world, comprising about 50 percent of Christians worldwide, according to a 2013 Pew Research Center report.[42] As a global church, Catholicism crosses a myriad of cultural, racial, and ethnic categories. Reflecting theologically on Catholic practice is hugely important—and fascinating. Practical theology stays within a mainline Protestant box at its peril, missing a large swath of global religious life. That said, religious identity today in many contexts is fluid, hybrid, fragmented. In my understanding, Catholic practical theology engages this reality. It does not

42 http://www.pewforum.org/2013/02/13/the-global-catholic-population/, accessed May 1, 2015.

seek to reify or ghettoize Catholicism but rather to explore the complexity, internal diversity, and hybridity of lived Catholicism.[43] Thus, Catholic scholarship in practical theology should not only engage "Catholic practice" but, more broadly, should engage cultural and religious practices from a Catholic theological perspective. While it draws upon the social sciences, Catholic practical theology brings a critical and committed theological engagement that goes beyond description.

As the discipline of practical theology expands to include more Catholic scholars and also turns more squarely to address interfaith and secular audiences, it becomes more and more important to recognize the internal pluralism of practical theologians and the wide diversity of contexts and communities into which practical theologians speak. Friedrich Schweitzer notes that until recently, "interdenominational cooperation in practical theology was rare, even if one can find instances of mutual influence between religious traditions from early on."[44] The time is ripe to expand dialogue and collaborative scholarship. The discipline of practical theology owes much to mainline Protestantism—but Catholic, evangelical, Pentecostal, Orthodox, intersecular, and interfaith approaches need space, recognition, and critical cultivation. Specifically, I would argue for greater inclusion of Catholic texts, practices, and issues in practical theology courses in Protestant and ecumenical settings. Continued efforts to articulate distinctive Catholic histories and traditions of practical theology and to engage with relevant Catholic theological scholarship (even if such scholars do not yet operate in recognized practical theology professional organizations) is imperative for the discipline as well. Moreover, greater attention to issues such as the role of doctrine, spirituality/mysticism, tradition, sacramentality, aesthetics, authority, and the vocation of the laity all would open practical theology more to Catholic perspectives, concerns, and imaginations. Likewise, Catholic pastoral and practical theologies, guided by the ecumenical spirit of Vatican II, can engage with a range of approaches in practical theology while introducing distinctive issues, discourse, and theological frameworks.

To take up the import of spirituality, returning thus to an issue that first cracked open this conundrum for me, I continue to seek to bridge the dis-

---

43 On these points with reference to Catholic Studies, see Jeannine Hill Fletcher, "A Definition of Catholic: Toward a Cosmopolitan Vision," in *The Catholic Studies Reader*, ed. James T. Fisher and Margaret M. McGuinness (New York: Fordham University Press, 2011), 129–147. See also Tom Beaudoin's chapter 1 on the problems of "christianicity" in this volume (pp. 8–32).

44 Schweitzer, "Continental Europe," 466.

courses of spirituality studies and practical theology. In previous publications, I have identified this intersection as an important area for practical theological scholarship, arguing, for example, that spirituality studies challenges practical theology to expand its sources to include mystical texts, bodies, and practices. Spirituality studies also provides an avenue for exploring practices across religious and secular traditions; a literature that addresses pedagogical questions about teaching practices, an area of great interest in practical theology; and explicit attention to the transformative and self-implicating aims of scholarship, discussions that are highly relevant to practical theology. In considering the importance of spirituality studies for practical theology, I frame this not as a matter of asserting a "subdiscipline" of practical theology, but rather more centrally about claiming the theological nature of practical theology and widening the discourse of the field to encompass language, practices, and concerns that are highly relevant in contemporary culture and in traditions beyond mainline Protestantism.[45] Indeed, the language of "spirituality" is becoming more widespread across religious and secular communities and may even provide a future bridge to a more dialogical practical theology.

What is at stake in negotiating the conundrum of Catholic practical theology? At stake is the breadth and scholarly range of the discipline of practical theology. Much also remains at stake for Catholic theology and formation. The language of practical theology is becoming more common in graduate schools of ministry, such as the Catholic Theological Union. Yet it is far less visible in undergraduate and doctoral theological education. The separation of prac-

45 See Claire E. Wolfteich, "'Practices of Unsaying': Michel de Certeau, Spirituality Studies, and Practical Theology," *Spiritus: A Journal of Christian Spirituality* 12 (2012): 161–171; Wolfteich, "Spirituality," in *The Wiley-Blackwell Companion to Practical Theology*, ed. Bonnie J. Miller McLemore (Malden, MA: Blackwell Publishers, 2012), 328–336; Wolfteich, "Animating Questions: Spirituality and Practical Theology," *International Journal of Practical Theology* 13 (2009): 121–143. My presidential address to the International Academy of Practical Theology specifically addressed gaps in practical theological attention to mysticism: "Words and Fire, Deserts and Dwellings: Toward Mystical Practical Theologies," Toronto, Canada, April 12, 2013. For an example of dialogical interdenominational and cross-regional scholarship, see too Claire E. Wolfteich and Jörg Schneider, "A Comparative Research Conversation: American Catholic and German Protestant Spirituality Studies." *International Journal of Practical Theology* 17, no. 1 (August 2013): 100–130. Note that David Tracy also argued for a turn to spirituality and aesthetics in his 2009 address to the International Academy of Practical Theology, a version of which is published as "A Correlational Model of Practical Theology Revisited," in Edward Foley, ed., *Religion, Diversity and Conflict* (Münster: LIT Verlag, 2011) and reprinted in Wolfteich, ed., *Invitation to Practical Theology*, pp. 70–86.

tical/pastoral theology (located primarily in schools or institutes dedicated to pastoral formation) and systematic theology (located primarily in departments of theology) perpetuates an intellectual separation between theology and practice that undermines the development of religious leadership and an educated laity.[46] Such structural and intellectual divides weaken the academic status of Catholic pastoral/practical theology and deprive it of essential dialogue partners in systematic theology and theological ethics. Moreover, the separation tends to reduce practical theology to pastoral formation—whereas the scope of practical theology actually includes a broader study of religious and cultural practice. Critical theological study of practice should be integral to Catholic theology and Catholic education, a core component of the formation of the laity. Integrating practical theology into the doctoral curriculum will improve the training of Catholic theological educators across the disciplines. And specifically, we need to improve doctoral training in the practical fields in Catholic contexts of theological education. Practical theology constitutes a significant but underdeveloped resource in these tasks. Practical theology provides complex theological rationales and methods for engagement with practice as *locus theologicus*; offers pedagogical strategies and reflections that fruitfully inform the development of an engaged lay leadership in the church; and contributes to the training of theological educators across disciplines and particularly in the practical fields.

The development of practical theology in Catholic contexts require institutional support, pedagogical shifts, and sustained collaboration among scholars in systematic, moral, and practical/pastoral theologies. We also need to foster explicit conversations between Catholic contextual theologies and practical theology. Rahner was prescient in calling for adjustments to institutional structures, adjustments which must accompany a correct understanding of practical theology as an independent science, not derivative of dogmatics or social science or pastoral ministry. Today the adjustments he briefly calls for still await realization in U.S. Catholic contexts of theological education: appointments to professorial chairs, curricular revision, finances.[47]

So too, collaboration across the different kinds of institutions and communities in which Catholic practical theology happens is vital. Following the spirit of Vatican II, practical theology is both a specialized academic discipline and a constitutive part of the ecclesial mission as the work of the whole people

46 See Bonnie Miller-McLemore's chapter 8 (pp. 190–218) in this volume on "The Politics of Knowledge."

47 Karl Rahner, "Practical Theology within the Totality of Theological Disciplines," 106.

of God. For example, one can see the range of institutions and communities reflected in *Invitation to Practical Theology*: university-based departments of theology at Jesuit institutions such as Fordham, Boston College, and Loyola Marymount as well as the Benedictine St. John's University, Collegeville and Dominican St. Thomas University in Miami; graduate schools of theology and ministry such as Catholic Theological Union; institutes such as the Instituto Fe y Vida in Los Angeles and the Institute of Black Catholic Studies at Xavier University of Louisiana in New Orleans; pastoral processes and *encuentros* sponsored by the bishops; spiritual direction; parish-based community organizing, and movements to develop lay "practical theological agency." Practical theology as an academic discipline can both study and help to guide the work of practical theology operating in multiple spheres and institutions.

By way of conclusion, in naming what is at stake in bridging Catholic theology and practical theology, let me return to my initial entry into the field. As described above, practical theology appealed to me as a scholarly path capable of integrating my concerns with living faith and living communities and an intellectual vocation as a teacher. Of all the doctoral fields of study, practical theology seemed most continuous, least disjointed, from my experience as a lay Catholic seeking out a vocation, from my experiences working in a New Haven soup kitchen or at St. Thomas parish on the south side of Chicago. In many ways, that attraction to practical theology is still at the root of my work. So here I offer a more personal and local reflection to indicate what is at stake in bridging practical theology and Catholicism. For me, being a "practicing" Catholic in Boston over the past decade has been a complicated task. What it means to be church and to practice our faith: these are living, and contested, questions, as seen most recently in the Synod on the Family debates about divorce and remarriage and the welcome of LGBT persons. In the last decade, the sexual abuse crisis revealed the moral failings and inept leadership of church leaders, with the tragedy of countless children injured by the church entrusted to protect, form, and nurture them. Church closings brought another layer of pain to many Catholics. My own parish was closed, for instance, bringing a sense of disorientation. During these same years, though, I have seen Catholics continue to stand for social justice—for the poor, for workers, for immigrants, for all forms of life. I have welcomed and baptized my three children in flourishing Catholic communities. I have seen them each go on to receive Communion, following lines of people up to the altar to take bread and wine, followed by lines of people behind them, all sharing in this same, central practice of ours. These practices root us and grow our knowledge of God and ourselves. If practical theology means anything, it must be able to speak to the issues of practice, formation, and leadership so intimately important to people seeking to be people of faith. As Tilley writes: "A tradition lives in practitioners living in and living out—practicing—the faith in different times and places."[48] And as Groome urges, we need a theology that moves "from life to Christian faith to renewed faith for life."[49] The question is: can the discipline of practical theology provide such a theology? How will we develop authentically Catholic modes of practical theology for the 21st century? And can contemporary theological institutions adequately make space for Catholic teaching and scholarship in practical theology?

Bibliography

Arnold, Franz Xaver, Karl Rahner, Viktor Schurr and Leonard Weber, eds. *Handbuch der Pastoraltheologie praktische Theologie der Kirche in ihrer Gegenwart.* Band I, Freiburg: Herder, 1964.

Bass, Dorothy C., and Craig R. Dykstra. *For Life Abundant: Practical Theology, Theological Education, and Christian Ministry*. Grand Rapids, MI: William B. Eerdmans Pub., 2008.

Beaudoin, Tom. "Secular Catholicism and Practical Theology." *International Journal of Practical Theology* 15, no. 1 (2011): 22–37.

Bridgers, Lynn. "Roman Catholicism." In *The Wiley-Blackwell Companion to Practical Theology*, edited by Bonnie J. Miller-McLemore, 565–576. Malden, MA: Blackwell Publishing, 2012.

Bridgers, Lynn. "The Resurrected Life: Roman Catholic Resources in Posttraumatic Pastoral Care." *International Journal of Practical Theology* 15, no. 1 (2011): 38–56.

Browning, Don S. *A Fundamental Practical Theology: Descriptive and Strategic Proposals*. Minneapolis, MN: Fortress Press, 1991.

Browning, Don S. "The Revival of Practical Theology." *Christian Century*, February 1, 1984, 134.

Brown, Sally A. "Hermeneutics in Protestant Practical Theology." In *Opening the Field of Practical Theology: An Introduction*, edited by Kathleen A. Cahalan and Gordon S. Mikoski, 115–132. Lanham, MD: Rowman & Littlefield, 2014.

Cahalan, Kathleen A. "Locating Practical Theology in Catholic Theological Discourse and Practice." *International Journal of Practical Theology* 15, no. 1 (2011): 1–21.

48 Terrence W. Tilley, "Practicing the Faith: Tradition in a Practical Theology" in Wolfteich, ed., *Invitation to Practical Theology: Catholic Voices and Visions*, 91.

49 Thomas Groome, "Practices of Teaching: A Pedagogy for Practical Theology," in Wolfteich, ed., *Invitation to Practical Theology: Catholic Voices and Visions*, 296.

Cahalan, Kathleen A. "Roman Catholic Pastoral Theology." In *Opening the Field of Practical Theology: An Introduction*, edited by Kathleen A. Cahalan and Gordon S. Mikoski, 217–232. Lanham, MD: Rowman & Littlefield, 2014.

Cahalan, Kathleen A., and Bryan Froehle. "A Developing Discipline: The Catholic Voice in Practical Theology." In *Invitation to Practical Theology: Catholic Voices and Visions*, edited by Claire E. Wolfteich, 27–51. New York: Paulist Press, 2014.

Cahalan, Kathleen A., and Gordon S. Mikoski, eds. *Opening the Field of Practical Theology: An Introduction*. Lanham, MD: Rowman & Littlefield, 2014.

Cartledge, Mark J. "Pentecostalism." In *The Wiley-Blackwell Companion to Practical Theology*, edited by Bonnie J. Miller-McLemore, 587–595. Malden, MA: Blackwell Publishing, 2012.

Catholic Theological Union. "General Information." Accessed July 31, 2015. http://www.ctu.edu/academics/general-information.

Copeland, M. Shawn. "Weaving Memory, Structuring Ritual, Evoking Mythos: Commemoration of the Ancestors." In *Invitation to Practical Theology: Catholic Voices and Visions*, edited by Claire E. Wolfteich, 125–148. New York: Paulist Press, 2014.

Driskill, Joseph D., and Bonnie J. Miller-McLemore. "Spirituality and the Disciples of Christ: Sanctifying the Ordinary." In *Chalice Introduction to Disciples Theology*, edited by Peter Goodwin Heltzel, 227–237. St. Louis, MO: Chalice Press, 2008.

Faggioli, Massimo. *Vatican II: The Battle for Meaning*. New York: Paulist Press, 2012.

Farley, Edward. *Theologia: The Fragmentation and Unity of Theological Education*. Philadelphia, PA: Fortress Press, 1983.

Fletcher, Jeannine Hill. "A Definition of Catholic: Toward a Cosmopolitan Vision." In *The Catholic Studies Reader*, edited by James Terence Fisher and Margaret M. McGuinness, 129–147. New York: Fordham University Press, 2011.

Foley, Edward. "Eucharistic Practice-Eucharistic Theology: The Fount and Summit of the Church's Life." In *Invitation to Practical Theology: Catholic Voices and Visions*, edited by Claire E. Wolfteich, 107–124. New York: Paulist Press, 2014.

Foley, Edward. "Eucharist, Postcolonial Theory and Developmental Disabilities: A Practical Theologian Revisits the Jesus Table." *International Journal of Practical Theology* 15, no. 1 (2011): 57–73.

Froehle, Bryan T. "Voting and Political Discourse as Practical Theology: Catholics, Bishops, and Obama in the U.S. Elections of 2008." *International Journal of Practical Theology* 15, no. 1 (2011): 74–93.

Gaillardetz, Richard R., ed. *When the Magisterium Intervenes: The Magisterium and Theologians in Today's Church*. Collegeville, MN: Liturgical, 2012.

Goizueta, Roberto S. *Caminemos Con Jesús: Toward a Hispanic/Latino Theology of Accompaniment*. Maryknoll, NY: Orbis Books, 1995.

Goizueta, Roberto S. "Practicing Beauty: Aesthetic Praxis, Justice, and U.S. Latino/a

Popular Religion." In *Invitation to Practical Theology: Catholic Voices and Visions*, edited by Claire E. Wolfteich, 149–167. New York: Paulist Press, 2014.

Groome, Thomas. "Practices of Teaching: A Pedagogy for Practical Theology." In *Invitation to Practical Theology: Catholic Voices and Visions*, edited by Claire E. Wolfteich, 277–300. New York: Paulist Press, 2014.

Haslinger, Herbert. "Vatican II, the Legacy of Rahner, and Catholic Distinctives in Practical Theology." In *Catholic Approaches in Practical Theology: International and Interdisciplinary Perspectives*, edited by Claire Wolfteich and Annemie Dillen. Leuven: Peeters Publishing, 2016, forthcoming.

Killen, Patricia O'Connell, and John De Beer. *The Art of Theological Reflection*. New York: Crossroad, 1994.

Kinast, Robert L. *Let Ministry Teach: A Guide to Theological Reflection*. Collegeville, MN: Liturgical Press, 1996.

Mikoski, Gordon S. "Mainline Protestantism." In *The Wiley-Blackwell Companion to Practical Theology*, edited by Bonnie J. Miller-McLemore, 557–566. Malden, MA: Blackwell Publishing, 2012.

Mikoski, Gordon S., and Richard Robert Osmer. *With Piety and Learning: The History of Practical Theology at Princeton Theological Seminary 1812–2012*. Zürich: LIT Verlag, 2011.

Miller-McLemore, Bonnie J. "Five Misunderstandings about Practical Theology." *International Journal of Practical Theology* 16, no. 1 (January 2012): 5–26.

Miller-McLemore, Bonnie J., ed. *The Wiley-Blackwell Companion to Practical Theology*. Malden, MA: Blackwell Publishing, 2012.

Nanko-Fernandez, Carmen. *Theologizing En Espanglish: Context, Community, and Ministry*. Maryknoll, NY: Orbis Books, 2010.

Pew Research Center Religion & Public Life. "The Global Catholic Population." Last modified, February 13, 2013. http://www.pewforum.org/2013/02/13/the-global-catholic-population/.

Rahner, Karl. "Practical Theology within the Totality of Theological Disciplines." In *Theological Investigations, Volume IX: Writings of 1965–67*. New York: Herder & Herder, 1972.

Rahner, Karl. *Theological Investigations, Volume IX: Writings of 1965–67*. New York: Herder & Herder, 1972.

Root, Andrew. "Evangelical Practical Theology." In *Opening the Field of Practical Theology: An Introduction*, edited by Kathleen A. Cahalan and Gordon S. Mikoski, 79–96. Lanham, MD: Rowman & Littlefield, 2014.

Scalise, Charles J. "Protestant Evangelicalism." In *The Wiley-Blackwell Companion to Practical Theology*, edited by Bonnie J. Miller-McLemore, 577–586. Malden, MA: Blackwell Publishing, 2012.

Schweitzer, Friedrich. "Continental Europe." In *The Wiley-Blackwell Companion to Practical Theology*, edited by Bonnie J. Miller-McLemore, 465–474. Malden, MA: Blackwell Publishing, 2012.

Sweeney, James, Gemma Simmonds, and David Lonsdale. *Keeping Faith in Practice: Aspects of Catholic Pastoral Theology*. London, UK: SCM Press, 2010.

Tilley, Terrence W. "Practicing the Faith: Tradition in a Practical Theology." In *Invitation to Practical Theology: Catholic Voices and Visions*, edited by Claire E. Wolfteich, 89–106. New York: Paulist Press, 2014.

Tracy, David. "A Correlational Model of Practical Theology Revisited." In *Religion, Diversity and Conflict*, edited by Edward Foley, 49–62. Münster: LIT Verlag, 2011 and reprinted in *Invitation to Practical Theology: Catholic Voices and Visions*, edited by Claire E. Wolfteich, 70–86. New York: Paulist Press, 2014.

Wheeler, Barbara G., and Edward Farley, eds. *Shifting Boundaries: Contextual Approaches to the Structure of Theological Education*. 1st ed. Louisville, KY: Westminster John Knox Press, 1991.

Whitehead, James D., and Evelyn Eaton Whitehead. *Method in Ministry: Theological Reflection and Christian Ministry*. Rev. and updated. Chicago: Sheed and Ward, 1995.

Wolfteich, Claire E. "Animating Questions: Spirituality and Practical Theology." *International Journal of Practical Theology* 13, no. 1 (2009): 121–43.

Wolfteich, Claire E. "Hermeneutical Approaches in Practical Theology: Catholic Perspectives." In *Opening the Field of Practical Theology: An Introduction*, edited by Kathleen A. Cahalan and Gordon S. Mikoski, 133–152. Lanham, MD: Rowman & Littlefield, 2014.

Wolfteich, Claire E., ed. *Invitation to Practical Theology: Catholic Voices and Visions*. New York: Paulist Press, 2014.

Wolfteich, Claire E. "Practices of 'Unsaying': Michel de Certeau, Spirituality Studies, and Practical Theology." *Spiritus: A Journal of Christian Spirituality* 12, no. 2 (2012): 161–71.

Wolfteich, Claire E. "Time Poverty, Women's Labor, and Catholic Social Teaching: A Practical Theological Exploration." *Journal of Moral Theology* 2, no. 2 (June 2013): 40–59.

Wolfteich, Claire E. "Spirituality." In *The Wiley-Blackwell Companion to Practical Theology*, edited by Bonnie J. Miller-McLemore, 328–336. Malden, MA: Blackwell Publishing, 2012.

Wolfteich, Claire E., and Annemie Dillen, eds. *Catholic Approaches in Practical Theology: International and Interdisciplinary Perspectives*. Leuven: Peeters Publishing, 2016, forthcoming.

Wolfteich, Claire E., and Jörg Schneider. "A Comparative Research Conversation: American Catholic and German Protestant Spirituality Studies." *International Journal of Practical Theology* 17, no. 1 (2013): 100–130.

Index of Names

Index of Subjects